Pandas in Action

Pandas in Action

BORIS PASKHAVER

MANNING
SHELTER ISLAND

For online information and ordering of this and other Manning books, please visit
www.manning.com. The publisher offers discounts on this book when ordered in quantity.
For more information, please contact

    Special Sales Department
    Manning Publications Co.
    20 Baldwin Road
    PO Box 761
    Shelter Island, NY 11964
    Email: orders@manning.com

Manning Publications Co.
20 Baldwin Road
PO Box 761
Shelter Island, NY 11964

Development editor: Sarah Miller
Technical development editor: Al Krinker
Review editor: Aleks Dragosavljević
Production editor: Deirdre S. Hiam
Copy editor: Keir Simpson
Proofreader: Jason Everett
Technical proofreader: Mathijs Affourtit
Typesetter and cover designer: Marija Tudor

ISBN 9781617297434
Printed in the United States of America

For Meredith Edwards, my ray of sunshine

contents

preface

Truth be told, I discovered pandas entirely by luck.

In 2015, I interviewed for a data operations analyst position at Indeed.com, the world's largest jobs site. For my final technical challenge, I was asked to derive insights from an internal data set, using the Microsoft Excel spreadsheet software. Eager to impress, I pulled out as many tricks as I could from my data analysis toolbox: column sorts, text manipulations, pivot tables, and of course the iconic VLOOKUP function. (OK, maybe *iconic* is a bit of an exaggeration.)

Strange as it may sound, at the time I didn't realize that there were any tools for data analysis besides Excel. Excel was ubiquitous: my parents used it, my teachers used it, and my colleagues used it. It felt like an established standard. So when I received a job offer, I immediately bought about $100 worth of Excel books and started studying. It was time to become a spreadsheet specialist!

I showed up for my first day of work with a printout of the 50 most-used Excel functions. Barely after I finished logging into my work computer, my manager pulled me into a conference room and informed me that priorities had shifted. The team's data sets had ballooned to a size that Excel could no longer support. My teammates were also looking for ways to automate the redundant steps in their daily and weekly reports. Luckily, my manager had figured out a solution to both problems. He asked me whether I'd heard of pandas.

"The furry animal?" I asked, perplexed.

"No," he said. "The Python data analysis library."

After all my prep, it was time to learn a new technology from scratch. I was a little nervous; I'd never written a line of code before. I was an Excel guy, wasn't I? Was I capable of doing this? There was only one way to find out. I started diving into the official pandas documentation, into YouTube videos, books, workshops, Stack Overflow questions, and whatever data sets I could get my hands on. I was relieved to discover how easy and joyful it was to get started with pandas. The code felt intuitive and straightforward. The library was fast. The features were well-developed and expansive. With pandas, I could accomplish a lot of data manipulation with a little code.

Stories like mine are common in the Python community. The language's astronomical growth over the past decade is often attributed to the ease with which new developers can pick it up. I am confident that if you're in a position similar to mine, you can learn pandas just as well. If you're looking to expand your data analysis skills beyond Excel spreadsheets, this book is your invitation.

When I felt comfortable with pandas, I continued to explore Python and then other programming languages. In many ways, pandas spearheaded my transition into full-time software engineering. I owe a lot to this powerful library, and I'm excited to pass on the torch of knowledge to you. I hope that you discover the magic of what code can do for you.

acknowledgments

It took a lot to get *Pandas in Action* to the finish line, and I want to express my utmost gratitude to the people who supported me in its two-year writing process.

First and foremost, a warm thank you to my wonderful girlfriend, Meredith. From the first sentence, she was steadfast in her support. She's a vivacious, funny, and kind soul who always picked me up when the going got tough. This book is better because of her. Thank you, Merbear.

Thank you to my parents, Irina and Dmitriy, for providing a welcoming home where I can always find respite.

Thank you to my twin sisters, Mary and Alexandra. They're remarkably clever, inquisitive, and hard-working for their age, and I couldn't be prouder of them. Good luck at college!

Thanks to Watson, our golden retriever. He's not much of a Python expert, but he makes up for it with his entertaining and friendly demeanor.

A big thank you to my editor, Sarah Miller, who was an absolute joy to work with. I am grateful for her patience and insights throughout the process. She was the true captain of the ship, and she kept everything sailing smoothly.

I would not be a software engineer without the opportunities I was given at Indeed. I want to offer my former manager, Srdjan Bodruzic, a hearty thank you for his generosity and mentorship (and for hiring me!). Thanks to my CX teammates—Tommy Winschel, Danny Moncada, JP Schultz, and Travis Wright—for their wisdom and humor. Thanks to other Indeedians who offered a helping hand during my tenure: Matthew Morin, Chris Hatton, Chip Borsi, Nicole Saglimbene, Danielle Scoli, Blairr Swayne, and George Improglou. Thanks to anybody I've shared a dinner with at Sophie's Cuban Cuisine!

I started writing this book as a software engineer at Stride Consulting. I want to thank many Striders for their support throughout the process: David "The Dominator" DiPanfilo, Min Kwak, Ben Blair, Kirsten Nordine, Michael "Bobby" Nunez, Jay Lee, James Yoo, Ray Veliz, Nathan Riemer, Julia Berchem, Dan Plain, Nick Char, Grant Ziolkowski, Melissa Wahnish, Dave Anderson, Chris Aporta, Michael Carlson, John Galioto, Sean Marzug-McCarthy, Travis Vander Hoop, Steve Solomon, and Jan Mlčoch.

Thank you to the friendly faces I've had the opportunity to work with as a software engineer and consultant: Francis Hwang, Inhak Kim, Liana Lim, Matt Bambach, Brenton Morris, Ian McNally, Josh Philips, Artem Kochnev, Andrew Kang, Andrew Fader, Karl Smith, Bradley Whitwell, Brad Popiolek, Eddie Wharton, Jen Kwok, and my favorite coffee crew: Adam McAmis and Andy Fritz.

Thank you to the following people for all they add to my life: Nick Bianco, Cam Stier, Keith David, Michael Cheung, Thomas Philippeau, Nicole DiAndrea, and James Rokeach.

Thanks to my favorite band, New Found Glory, for providing the soundtrack to many writing sessions. Pop punk's not dead!

Thank you to the Manning staff who shepherded the project to completion and helped with marketing efforts: Jennifer Houle, Aleksandar Dragosavljević, Radmila Ercegovac, Candace Gillhoolley, Stjepan Jureković, and Lucas Weber. Thanks also to the Manning staff who oversaw the content: Sarah Miller, my developmental editor; Deirdre Hiam, my product manager; Keir Simpson, my copyeditor; and Jason Everett, my proofreader.

Thanks to the technical reviewers who helped me iron out the kinks: Al Pezewski, Alberto Ciarlanti, Ben McNamara, Björn Neuhaus, Christopher Kottmyer, Dan Sheikh, Dragos Manailoiu, Erico Lendzian, Jeff Smith, Jérôme Bâton, Joaquin Beltran, Jonathan Sharley, Jose Apablaza, Ken W. Alger, Martin Czygan, Mathijs Affourtit, Matthias Busch, Mike Cuddy, Monica E. Guimaraes, Ninoslav Cerkez, Rick Prins, Syed Hasany, Viton Vitanis, and Vybhavreddy Kammireddy Changalreddy. I am a better writer and educator thanks to your efforts.

Finally, to the city of Hoboken, my home for the past six years. I wrote many parts of this manuscript in its public library, local cafes, and bubble tea shops. I made many forward strides in my life in this town, and it is forever etched into my history. Thank you, Hoboken!

about this book

Who should read this book

Pandas in Action is a comprehensive introduction to the pandas library for data analysis. Pandas enables you to perform a multitude of data manipulations with ease: sorting, joining, pivoting, cleaning, deduping, aggregating, and more. The book approaches the subject matter incrementally. It introduces pandas one piece at a time, starting with its smaller building blocks and proceeding to its larger data structures.

Pandas in Action is written for data analysts who have intermediate experience with spreadsheet software (such as Microsoft Excel, Google Sheets, and Apple Numbers) and/or alternative data analysis tools (such as R and SAS). It is also a fitting title for Python developers who are curious to learn more about data analysis.

How this book is organized: A road map

Pandas in Action consists of 14 chapters spread across two parts.

Part 1, "Core pandas," introduces the base mechanics of the pandas library in an incremental manner:

- Chapter 1 analyzes a sample dataset with pandas to present a big-picture overview of what the library is capable of.
- Chapter 2 introduces the `Series` object, a core pandas data structure that stores a collection of ordered data.
- Chapter 3 dives into the `Series` object in greater depth. We explore various `Series` operations, including sorting values, dropping duplicates, extracting minimums and maximums, and more.
- Chapter 4 introduces the `DataFrame`, a two-dimensional table of data. We apply concepts from the previous chapters to the new data structure and introduce additional manipulations.

- Chapter 5 shows you how to filter subsets of rows from a `DataFrame` by using various logical conditions: equality, inequality, comparison, inclusion, exclusion, and more.

Part 2, "Applied pandas," focuses on more-advanced pandas features and the problems they solve in real-world datasets:

- Chapter 6 teaches you how to work with imperfect text data in pandas. We discuss how to solve issues such as removing whitespace, fixing character casing, and extracting multiple values from a single column.
- Chapter 7 discusses the `MultiIndex`, which allows us to combine multiple column values into a single identifier for a row of data.
- Chapter 8 describes how to aggregate our data in a pivot table, shift headers from the row axis to the column axis, and convert our data from wide format to narrow format.
- Chapter 9 explores how to group rows into buckets and aggregate the resulting collections via the `GroupBy` object.
- Chapter 10 walks you through combining multiple data sets into a single one by using various joins.
- Chapter 11 demonstrates how to work with dates and times in pandas. It covers topics such as sorting dates, calculating durations, and determining whether a date falls at the start of a month or quarter.
- Chapter 12 shows you how to import additional file types into pandas, including Excel and JSON. We also learn how to export data from pandas.
- Chapter 13 focuses on configuring the library's settings. We dive into how to modify the number of displayed rows, alter the precision of floating-point numbers, round values below a threshold, and more.
- Chapter 14 explores data visualization using the matplotlib library. We see how to use pandas data to create line charts, bar graphs, pie charts, and more.

Each chapter builds upon the preceding one. For those who are learning pandas from scratch, I recommend proceeding through the chapters in linear order. Simultaneously, to ensure that the book is helpful as a reference guide, I've written each chapter as an independent tutorial with its own data sets. We start writing our code from scratch at the beginning of each chapter, so you can start with any chapter you like.

Most chapters conclude with a coding challenge that allows you to practice its concepts. I strongly recommend taking a shot at these exercises.

Pandas is built on the Python programing language, and basic knowledge of the language's mechanics is recommended before you get started. For those who have limited experience in Python, appendix B offers a hearty introduction to the language.

About the code

This book contains many examples of source code, which is formatted in a fixed-width font `like this` to separate it from ordinary text.

The source code for the book's examples is available at the following GitHub repository: https://github.com/paskhaver/pandas-in-action. For those who are new to Git and GitHub, look for a Download Zip button on the repository page. Those who are experienced with Git and GitHub are welcome to clone the repo from the command line.

The repository also includes the complete data sets for the text. When I was learning pandas, one of my biggest frustrations was that tutorials loved to rely on randomly generated data. There was no consistency, no context, no story, no fun. In this book, we'll work with many real-world data sets that cover everything from basketball players' salaries to Pokémon types to restaurant health inspections. Data is everywhere around us, and pandas is one of the best tools available today to make sense of it. I hope that you enjoy the casual focus of the data sets.

liveBook discussion forum

Purchase of *Pandas in Action* includes free access to a private web forum run by Manning Publications where you can make comments about the book, ask technical questions, and receive help from the author and from other users. To access the forum, go to https://livebook.manning.com/#!/book/pandas-in-action/discussion. You can also learn more about Manning's forums and the rules of conduct at https://livebook.manning.com/#!/discussion.

Manning's commitment to our readers is to provide a venue where meaningful dialogue between individual readers and between readers and the author can take place. It is not a commitment to any specific amount of participation on the part of the author, whose contribution to the forum remains voluntary (and unpaid). We suggest that you try asking the author some challenging questions lest their interest stray! The forum and the archives of previous discussions will be accessible from the publisher's website as long as the book is in print.

Other online resources

- The official pandas documentation is available at https://pandas.pydata.org/docs.
- In my spare time, I create technical video courses on Udemy. You can find the courses at https://www.udemy.com/user/borispaskhaver; they include a 20-hour pandas course and a 60-hour Python course.
- Feel free to reach out to me via Twitter (https://twitter.com/borispaskhaver) or LinkedIn (https://www.linkedin.com/in/boris-paskhaver).

about the author

BORIS PASKHAVER is a full-stack software engineer, consultant, and online educator based in New York City. He has six courses on the e-learning platform Udemy with over 140 hours of videos, 300,000 students, 20,000 reviews, and 1 million minutes of content consumed monthly. Before becoming a software engineer, Boris worked as a data analyst and systems administrator. He graduated from New York University in 2013 with a double major in business economics and marketing.

about the cover illustration

The figure on the cover of *Pandas in Action* is captioned "Dame de Calais," or Lady from Calais. The illustration is taken from a collection of dress costumes from various countries by Jacques Grasset de Saint-Sauveur (1757–1810), titled *Costumes de Différents Pays*, published in France in 1797. Each illustration is finely drawn and colored by hand. The rich variety of Grasset de Saint-Sauveur's collection reminds us vividly of how culturally apart the world's towns and regions were only 200 years ago. Isolated from one another, people spoke different dialects and languages. In the streets or in the countryside, it was easy to identify by their dress alone where they lived and what their trade or station in life was.

The way we dress has changed since then, and diversity by region, so abundant at the time, has faded away. Now it is hard to tell apart the inhabitants of different continents, let alone different towns, regions, or countries. Perhaps we have traded cultural diversity for a more varied personal life—certainly for a more varied and fast-paced technological life.

At a time when it is hard to tell one computer book from another, Manning celebrates the inventiveness and initiative of the computer business with book covers based on the deep diversity of regional life of two centuries ago, brought back to life by Grasset de Saint-Sauveur's pictures.

Part 1

Core pandas

Welcome! In this section, we'll familiarize ourselves with the core mechanics of pandas and its two primary data structures: the one-dimensional `Series` and the two-dimensional `DataFrame`. Chapter 1 begins with an analysis of a data set with pandas so you can immediately get a sense of what is possible with the library. From there, we proceed to an in-depth exploration of the `Series` in chapters 2 and 3. We learn how to create a `Series` from scratch; import it from an external data set; and apply a slew of mathematical, statistical, and logical operations to it. In chapter 4, we introduce the tabular `DataFrame` and various ways to extract rows, columns, and values from its data. Finally, chapter 5 focuses on extracting subsets of `DataFrame` rows by applying logical criteria. Along the way, we'll work through eight datasets that cover everything from box-office grosses to NBA players to Pokémon.

This part covers the essentials of pandas, the fundamentals you need to know to work effectively with the library. I've made every effort to start from square one, from the smallest building blocks possible, and proceed to the larger and more complex elements. The following five chapters build the foundation for your mastery of pandas. Good luck!

Introducing pandas 1

This chapter covers

- The growth of data science in the 21st century
- The history of the pandas library for data analysis
- The pros and cons of pandas and its competitors
- Data analysis in Excel versus data analysis with a programming language
- A tour of the library's features through a working example

Welcome to *Pandas in Action*! Pandas is a library for data analysis built on top of the Python programming language. A *library* (also called a *package*) is a collection of code for solving problems in a specific field of endeavor. Pandas is a toolbox for data manipulation operations: sorting, filtering, cleaning, deduping, aggregating, pivoting, and more. The epicenter of Python's vast data science ecosystem, pandas pairs well with other libraries for statistics, natural language processing, machine learning, data visualization, and more.

In this introductory chapter, we'll explore the history and evolution of modern data analytics tools. We'll see how pandas grew from one financial analyst's pet project to an industry standard used by companies such as Stripe, Google, and J.P. Morgan. We'll compare the library with its competitors, including Excel and R. We'll discuss the differences between working with a programming language and working with a graphical spreadsheet application. Finally, we'll use pandas to analyze a real-world data set. Consider this chapter to be a sneak preview of the concepts you'll master throughout the book. Let's dive in!

1.1   Data in the 21st century

"It is a capital mistake to theorize before one has data," Sherlock Holmes advises his assistant John Watson in "A Scandal in Bohemia," the first of Sir Arthur Conan Doyle's classic short stories pairing the duo. "Insensibly one begins to twist facts to suit theories, instead of theories to suit facts."

The wise detective's words continue to ring true more than a century after the publication of Doyle's work, in a world in which data is becoming increasingly prevalent in every facet of our lives. "The world's most valuable resource is no longer oil, but data," declared *The Economist* in a 2017 opinion piece. Data is *evidence*, and evidence is critical to businesses, governments, institutions, and individuals solving increasingly complex problems in our interconnected world. Across a breadth of industries, the world's most successful companies, from Facebook to Amazon to Netflix, cite data as the most prized asset in their portfolios. United Nations Secretary-General António Guterres called accurate data "the lifeblood of good policy and decision-making." Data powers everything from movie recommendations to medical treatments, from supply chain logistics to poverty-reduction initiatives. The success of communities, companies, and even countries in the 21st century will depend on their ability to acquire, aggregate, and analyze data.

1.2   Introducing pandas

The technological ecosystem of tools for working with data has grown tremendously over the past decade. Today, the open source pandas library is one of the most popular solutions available for data analysis and manipulation. *Open source* means that the library's source code is publicly available to download, use, modify, and distribute. Its license grants users more permissions than proprietary software such as Excel. Pandas is free to use. A global team of volunteer software developers maintains the library, and you can find its complete source code on GitHub (https://github.com/pandas-dev/pandas).

Pandas is comparable to Microsoft's Excel spreadsheet software and Google's in-browser Sheets application. In all three technologies, a user interacts with tables consisting of rows and columns of data. A row represents a record or, equivalently, one collection of values for the columns. Transformations are applied to coax the data into the desired state.

Figure 1.1 displays a sample transformation of a data set. The analyst applies an operation to the four-row data set on the left to arrive at the two-row data set on the

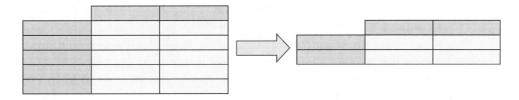

Figure 1.1   A sample transformation of a tabular data set

right. They may select rows that fit a criterion, for example, or remove duplicate rows from the original data set.

What makes pandas unique is the balance it strikes between processing power and user productivity. By relying on lower-level languages such as C for many of its calculations, the library can efficiently transform million-row data sets in milliseconds. At the same time, it maintains a simple and intuitive set of commands. It is easy to accomplish a lot with a little code in pandas.

Figure 1.2 shows some sample pandas code that imports and sorts a CSV data set. Don't worry about the code yet, but take a second to notice that the entire operation takes only two lines of code.

```
In [2]: populations = pd.read_csv("populations.csv")
        populations.sort_values(by = "Population", ascending = False)
```

Out[2]:

	Country	Population
144	China	1433783686
21	India	1366417754
156	United States	329064917
76	Indonesia	270625568
147	Pakistan	216565318
79	Brazil	211049527
6	Nigeria	200963599
123	Bangladesh	163046161

Figure 1.2   A sample of code that imports and sorts a data set in pandas

Pandas works seamlessly with numbers, text, dates, times, missing data, and more. We'll explore its incredible versatility as we proceed through the more than 30 data sets included with this book.

The first version of pandas was developed in 2008 by software developer Wes McKinney, who was working at New York's AQR Capital Management investment firm. Dissatisfied with both Excel and the statistical programming language R, McKinney searched for a tool that would make it easy to solve common data problems in the financial industry, particularly cleanup and aggregation. Unable to find an ideal product, he decided to build one himself. At the time, Python was far from the powerhouse it is today, but the beauty of the language inspired McKinney to build his library on top of its foundation. "I loved [Python] for its economy of expressions," he stated in Quartz (http://mng.bz/w0Na). "You can express complicated ideas in Python with very little code, and it is very easy to read."

Pandas has seen continual, extensive growth since its release to the public in December 2009. User counts are estimated to be between five and ten million.[1] As of June 2021, pandas has been downloaded more than 750 million times from PyPi, the centralized online repository of Python packages (https://pepy.tech/project/pandas). Its GitHub code repository has more than 30,000 stars (a star is equivalent to a "like" on the platform). Pandas questions make up a growing percentage of questions on the question-answer aggregator Stack Overflow, suggesting increased user interest.

I would argue that we can even credit pandas for the astronomical growth of Python itself. The language has exploded in popularity because of its prevalence in data science, a field to which pandas contributes greatly. Python is now the most common first language taught at colleges and universities. The TIOBE index, a ranking of programming language popularity by search engine traffic, declared Python to be the fastest-growing language of 2018.[2] "If Python can keep this pace, it will probably replace C and Java in 3 to 4 years' time, thus becoming the most popular programming language of the world," wrote TIOBE in a press release. As you learn pandas, you'll also be learning Python, which is another perk of the library.

1.2.1   *Pandas vs. graphical spreadsheet applications*

Pandas requires a different mindset from a graphical spreadsheet app such as Excel. Programming is inherently more verbal than it is visual. We communicate with the computer through commands, not clicks. Because it makes fewer assumptions about what you're trying to accomplish, a programming language tends to be more unforgiving. It needs to be *told* what to do with no uncertainty. We need to issue the correct instructions with the correct inputs in the correct order; otherwise, the program will not work.

Due to these stricter requirements, pandas has a steeper learning curve than Excel or Sheets. But if you have limited experience in Python or programming in general, there's no need to worry! When you're fiddling with functions such as SUMIF and VLOOKUP in Excel, you're already thinking like a programmer. The process is the same: identify the correct function to use and then supply the right inputs in the proper order. Pandas requires an identical set of skills; the difference is that we're communicating with the computer in a more verbose language.

---

[1]   See "What's the future of the pandas library?," *Data School*, https://www.dataschool.io/future-of-pandas.

[2]   See Oliver Peckham, "TIOBE Index: Python Reaches Another All-Time High," *HPC Wire*, http://mng.bz/w0XP.

When you become familiar with its complexities, pandas grants you greater power and flexibility in your data manipulations. In addition to extending the range of your available procedures, programming allows you to automate them. You can write a piece of code once and reuse it across multiple files—perfect for those pesky daily and weekly reports. It's important to note that Excel comes bundled with Visual Basic for Applications (VBA), a programming language that also enables you to automate spreadsheet procedures. I would argue, however, that Python is easier to pick up than VBA and has uses beyond data analysis, making it a better investment of your time.

There are additional benefits to making the jump from Excel to Python. Jupyter Notebook, the coding environment often paired with pandas, allows for more dynamic, interactive, and comprehensive reports. A Jupyter Notebook consists of cells, each of which contains a chunk of executable code. An analyst can integrate these cells with headers, charts, descriptions, annotations, images, videos, diagrams, and more. Readers can follow the analyst's step-by-step logic to see how they reached their conclusion, not only their final result.

Another advantage of pandas is Python's large data science ecosystem. Pandas integrates easily with libraries for statistics, natural language processing, machine learning, web scraping, data visualization, and more. New libraries appear yearly. Experimentation is welcomed. Innovation is constant. These robust tools sometimes remain underdeveloped in corporate competitors, which lack the support of a large, global community of contributors.

Graphical spreadsheet applications also begin to struggle as data sets grow; pandas is significantly more powerful than Excel in this aspect. The capacity of the library is limited only by the computer's memory and processing power. On most modern machines, pandas plays well with multigigabyte data sets with millions of rows, especially when a developer knows how to exploit all its performance optimizations. In a blog post describing the limitations of the library, creator Wes McKinney wrote, "Nowadays, my rule of thumb for pandas is that you should have 5 to 10 times more RAM as the size of your data set" (http://mng.bz/qeK6).

Part of the challenge in choosing the best tool for the job is defining what terms such as *data analysis* and *big data* mean to your organization and your project. Excel, which is used by approximately 750 million working professionals globally, limits its spreadsheets to 1,048,576 rows of data.[3] For some analysts, 1 million rows of data are more than any report requires; for others, 1 million rows only scratch the surface.

I would advise you to look at pandas as being not the best data analysis solution but a powerful option to use alongside other modern technologies. Excel is still an excellent choice for quick, easy data manipulations. A spreadsheet application usually makes assumptions about your intent, which is why it takes only a few clicks to import a CSV file or sort a column of 100 values. There's no real advantage to using pandas for simple tasks like these (although it's more than capable of doing them). But what

---

[3] See Andy Patrizio, "Excel: Your entry into the world of data analytics," *Computer World*, http://mng.bz/qe6r.

do you use when you need to clean text values in two data sets of ten million rows each, remove their duplicate records, join them, and replicate that logic for 100 batches of files? For those scenarios, it's easier and less time-consuming to do the work with Python and pandas.

1.2.2   *Pandas vs. its competitors*

Data science enthusiasts frequently compare pandas with the open source programming language R and the proprietary software suite SAS. Each solution has its own community of advocates.

R is a specialized language with a foundation in statistics, whereas Python is a generalist language used in multiple technical domains. Predictably, the two languages tend to attract users with expertise in specific fields. Hadley Wickham, a prominent developer in the R community who built a collection of data science packages called tidyverse, advises users to see the two languages as collaborators rather than rivals. "These things exist independently and are both awesome in different ways," he said in *Quartz* (http://mng.bz/Jv9V). "A pattern that I see is that the data science team in a company uses R and the data engineering team uses Python. The Python people tend to have a background in software engineering and are very confident about their programming skills. . . . [The R users] really like R, but can't argue with the engineering team because they don't have the language to make that argument." One language may have an advanced feature that the other does not, but the two have achieved near parity when it comes to common tasks in data analysis. Developers and data scientists simply gravitate to what they know best.

A suite of complementary software tools that supports statistics, data mining, econometrics, and more, SAS is a commercial product developed by the North Carolina-based SAS Institute. It charges an annual user subscription fee that varies based on the bundle of selected software. The advantages conferred by a corporate-backed product include technical and visual consistency across tools, robust documentation, and a product road map geared towards enterprise clients' needs. Open source technology like pandas enjoys a more free-for-all approach; developers work for their needs and for other developers' needs, which sometimes miss market trends.

Certain technologies share features with pandas but serve intrinsically different purposes. SQL is one example. *SQL* (Structured Query Language) is a language for communicating with relational databases. A *relational database* consists of tables of data linked by common keys. We can use SQL for basic data manipulations such as extracting columns from tables and filtering rows by a criterion, but its functionalities are greater in scope and fundamentally revolve around data management. Databases are built to *store* data; data analysis is a secondary use case. SQL can create new tables, update existing records with new values, delete existing records, and so on. By comparison, pandas is built entirely for data analysis: statistical calculations, data wrangling, data merges, and more. In a typical work environment, the two tools often serve as complements. An analyst might use SQL to extract an initial cluster of data and then use pandas to manipulate it.

In summary, pandas is not the only tool in town, but it is a powerful, popular, and valuable solution for solving most data analysis problems. Again, Python truly shines in its focus on brevity and productivity. As its creator, Guido van Rossum, remarked, "The joy of coding Python should be in seeing short, concise, readable [data structures] that express a lot of action in a small amount of clear code" (http://mng.bz/7jo7). Pandas lives up to that standard and is an excellent next step for spreadsheet analysts who are eager to grow their programming skills with a powerful, modern data analysis toolkit.

1.3 A tour of pandas

The best way to grasp the power of pandas is to see it in action. Let's take a quick tour of the library by analyzing a data set of the 700 highest-grossing movies of all time. I hope you are pleasantly surprised by how intuitive the syntax of pandas can be, even if you are new to programming.

As you proceed through the rest of the chapter, try not to overanalyze the code samples; you don't even need to copy them. Our goal right now is to get a bird's-eye view of the features and functionalities of pandas. Think about what the library can do; we'll worry about how in greater detail later.

We'll be using the Jupyter Notebook development environment to write our code throughout the book. If you need help setting up pandas and Jupyter Notebook on your computer, see appendix A. You can download all data sets and completed Jupyter Notebooks at https://www.github.com/paskhaver/pandas-in-action.

1.3.1 Importing a data set

Let's get started! First, we'll create a new Jupyter Notebook inside the same directory as the movies.csv file; then we'll import the pandas library to gain access to its features:

```
In [1] import pandas as pd
```

The box to the left of the code (displaying the number 1 in the previous example) marks the cell's execution order relative to the launch or restart of the Jupyter Notebook. You can execute the cells in any order, and you can execute the same cell multiple times.

As you read through the book, you are encouraged to experiment by executing different snippets of code in your Jupyter cells. Thus, it is OK if your execution numbers do not match those in the text.

Our data is stored in a single movies.csv file. A CSV (comma-separated values) file is a plain-text file that separates each row of data with a line break and each row value with a comma. The first row in the file holds the column headers for the data. Here's a preview of the first three rows of movies.csv:

```
Rank,Title,Studio,Gross,Year
1,Avengers: Endgame,Buena Vista,"$2,796.30",2019
2,Avatar,Fox,"$2,789.70",2009
```

The first row lists the five columns in the data set: Rank, Title, Studio, Gross, and Year. The second row holds the first record or, equivalently, the data for the first movie. The film has a Rank of 1, a Title of "Avengers: Endgame", a Studio of "Buena Vista", a Gross of "$2,796.30", and a Year of 2019. The next line holds the values for the next movie, and the pattern repeats for the remaining 750-plus rows in the data set.

Pandas can import various file types, each of which has an associated import function at the top level of the library. A *function* in pandas is equivalent to a function in Excel. It's a command that we issue, either to the library or an entity within it. In this scenario, we'll use the read_csv function to import the movies.csv file:

```
In  [2] pd.read_csv("movies.csv")

Out [2]
```

	Rank	Title	Studio	Gross	Year
0	1	Avengers: Endgame	Buena Vista	$2,796.30	2019
1	2	Avatar	Fox	$2,789.70	2009
2	3	Titanic	Paramount	$2,187.50	1997
3	4	Star Wars: The Force Awakens	Buena Vista	$2,068.20	2015
4	5	Avengers: Infinity War	Buena Vista	$2,048.40	2018
...	...	...	...	...	...
777	778	Yogi Bear	Warner Brothers	$201.60	2010
778	779	Garfield: The Movie	Fox	$200.80	2004
779	780	Cats & Dogs	Warner Brothers	$200.70	2001
780	781	The Hunt for Red October	Paramount	$200.50	1990
781	782	Valkyrie	MGM	$200.30	2008

782 rows × 5 columns

Pandas imports the CSV file's contents into an object called a DataFrame. Think of an object as a container for storing data. Different objects are optimized for different types of data, and we interact with them in different ways. Pandas uses one type of object (the DataFrame) to store multicolumn data sets and another type of object (the Series) to store single-column data sets. A DataFrame is comparable to a multi-column table in Excel.

To avoid cluttering the screen, pandas displays only the first five and last five rows of the DataFrame. A row of ellipses (...) marks where the data gap occurs.

This DataFrame consists of five columns (Rank, Title, Studio, Gross, Year) and an index. The index is the range of ascending numbers on the left side of the Data-Frame. Index labels serve as identifiers for rows of data. We can set any column as the index of the DataFrame. When we do not explicitly tell pandas which column to use, the library generates a numeric index starting from 0.

What column is a good candidate for the index? It's one whose values can act as a primary identifier or point of reference for each row. Among our five columns, Rank and Title are the two best options. Let's swap the autogenerated numeric index with the values from the Title column. We can do so directly during the CSV import:

```
In  [3] pd.read_csv("movies.csv", index_col = "Title")

Out [3]
```

	Rank	Studio	Gross	Year
Title				
Avengers: Endgame	1	Buena Vista	$2,796.30	2019
Avatar	2	Fox	$2,789.70	2009
Titanic	3	Paramount	$2,187.50	1997
Star Wars: The Force Awakens	4	Buena Vista	$2,068.20	2015
Avengers: Infinity War	5	Buena Vista	$2,048.40	2018
...	...	...	...	...
Yogi Bear	778	Warner Brothers	$201.60	2010
Garfield: The Movie	779	Fox	$200.80	2004
Cats & Dogs	780	Warner Brothers	$200.70	2001
The Hunt for Red October	781	Paramount	$200.50	1990
Valkyrie	782	MGM	$200.30	2008

782 rows × 4 columns

Next, we'll assign the DataFrame to a movies variable so that we can reference it else-where in our program. A *variable* is a user-assigned name for an object in the program:

```
In  [4] movies = pd.read_csv("movies.csv", index_col = "Title")
```

For more on variables, check out appendix B.

1.3.2 Manipulating a DataFrame

We can look at the DataFrame from a variety of angles. We can extract a few rows from the beginning:

```
In  [5] movies.head(4)

Out [5]
```

	Rank	Studio	Gross	Year
Title				
Avengers: Endgame	1	Buena Vista	$2,796.30	2019
Avatar	2	Fox	$2,789.70	2009
Titanic	3	Paramount	$2,187.50	1997
Star Wars: The Force Awakens	4	Buena Vista	$2,068.20	2015

Or we can peek at the end of the data set instead:

```
In  [6] movies.tail(6)

Out [6]
```

	Rank	Studio	Gross	Year
Title				
21 Jump Street	777	Sony	$201.60	2012
Yogi Bear	778	Warner Brothers	$201.60	2010
Garfield: The Movie	779	Fox	$200.80	2004
Cats & Dogs	780	Warner Brothers	$200.70	2001
The Hunt for Red October	781	Paramount	$200.50	1990
Valkyrie	782	MGM	$200.30	2008

We can find out how many rows the `DataFrame` has:

```
In  [7] len(movies)

Out [7] 782
```

We can ask pandas for the number of rows and columns in the `DataFrame`. This data set has 782 rows and 4 columns:

```
In  [8] movies.shape

Out [8] (782, 4)
```

We can inquire about the total number of cells:

```
In  [9] movies.size

Out [9] 3128
```

We can ask for the data types of the four columns. In the following output, `int64` denotes an integer column, and `object` denotes a text column:

```
In  [10] movies.dtypes

Out [10]

Rank        int64
Studio     object
Gross      object
Year        int64
dtype: object
```

We can extract a row from the data set by its numeric order in line, also called its index position. In most programming languages, the index starts counting at 0. Thus, if we wanted to pull out the 500th movie in the data set, we would target index position 499:

```
In  [11] movies.iloc[499]

Out [11] Rank              500
         Studio            Fox
         Gross         $288.30
         Year             2018
         Name: Maze Runner: The Death Cure, dtype: object
```

Pandas returns a new object here called a `Series`, a one-dimensional labeled array of values. Think of it as a single column of data with an identifier for each row. Notice that the `Series'` index labels (Rank, Studio, Gross, and Year) are the four columns from the `movies` DataFrame. Pandas has altered the presentation of the original row's values.

We can also use an index label to access a `DataFrame` row. As a reminder, our `DataFrame` index holds the films' titles. Let's extract the row values for everyone's favorite tearjerker, *Forrest Gump*. The next example extracts a row by its index label rather than its numeric position:

```
In  [12] movies.loc["Forrest Gump"]

Out [12] Rank              119
         Studio      Paramount
         Gross          $677.90
         Year             1994
         Name: Forrest Gump, dtype: object
```

Index labels can contain duplicates. Two movies in the DataFrame have the title "101 Dalmatians", for example (the 1961 original and the 1996 remake):

```
In  [13] movies.loc["101 Dalmatians"]

Out [13]
```

Title	Rank	Studio	Gross	Year
101 Dalmatians	425	Buena Vista	$320.70	1996
101 Dalmatians	708	Buena Vista	$215.90	1961

Although pandas permits duplicates, I recommend keeping index labels unique if possible. A unique collection of labels accelerates the speed at which pandas can locate and extract a specific row.

The films in the CSV are sorted by values in the Rank column. What if we wanted to see the five movies with the most recent release date? We can sort the DataFrame by the values in another column, such as Year:

```
In  [14] movies.sort_values(by = "Year", ascending = False).head()

Out [14]
```

Title	Rank	Studio	Gross	Year
Avengers: Endgame	1	Buena Vista	2796.3	2019
John Wick: Chapter 3 - Parab...	458	Lionsgate	304.7	2019
The Wandering Earth	114	China Film Corporation	699.8	2019
Toy Story 4	198	Buena Vista	519.8	2019
How to Train Your Dragon: Th...	199	Universal	519.8	2019

We can also sort DataFrames by values across multiple columns. Let's sort movies first by the Studio column's values and then by the Year column's values. Now we can see the films organized alphabetically by both studio and release date:

```
In  [15] movies.sort_values(by = ["Studio", "Year"]).head()

Out [15]
```

Title	Rank	Studio	Gross	Year
The Blair Witch Project	588	Artisan	$248.60	1999
101 Dalmatians	708	Buena Vista	$215.90	1961
The Jungle Book	755	Buena Vista	$205.80	1967
Who Framed Roger Rabbit	410	Buena Vista	$329.80	1988
Dead Poets Society	636	Buena Vista	$235.90	1989

We can also sort the index, which is helpful if we want to see the movies in alphabetical order:

```
In  [16] movies.sort_index().head()

Out [16]
```

Title	Rank	Studio	Gross	Year
10,000 B.C.	536	Warner Brothers	$269.80	2008
101 Dalmatians	708	Buena Vista	$215.90	1961
101 Dalmatians	425	Buena Vista	$320.70	1996
2 Fast 2 Furious	632	Universal	$236.40	2003
2012	93	Sony	$769.70	2009

The operations we've performed so far return *new* DataFrame objects. Pandas has not altered the original movies DataFrame from the CSV file. The nondestructive nature of these operations is beneficial; it actively encourages experimentation. We can always confirm that a result is correct before making it permanent.

1.3.3   *Counting values in a Series*

Let's try a more sophisticated analysis. What if we wanted to find out which movie studio had the greatest number of highest-grossing films? To solve this problem, we'll need to count the number of times each studio appears in the Studio column.

We can extract a single column of data from a DataFrame as a Series. Notice that pandas preserves the DataFrame's index, the movie titles, in the Series:

```
In  [17] movies["Studio"]

Out [17] Title
         Avengers: Endgame             Buena Vista
         Avatar                                Fox
         Titanic                         Paramount
         Star Wars: The Force Awakens  Buena Vista
         Avengers: Infinity War        Buena Vista
                                             ...
         Yogi Bear                   Warner Brothers
         Garfield: The Movie                   Fox
         Cats & Dogs                 Warner Brothers
         The Hunt for Red October        Paramount
         Valkyrie                              MGM
         Name: Studio, Length: 782, dtype: object
```

If a Series has a large number of rows, pandas truncates the data set to show only the first five and the last five rows.

Now that we've isolated the Studio column, we can count each unique value's number of occurrences. Let's limit our results to the top 10 studios:

```
In  [18] movies["Studio"].value_counts().head(10)

Out [18] Warner Brothers    132
         Buena Vista        125
         Fox                117
```

```
Universal            109
Sony                  86
Paramount             76
Dreamworks            27
Lionsgate             21
New Line              16
MGM                   11
Name: Studio, dtype: int64
```

The return value above is yet another `Series` object! This time around, pandas uses the studios from the Studio column as the index labels and their counts as the `Series` values.

1.3.4 *Filtering a column by one or more criteria*

You'll often want to extract a subset of rows based on one or more criteria. Excel offers the Filter tool for this exact purpose.

What if we wanted to find only the films released by Universal Studios? We can accomplish this task with one line of code in pandas:

```
In [19] movies[movies["Studio"] == "Universal"]

Out [19]
```

Title	Rank	Studio	Gross	Year
Jurassic World	6	Universal	$1,671.70	2015
Furious 7	8	Universal	$1,516.00	2015
Jurassic World: Fallen Kingdom	13	Universal	$1,309.50	2018
The Fate of the Furious	17	Universal	$1,236.00	2017
Minions	19	Universal	$1,159.40	2015
...	...	...	...	...
The Break-Up	763	Universal	$205.00	2006
Everest	766	Universal	$203.40	2015
Patch Adams	772	Universal	$202.30	1998
Kindergarten Cop	775	Universal	$202.00	1990
Straight Outta Compton	776	Universal	$201.60	2015

```
109 rows × 4 columns
```

We can assign the filtering condition to a variable to provide context for readers:

```
In [20] released_by_universal = (movies["Studio"] == "Universal")
        movies[released_by_universal].head()

Out [20]
```

Title	Rank	Studio	Gross	Year
Jurassic World	6	Universal	$1,671.70	2015
Furious 7	8	Universal	$1,516.00	2015
Jurassic World: Fallen Kingdom	13	Universal	$1,309.50	2018
The Fate of the Furious	17	Universal	$1,236.00	2017
Minions	19	Universal	$1,159.40	2015

We can also filter `DataFrame` rows by multiple criteria. The next example targets all movies released by Universal Studios *and* released in 2015:

```
In  [21] released_by_universal = movies["Studio"] == "Universal"
         released_in_2015 = movies["Year"] == 2015
         movies[released_by_universal & released_in_2015]
```

Out [21]

Title	Rank	Studio	Gross	Year
Jurassic World	6	Universal	$1,671.70	2015
Furious 7	8	Universal	$1,516.00	2015
Minions	19	Universal	$1,159.40	2015
Fifty Shades of Grey	165	Universal	$571.00	2015
Pitch Perfect 2	504	Universal	$287.50	2015
Ted 2	702	Universal	$216.70	2015
Everest	766	Universal	$203.40	2015
Straight Outta Compton	776	Universal	$201.60	2015

The previous example includes rows that satisfied both conditions. We can also filter for films that fit either condition: released by Universal *or* released in 2015. The resulting `DataFrame` is longer because more films have a chance of satisfying one of the two conditions instead of both:

```
In  [22] released_by_universal = movies["Studio"] == "Universal"
         released_in_2015 = movies["Year"] == 2015
         movies[released_by_universal | released_in_2015]
```

Out [22]

Title	Rank	Studio	Gross	Year
Star Wars: The Force Awakens	4	Buena Vista	$2,068.20	2015
Jurassic World	6	Universal	$1,671.70	2015
Furious 7	8	Universal	$1,516.00	2015
Avengers: Age of Ultron	9	Buena Vista	$1,405.40	2015
Jurassic World: Fallen Kingdom	13	Universal	$1,309.50	2018
...	...	...	...	...
The Break-Up	763	Universal	$205.00	2006
Everest	766	Universal	$203.40	2015
Patch Adams	772	Universal	$202.30	1998
Kindergarten Cop	775	Universal	$202.00	1990
Straight Outta Compton	776	Universal	$201.60	2015

140 rows × 4 columns

Pandas provides additional ways to filter a `DataFrame`. We can target column values less than or greater than a specific value, for example. Here, we target movies released before 1975:

```
In  [23] before_1975 = movies["Year"] < 1975
         movies[before_1975]

Out [23]
```

Title	Rank	Studio	Gross	Year
The Exorcist	252	Warner Brothers	$441.30	1973
Gone with the Wind	288	MGM	$402.40	1939
Bambi	540	RKO	$267.40	1942
The Godfather	604	Paramount	$245.10	1972
101 Dalmatians	708	Buena Vista	$215.90	1961
The Jungle Book	755	Buena Vista	$205.80	1967

We can also specify a range between which all values must fall. The next example pulls out movies released between 1983 and 1986:

```
In  [24] mid_80s = movies["Year"].between(1983, 1986)
         movies[mid_80s]

Out [24]
```

Title	Rank	Studio	Gross	Year
Return of the Jedi	222	Fox	$475.10	1983
Back to the Future	311	Universal	$381.10	1985
Top Gun	357	Paramount	$356.80	1986
Indiana Jones and the Temple of Doom	403	Paramount	$333.10	1984
Crocodile Dundee	413	Paramount	$328.20	1986
Beverly Hills Cop	432	Paramount	$316.40	1984
Rocky IV	467	MGM	$300.50	1985
Rambo: First Blood Part II	469	TriStar	$300.40	1985
Ghostbusters	485	Columbia	$295.20	1984
Out of Africa	662	Universal	$227.50	1985

We can also use the `DataFrame` index to filter rows. The next example lowercases the movie titles in the index and finds all movies with the word `"dark"` in their title:

```
In  [25] has_dark_in_title = movies.index.str.lower().str.contains("dark")
         movies[has_dark_in_title]

Out [25]
```

Title	Rank	Studio	Gross	Year
Transformers: Dark of the Moon	23	Paramount	$1,123.80	2011
The Dark Knight Rises	27	Warner Brothers	$1,084.90	2012
The Dark Knight	39	Warner Brothers	$1,004.90	2008
Thor: The Dark World	132	Buena Vista	$644.60	2013
Star Trek Into Darkness	232	Paramount	$467.40	2013
Fifty Shades Darker	309	Universal	$381.50	2017
Dark Shadows	600	Warner Brothers	$245.50	2012
Dark Phoenix	603	Fox	$245.10	2019

Notice that pandas finds all movies containing the word `"dark"` irrespective of where the text appears in the title.

1.3.5   *Grouping data*

Our next challenge is the most complex one yet. We might be curious which studio had the highest total grosses across all films. Let's aggregate the values in the Gross column by studio.

Our first dilemma is that the Gross column's values are stored as text rather than as numbers. Pandas imported the column's values as text to preserve the dollar signs and comma symbols in the original CSV. We can convert the column's values to decimal numbers, but only if we remove both of those characters. The next example replaces all occurrences of "$" and "," with empty text. This operation is similar to Find and Replace in Excel:

```
In  [26] movies["Gross"].str.replace(
             "$", "", regex = False
         ).str.replace(",", "", regex = False)
```

```
Out [26] Title
         Avengers: Endgame              2796.30
         Avatar                         2789.70
         Titanic                        2187.50
         Star Wars: The Force Awakens   2068.20
         Avengers: Infinity War         2048.40
                                          ...
         Yogi Bear                       201.60
         Garfield: The Movie             200.80
         Cats & Dogs                     200.70
         The Hunt for Red October        200.50
         Valkyrie                        200.30
         Name: Gross, Length: 782, dtype: object
```

With the symbols gone, we can convert the Gross column's values from text to floating-point numbers:

```
In  [27] (
             movies["Gross"]
             .str.replace("$", "", regex = False)
             .str.replace(",", "", regex = False)
             .astype(float)
         )
```

```
Out [27] Title
         Avengers: Endgame              2796.3
         Avatar                         2789.7
         Titanic                        2187.5
         Star Wars: The Force Awakens   2068.2
         Avengers: Infinity War         2048.4
                                          ...
         Yogi Bear                       201.6
         Garfield: The Movie             200.8
         Cats & Dogs                     200.7
         The Hunt for Red October        200.5
         Valkyrie                        200.3
         Name: Gross, Length: 782, dtype: float64
```

Once again, these operations are temporary and do not modify the original Gross Series. In all the previous examples, pandas created a copy of the original data structure, performed the operation, and returned a new object. The next example explicitly overwrites the Gross column in movies with a new column of decimal-point numbers. Now the transformation is permanent:

```
In  [28] movies["Gross"] = (
             movies["Gross"]
             .str.replace("$", "", regex = False)
             .str.replace(",", "", regex = False)
             .astype(float)
         )
```

Our data type conversion opens the door to more calculations and manipulations. The next example calculates the average box-office gross of the movies:

```
In  [29] movies["Gross"].mean()

Out [29] 439.0308184143222
```

Let's return to our original problem: calculating the aggregate box-office grosses per film studio. First, we'll need to identify the studios and bucket the movies (or rows) that belong to each one. This process is called *grouping*. In the next example, we group the DataFrame's rows based on values in the Studio column:

```
In  [30] studios = movies.groupby("Studio")
```

We can ask pandas to count the number of films per studio:

```
In  [31] studios["Gross"].count().head()

Out [31] Studio
         Artisan                  1
         Buena Vista            125
         CL                       1
         China Film Corporation   1
         Columbia                 5
         Name: Gross, dtype: int64
```

The previous results are sorted alphabetically by studio name. We can instead sort the Series by count of films, from most to least:

```
In  [32] studios["Gross"].count().sort_values(ascending = False).head()

Out [32] Studio
         Warner Brothers   132
         Buena Vista       125
         Fox               117
         Universal         109
         Sony               86
         Name: Gross, dtype: int64
```

Next, let's add the values of the Gross column per studio. Pandas will identify the subset of movies that belong to each studio, pull out their row's respective Gross values, and sum them together:

```
In   [33] studios["Gross"].sum().head()

Out [33] Studio
         Artisan                      248.6
         Buena Vista                73585.0
         CL                           228.1
         China Film Corporation       699.8
         Columbia                    1276.6
         Name: Gross, dtype: float64
```

Again, pandas sorts the results by studio name. We want to identify the studios with the highest grosses, so let's sort the `Series` values in descending order. Here are the five studios with the greatest grosses:

```
In   [34] studios["Gross"].sum().sort_values(ascending = False).head()

Out [34] Studio
         Buena Vista        73585.0
         Warner Brothers    58643.8
         Fox                50420.8
         Universal          44302.3
         Sony               32822.5
         Name: Gross, dtype: float64
```

With a few lines of code, we can derive some fun insights from this complex data set. The Warner Brothers studio, for example, has more movies in the list than Buena Vista, but Buena Vista has a higher cumulative gross for all films. This fact indicates that the average gross of a Buena Vista film is greater than that of a Warner Brothers film.

We have barely scratched the surface of what pandas is capable of doing. I hope that these examples have shed light on the diverse ways we can manipulate and transform data with this powerful library. We'll discuss all the code used in this chapter in much greater detail throughout the book. Next, we'll dive into a core building block of pandas: the `Series` object.

Summary

- Pandas is a data analysis library built on top of the Python programming language.
- Pandas excels at performing complex operations on large data sets with a terse syntax.
- Competitors to pandas include the graphical spreadsheet application Excel, the statistical programming language R, and the SAS software suite.
- Programming requires a different skill set than working with Excel or Sheets.
- Pandas can import a variety of file formats. A popular format is CSV, which separates rows with line breaks and row values with commas.

- The `DataFrame` is the primary data structure in pandas. It is effectively a table of data with multiple columns.
- The `Series` is a one-dimensional labeled array. Think of it as a single column of data.
- We can access a row in a `Series` or `DataFrame` by its row number or index label.
- We can sort a `DataFrame` by values across one or more columns.
- We can use logical conditions to extract subsets of data from a `DataFrame`.
- We bucket `DataFrame` rows based on a column's values. We can also perform aggregate operations such as sums on the resulting groups.

The Series object 2

This chapter covers

- Instantiating `Series` objects from lists, dictionaries, tuples, and more
- Setting a custom index on a `Series`
- Accessing attributes and invoking methods on a `Series`
- Performing mathematical operations on one or more `Series`
- Passing the `Series` to Python's built-in functions

One of pandas' core data structures, the `Series` is a one-dimensional labeled array for homogeneous data. An *array* is an ordered collection of values comparable to a Python list. The term *homogeneous* means that the values are of the same data type (all integers or all Booleans, for example).

Pandas assigns each `Series` value a *label*—an identifier we can use to locate the value. The library also assigns each `Series` value an *order*—a position in line. The order starts counting from 0; the first `Series` value occupies position 0, the second value occupies position 1, and so on. The `Series` is a one-dimensional data structure because we need one reference point to access a value: either a label or a position.

A `Series` combines and expands the best features of Python's native data structures. Like a list, it holds its values in a sequenced order. Like a dictionary, it assigns a key/label to each value. We gain the benefits of both of those objects plus more than 180 methods for data manipulation.

In this chapter, we'll familiarize ourselves with the mechanics of a `Series` object, learn how to calculate the sum and average of `Series` values, apply mathematical operations to each `Series` value, and more. As a building block of pandas, the `Series` is a perfect starting point for our exploration of the library.

2.1 Overview of a Series

Let's create some `Series` objects, shall we? We'll begin by importing the pandas and NumPy packages with the `import` keyword; we'll use the latter library in section 2.1.4. The popular community aliases for `pandas` and `numpy` are `pd` and `np`. We can assign an alias to an import with the `as` keyword:

```
In  [1] import pandas as pd
        import numpy as np
```

The `pd` namespace holds the top-level exports of the `pandas` package, a bundle of more than 100 classes, functions, exceptions, constants, and more. For more information on these concepts, see appendix B.

Think of `pd` as being the lobby to the library—an entrance room where we can access pandas' available features. The library's exports are available as attributes on `pd`. We can access an attribute with dot syntax:

```
pd.attribute
```

Jupyter Notebook provides a convenient autocomplete feature for use in searching for attributes. Enter the library's name, add a dot, and press the Tab key to reveal a modal of the package's exports. As you type additional characters, the Notebook filters the results to those that match your search term.

Figure 2.1 shows the autocomplete feature in action. After entering the capital letter `S`, we can press Tab to reveal all `pd` exports starting with that character. Note that the search is case-sensitive. If the autocomplete feature is not working, add the following code to a cell in your Notebook, execute it, and try searching again:

```
%config Completer.use_jedi = False
```

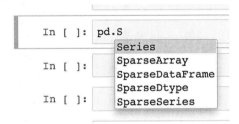

Figure 2.1 Using Jupyter Notebook's autocomplete features to show pandas exports that start with `S`

We can use our keyboard's up- and down-arrow keys to navigate the modal's search results. Luckily, the Series class is our first search result. Press the Enter key to auto-complete its name.

2.1.1   Classes and instances

A *class* is a blueprint for a Python object. The pd.Series class is a template, and the next step is to create a concrete instance of it. We instantiate an object from a class with a pair of opening and closing parentheses. Let's create a Series object from the Series class:

```
In  [2] pd.Series()

Out [2] Series([], dtype: float64)
```

A warning might appear in a red box alongside the output:

```
DeprecationWarning: The default dtype for empty Series will be 'object'
    instead of 'float64' in a future version. Specify a dtype explicitly to
    silence this warning.
```

Because we did not provide any values to store, pandas could not infer the data type that the Series should hold. No need to worry; the warning is expected behavior.

We've successfully created our first Series object! Unfortunately, it stores no data. Let's populate our Series with some values.

2.1.2   Populating the Series with values

A *constructor* is a method that builds an object from a class. When we wrote pd.Series() in section 2.1.1, we used the Series constructor to create a new Series object.

When we create an object, we'll often want to define its starting state. We can think of an object's starting state as being its initial configuration—its "settings." We can often set state by passing arguments to the constructor that we use to create the object. An *argument* is an input we pass to a method.

Let's practice creating some Series from manual data. The goal is to get comfortable with the look and feel of the data structure. In the future, we'll use an imported data set to populate our Series' values.

The first argument to the Series constructor is an iterable object whose values will populate the Series. We can pass various inputs, including lists, dictionaries, tuples, and NumPy ndarrays.

Let's create a Series object with data from a Python list. The next example declares a list of four strings, assigns the list to an ice_cream_flavors variable, and then passes the list to the Series constructor:

```
In  [3] ice_cream_flavors = [
            "Chocolate",
            "Vanilla",
            "Strawberry",
            "Rum Raisin",
        ]
```

```
pd.Series(ice_cream_flavors)
```

```
Out [3]  0     Chocolate
         1       Vanilla
         2    Strawberry
         3    Rum Raisin
         dtype: object
```

Excellent—we've created a new `Series` with the four values from our `ice_cream_` `flavors` list. Notice that pandas preserves the order of the strings from the input list. We'll come back to the numbers on the left of the `Series` in a moment.

A *parameter* is a name given to an expected input to a function or method. Behind the scenes, Python matches every argument we pass to a constructor with a parameter. We can view a constructor's parameters directly in Jupyter Notebook. Enter `pd.Series()` in a new cell, place the mouse cursor between the parentheses, and press Shift+Tab. Figure 2.2 shows the documentation modal that appears.

Figure 2.2   A documentation modal with the parameters and default arguments for a
`Series` **constructor**

Press Shift+Tab repeatedly to reveal more information. Eventually, Jupyter will fix the documentation panel to the bottom of the screen.

The `Series` constructor defines six parameters: `data`, `index`, `dtype`, `name`, `copy`, and `fastpath`. We can use these parameters to set the object's initial state. We can think of the parameters as being configuration options for the `Series`.

The documentation displays each parameter alongside its default argument. A *default argument* is a fallback value that Python uses if we do not provide an argument for the parameter. If we do not pass a value for the `name` parameter, for example, Python will use `None`. A parameter with a default argument is inherently optional. It will always have some argument, either explicitly from its invocation or implicitly from its definition. We were able to instantiate a `Series` without arguments earlier because all six of its constructor's parameters are optional.

The `Series` constructor's first parameter, `data`, expects the object whose values will populate the `Series`. If we pass arguments to the constructor without parameter names, Python will assume that we are passing them sequentially. In the preceding code example, we passed the `ice_cream_flavors` list as the first argument to the constructor; thus, Python matched it with `data`, the first constructor parameter. Python also fell back to default arguments of `None` for the `index`, `dtype`, and `name` parameters and `False` for the `copy` and `fastpath` parameters.

We can connect parameters and arguments explicitly with keyword arguments (see appendix B). Enter the parameter, followed by an equal sign and its argument. In the following example, the first line uses positional arguments, and the second one uses keyword arguments, but the result is the same:

```
In   [4] # The two lines below are equivalent
         pd.Series(ice_cream_flavors)
         pd.Series(data = ice_cream_flavors)

Out [4] 0       Chocolate
        1         Vanilla
        2      Strawberry
        3      Rum Raisin
        dtype: object
```

Keyword arguments are advantageous because they provide context for what each constructor argument represents. The second line in the example better communicates that `ice_cream_flavors` represents the `data` for the `Series`.

2.1.3 *Customizing the Series index*

Let's take a closer look at our `Series`:

```
0       Chocolate
1         Vanilla
2      Strawberry
3      Rum Raisin
dtype: object
```

Earlier, we mentioned that pandas assigns a position in line to each `Series` value. The collection of incrementing integers on the left side of the output is called the index. Each number signifies a value's order within the `Series`. The index starts counting from 0. The string `"Chocolate"` occupies index 0, the string `"Vanilla"` occupies index 1, and so on. In graphical spreadsheet applications, the first row of data starts counting at 1—an important difference between pandas and Excel.

The term *index* describes both the collection of identifiers and an individual identifier. Both of these two expressions are valid: "The index of the `Series` consists of integers" and "The value `'Strawberry'` is found at index 2 in the `Series`."

The last index position will always be 1 less than the total number of values. The current `Series` has four ice cream flavors, so the index counts up to 3.

In addition to an index position, we can assign each `Series` value an index label. Index labels can be of any immutable data type: strings, tuples, datetimes, and more. This flexibility makes a `Series` powerful: we can reference a value by its order or by a key/label. In a sense, each value has two identifiers.

The `Series` constructor's second parameter, `index`, sets the index labels of the `Series`. If we do not pass an argument to the parameter, pandas defaults to a numeric index starting from 0. With this type of index, the label and the position identifiers are one and the same.

Let's construct a `Series` with a custom index. We can pass objects of different data types to the `data` and `index` parameters, but they must have the same length so that pandas can associate their values. The next example passes a list of strings for the `data` parameter and a tuple of strings to the `index` parameter. Both the list and the tuple have a length of 4:

```
In  [5] ice_cream_flavors = [
            "Chocolate",
            "Vanilla",
            "Strawberry",
            "Rum Raisin",
        ]

        days_of_week = ("Monday", "Wednesday", "Friday", "Saturday")

        # The two lines below are equivalent
        pd.Series(ice_cream_flavors, days_of_week)
        pd.Series(data = ice_cream_flavors, index = days_of_week)

Out [5] Monday          Chocolate
        Wednesday         Vanilla
        Friday         Strawberry
        Saturday       Rum Raisin
        dtype: object
```

Pandas uses shared index positions to associate the values from the `ice_cream_flavors` list and the `days_of_week` tuple. The library sees `"Rum Raisin"` and `"Saturday"` at index position 3 in their respective objects, for example; thus, it ties them together in the `Series`.

Even though the index consists of string labels, pandas still assigns each `Series` value an index position. In other words, we can access the value `"Vanilla"` either by the index label `"Wednesday"` or by index position 1. We'll explore how to access `Series` elements by row and label in chapter 4.

The index permits duplicates, a detail that distinguishes a `Series` from a Python dictionary. In the next example, the string `"Wednesday"` appears twice in the `Series`' index labels:

```
In  [6] ice_cream_flavors = [
            "Chocolate",
            "Vanilla",
            "Strawberry",
            "Rum Raisin",
        ]

        days_of_week = ("Monday", "Wednesday", "Friday", "Wednesday")
```

```
        # The two lines below are equivalent
        pd.Series(ice_cream_flavors, days_of_week)
        pd.Series(data = ice_cream_flavors, index = days_of_week)
```

```
Out [6] Monday        Chocolate
        Wednesday       Vanilla
        Friday       Strawberry
        Wednesday    Rum Raisin
        dtype: object
```

Although pandas permits duplicates, it is ideal to avoid them whenever possible, because a unique index allows the library to locate index labels more quickly.

One additional advantage of keyword arguments is that they permit us to pass parameters in any order. By comparison, sequential/positional arguments require us to pass arguments in the order in which the constructor expects them. The next example swaps the order of the index and data keyword parameters. Pandas creates the same Series:

```
In  [7] pd.Series(index = days_of_week, data = ice_cream_flavors)
```

```
Out [7] Monday        Chocolate
        Wednesday       Vanilla
        Friday       Strawberry
        Wednesday    Rum Raisin
        dtype: object
```

There's one piece of the output that we haven't discussed yet: the dtype statement at the bottom reflects the data type of the values in the Series. For most data types, pandas will display a predictable type (such as bool, float, or int). For strings and more-complex objects (such as nested data structures), pandas will show dtype: object.[1]

The next examples create Series objects from lists of Boolean, integer, and floating-point values. Observe the similarities and differences in the Series:

```
In  [8] bunch_of_bools = [True, False, False]
        pd.Series(bunch_of_bools)
```

```
Out [8] 0     True
        1    False
        2    False
        dtype: bool
```

```
In  [9] stock_prices = [985.32, 950.44]
        time_of_day = ["Open", "Close"]
        pd.Series(data = stock_prices, index = time_of_day)
```

```
Out [9] Open     985.32
        Close    950.44
        dtype: float64
```

---

[1] See http://mng.bz/7j6v for a discussion of why pandas lists "object" as the dtype for strings.

```
In  [10] lucky_numbers = [4, 8, 15, 16, 23, 42]
         pd.Series(lucky_numbers)

Out [10] 0     4
         1     8
         2    15
         3    16
         4    23
         5    42
         dtype: int64
```

The `float64` and `int64` data types indicate that each floating-point/integer value in the `Series` occupies 64 bits (8 bytes) of your computer's RAM. Bits and bytes are storage units for memory. We don't need to dive extensively into these computer science concepts right now to work effectively with pandas.

Pandas does its best to infer an appropriate data type for the `Series` from the `data` parameter's values. We can force coercion to a different type via the constructor's `dtype` parameter. The next example passes an integer list to the constructor but asks for a floating-point `Series`:

```
In  [11] lucky_numbers = [4, 8, 15, 16, 23, 42]
         pd.Series(lucky_numbers, dtype = "float")

Out [11] 0     4.0
         1     8.0
         2    15.0
         3    16.0
         4    23.0
         5    42.0
         dtype: float64
```

The previous example used both positional arguments and keyword arguments. We passed the `lucky_numbers` list sequentially to the `data` parameter. We also passed the `dtype` parameter explicitly with keyword arguments. The `Series` constructor expects the `dtype` parameter to be third in line, so we cannot pass it directly after `lucky_numbers`; we have to use keyword arguments.

2.1.4   *Creating a Series with missing values*

So far, so good. Our `Series` so far have been simple and complete. It's easy to have perfect data when we're crafting our own data sets. In the real world, data is a lot messier. Perhaps the most frequent problem that analysts encounter is missing values.

When pandas sees a missing value during a file import, the library substitutes NumPy's nan object. The acronym nan is short for *not a number* and is a catch-all term for an undefined value. In other words, nan is a placeholder object that represents nullness or absence.

Let's sneak a missing value into a `Series`. We assigned the NumPy library to the alias np when we imported it earlier. The nan attribute is available as a top-level export of the library. The next example nestles a np.nan inside a list of temperatures that we pass to the `Series` constructor. Notice the `NaN` at index position 2 in the output. Get used to this trio of letters; we're going to be seeing them a lot throughout the book:

```
In   [12] temperatures = [94, 88, np.nan, 91]
          pd.Series(data = temperatures)

Out  [12] 0     94.0
          1     88.0
          2      NaN
          3     91.0
          dtype: float64
```

Notice that the `Series` dtype is `float64`. Pandas automatically converts numeric values from integers to floating-points when it spots a `nan` value; this internal technical requirement allows the library to store numeric values and missing values in the same homogeneous `Series`.

2.2   *Creating a Series from Python objects*

The `Series` constructor's `data` parameter accepts various inputs, including native Python data structures and objects from other libraries. In this section, we'll explore how the `Series` constructor deals with dictionaries, tuples, sets, and NumPy arrays. The `Series` object that pandas returns operates the same way irrespective of its data source.

A *dictionary* is a collection of key-value pairs (see appendix B). When passed a dictionary, the constructor sets each key as a corresponding index label in the `Series`:

```
In   [13] calorie_info = {
              "Cereal": 125,
              "Chocolate Bar": 406,
              "Ice Cream Sundae": 342,
          }

          diet = pd.Series(calorie_info)
          diet

Out  [13] Cereal              125
          Chocolate Bar       406
          Ice Cream Sundae    342
          dtype: int64
```

A *tuple* is an immutable list. We cannot add, remove, or replace elements in a tuple after creating it (see appendix B). When passed a tuple, the constructor populates the `Series` in an expected manner:

```
In   [14] pd.Series(data = ("Red", "Green", "Blue"))

Out  [14] 0      Red
          1     Green
          2      Blue
          dtype: object
```

To create a `Series` that stores tuples, wrap the tuples in a list. Tuples work well for row values that consist of multiple parts or components, such as an address:

```
In  [15] rgb_colors = [(120, 41, 26), (196, 165, 45)]
         pd.Series(data = rgb_colors)

Out [15] 0       (120, 41, 26)
         1       (196, 165, 45)
         dtype: object
```

A *set* is an unordered collection of unique values. We can declare it with a pair of curly braces, exactly like a dictionary. Python uses the presence of key-value pairs to distinguish between the two data structures (see appendix B).

If we pass a set to the `Series` constructor, pandas raises a `TypeError` exception. A set has neither the concept of order (such as a list) nor the concept of association (such as a dictionary). Thus, the library cannot assume an order in which to store the set's values:[2]

```
In  [16] my_set = {"Ricky", "Bobby"}
         pd.Series(my_set)

---------------------------------------------------------------------
TypeError                              Traceback (most recent call last)
<ipython-input-16-bf85415a7772> in <module>
      1 my_set = { "Ricky", "Bobby" }
----> 2 pd.Series(my_set)

TypeError: 'set' type is unordered
```

If your program involves a set, transform it to an ordered data structure before passing it to the `Series` constructor. The next example converts `my_set` to a list by using Python's built-in `list` function:

```
In  [17] pd.Series(list(my_set))

Out [17] 0       Ricky
         1       Bobby
         dtype: object
```

Because a set is unordered, we cannot guarantee the order of list elements (or the `Series` elements).

The `Series` constructor's `data` parameter also accepts a NumPy `ndarray` object. Many data science libraries use NumPy arrays, which are common storage formats for moving data around. The next example feeds the `Series` constructor an `ndarray` generated by NumPy's `randint` function (see appendix C):

---

[2] See "Constructing a Series with a set returns a set and not a Series," https://github.com/pandas-dev/pandas/issues/1913.

```
In  [18] random_data = np.random.randint(1, 101, 10)
         random_data

Out [18] array([27, 16, 13, 83,  3, 38, 34, 19, 27, 66])

In  [19] pd.Series(random_data)

Out [19] 0    27
         1    16
         2    13
         3    83
         4     3
         5    38
         6    34
         7    19
         8    27
         9    66
         dtype: int64
```

As with all other inputs, pandas preserves the order of the ndarray's values in the Series.

2.3   *Series attributes*

An *attribute* is a piece of data belonging to an object. Attributes reveal information about the object's internal state. An attribute's value may be another object. See appendix B for an in-depth overview.

A Series is composed of several smaller objects. Think of these objects as being puzzle pieces that join to make a greater whole. Consider the calorie_info Series from section 2.2:

```
Cereal            125
Chocolate Bar     406
Ice Cream Sundae  342
dtype: int64
```

This Series uses the NumPy library's ndarray object to store the calorie counts and the pandas library's Index object to store the food names in the index. We can access these nested objects through Series attributes. The values attribute, for example, exposes the ndarray object that stores the values:

```
In  [20] diet.values

Out [20] array([125, 406, 342])
```

If we're ever uncertain what type an object is or what library it comes from, we can pass the object to Python's built-in type function. The function will return the class from which the object was instantiated:

```
In  [21] type(diet.values)

Out [21] numpy.ndarray
```

Let's pause here to reflect for a second. Pandas delegates the responsibility of storing `Series` values to an object from a different library. That's why NumPy is a dependency of pandas. The `ndarray` object optimizes for speed and efficiency by relying on the lower-level C programming language for many of its calculations. In many ways, the `Series` is a wrapper—an additional layer of functionality around a core NumPy library object.

Pandas has its own objects, of course. The `index` attribute, for example, returns the `Index` object that stores the `Series` labels:

```
In  [22] diet.index

Out [22] Index(['Cereal', 'Chocolate Bar', 'Ice Cream Sundae'],
             dtype='object')
```

Index objects such as `Index` are built into pandas:

```
In  [23] type(diet.index)

Out [23] pandas.core.indexes.base.Index
```

Some attributes reveal helpful details about the object. `dtype`, for example, returns the data type of the `Series`' values:

```
In  [24] diet.dtype

Out [24] dtype('int64')
```

The `size` attribute returns the number of values in the `Series`:

```
In  [25] diet.size

Out [25] 3
```

The complementary `shape` attribute returns a tuple with the dimensions of a pandas data structure. For the one-dimensional `Series`, the tuple's only value will be the `Series`' size. The comma after the 3 is a standard visual output for one-element tuples in Python:

```
In  [26] diet.shape

Out [26] (3,)
```

The `is_unique` attribute returns `True` if all `Series` values are unique:

```
In  [27] diet.is_unique

Out [27] True
```

The `is_unique` attribute returns `False` if the `Series` contains duplicates:

```
In  [28] pd.Series(data = [3, 3]).is_unique

Out [28] False
```

The `is_monotonic` attribute returns `True` if each `Series` value is greater than the previous one. The increments between values do not have to be equal:

```
In  [29] pd.Series(data = [1, 3, 6]).is_monotonic

Out [29] True
```

The `is_monotonic` attribute returns `False` if any element is smaller than the previous one:

```
In  [30] pd.Series(data = [1, 6, 3]).is_monotonic

Out [30] False
```

In summary, attributes ask an object for information on its internal state. Attributes reveal nested objects, which can have their own functionalities. In Python, everything is an object, including integers, strings, and Booleans. Thus, an attribute that returns a number is no technically different from one that returns a complex object such as an `ndarray`.

2.4   *Retrieving the first and last rows*

By now, you should feel comfortable creating `Series` objects. It's OK if the technical terminology is a bit overwhelming; we've presented a lot of information up front, and we'll review it many times throughout the book. In this section, we'll start exploring what we can do with `Series` objects.

A Python object has both attributes and methods. An *attribute* is a piece of data belonging to an object—a characteristic or detail that the data structure can reveal about itself. In section 2.3, we accessed `Series` attributes such as `size`, `shape`, `values`, and `index`.

By comparison, a *method* is a function that belongs to an object—an action or command that we ask the object to perform. Methods typically involve some analysis, calculation, or manipulation of the object's attributes. Attributes define an object's *state*, and methods define an object's *behavior*.

Let's create our largest `Series` yet. We'll use Python's built-in `range` function to generate a sequence of all numbers between a starting point and an endpoint. The `range` function's three arguments are a lower bound, the upper bound, and a step sequence (the interval between every two numbers).

The next example generates a 100-value range of numbers between 0 and 500 in increments of 5 and then pass the range object into the `Series` constructor:

```
In  [31] values = range(0, 500, 5)
         nums = pd.Series(data = values)
         nums

Out [31] 0        0
         1        5
         2        10
         3        15
         4        20
```

```
          . . .
95        475
96        480
97        485
98        490
99        495
Length: 100, dtype: int64
```

Now we have a `Series` with 100 values. Fancy! Take note of the ellipses (the three dots) that appear in the middle of the output. Pandas is telling us that it condensed the output by hiding some rows. The library conveniently truncates the `Series` to show only the first five and the last five rows. Too many rows of printed data can slow Jupyter Notebook.

We invoke a method with a pair of parentheses after its name. Let's invoke some simple `Series` methods. We'll start with the `head` method, which returns rows from the beginning or top of the data set. It accepts a single argument n, which sets the number of rows to extract:

```
In   [32] nums.head(3)

Out  [32] 0      0
          1      5
          2     10
          dtype: int64
```

We can pass keyword arguments in method calls, as in constructors and functions. The following code produces the same result as the preceding code:

```
In   [33] nums.head(n = 3)

Out  [33] 0      0
          1      5
          2     10
          dtype: int64
```

Like functions, methods can declare default arguments for their parameters. The `head` method's n parameter has a default argument of 5. If we do not pass an explicit argument for n, pandas returns five rows (a design decision of the pandas development team):

```
In   [34] nums.head()

Out  [34] 0      0
          1      5
          2     10
          3     15
          4     20
          dtype: int64
```

The complementary `tail` method returns rows from the bottom or end of a `Series`:

```
In  [35] nums.tail(6)

Out [35] 94     470
         95     475
         96     480
         97     485
         98     490
         99     495
         dtype: int64
```

The `tail` method's n parameter also has a default argument of 5:

```
In  [36] nums.tail()

Out [36] 95     475
         96     480
         97     485
         98     490
         99     495
         dtype: int64
```

`head` and `tail` are the two methods I use most frequently; we can use them to pre-view the beginning and end of a data set quickly. Next, let's dive into some more-advanced `Series` methods.

2.5   *Mathematical operations*

A `Series` object includes plenty of statistical and mathematical methods. Let's see a few of these methods in action. Feel free to breeze through this section and revisit it when you need to track down a specific function.

2.5.1   *Statistical operations*

We'll begin by creating a `Series` from a list of ascending numbers, sneaking in an `np.nan` value in the middle. Remember that if a data source has even a single missing value, pandas will coerce the integers to floating-point values:

```
In  [37] numbers = pd.Series([1, 2, 3, np.nan, 4, 5])
         numbers

Out [37] 0     1.0
         1     2.0
         2     3.0
         3     NaN
         4     4.0
         5     5.0
         dtype: float64
```

The `count` method counts the number of non-null values:

```
In  [38] numbers.count()

Out [38] 5
```

The sum method adds the Series' values together:

```
In  [39] numbers.sum()

Out [39] 15.0
```

Most mathematical methods ignore missing values by default. We can pass an argument of False to the skipna parameter to force the inclusion of missing values.

The next example invokes the sum method with the parameter. Pandas returns a nan because it cannot add the unknown nan value at index 3 to the cumulative sum:

```
In  [40] numbers.sum(skipna = False)

Out [40] nan
```

The sum method's min_count parameter sets the minimum number of valid values a Series must hold for pandas to calculate its sum. Our six-element numbers Series contains five present values and one nan value

In the next example, the Series meets the threshold of three present values, so pandas returns the sum:

```
In  [41] numbers.sum(min_count = 3)

Out [41] 15.0
```

By comparison, the next invocation demands a minimum of six values for pandas to calculate the sum. The threshold is unmet, so the sum method returns nan:

```
In  [42] numbers.sum(min_count = 6)

Out [42] nan
```

TIP If you're ever curious about a method's parameters, press Shift+Tab between a method's parentheses to bring up the documentation in Jupyter Notebook.

The product method multiplies all Series values together:

```
In  [43] numbers.product()

Out [43] 120.0
```

The method also accepts skipna and min_count parameters. Here, we ask pandas to include nan values in the calculation:

```
In  [44] numbers.product(skipna = False)

Out [44] nan
```

The next example asks for the product of all Series values if it has at least three present ones:

```
In  [45] numbers.product(min_count = 3)

Out [45] 120.0
```

The `cumsum` (cumulative sum) method returns a new `Series` with a rolling sum of values. Each index position holds the sum of values up to and including the value at that index. A cumulative sum helps determine which values contribute most to the total:

```
In   [46] numbers

Out [46] 0      1.0
         1      2.0
         2      3.0
         3      NaN
         4      4.0
         5      5.0
         dtype: float64

In   [47] numbers.cumsum()

Out [47] 0       1.0
         1       3.0
         2       6.0
         3       NaN
         4      10.0
         5      15.0
         dtype: float64
```

Let's walk through some of the calculations in the result:

- The cumulative sum at index 0 is 1.0, the first value in the `numbers` Series. There is nothing to add yet.
- The cumulative sum at index 1 is 3.0, the sum of 1.0 at index 0 and 2.0 at index position 1.
- The cumulative sum at index 2 is 6.0, the sum of 1.0, 2.0, and 3.0.
- The `numbers` Series has a `nan` at index 3. Pandas cannot add a missing value to the cumulative sum, so it places a `nan` at the same index in the returned `Series`.
- The cumulative sum at index 4 is 10.0. Pandas adds the previous cumulative sum with the current index's value (1.0 + 2.0 + 3.0 + 4.0).

If we pass the `skipna` an argument of `False`, the `Series` will list the cumulative sum up to the index with the first missing value and then NaN for the remaining values:

```
In   [48] numbers.cumsum(skipna = False)

Out [48] 0      1.0
         1      3.0
         2      6.0
         3      NaN
         4      NaN
         5      NaN
         dtype: float64
```

The `pct_change` (percent change) method returns the percentage difference from one `Series` value to the next. At each index, pandas adds the last index's value and the current index's value and then divides the sum by the last index's value. Pandas can calculate a percentage difference only if both indexes have valid values.

The `pct_change` method defaults to a *forward-fill* strategy for missing values. With this strategy, pandas replaces a `nan` with the last valid value it encountered. Let's invoke the method and then walk through the calculations:

```
In  [49] numbers

Out [49] 0    1.0
         1    2.0
         2    3.0
         3    NaN
         4    4.0
         5    5.0
         dtype: float64

In  [50] numbers.pct_change()

Out [50] 0         NaN
         1    1.000000
         2    0.500000
         3    0.000000
         4    0.333333
         5    0.250000
         dtype: float64
```

Here's how pandas operates:

- At index 0, pandas cannot compare the value 1.0 in the `numbers` `Series` with any previous value. Thus, index 0 in the returned `Series` has a `NaN` value.
- At index 1, pandas compares index 1's value of 2.0 with index 0's value of 1.0. The percentage change between 2.0 and 1.0 is 100 (double), which translates to 1.00000 at index 1 in the returned `Series`.
- At index 2, pandas repeats the same operation.
- At index 3, the `numbers` `Series` has a `NaN` missing value. Pandas substitutes the last encountered value (3.0 from index 2) in its place. The percentage change between the substituted 3.0 at index 3 and the 3.0 at index 2 is 0.
- At index 4, pandas compares index 4's value of 4.0 with the previous row's value. It again substitutes the `nan` with the last valid value it saw, 3.0. The percentage change between 4 and 3 is 0.333333 (a 33 percent increase).

Figure 2.3 shows a visual representation of a forward-fill percentage-change calculation. The `Series` on the left is the starting point. The `Series` in the middle shows the intermediate calculations that pandas performs. The `Series` on the right is the final result.

0	1.0
1	2.0
2	3.0
3	NaN
4	4.0
5	5.0

0	NaN
1	(2.0 - 1.0) / 1.0
2	(3.0 - 2.0) / 2.0
3	(3.0 - 3.0) / 3.0
4	(4.0 - 3.0) / 3.0
5	(5.0 - 4.0) / 4.0

0	NaN
1	1.000000
2	0.500000
3	0.000000
4	0.333333
5	0.250000

Figure 2.3 **A walkthrough of how the `pct_change` method calculates values with a forward-fill solution**

The `fill_method` parameter customizes the protocol by which `pct_change` substitutes NaN values. This parameter is available across many methods, so it's worth taking the time to familiarize yourself with it. As mentioned earlier, with the default forward-fill strategy, pandas replaces a nan value with the *last* valid observation. We can pass the `fill_method` parameter an explicit argument of `"pad"` or `"ffill"` to achieve the same result:

```
In  [51] # The three lines below are equivalent
         numbers.pct_change()
         numbers.pct_change(fill_method = "pad")
         numbers.pct_change(fill_method = "ffill")

Out [51] 0         NaN
         1    1.000000
         2    0.500000
         3    0.000000
         4    0.333333
         5    0.250000
         dtype: float64
```

An alternative strategy for dealing with missing values is a *backfill* solution. With this option, pandas replaces a nan value with the next valid observation. Let's pass the `fill_method` parameter a value of `"bfill"` to see the results and then walk through them step by step:

```
In  [52] # The two lines below are equivalent
         numbers.pct_change(fill_method = "bfill")
         numbers.pct_change(fill_method = "backfill")

Out [52] 0         NaN
         1    1.000000
         2    0.500000
         3    0.333333
         4    0.000000
         5    0.250000
         dtype: float64
```

Notice that the values at index positions 3 and 4 differ between the forward-fill and backfill solutions. Here's how pandas arrives at the previous calculations:

- At index 0, pandas cannot compare the value 1.0 in the numbers Series with any previous value. Thus, index 0 in the returned Series has a NaN value.
- At index 3, pandas runs into a NaN in the numbers Series. Pandas substitutes the next valid value (4.0 at index 4) in its place. The percentage change between 4.0 at index 3 and 3.0 at index 2 in numbers is 0.33333.
- At index 4, pandas compares 4.0 with index 3's value. It again replaces the NaN at index 3 with 4.0, the next valid value available in the numbers Series. The percentage change between 4 and 4 is 0.0.

Figure 2.4 shows a visual representation of a backfill percentage-change calculation. The Series on the left is the starting point. The Series in the middle shows the intermediate calculations that pandas performs. The Series on the right is the final result.

0	1.0
1	2.0
2	3.0
3	NaN
4	4.0
5	5.0

0	NaN
1	(2.0 - 1.0) / 1.0
2	(3.0 - 2.0) / 2.0
3	(4.0 - 3.0) / 3.0
4	(4.0 - 4.0) / 4.0
5	(5.0 - 4.0) / 4.0

0	NaN
1	1.000000
2	0.500000
3	0.333333
4	0.000000
5	0.250000

Figure 2.4   A walkthrough of how the `pct_change` method calculates values with a backfill solution

The mean method returns the average of the values in the Series. An average is the result of dividing the sum of values by the count of values:

```
In  [53] numbers.mean()

Out [53] 3.0
```

The median method returns the middle number in a sorted Series of values. Half of the Series values will be below the median, and half of the values will be above the median:

```
In  [54] numbers.median()

Out [54] 3.0
```

The std method returns the *standard deviation*, a measure of the variation in the data:

```
In  [55] numbers.std()

Out [55] 1.5811388300841898
```

The max and min methods retrieve the largest and smallest value from the Series:

```
In  [56] numbers.max()

Out [56] 5.0
```

```
In   [57] numbers.min()

Out [57] 1.0
```

Pandas sorts a string Series alphabetically. The "smallest" string is the one closest to the start of the alphabet, and the "largest" string is the one closest to the end of the alphabet. Here's a simple example with a small Series:

```
In   [58] animals = pd.Series(["koala", "aardvark", "zebra"])
          animals

Out [58] 0          koala
          1      aardvark
          2          zebra
          dtype: object

In   [59] animals.max()

Out [59] 'zebra'

In   [60] animals.min()

Out [60] 'aardvark'
```

If you're looking for a single method to summarize a Series effectively, the powerful describe method does the trick. It returns a Series of statistical evaluations, including count, mean, and standard deviation:

```
In   [61] numbers.describe()

Out [61] count     5.000000
          mean      3.000000
          std       1.581139
          min       1.000000
          25%       2.000000
          50%       3.000000
          75%       4.000000
          max       5.000000
          dtype: float64
```

The sample method selects a random assortment of values from the Series. It is possible for the order of values to differ between the new Series and the original Series. In the next example, notice that the lack of NaN values from the random selection allows pandas to return a Series of integers. If NaN was even one of the values, pandas would return a Series of floats instead:

```
In   [62] numbers.sample(3)

Out [62] 1     2
          3     4
          2     3
          dtype: int64
```

The unique method returns a NumPy ndarray of unique values from the Series. In the next example, the string "Orwell" appears twice in the authors Series but only once in the returned ndarray:

```
In  [63] authors = pd.Series(
             ["Hemingway", "Orwell", "Dostoevsky", "Fitzgerald", "Orwell"]
         )

         authors.unique()

Out [63] array(['Hemingway', 'Orwell', 'Dostoevsky', 'Fitzgerald'],
         dtype=object)
```

The complementary `nunique` method returns the number of unique values in the `Series`:

```
In  [64] authors.nunique()

Out [64] 4
```

The `nunique` method's return value will be equal to the length of the array that the `unique` method returns.

2.5.2 *Arithmetic operations*

In section 2.5.1, we practiced invoking numerous mathematical methods on our `Series` objects. Pandas gives us additional ways to perform arithmetic calculations with a `Series`. Let's start by creating a `Series` of integers with one missing value:

```
In  [65] s1 = pd.Series(data = [5, np.nan, 15], index = ["A", "B", "C"])
         s1

Out [65] A     5.0
         B     NaN
         C    15.0
         dtype: float64
```

We can perform arithmetic on a `Series` with Python's standard mathematical operators:

- + for addition
- – for subtraction
- * for multiplication
- / for division

The syntax is intuitive: treat the `Series` as a regular operand on one side of a mathematical operator. Place the complementary value on the other side of the operator. Note that any mathematical operation with a nan yields another nan. The next example adds 3 to each value in the s1 `Series`:

```
In  [66] s1 + 3

Out [66] A     8.0
         B     NaN
         C    18.0
         dtype: float64
```

Some software developers might find the result surprising. How can we add an integer to a data structure? The types are seemingly incompatible. Behind the scenes, pandas is smart enough to parse our syntax and understand that we'd like to add an integer to every value in the `Series`, not to the `Series` object itself.

If you prefer a method-based approach, the `add` method achieves the same result:

```
In  [67] s1.add(3)

Out [67] A      8.0
         B      NaN
         C     18.0
         dtype: float64
```

The next three examples show the complementary syntax options for subtraction (-), multiplication (*), and division (/). Often, there are multiple ways to accomplish the same operation in pandas:

```
In  [68] # The three lines below are equivalent
         s1 - 5
         s1.sub(5)
         s1.subtract(5)

Out [68] A      0.0
         B      NaN
         C     10.0
         dtype: float64

In  [69] # The three lines below are equivalent
         s1 * 2
         s1.mul(2)
         s1.multiply(2)

Out [69] A     10.0
         B      NaN
         C     30.0
         dtype: float64

In  [70] # The three lines below are equivalent
         s1 / 2
         s1.div(2)
         s1.divide(2)

Out [70] A      2.5
         B      NaN
         C      7.5
         dtype: float64
```

The floor division operator (//) performs a division and removes any digits after the decimal point in the result. The regular division of 15 by 4, for example, yields 3.75. By comparison, the floor division of 15 by 4 yields 3. We can apply the operator to a `Series`; the alternative is to invoke the `floordiv` method:

```
In  [71] # The two lines below are equivalent
         s1 // 4
         s1.floordiv(4)

Out [71] A    1.0
         B    NaN
         C    3.0
         dtype: float64
```

The modulo operator (%) returns the remainder of a division. Here's an example:

```
In  [72] # The two lines below are equivalent
         s1 % 3
         s1.mod(3)

Out [72] A    2.0
         B    NaN
         C    0.0
         dtype: float64
```

In the previous example,

- Pandas divides the value of 5.0 at index label A by 3 and leaves a remainder of 2.0.
- Pandas cannot divide the NaN at index label B.
- Pandas divides the value of 15.0 at index label C by 3 and leaves a reminder of 0.0.

2.5.3 *Broadcasting*

Recall that pandas stores its Series values in a NumPy ndarray under the hood. When we use syntax such as s1 + 3 or s1 – 5, pandas delegates the mathematical calculations to NumPy.

The NumPy documentation uses the term *broadcasting* to describe the derivation of one array of values from another. Without diving too much into the technical details (you don't need to understand NumPy's complexities to work effectively with pandas), the term *broadcasting* comes from a radio broadcast tower, which transmits the same signal to all recipients listening in. Syntax like s1 + 3 means "Apply the same operation (add 3) to each value in the Series." Each Series value gets the same message, much as every person listening to the same radio station at the same time hears the same song.

Broadcasting also describes mathematical operations between multiple Series objects. As a rule of thumb, pandas uses shared index labels to align values across different data structures. Let's demonstrate this concept through an example. Let's instantiate two Series with the same three-element index:

```
In  [73] s1 = pd.Series([1, 2, 3], index = ["A", "B", "C"])
         s2 = pd.Series([4, 5, 6], index = ["A", "B", "C"])
```

When we use the + operator with the two `Series` as operands, pandas adds the values at the same index positions:

- At index A, pandas adds the values 1 and 4 to arrive at 5.
- At index B, pandas adds the values 2 and 5 to arrive at 7.
- At index C, pandas adds the values 3 and 6 to arrive at 9.

```
In  [74] s1 + s2

Out [74] A    5
         B    7
         C    9
         dtype: int64
```

Figure 2.5 offers a visualization of how pandas aligns the two `Series`.

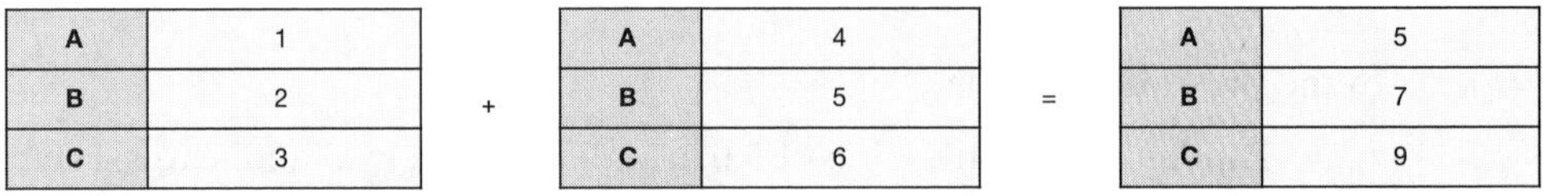

Figure 2.5   Pandas aligns `Series` by shared index labels when performing a mathematical operation.

Here's another example of how pandas uses shared index labels to align data. Let's create another two `Series` with the standard numeric index. We'll add a missing value to each collection:

```
In  [75] s1 = pd.Series(data = [3, 6, np.nan, 12])
         s2 = pd.Series(data = [2, 6, np.nan, 12])
```

Python's equality operator (==) compares the equality of two objects. We can use this operator to compare values across two `Series`, as in the following example. Note that pandas considers a nan value to be unequal to another nan; it cannot assume that an absent value is equal to another absent value. The method equivalent for the equality operator is eq:

```
In  [76] # The two lines below are equivalent
         s1 == s2
         s1.eq(2)

Out [76] 0    False
         1     True
         2    False
         3     True
         dtype: bool
```

The inequality operator (!=) confirms whether two values are unequal. Its method equivalent is ne:

```
In  [77] # The two lines below are equivalent
         s1 != s2
         s1.ne(s2)

Out [77] 0    True
         1    False
         2    True
         3    False
         dtype: bool
```

Comparison operations between `Series` become trickier when the indices differ. One index may have a greater or smaller number of labels, or there may be a mismatch between the labels themselves.

The next example creates two `Series` that share only two index labels, B and C:

```
In  [78] s1 = pd.Series(
             data = [5, 10, 15], index = ["A", "B", "C"]
         )

         s2 = pd.Series(
             data = [4, 8, 12, 14], index = ["B", "C", "D", "E"]
         )
```

What happens when we try to add `s1` and `s2`? Pandas adds the values at the B and C labels and returns `NaN` values for the remaining indices (A, D, and E). As a reminder, any arithmetic operation with a `NaN` value always results in a `NaN`:

```
In  [79] s1 + s2

Out [79] A    NaN
         B    14.0
         C    23.0
         D    NaN
         E    NaN
         dtype: float64
```

Figure 2.6 shows how pandas aligns the `s1` and `s2` `Series` and then adds their associated index values.

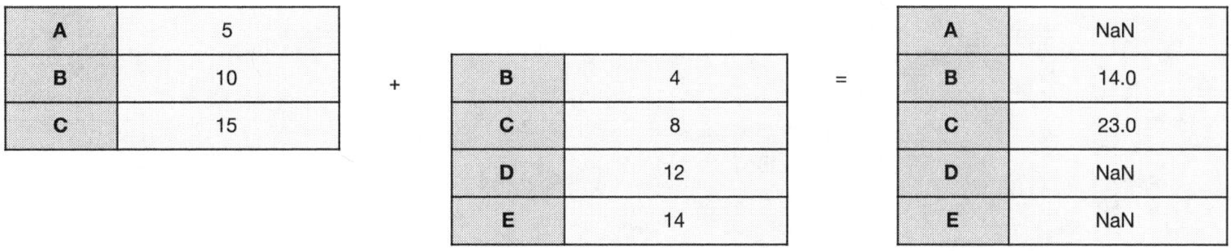

Figure 2.6   Pandas returns `NaN` whenever the `Series` do not share an index label.

In summary, pandas aligns data by shared index labels across two `Series`, substituting `NaN`s where needed.

2.6   *Passing the Series to Python's built-in functions*

Python's developer community likes to rally around certain design principles to ensure consistency across codebases. One example is seamless integration between library objects and Python's built-in functions. Pandas is no exception. We can pass a Series to any of Python's built-in functions and yield a predictable result. Let's create a small Series of cities in the United States:

```
In  [80] cities = pd.Series(
             data = ["San Francisco", "Los Angeles", "Las  Vegas", np.nan]
         )
```

The len function returns the number of rows in a Series. The count includes missing values (NaNs):

```
In  [81] len(cities)

Out [81] 4
```

As we saw earlier, the type function returns the class of an object. Use this function when you're uncertain about the data structure you're working with or the library it's coming from:

```
In  [82] type(cities)

Out [82] pandas.core.series.Series
```

The dir function returns a list of an object's attributes and methods as strings. Note that the next example displays an abbreviated version of the output:

```
In  [83] dir(cities)

Out [83] ['T',
          '_AXIS_ALIASES',
          '_AXIS_IALIASES',
          '_AXIS_LEN',
          '_AXIS_NAMES',
          '_AXIS_NUMBERS',
          '_AXIS_ORDERS',
          '_AXIS_REVERSED',
          '_HANDLED_TYPES',
          '__abs__',
          '__add__',
          '__and__',
          '__annotations__',
          '__array__',
          '__array_priority__',
          #...
         ]
```

A Series' values can populate a native Python data structure. The next example creates a list from our cities Series by using Python's list function:

```
In  [84] list(cities)

Out [84] ['San Francisco', 'Los Angeles', 'Las  Vegas', nan]
```

We can pass the `Series` to Python's built-in `dict` function to create a dictionary. Pandas maps the `Series`' index labels and values to the dictionary's keys and values:

```
In  [85] dict(cities)

Out [85] {0: 'San Francisco', 1: 'Los Angeles', 2: 'Las  Vegas', 3: nan}
```

In Python, we use the `in` keyword to check for inclusion. In pandas, we can use the `in` keyword to check whether a given value exists in the `Series`' index. Here's a reminder of what `cities` looks like:

```
In  [86] cities

Out [86] 0    San Francisco
         1      Los Angeles
         2       Las  Vegas
         3              NaN
         dtype: object
```

The next two examples query for `"Las Vegas"` and `2` in the `Series`' index:

```
In  [87] "Las Vegas" in cities

Out [87] False

In  [88] 2 in cities

Out [88] True
```

To check for inclusion among the `Series`' values, we can pair the `in` keyword with the `values` attribute. Remember that `values` exposes the `ndarray` object that holds the data itself:

```
In  [89] "Las Vegas" in cities.values

Out [89] True
```

We can use the inverse `not in` operator to check for exclusion. The operator returns `True` if pandas cannot find the value in the `Series`:

```
In  [90] 100 not in cities

Out [90] True

In  [91] "Paris" not in cities.values

Out [91] True
```

A pandas object will often integrate with Python's built-in functions and offer its own attribute/method to return the same data. Choose the syntax option that works best for you.

2.7   *Coding challenge*

Welcome to the book's first coding challenge! The goal of these exercises is to help you apply and review the concepts introduced throughout the chapter. You'll find the solutions immediately after the questions. Good luck!

2.7.1   *Problems*

Suppose that you're given these two data structures:

```
In  [92] superheroes = [
            "Batman",
            "Superman",
            "Spider-Man",
            "Iron Man",
            "Captain America",
            "Wonder Woman"
         ]

In  [93] strength_levels = (100, 120, 90, 95, 110, 120)
```

Here are your challenges:

1 Use the list of superheroes to populate a new `Series` object.
2 Use the tuple of strengths to populate a new `Series` object.
3 Create a `Series` with the superheroes as index labels and the strength levels as the values. Assign the `Series` to a `heroes` variable.
4 Extract the first two rows of the `heroes` `Series`.
5 Extract the last four rows of the `heroes` `Series`.
6 Determine the number of unique values in your `heroes` `Series`.
7 Calculate the average strength of the superheroes in `heroes`.
8 Calculate the maximum and minimum strengths in `heroes`.
9 Calculate what each superhero's strength level would be if it doubled.
10 Convert the `heroes` `Series` to a Python dictionary.

2.7.2   *Solutions*

Let's explore the solutions to the problems in section 2.7.1:

1 To create a new `Series` object, we can use the `Series` constructor at the top level of the pandas library. Pass in the source of data as the first positional argument:

```
In  [94] pd.Series(superheroes)

Out [94] 0              Batman
         1            Superman
         2          Spider-Man
         3            Iron Man
         4     Captain America
         5        Wonder Woman
         dtype: object
```

2 The solution to this problem is identical to the previous one; we only have to pass in our tuple of strengths to the `Series` constructor. This time around, let's write out the `data` keyword parameter explicitly:

```
In  [95] pd.Series(data = strength_levels)

Out [95] 0    100
         1    120
         2     90
         3     95
         4    110
         5    120
         dtype: int64
```

3 To create a `Series` with a custom index, we can pass the `index` parameter to the constructor. Here, we set the strength levels as the `Series`' values and the superhero names as the index labels:

```
In  [96] heroes = pd.Series(
             data = strength_levels, index = superheroes
         )

         heroes

Out [96] Batman             100
         Superman           120
         Spider-Man          90
         Iron Man            95
         Captain America    110
         Wonder Woman       120
         dtype: int64
```

4 As a reminder, a *method* is an action or a command we can give to an object. We can use the `head` method to extract rows from the top of a pandas data structure. The method's only parameter, n, sets the number of rows to pull out. The head method returns a new `Series`:

```
In  [97] heroes.head(2)

Out [97] Batman      100
         Superman    120
         dtype: int64
```

5 The complementary `tail` method extracts rows from the end of a pandas data structure. To target the last four rows, we'll pass in an argument of 4:

```
In  [98] heroes.tail(4)

Out [98] Spider-Man          90
         Iron Man            95
         Captain America    110
         Wonder Woman       120
         dtype: int64
```

6   To identify the number of unique values in a `Series`, we can invoke the `nunique` method. The heroes `Series` has six total values and five unique values; the value `120` appears twice:

```
In  [99] heroes.nunique()

Out [99] 5
```

7   To calculate the average of a `Series`' values, we can invoke the `mean` method:

```
In  [100] heroes.mean()

Out [100] 105.83333333333333
```

8   The next challenge is to identify the largest and smallest values in the `Series`. The `max` and `min` methods do the trick:

```
In  [101] heroes.max()

Out [101] 120

In  [102] heroes.min()

Out [102] 90
```

9   How can we double each superhero's strength level? We can multiply each `Series` value by 2. The following solution uses the multiplication operator, but the `mul` and `multiply` methods are also suitable options:

```
In  [103] heroes * 2

Out [103] Batman              200
          Superman            240
          Spider-Man          180
          Iron Man            190
          Captain America     220
          Wonder Woman        240
          dtype: int64
```

10   The last challenge is to convert the `heroes` `Series` to a Python dictionary. To solve this problem, we can pass the data structure into Python's `dict` constructor/function. Pandas sets the index labels as the dictionary keys and the `Series` values as the dictionary values:

```
In  [104] dict(heroes)

Out [104] {'Batman': 100,
           'Superman': 120,
           'Spider-Man': 90,
           'Iron Man': 95,
           'Captain America': 110,
           'Wonder Woman': 120}
```

Congratulations on completing your first coding challenge!

Summary

- A `Series` is a one-dimensional homogeneous labeled array that holds values and an index.
- A `Series`' values can be of any data type. The index labels can be of any immutable data type.
- Pandas assigns both an index *position* and an index *label* to each `Series` value.
- We can populate a `Series` with data from lists, dictionaries, tuples, NumPy arrays, and more.
- The `head` method retrieves the first rows of a `Series`.
- The `tail` method retrieves the last rows of a `Series`.
- A `Series` supports common statistical operations such as sum, mean, median, and standard deviation.
- Pandas uses shared index labels to apply arithmetic operations across multiple `Series`.
- A `Series` plays friendly with Python's built-in functions, including `dict`, `list`, and `len`.

Series methods 3

This chapter covers

- Importing CSV data sets with the `read_csv` function
- Sorting `Series` values in ascending and descending order
- Retrieving the largest and smallest values in a `Series`
- Counting occurrences of unique values in a `Series`
- Invoking a function with every value in a `Series`

In chapter 2, we began exploring the `Series` object, a one-dimensional labeled array of homogeneous values. We populated our `Series` with data from different sources, including lists, dictionaries, and NumPy `ndarrays`. We observed how pandas assigned each `Series` value an index label and an index position. We learned how to apply mathematical operations to `Series`.

With the basics under our belt, we're ready to explore some real-world data sets! In this chapter, we'll introduce lots of advanced `Series` operations, including sorting, counting, and bucketing. We'll also start to see how these methods can help us derive insights from our data. Let's dive in.

3.1 *Importing a data set with the read_csv function*

A *CSV* is a plain-text file that separates each row of data with a line break and each row value with a comma. The first row in the file holds the column headers for the data. This chapter has three CSV files for us to play with:

- *pokemon.csv*—A list of more than 800 Pokémon, the cartoon monsters from Nintendo's popular media franchise. Each Pokémon has one or more associated *types*, such as Fire, Water, and Grass.
- *google_stock.csv*—A collection of daily stock prices in U.S. dollars for the technology company Google from its market debut in August 2004 to October 2019.
- *revolutionary_war.csv*—A record of battles during the American Revolutionary War. Each skirmish is associated with a start date and a U.S. state.

Let's begin by importing the data sets. As we proceed, we'll talk through some optimizations we can make to pave the way for easier analysis.

Our first step is spinning up a new Jupyter Notebook and importing the pandas library. Make sure to create the notebook in the same directory as the CSV files:

```
In [1] import pandas as pd
```

Pandas has more than a dozen import functions to load various file formats. The functions are available at the library's top level and begin with the prefix `read`. In our case, to import a CSV, we want the `read_csv` function. The function's first parameter, `filepath_or_buffer`, expects a string with the filename. Make sure that the string includes the .csv extension (`"pokemon.csv"`, for example, instead of `"pokemon"`). By default, pandas looks for the file in the same directory as the Notebook:

```
In  [2] # The two lines below are equivalent
        pd.read_csv(filepath_or_buffer = "pokemon.csv")
        pd.read_csv("pokemon.csv")
```

```
Out [2]
```

	Pokemon	Type
0	Bulbasaur	Grass / Poison
1	Ivysaur	Grass / Poison
2	Venusaur	Grass / Poison
3	Charmander	Fire
4	Charmeleon	Fire
...	...	...
804	Stakataka	Rock / Steel
805	Blacephalon	Fire / Ghost
806	Zeraora	Electric
807	Meltan	Steel
808	Melmetal	Steel

809 rows × 2 columns

Regardless of the number of columns in a data set, the read_csv function always imports the data into a DataFrame, a two-dimensional pandas data structure that supports multiple rows and columns. We'll introduce this object in greater detail in chapter 4. There's nothing wrong with using the DataFrame, but we want to practice a bit more with the Series, so let's store the CSV's data in the smaller data structure.

Our first issue is that the data set has two columns (Pokemon and Type), but a Series supports only one column of data. One simple solution is setting one of the data set's columns as the Series index. We can use the index_col parameter to set the index column. Be mindful of case sensitivity: the string must match the header in the data set. Let's pass "Pokemon" as the argument to index_col:

```
In  [3] pd.read_csv("pokemon.csv", index_col = "Pokemon")

Out [3]
```

	Type
Pokemon	
Bulbasaur	Grass / Poison
Ivysaur	Grass / Poison
Venusaur	Grass / Poison
Charmander	Fire
Charmeleon	Fire
...	...
Stakataka	Rock / Steel
Blacephalon	Fire / Ghost
Zeraora	Electric
Meltan	Steel
Melmetal	Steel

```
809 rows × 1 columns
```

We've successfully set the Pokemon column as the Series index, but pandas still defaults to importing the data into a DataFrame. After all, a container capable of holding multiple columns of data can technically hold one column of data. To force pandas to use a Series, we need to add another parameter called squeeze and pass it an argument of True. The squeeze parameter coerces a one-column DataFrame into a Series:

```
In  [4] pd.read_csv("pokemon.csv", index_col = "Pokemon", squeeze = True)

Out [4] Pokemon
        Bulbasaur       Grass / Poison
        Ivysaur         Grass / Poison
        Venusaur        Grass / Poison
        Charmander               Fire
        Charmeleon               Fire

                         . . .
        Stakataka         Rock / Steel
        Blacephalon       Fire / Ghost
        Zeraora               Electric
        Meltan                   Steel
        Melmetal                 Steel
        Name: Type, Length: 809, dtype: object
```

We officially have a `Series`. Hooray! The index labels are the Pokémon names, and the values are the Pokémon types.

The output below the values reveals some important details:

- Pandas has assigned the `Series` a name of Type, the column's name from the CSV file.
- The `Series` has 809 values.
- `dtype: object` tells us that it's a `Series` of string values. `object` is pandas' internal lingo for strings and more-complex data structures.

The final step is assigning the `Series` to a variable. `pokemon` feels suitable here:

```
In  [5] pokemon = pd.read_csv(
           "pokemon.csv", index_col = "Pokemon", squeeze = True
        )
```

The remaining two data sets carry some additional complexity. Let's take a peek at google_stock.csv:

```
In  [6] pd.read_csv("google_stocks.csv").head()

Out [6]
```

	Date	Close
0	2004-08-19	49.98
1	2004-08-20	53.95
2	2004-08-23	54.50
3	2004-08-24	52.24
4	2004-08-25	52.80

When importing a data set, pandas infers the most suitable data type for each column. Sometimes, the library plays it safe and avoids making assumptions about our data. google_stocks.csv, for example, includes a Date column with datetime values in YYYY-MM-DD format (such as 2010-08-04). Unless we tell pandas to treat the values as datetimes, the library defaults to importing them as strings. A string is a more generic and versatile data type; it can represent any value.

Let's explicitly tell pandas to convert the values in the Date column to datetimes. Although we won't cover datetimes until chapter 11, it's considered to be a best practice to store each column's data in the most accurate type. When pandas knows that it has datetimes, it enables additional methods that are not available on plain strings, such as calculating the weekday of a date.

The `read_csv` function's `parse_dates` parameter accepts a list of strings denoting the columns whose text values pandas should convert to datetimes. The next example passes a list containing `"Date"`:

```
In  [7] pd.read_csv("google_stocks.csv", parse_dates = ["Date"]).head()

Out [7]
```

	Date	Close
0	2004-08-19	49.98
1	2004-08-20	53.95

```
2   2004-08-23   54.50
3   2004-08-24   52.24
4   2004-08-25   52.80
```

There is no visual difference in the output, but pandas is storing a different data type for the Date column under the hood. Let's set the Date column as the `Series` index with the `index_col` parameter; a `Series` works fine with datetime indexes. Finally, let's add the `squeeze` parameter to force a `Series` object instead of a `DataFrame`:

```
In  [8] pd.read_csv(
          "google_stocks.csv",
          parse_dates = ["Date"],
          index_col = "Date",
          squeeze = True
        ).head()

Out [8] Date
        2004-08-19    49.98
        2004-08-20    53.95
        2004-08-23    54.50
        2004-08-24    52.24
        2004-08-25    52.80
        Name: Close, dtype: float64
```

Looks good. We have a `Series` of datetime index labels and floating-point values. Let's save this `Series` to a `google` variable:

```
In  [9] google = pd.read_csv(
          "google_stocks.csv",
          parse_dates = ["Date"],
          index_col = "Date",
          squeeze = True
        )
```

We have one more data set to import: Revolutionary War battles. This time around, let's preview the last five rows on import. We'll chain the `tail` method to the `Data-Frame` returned by the `read_csv` function:

```
In  [10] pd.read_csv("revolutionary_war.csv").tail()

Out [10]
```

	Battle	Start Date	State
227	Siege of Fort Henry	9/11/1782	Virginia
228	Grand Assault on Gibraltar	9/13/1782	NaN
229	Action of 18 October 1782	10/18/1782	NaN
230	Action of 6 December 1782	12/6/1782	NaN
231	Action of 22 January 1783	1/22/1783	Virginia

Take a look at the State column. Uh-oh—this data set has some missing values. As a reminder, pandas uses the NaN (not a number) designation to mark absent values. NaN is a NumPy object used to represent nothingness or the absence of a value. This data set contains missing/absent values for battles without a definitive start date or those fought outside U.S. territory.

Let's set the Start Date column as the index. We'll again use the `index_col` parameter to set the index and the `parse_dates` parameter to convert the Start Date strings to datetime values. Pandas can recognize this data set's date format (M/D/YYYY):

```
In  [11] pd.read_csv(
            "revolutionary_war.csv",
            index_col = "Start Date",
            parse_dates = ["Start Date"],
        ).tail()


Out [11]
```

	Battle	State
Start Date		
1782-09-11	Siege of Fort Henry	Virginia
1782-09-13	Grand Assault on Gibraltar	NaN
1782-10-18	Action of 18 October 1782	NaN
1782-12-06	Action of 6 December 1782	NaN
1783-01-22	Action of 22 January 1783	Virginia

By default, the `read_csv` function imports all columns from a CSV. We'll have to limit the import to two columns if we want a `Series`: one column for the index and the other for the values. The `squeeze` parameter by itself is insufficient in this scenario; pandas will ignore the parameter if there is more than one column of data.

The `read_csv` function's `usecols` parameter accepts a list of columns that pandas should import. Let's include only Start Date and State:

```
In  [12] pd.read_csv(
            "revolutionary_war.csv",
            index_col = "Start Date",
            parse_dates = ["Start Date"],
            usecols = ["State", "Start Date"],
            squeeze = True
        ).tail()

Out [12] Start Date
         1782-09-11     Virginia
         1782-09-13          NaN
         1782-10-18          NaN
         1782-12-06          NaN
         1783-01-22     Virginia
         Name: State, dtype: object
```

Perfect! We have a `Series` consisting of a datetime index and string values. Let's assign this one to a `battles` variable:

```
In  [13] battles = pd.read_csv(
            "revolutionary_war.csv",
            index_col = "Start Date",
            parse_dates = ["Start Date"],
            usecols = ["State", "Start Date"],
            squeeze = True
         )
```

Now that we've imported our data sets into `Series` objects, let's see what we can do with them.

3.2 Sorting a Series

We can sort a `Series` by its values or its index, in ascending or descending order.

3.2.1 Sorting by values with the sort_values method

Suppose that we're curious about the lowest and highest stock prices that Google has had. The `sort_values` method returns a new `Series` with the values sorted in ascending order. *Ascending* means increasing in size—in other words, smallest to greatest. The index labels move with their value counterparts:

```
In  [14] google.sort_values()

Out [14] Date
         2004-09-03       49.82
         2004-09-01       49.94
         2004-08-19       49.98
         2004-09-02       50.57
         2004-09-07       50.60
                           ...
         2019-04-23     1264.55
         2019-10-25     1265.13
         2018-07-26     1268.33
         2019-04-26     1272.18
         2019-04-29     1287.58
         Name: Close, Length: 3824, dtype: float64
```

Pandas sorts a `Series` of strings in alphabetical order. *Ascending* means from the start of the alphabet to the end of the alphabet:

```
In  [15] pokemon.sort_values()

Out [15] Pokemon
         Illumise                Bug
         Silcoon                 Bug
         Pinsir                  Bug
         Burmy                   Bug
         Wurmple                 Bug
                      ...
         Tirtouga        Water / Rock
         Relicanth       Water / Rock
         Corsola         Water / Rock
         Carracosta      Water / Rock
         Empoleon       Water / Steel
         Name: Type, Length: 809, dtype: object
```

Pandas sorts uppercase characters before lowercase characters. Thus, a capital `"Z"` comes before a lowercase `"a"`. In the next example, notice that the string `"adam"` appears *after* `"Ben"`:

```
In  [16] pd.Series(data = ["Adam", "adam", "Ben"]).sort_values()

Out [16] 0     Adam
         2      Ben
         1     adam
         dtype: object
```

The ascending parameter sets the sort order, and it has a default argument of True.
To sort Series values in descending order (largest to smallest), pass the parameter
an argument of False:

```
In  [17] google.sort_values(ascending = False).head()

Out [17] Date
         2019-04-29     1287.58
         2019-04-26     1272.18
         2018-07-26     1268.33
         2019-10-25     1265.13
         2019-04-23     1264.55
         Name: Close, dtype: float64
```

A descending sort will arrange a Series of strings in reverse alphabetical order.
Descending means from the end of the alphabet to the start of the alphabet:

```
In  [18] pokemon.sort_values(ascending = False).head()

Out [18] Pokemon
         Empoleon       Water / Steel
         Carracosta     Water / Rock
         Corsola        Water / Rock
         Relicanth      Water / Rock
         Tirtouga       Water / Rock
         Name: Type, dtype: object
```

The na_position parameter configures the placement of NaN values in the returned
Series and has a default argument of "last". By default, pandas places missing values at the end of a sorted Series:

```
In  [19] # The two lines below are equivalent
         battles.sort_values()
         battles.sort_values(na_position = "last")

Out [19] Start Date
         1781-09-06     Connecticut
         1779-07-05     Connecticut
         1777-04-27     Connecticut
         1777-09-03        Delaware
         1777-05-17         Florida
                             ...
         1782-08-08             NaN
         1782-08-25             NaN
         1782-09-13             NaN
         1782-10-18             NaN
         1782-12-06             NaN
         Name: State, Length: 232, dtype: object
```

To display the missing values first, pass the `na_position` parameter an argument of `"first"`. The resulting `Series` shows all NaNs first, followed by the sorted values:

```
In  [20] battles.sort_values(na_position = "first")

Out [20] Start Date
         1775-09-17          NaN
         1775-12-31          NaN
         1776-03-03          NaN
         1776-03-25          NaN
         1776-05-18          NaN
                      . . .
         1781-07-06     Virginia
         1781-07-01     Virginia
         1781-06-26     Virginia
         1781-04-25     Virginia
         1783-01-22     Virginia
         Name: State, Length: 232, dtype: object
```

What if we wanted to remove NaN values? The `dropna` method returns a `Series` with all missing values removed. Note that the method targets only NaNs in the `Series`' values, not the index. The next example filters our battles to those with a present location:

```
In  [21] battles.dropna().sort_values()

Out [21] Start Date
         1781-09-06     Connecticut
         1779-07-05     Connecticut
         1777-04-27     Connecticut
         1777-09-03       Delaware
         1777-05-17        Florida
                      . . .
         1782-08-19      Virginia
         1781-03-16      Virginia
         1781-04-25      Virginia
         1778-09-07      Virginia
         1783-01-22      Virginia
         Name: State, Length: 162, dtype: object
```

The previous `Series` is predictably shorter than `battles`. Pandas has removed 70 NaN values from `battles`.

3.2.2 Sorting by index with the sort_index method

Sometimes, our area of focus may lie in the index rather than the values. Luckily, we can sort a `Series` by index as well with the `sort_index` method. With this option, the values move alongside their index counterparts. Like `sort_values`, `sort_index` accepts an `ascending` parameter, and its default argument is also `True`:

```
In  [22] # The two lines below are equivalent
         pokemon.sort_index()
         pokemon.sort_index(ascending = True)
```

```
Out [22] Pokemon
         Abomasnow         Grass / Ice
         Abra                  Psychic
         Absol                    Dark
         Accelgor                  Bug
         Aegislash       Steel / Ghost
                          ...
         Zoroark                  Dark
         Zorua                    Dark
         Zubat          Poison / Flying
         Zweilous        Dark / Dragon
         Zygarde       Dragon / Ground
         Name: Type, Length: 809, dtype: object
```

When sorting a collection of datetimes in ascending order, pandas sorts from the earliest date to the latest. The `battles` Series offers a great opportunity to see this sort in action:

```
In  [23] battles.sort_index()

Out [23] Start Date
         1774-09-01     Massachusetts
         1774-12-14     New Hampshire
         1775-04-19     Massachusetts
         1775-04-19     Massachusetts
         1775-04-20          Virginia
                       ...
         1783-01-22          Virginia
         NaT            New Jersey
         NaT                 Virginia
         NaT                      NaN
         NaT                      NaN
         Name: State, Length: 232, dtype: object
```

We see a new type of value toward the end of the sorted `Series`. Pandas uses another NumPy object, `NaT`, in place of missing date values (`NaT` stands for not a time). The `NaT` object maintains data integrity with the index's datetime type.

The `sort_index` method also includes the `na_position` parameter for altering the placement of NaN values. The next example displays the missing values first, followed by the sorted datetimes:

```
In  [24] battles.sort_index(na_position = "first").head()

Out [24] Start Date
         NaT            New Jersey
         NaT                 Virginia
         NaT                      NaN
         NaT                      NaN
         1774-09-01     Massachusetts
         Name: State, dtype: object
```

To sort in descending order, we can pass the `ascending` parameter an argument of `False`. A descending sort displays dates from latest to earliest:

```
In  [25] battles.sort_index(ascending = False).head()

Out [25] Start Date
         1783-01-22    Virginia
         1782-12-06         NaN
         1782-10-18         NaN
         1782-09-13         NaN
         1782-09-11    Virginia
         Name: State, dtype: object
```

The data set's earliest battle took place on January 22, 1783, in Virginia.

3.2.3 *Retrieving the smallest and largest values with the nsmallest and nlargest methods*

Suppose that we wanted to find the five dates on which Google's stock performed best. One option is to sort the `Series` in descending order and then limit the results to the first five rows:

```
In  [26] google.sort_values(ascending = False).head()

Out [26] Date
         2019-04-29    1287.58
         2019-04-26    1272.18
         2018-07-26    1268.33
         2019-10-25    1265.13
         2019-04-23    1264.55
         Name: Close, dtype: float64
```

The operation is fairly common, so pandas offers a helper method to save us a few characters. The `nlargest` method returns the largest values from a `Series`. Its first parameter, n, sets the number of records to return. The n parameter has a default argument of 5. Pandas sorts the values in descending order in the returned `Series`:

```
In  [27] # The two lines below are equivalent
         google.nlargest(n = 5)
         google.nlargest()

Out [27] Date
         2019-04-29    1287.58
         2019-04-26    1272.18
         2018-07-26    1268.33
         2019-10-25    1265.13
         2019-04-23    1264.55
         Name: Close, dtype: float64
```

The complementary `nsmallest` method returns the smallest values from a `Series`, sorted in ascending order. Its n parameter also has a default argument of 5:

```
In  [28] # The two lines below are equivalent
         google.nsmallest(n = 5)
         google.nsmallest(5)
```

```
Out [28] Date
         2004-09-03    49.82
         2004-09-01    49.94
         2004-08-19    49.98
         2004-09-02    50.57
         2004-09-07    50.60
         2004-08-30    50.81
         Name: Close, dtype: float64
```

Note that neither of these methods works on `Series` of strings.

3.3 *Overwriting a Series with the inplace parameter*

All the methods that we've invoked in this chapter return new `Series` objects. The original `Series` objects referenced by our `pokemon`, `google`, and `battles` variables have remained unaffected throughout our operations thus far. As an example, let's observe `battles` before and after a method call; the `Series` does not change:

```
In  [29] battles.head(3)
```

```
Out [29] Start Date
         1774-09-01    Massachusetts
         1774-12-14    New Hampshire
         1775-04-19    Massachusetts
         Name: State, dtype: object
```

```
In  [30] battles.sort_values().head(3)
```

```
Out [30] Start Date
         1781-09-06    Connecticut
         1779-07-05    Connecticut
         1777-04-27    Connecticut
         Name: State, dtype: object
```

```
In  [31] battles.head(3)
```

```
Out [31] Start Date
         1774-09-01    Massachusetts
         1774-12-14    New Hampshire
         1775-04-19    Massachusetts
         Name: State, dtype: object
```

What if we wanted to modify the `battles` `Series`? Many methods in pandas include an `inplace` parameter that, when passed an argument of `True`, appears to modify the object on which the method is invoked.

Compare the previous example with the next one. Here, we once again invoke the `sort_values` method, but this time around, we pass an argument of `True` to the `inplace` parameter. If we use `inplace`, the method returns `None`, leading to no output in Jupyter Notebook. When we output `battles`, we can see that it has changed:

```
In  [32] battles.head(3)
```

```
Out [32] Start Date
         1774-09-01    Massachusetts
         1774-12-14    New Hampshire
         1775-04-19    Massachusetts
         Name: State, dtype: object
```

```
In  [33] battles.sort_values(inplace = True)

In  [34] battles.head(3)

Out [34] Start Date
         1781-09-06     Connecticut
         1779-07-05     Connecticut
         1777-04-27     Connecticut
         Name: State, dtype: object
```

The `inplace` parameter is a frequent point of confusion. Its name suggests that it modifies or mutates the existing object rather than creating a copy. Developers are tempted to use `inplace` because reducing the number of copies we create decreases memory use. But even with the `inplace` parameter, pandas creates a copy of an object whenever we invoke a method. The library *always* creates a duplicate; the `inplace` parameter reassigns our existing variable to the new object. Thus, contrary to popular belief, the `inplace` parameter does not offer any performance benefits. These two lines are technically equivalent:

```
battles.sort_values(inplace = True)
battles = battles.sort_values()
```

Why did the pandas developers choose this implementation? What advantage do we gain from always creating copies? You can find more detailed explanations online, but the short answer is that immutable data structures tend to lead to fewer bugs. Remember that an immutable object is incapable of change. We can copy an immutable object and manipulate the copy, but we can't alter the original object. A Python string is an example. An immutable object is less likely to enter a corrupted or invalid state; it is also easier to test.

The pandas development team has discussed removing the `inplace` parameter from the library in future versions. My recommendation is to avoid using it if possible. The alternative solution is to reassign a method's return value to the same variable or create a separate, more descriptive variable. We can assign the `sort_values` method return value to a variable such as `sorted_battles`, for example.

3.4   *Counting values with the value_counts method*

Here's a reminder of what the `pokemon` Series looks like:

```
In  [35] pokemon.head()

Out [35] Pokemon
         Bulbasaur      Grass / Poison
         Ivysaur        Grass / Poison
         Venusaur       Grass / Poison
         Charmander              Fire
         Charmeleon              Fire
         Name: Type, dtype: object
```

How can we find out the most common types of Pokémon? We need to group the values into buckets and count the number of elements in each bucket. The value_counts method, which counts the number of occurrences of each `Series` value, solves the problem perfectly:

```
In  [36] pokemon.value_counts()

Out [36] Normal            65
         Water             61
         Grass             38
         Psychic           35
         Fire              30
                        ..
         Fire / Dragon      1
         Dark / Ghost       1
         Steel / Ground     1
         Fire / Psychic     1
         Dragon / Ice       1
         Name: Type, Length: 159, dtype: int64
```

The `value_counts` method returns a new `Series` object. The index labels are the pokemon `Series'` values, and the values are their respective counts. Sixty-five of the Pokémon are classified as Normal, 61 are classified as Water, and so on. For those who are curious, "Normal" Pokémon are those that excel in physical attacks.

The length of the `value_counts` `Series` is equal to the number of unique values in the pokemon `Series`. As a reminder, the `nunique` method returns this piece of information:

```
In  [37] len(pokemon.value_counts())

Out [37] 159

In  [38] pokemon.nunique()

Out [38] 159
```

Data integrity is paramount in situations like these. The presence of an extra space or the different casing of a character will cause pandas to deem two values unequal and count them separately. We'll discuss data cleanup in chapter 6.

The `value_counts` method's `ascending` parameter has a default argument of `False`. Pandas sorts the values in descending order, from most occurrences to least occurrences. To sort the values in ascending order, pass the `ascending` parameter a value of `True`:

```
In  [39] pokemon.value_counts(ascending = True)

Out [39] Rock / Poison        1
         Ghost / Dark         1
         Ghost / Dragon       1
         Fighting / Steel     1
         Rock / Fighting      1
                           ..
         Fire                30
         Psychic             35
         Grass               38
         Water               61
         Normal              65
```

We may be more interested in the ratio of a Pokémon type relative to all the types. Set the `value_counts` method's `normalize` parameter to `True` to return the frequencies of each unique value. A value's frequency is the portion of the data set that the value makes up:

```
In  [40] pokemon.value_counts(normalize = True).head()

Out [40] Normal          0.080346
         Water           0.075402
         Grass           0.046972
         Psychic         0.043263
         Fire            0.037083
```

We can multiply the values in the frequency `Series` by 100 to get the percentage each Pokémon type contributes to the whole. Do you recall the syntax from chapter 2? We can use a plain mathematical operator like a multiplication symbol with a `Series`. Pandas will apply the operation to each value:

```
In  [41] pokemon.value_counts(normalize = True).head() * 100

Out [41] Normal          8.034611
         Water           7.540173
         Grass           4.697157
         Psychic         4.326329
         Fire            3.708282
```

Normal Pokémon make up 8.034611% of the data set, Water Pokémon make up 7.540173%, and so on. Interesting!

Let's say we wanted to limit the precision of the percentages. We can round a `Series`' values with the `round` method. The method's first parameter, `decimals`, sets the number of digits to leave after the decimal point. The next example rounds the values to two digits; it wraps code from the previous example in parentheses to avoid a syntactical error. We want to make sure that pandas first multiplies each value by 100 and then invokes `round` on the resulting `Series`:

```
In  [42] (pokemon.value_counts(normalize = True) * 100).round(2)

Out [42] Normal               8.03
         Water                7.54
         Grass                4.70
         Psychic              4.33
         Fire                 3.71
                              ...
         Rock / Fighting      0.12
         Fighting / Steel     0.12
         Ghost / Dragon       0.12
         Ghost / Dark         0.12
         Rock / Poison        0.12
         Name: Type, Length: 159, dtype: float64
```

The `value_counts` method operates identically on a numeric `Series`. The next example counts the occurrences of each unique stock price in the `google` `Series`. It turns out that no stock price appears more than three times in the data set:

```
In   [43] google.value_counts().head()

Out  [43] 237.04     3
          288.92     3
          287.68     3
          290.41     3
          194.27     3
```

To identify trends in numeric data sets, it can be more beneficial to group values into predefined intervals rather than count distinct values. Let's begin by determining the difference between the smallest and largest values within the `google` Series. The Series' max and min methods work well here. An alternative option is passing the Series into Python's built-in max and min functions:

```
In   [44] google.max()

Out  [44] 1287.58

In   [45] google.min()

Out  [45] 49.82
```

We have a range of ~1,250 between the smallest and largest values. Let's group the stock prices into buckets of 200, starting at 0 and working up to 1,400. We can define these intervals as values in a list and pass the list to the `value_counts` method's `bins` parameter. Pandas will use every two subsequent list values as the lower and upper ends of an interval:

```
In   [46] buckets = [0, 200, 400, 600, 800, 1000, 1200, 1400]
          google.value_counts(bins = buckets)

Out  [46] (200.0, 400.0]      1568
          (-0.001, 200.0]      595
          (400.0, 600.0]       575
          (1000.0, 1200.0]     406
          (600.0, 800.0]       380
          (800.0, 1000.0]      207
          (1200.0, 1400.0]      93
          Name: Close, dtype: int64
```

The output tells us that Google's stock price was between $200 and $400 for 1,568 values in the data set.

Note that pandas sorted the previous Series in descending order by the number of values in each bucket. What if we wanted to sort the results by the intervals instead? We simply have to mix and match a few pandas methods. The intervals are the index labels in the returned Series, so we can use the `sort_index` method to sort them. This technique of invoking multiple methods in sequence is called *method chaining*:

```
In   [47] google.value_counts(bins = buckets).sort_index()

Out  [47] (-0.001, 200.0]      595
          (200.0, 400.0]      1568
          (400.0, 600.0]       575
          (600.0, 800.0]       380
```

```
          (800.0, 1000.0]       207
          (1000.0, 1200.0]      406
          (1200.0, 1400.0]       93
          Name: Close, dtype: int64
```

We can achieve an identical result by passing a value of False to the sort parameter of the value_counts method:

```
In   [48] google.value_counts(bins = buckets, sort = False)

Out [48] (-0.001, 200.0]       595
          (200.0, 400.0]       1568
          (400.0, 600.0]        575
          (600.0, 800.0]        380
          (800.0, 1000.0]       207
          (1000.0, 1200.0]      406
          (1200.0, 1400.0]       93
          Name: Close, dtype: int64
```

Notice that the first interval includes the value -0.001 instead of 0. When pandas organizes the Series' values into buckets, it may extend any bin's range up to .1% in either direction. The symbols around intervals have significance:

- A parenthesis marks a value as *excluded* from the interval.
- A square bracket marks a value as *included* in the interval.

Consider the interval (-0.001, 200.0]. -0.001 is excluded, and 200 is included. Thus, the interval captures all values greater than -0.001 and less than or equal to 200.0.

A *closed interval* includes both endpoints. An example is [5, 10] (greater than or equal to 5, less than or equal to 10).

An *open interval* excludes both endpoints. An example is (5, 10) (greater than 5, less than 10).

The value_counts method with a bin parameter returns *half-open* intervals. Pandas will include one of the endpoints and exclude the other.

The value_counts method's bins parameter also accepts an integer argument. Pandas will automatically calculate the difference between the maximum and minimum values in the Series and divide the range into the specified number of bins. The next example splits the stock prices in google into six bins. Note that the bins/ buckets may not be perfectly equal in size (due to the possible .1% extension of any interval in any direction) but will be reasonably close:

```
In   [49] google.value_counts(bins = 6, sort = False)

Out [49] (48.581, 256.113]     1204
          (256.113, 462.407]    1104
          (462.407, 668.7]       507
          (668.7, 874.993]       380
          (874.993, 1081.287]    292
          (1081.287, 1287.58]    337
          Name: Close, dtype: int64
```

What about our `battles` data set? We haven't seen it for a while:

```
In  [50] battles.head()

Out [50] Start Date
         1781-09-06    Connecticut
         1779-07-05    Connecticut
         1777-04-27    Connecticut
         1777-09-03       Delaware
         1777-05-17        Florida
         Name: State, dtype: object
```

We can use the `value_counts` method to see which states had the most battles in the Revolutionary War:

```
In  [51] battles.value_counts().head()

Out [51] South Carolina    31
         New York          28
         New Jersey        24
         Virginia          21
         Massachusetts     11
         Name: State, dtype: int64
```

Pandas will exclude NaN values from the `value_counts` Series by default. Pass the `dropna` parameter an argument of `False` to count null values as a distinct category:

```
In  [52] battles.value_counts(dropna = False).head()

Out [52] NaN               70
         South Carolina    31
         New York          28
         New Jersey        24
         Virginia          21
         Name: State, dtype: int64
```

A `Series` index also supports the `value_counts` method. We have to access the index object via the `index` attribute before invoking the method. Let's find out which dates had the most battles during the Revolutionary War:

```
In  [53] battles.index

Out [53]

DatetimeIndex(['1774-09-01', '1774-12-14', '1775-04-19', '1775-04-19',
               '1775-04-20', '1775-05-10', '1775-05-27', '1775-06-11',
               '1775-06-17', '1775-08-08',
               ...
               '1782-08-08', '1782-08-15', '1782-08-19', '1782-08-26',
               '1782-08-25', '1782-09-11', '1782-09-13', '1782-10-18',
               '1782-12-06', '1783-01-22'],
              dtype='datetime64[ns]', name='Start Date', length=232,
              freq=None)
```

```
In  [54] battles.index.value_counts()

Out [54] 1775-04-19    2
         1781-05-22    2
         1781-04-15    2
         1782-01-11    2
         1780-05-25    2
                      ..
         1778-05-20    1
         1776-06-28    1
         1777-09-19    1
         1778-08-29    1
         1777-05-17    1
         Name: Start Date, Length: 217, dtype: int64
```

It looks as though no date saw more than two battles.

3.5   *Invoking a function on every Series value with the apply method*

A function is a *first-class object* in Python, which means that the language treats it like any other data type. A function may feel like a more abstract entity, but it's as valid a data structure as any other.

Here's the simplest way to think about first-class objects. Anything that you can do with a number, you can do with a function. You can do all the following things, for example:

- Store a function in a list.
- Assign a function as a value for a dictionary key.
- Pass a function into another function as an argument.
- Return a function from another function.

It's important to distinguish between a function and a function invocation. A *function* is a sequence of instructions that produces an output; it is a "recipe" that has not been cooked yet. By comparison, a *function invocation* is the actual execution of the instructions; it is the cooking of the recipe.

The next example declares a funcs list that stores three Python built-in functions. The len, max, and min functions are not invoked within the list. The list stores references to the functions themselves:

```
In  [55] funcs = [len, max, min]
```

The next example iterates over the funcs list with a for loop. Over three iterations, the current_func iterator variable represents the uninvoked len, max, and min functions. During each iteration, the loop invokes the dynamic current_func function, passes in the google Series, and prints the return value:

```
In  [56] for current_func in funcs:
             print(current_func(google))

Out [56] 3824
         1287.58
         49.82
```

The output includes the sequential return values of the three functions: the length of the `Series`, the maximum value in the `Series`, and the minimum value in the `Series`.

The key takeaway here is that we can treat a function like any other object in Python. So how does this fact apply to pandas? Suppose that we want to round each floating-point value in our `google` `Series` up or down to the closest integer. Python has a convenient `round` function for this purpose. The function rounds a value above 0.5 up and any value below 0.5 down:

```
In  [57] round(99.2)

Out [57] 99

In  [58] round(99.49)

Out [58] 99

In  [59] round(99.5)

Out [59] 100
```

Wouldn't it be great if we could apply this `round` function to every value in our `Series`? We're in luck. The `Series` has a method called `apply` that invokes a function once for each `Series` value and returns a new `Series` consisting of the return values of the function invocations. The `apply` method expects the function it will invoke as its first parameter, `func`. The next example passes Python's built-in `round` function:

```
In  [60] # The two lines below are equivalent
         google.apply(func = round)
         google.apply(round)

Out [60] Date
         2004-08-19        50
         2004-08-20        54
         2004-08-23        54
         2004-08-24        52
         2004-08-25        53
                          ...
         2019-10-21      1246
         2019-10-22      1243
         2019-10-23      1259
         2019-10-24      1261
         2019-10-25      1265
         Name: Close, Length: 3824, dtype: int64
```

We've rounded every `Series` value!

Again, please take a moment to notice that we're passing the `apply` method the uninvoked `round` function. We're passing in the recipe. Somewhere in the internals of pandas, the `apply` method knows to invoke our function on every `Series` value. Pandas abstracts away the complexity of the operation.

The `apply` method also accepts custom functions. Define the function to accept a single parameter and have it return the value that you'd like pandas to store in the aggregated `Series`.

Let's say we wanted to find out how many of our Pokémon have one type (such as Fire) and how many have two or more types. We need to apply the same logic, the categorization of a Pokémon, to each `Series` value. A function is an ideal container for encapsulating that logic. Let's define a utility function called `single_or_multi` that accepts a single Pokémon type and determines whether it has one or several types. If a Pokémon has multiple types, the string separates them with a slash (`"Fire / Ghost"`). We can use Python's `in` operator to check for the inclusion of a forward slash in the argument string. The `if` statement executes a block only if its condition evaluates to `True`. In our case, if a `/` is present, the function will return the string `"Multi"`; otherwise, it'll return `"Single"`:

```
In  [61] def single_or_multi(pokemon_type):
             if "/" in pokemon_type:
                 return "Multi"

             return "Single"
```

Now we can pass the `single_or_multi` function to the `apply` method. Here's a quick refresher on what `pokemon` looks like:

```
In  [62] pokemon.head(4)

Out [62] Pokemon
         Bulbasaur      Grass / Poison
         Ivysaur        Grass / Poison
         Venusaur       Grass / Poison
         Charmander              Fire
         Name: Type, dtype: object
```

The next example calls the `apply` method with the `single_or_multi` function as its argument. Pandas invokes the `single_or_multi` function for every `Series` value:

```
In  [63] pokemon.apply(single_or_multi)

Out [63] Pokemon
         Bulbasaur      Multi
         Ivysaur        Multi
         Venusaur       Multi
         Charmander     Single
         Charmeleon     Single
                         ...
         Stakataka      Multi
         Blacephalon    Multi
         Zeraora        Single
         Meltan         Single
         Melmetal       Single
         Name: Type, Length: 809, dtype: object
```

Our first specimen, Bulbasaur, is classified as a Grass / Poison Pokémon, so the `single_or_multi` function returns `"Multi"`. By comparison, our fourth specimen, Charmander, is classified as a Fire Pokémon, so the function returns `"Single"`. The same logic repeats for the remaining `pokemon` values.

We have a new `Series` object! Let's find out how many Pokémon fall into each classification by invoking `value_counts`:

```
In  [64] pokemon.apply(single_or_multi).value_counts()

Out [64] Multi    405
         Single   404
         Name: Type, dtype: int64
```

It turns out that there's a fairly even split of single-power and multipower Pokémon. I hope that this knowledge will prove to be useful at some point in your life.

3.6 *Coding challenge*

Let's tackle a challenge that combines several ideas introduced in this chapter and chapter 2.

3.6.1 *Problems*

Suppose that a historian reaches out to us and asks us to determine which day of the week saw the most battles during the Revolutionary War. The final output should be a `Series` with the days (Sunday, Monday, and so on) as index labels and a count of battles on each day as the values. Starting from scratch, import the revolutionary_war.csv data set, and perform the necessary operations to arrive at the following data:

```
Saturday    39
Friday      39
Wednesday   32
Thursday    31
Sunday      31
Tuesday     29
Monday      27
```

You'll need one additional piece of Python knowledge to solve this problem. If you have a single datetime object, you can invoke the `strftime` method on it with an argument of `"%A"` to return the day of a week a date falls on (such as `"Sunday"`). See the following example and appendix B for a more-extensive overview of a datetime object:

```
In  [65] import datetime as dt
         today = dt.datetime(2020, 12, 26)
         today.strftime("%A")

Out [65] 'Saturday'
```

> **HINT** Declaring a custom function to calculate a date's day of the week may prove to be helpful.

Good luck!

3.6.2 *Solutions*

Let's reimport the revolutionary_war.csv data set and remind ourselves of its original shape:

```
In  [66] pd.read_csv("revolutionary_war.csv").head()
```

```
Out [66]
```

	Battle	Start Date	State
0	Powder Alarm	9/1/1774	Massachusetts
1	Storming of Fort William and Mary	12/14/1774	New Hampshire
2	Battles of Lexington and Concord	4/19/1775	Massachusetts
3	Siege of Boston	4/19/1775	Massachusetts
4	Gunpowder Incident	4/20/1775	Virginia

We do not need the Battle and State columns for this analysis. You're welcome to use either column as the index or stick with the default numeric one.

The critical step is coercing the string values in the Start Date column to datetimes. If we're working with dates, we can invoke date-related methods such as strftime. We do not have the same power with plain strings. Let's select the Start Date column with the usecols parameter and convert its values to datetimes with the parse_dates parameter. Finally, remember to pass True to the squeeze parameter to create a Series instead of a DataFrame:

```
In  [67] days_of_war = pd.read_csv(
             "revolutionary_war.csv",
             usecols = ["Start Date"],
             parse_dates = ["Start Date"],
             squeeze = True,
         )

         days_of_war.head()
```

```
Out [67] 0    1774-09-01
         1    1774-12-14
         2    1775-04-19
         3    1775-04-19
         4    1775-04-20
         Name: Start Date, dtype: datetime64[ns]
```

Our next challenge is extracting the day of the week for each date. One solution (using only the tools we know now) is to pass each Series value to a function that will return that date's day of the week. Let's declare that function now:

```
In  [68] def day_of_week(date):
             return date.strftime("%A")
```

How can we invoke the day_of_week function once for each Series value? We can pass the day_of_week function as the argument to the apply method. We expect to get the days of the week, except that...

```
In  [69] days_of_war.apply(day_of_week)

-------------------------------------------------------------------------
ValueError                                 Traceback (most recent call last)
<ipython-input-411-c133befd2940> in <module>
----> 1 days_of_war.apply(day_of_week)

ValueError: NaTType does not support strftime
```

Uh-oh—our Start Date column has missing values. Unlike a datetime object, a NaT object does not have a `strftime` method, so pandas runs into trouble when passing it into the `day_of_week` function. The simple solution is to drop all missing datetime values from the `Series` before we call the `apply` method. We can do so with the `dropna` method:

```
In  [70] days_of_war.dropna().apply(day_of_week)

Out [70] 0         Thursday
         1        Wednesday
         2        Wednesday
         3        Wednesday
         4         Thursday
                    ...
         227      Wednesday
         228         Friday
         229         Friday
         230         Friday
         231      Wednesday
         Name: Start Date, Length: 228, dtype: object
```

Now we're getting somewhere! We need a way to count the number of occurrences for each weekday. The `value_counts` method does the trick:

```
In  [71] days_of_war.dropna().apply(day_of_week).value_counts()

Out [71] Saturday      39
         Friday        39
         Wednesday     32
         Thursday      31
         Sunday        31
         Tuesday       29
         Monday        27
         Name: Start Date, dtype: int64
```

Perfect! The result is a tie between Friday and Saturday. Congratulations on completing the coding challenge!

Summary

- The `read_csv` function imports a CSV's contents into a pandas data structure.
- The `read_csv` function's parameters can customize the imported columns, the index, the data types, and more.

- The `sort_values` method sorts a `Series`' values in ascending or descending order.
- The `sort_index` method sorts a `Series`' index in ascending or descending order.
- We can use the `inplace` parameter to reassign the copy returned from a method to the original variable holding an object. There are no performance benefits to using `inplace`.
- The `value_counts` method counts the occurrences of each unique value in a `Series`.
- The `apply` method invokes a function on each `Series` value and returns the results in a new `Series`.

The DataFrame object

4

This chapter covers

- Instantiating `DataFrame` objects from dictionaries and NumPy `ndarrays`
- Importing `DataFrame`s from CSV files with the `read_csv` function
- Sorting `DataFrame` columns
- Accessing rows and columns in a `DataFrame`
- Setting and resetting a `DataFrame` index
- Renaming columns and index labels in a `DataFrame`

The pandas `DataFrame` is a two-dimensional table of data with rows and columns. As with a `Series`, pandas assigns an index label and an index position to each `DataFrame` row. Pandas also assigns a label and a position to each column. The `DataFrame` is two-dimensional because it requires two points of reference—a row and a column—to isolate a value from the data set. Figure 4.1 displays a visual example of a pandas `DataFrame`.

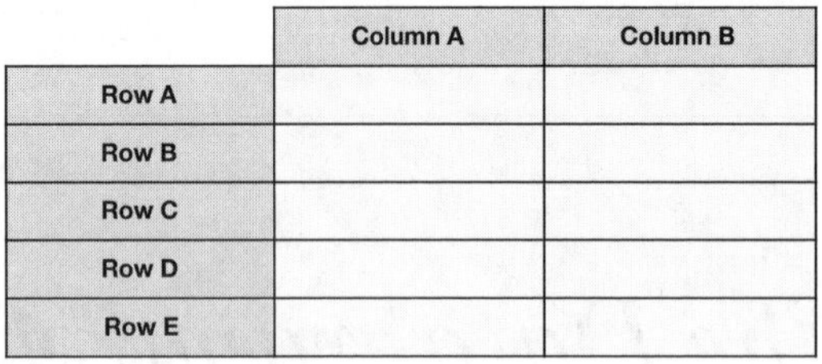

	Column A	Column B
Row A		
Row B		
Row C		
Row D		
Row E		

Figure 4.1   A visual representation of a pandas DataFrame with five rows and two columns

The DataFrame is the workhorse of the pandas library and the data structure you'll be working with most on a daily basis, so we'll be spending the remainder of this book exploring its vast features.

4.1   Overview of a DataFrame

As always, let's spin up a new Jupyter Notebook and import pandas. We also need the NumPy library, which we'll use in section 4.1.2 to generate random data. NumPy is usually assigned the alias np:

```
In  [1] import pandas as pd
        import numpy as np
```

The DataFrame class constructor is available at the top level of pandas. The syntax for instantiating a DataFrame object is identical to the one for instantiating a Series. We access the DataFrame class and instantiate with a pair of parentheses: pd.DataFrame().

4.1.1   Creating a DataFrame from a dictionary

The constructor's first parameter, data, expects the data that will populate the DataFrame. One suitable input is a Python dictionary in which the keys are column names and the values are column values. The next example passes a dictionary of string keys and list values. Pandas returns a DataFrame with three columns. Each list element becomes a value in its respective column:

```
In  [2] city_data = {
            "City": ["New York City", "Paris", "Barcelona", "Rome"],
            "Country": ["United States", "France", "Spain", "Italy"],
            "Population": [8600000, 2141000, 5515000, 2873000]
        }

        cities = pd.DataFrame(city_data)
        cities
```

```
Out [2]
```

	City	Country	Population
0	New York City	United States	8600000
1	Paris	France	2141000
2	Barcelona	Spain	5515000
3	Rome	Italy	2873000

We officially have a `DataFrame`! Notice that the data structure is rendered differently from a `Series`.

A `DataFrame` holds an index of row labels. We did not provide the constructor a custom index, so pandas generated a numeric one starting at 0. The logic operates the same way it does on a `Series`.

A `DataFrame` can hold multiple columns of data. It's helpful to think of the column headers as a second index. City, Country, and Population are three index labels on the column axis; pandas assigns them the index positions 0, 1, and 2, respectively.

What if we wanted to swap the column headers with the index labels? Two options are available here. We can invoke the `transpose` method on the `DataFrame` or access its `T` attribute:

```
In  [3] # The two lines below are equivalent
        cities.transpose()
        cities.T
```

```
Out [3]
```

	0	1	2	3
City	New York City	Paris	Barcelona	Rome
Country	United States	France	Spain	Italy
Population	8600000	2141000	5515000	2873000

The previous example serves as a reminder that pandas can store index labels of different data types. In the previous output, the columns use the same value for index labels and index positions. The rows have different labels (City, Country, Population) and positions (0, 1, and 2).

4.1.2 Creating a DataFrame from a NumPy ndarray

Let's try one more example. The `DataFrame` constructor's `data` parameter also accepts a NumPy `ndarray`. We can generate an `ndarray` of any size with the `randint` function in NumPy's `random` module. The next example creates a 3 x 5 `ndarray` of integers between 1 and 101 (exclusive):

```
In  [4] random_data = np.random.randint(1, 101, [3, 5])
        random_data
```

```
Out [4] array([[25, 22, 80, 43, 42],
               [40, 89,  7, 21, 25],
               [89, 71, 32, 28, 39]])
```

If you'd like more information on random data generation in NumPy, see appendix C.

Next, let's pass our `ndarray` into the `DataFrame` constructor. The `ndarray` has neither row labels nor column labels. Thus, pandas uses a numeric index for both the row axis and column axis:

```
In  [5] pd.DataFrame(data = random_data)

Out [5]
```

	0	1	2	3	4
0	25	22	80	43	42
1	40	89	7	21	25
2	89	71	32	28	39

We can manually set the row labels with the DataFrame constructor's index parameter, which accepts any iterable object, including a list, tuple, or ndarray. Note that the iterable's length must be equal to the data set's number of rows. We're passing a 3 x 5 ndarray, so we must provide three row labels:

```
In  [6] row_labels = ["Morning", "Afternoon", "Evening"]
        temperatures = pd.DataFrame(
            data = random_data, index = row_labels
        )
        temperatures

Out [6]
```

	0	1	2	3	4
Morning	25	22	80	43	42
Afternoon	40	89	7	21	25
Evening	89	71	32	28	39

We can set the column names with the constructor's columns parameter. The ndarray includes five columns, so we must pass an iterable with five items. The next example passes the column names in a tuple:

```
In  [7] row_labels = ["Morning", "Afternoon", "Evening"]
        column_labels = (
            "Monday",
            "Tuesday",
            "Wednesday",
            "Thursday",
            "Friday",
        )

        pd.DataFrame(
            data = random_data,
            index = row_labels,
            columns = column_labels,
        )

Out [7]
```

	Monday	Tuesday	Wednesday	Thursday	Friday
Morning	25	22	80	43	42
Afternoon	40	89	7	21	25
Evening	89	71	32	28	39

Pandas permits duplicates in the row and column indices. In the next example, "Morning" appears twice in the rows' index labels, and "Tuesday" appears twice in the columns' index labels:

```
In  [8] row_labels = ["Morning", "Afternoon", "Morning"]
        column_labels = [
            "Monday",
            "Tuesday",
            "Wednesday",
            "Tuesday",
            "Friday"
        ]

        pd.DataFrame(
            data = random_data,
            index = row_labels,
            columns = column_labels,
        )
```

Out [8]

	Monday	Tuesday	Wednesday	Tuesday	Friday
Morning	25	22	80	43	42
Afternoon	40	89	7	21	25
Evening	89	71	32	28	39

As we mentioned in earlier chapters, it's ideal to have unique indices when possible. If there are no duplicates, it is easier for pandas to extract a specific row or column.

4.2   Similarities between Series and DataFrames

Many `Series` attributes and methods are also available on `DataFrames`. Their implementations can vary; pandas must account for multiple columns and two separate axes now.

4.2.1   Importing a DataFrame with the read_csv function

The nba.csv data set is a list of professional basketball players in the National Basketball Association (NBA) during the 2019–20 season. Each row includes a player's name, team, position, birthday, and salary. A good mix of data types is scattered throughout, making this data set excellent for exploring the basics of `DataFrames`.

Let's use the `read_csv` function at the top level of pandas to import the file (we introduced this function in chapter 3). The function accepts a filename as its first argument and returns a `DataFrame` by default. Before you execute the following code, please make sure that the data set is in the same directory as your Jupyter Notebook:

```
In  [9] pd.read_csv("nba.csv")
```

Out [9]

	Name	Team	Position	Birthday	Salary
0	Shake Milton	Philadelphia 76ers	SG	9/26/96	1445697
1	Christian Wood	Detroit Pistons	PF	9/27/95	1645357
2	PJ Washington	Charlotte Hornets	PF	8/23/98	3831840
3	Derrick Rose	Detroit Pistons	PG	10/4/88	7317074
4	Marial Shayok	Philadelphia 76ers	G	7/26/95	79568
...	...	...	...	...	...
445	Austin Rivers	Houston Rockets	PG	8/1/92	2174310
446	Harry Giles	Sacramento Kings	PF	4/22/98	2578800

```
447       Robin Lopez       Milwaukee Bucks           C    4/1/88     4767000
448     Collin Sexton   Cleveland Cavaliers          PG    1/4/99     4764960
449       Ricky Rubio          Phoenix Suns          PG   10/21/90   16200000
```

450 rows × 5 columns

At the bottom of the output, pandas informs us that the data has 450 rows and 5 columns.

Before we assign the DataFrame to a variable, let's make one optimization. Pandas imports the Birthday column values as strings rather than as datetimes, limiting the number of operations we can perform on them. We can use the parse_dates parameter to coerce the values into datetimes:

```
In  [10] pd.read_csv("nba.csv", parse_dates = ["Birthday"])
```

Out [10]

	Name	Team	Position	Birthday	Salary
0	Shake Milton	Philadelphia 76ers	SG	1996-09-26	1445697
1	Christian Wood	Detroit Pistons	PF	1995-09-27	1645357
2	PJ Washington	Charlotte Hornets	PF	1998-08-23	3831840
3	Derrick Rose	Detroit Pistons	PG	1988-10-04	7317074
4	Marial Shayok	Philadelphia 76ers	G	1995-07-26	79568
...	...	...	...	...	...
445	Austin Rivers	Houston Rockets	PG	1992-08-01	2174310
446	Harry Giles	Sacramento Kings	PF	1998-04-22	2578800
447	Robin Lopez	Milwaukee Bucks	C	1988-04-01	4767000
448	Collin Sexton	Cleveland Cavaliers	PG	1999-01-04	4764960
449	Ricky Rubio	Phoenix Suns	PG	1990-10-21	16200000

450 rows × 5 columns

Much better! Now we have a column of datetimes. Pandas displays the datetime values in conventional YYYY-MM-DD format. I'm happy with the import, so we can assign the DataFrame to a variable like nba:

```
In  [11] nba = pd.read_csv("nba.csv", parse_dates = ["Birthday"])
```

It's helpful to think of a DataFrame as being a collection of Series objects with a common index. In this example, the five columns in nba (Name, Team, Position, Birthday, and Salary) share the same row index. Let's get to work exploring the DataFrame.

4.2.2   Shared and exclusive attributes of Series and DataFrames

Attributes and methods may differ between Series and DataFrames, both in name and implementation. Here's an example. A Series has a dtype attribute that reveals the data type of its values (see chapter 2). Notice that the dtype attribute is singular because a Series can store only one data type:

```
In  [12] pd.Series([1, 2, 3]).dtype
```

Out [12] dtype('int64')

By comparison, a `DataFrame` can hold heterogeneous data. *Heterogeneous* means mixed or varied. One column can hold integers, and another can hold strings. A `DataFrame` has a unique `dtypes` attribute. (Notice that the name is plural.) The attribute returns a `Series` with the `DataFrame`'s columns as the index labels and the columns' data types as the values:

```
In  [13] nba.dtypes

Out [13] Name                    object
         Team                    object
         Position                object
         Birthday        datetime64[ns]
         Salary                   int64
         dtype: object
```

The Name, Team, and Position columns list `object` as their data type. The `object` data type is pandas' lingo for complex objects including strings. Thus, the nba `DataFrame` has three string columns, one datetime column, and one integer column.

We can invoke the `value_counts` method on the `Series` to count the number of columns storing each data type:

```
In  [14] nba.dtypes.value_counts()

Out [14] object            3
         datetime64[ns]    1
         int64             1
         dtype: int64
```

`dtype` versus `dtypes` is one example of the different attributes between `Series` and `DataFrames`. But the two data structures also have many attributes and methods in common.

A `DataFrame` consists of several smaller objects: an index that holds the row labels, an index that holds the column labels, and a data container that holds the values. The `index` attribute exposes the index of the `DataFrame`:

```
In  [15] nba.index

Out [15] RangeIndex(start=0, stop=450, step=1)
```

Here, we have a `RangeIndex`, an index optimized for storing a sequence of numeric values. A `RangeIndex` object includes three attributes: `start` (the inclusive lower bound), `stop` (the exclusive upper bound), and `step` (the interval or step sequence between every two values). The output above tells us that nba's index starts counting at 0 and proceeds to 450 in increments of 1.

Pandas uses a separate index object to store a `DataFrame`'s columns. We can access it via the `columns` attribute:

```
In  [16] nba.columns

Out [16] Index(['Name', 'Team', 'Position', 'Birthday', 'Salary'],
         dtype='object'
```

This object is another type of index object: `Index`. Pandas uses this option when an index consists of text values.

The `index` attribute is an example of an attribute that a `DataFrame` shares with a `Series`. The `columns` attribute is an example of an attribute that is exclusive to a `DataFrame`. A `Series` has no concept of columns.

The `ndim` attribute returns the number of dimensions in a pandas object. A Data-Frame has two:

```
In  [17] nba.ndim

Out [17] 2
```

The `shape` attribute returns the `DataFrame`'s dimensions in a tuple. The nba data set has 450 rows and 5 columns:

```
In  [18] nba.shape

Out [18] (450, 5)
```

The `size` attribute calculates the total number of values in the data set. Missing values (such as `NaNs`) are included in the count:

```
In  [19] nba.size

Out [19] 2250
```

If we want to exclude missing values, the `count` method returns a `Series` with the counts of present values per column:

```
In  [20] nba.count()

Out [20] Name         450
         Team         450
         Position     450
         Birthday     450
         Salary       450
         dtype: int64
```

We can add all these `Series` values with the `sum` method to arrive at the number of non-null values in the `DataFrame`. The nba `DataFrame` data set holds no missing values, so the `size` attribute and the `sum` method return the same result:

```
In  [21] nba.count().sum()

Out [21] 2250
```

Here's an example illustrating the differences between the `size` attribute and the `count` method. Let's create a `DataFrame` with a missing value. We can access nan as a top-level attribute on the NumPy package:

```
In  [22] data = {
             "A": [1, np.nan],
             "B": [2, 3]
```

```
                    }
                    df = pd.DataFrame(data)
                    df
```

Out [22]

	A	B
0	1.0	2
1	NaN	3

The `size` attribute returns 4 because the `DataFrame` has four cells:

```
In  [23] df.size
```

Out [23] 4

By comparison, the `sum` method returns 3 because the `DataFrame` has three non-null values:

```
In  [24] df.count()
```

```
Out [24] A    1
         B    2
         dtype: int64
```

```
In  [25] df.count().sum()
```

Out [25] 3

The A column has one present value, and the B column has two present values.

4.2.3 Shared methods of Series and DataFrames

`DataFrames` and `Series` have methods in common too. We can use the `head` method to extract rows from the top of a `DataFrame`, for example:

```
In  [26] nba.head(2)
```

Out [26]

	Name	Team	Position	Birthday	Salary
0	Shake Milton	Philadelphia 76ers	SG	1996-09-26	1445697
1	Christian Wood	Detroit Pistons	PF	1995-09-27	1645357

The `tail` method returns rows from the bottom of the `DataFrame`:

```
In  [27] nba.tail(n = 3)
```

Out [27]

	Name	Team	Position	Birthday	Salary
447	Robin Lopez	Milwaukee Bucks	C	1988-04-01	4767000
448	Collin Sexton	Cleveland Cavaliers	PG	1999-01-04	4764960
449	Ricky Rubio	Phoenix Suns	PG	1990-10-21	16200000

The two methods default to returning five rows when invoked without an argument:

```
In  [28] nba.tail()

Out [28]
```

	Name	Team	Position	Birthday	Salary
445	Austin Rivers	Houston Rockets	PG	1992-08-01	2174310
446	Harry Giles	Sacramento Kings	PF	1998-04-22	2578800
447	Robin Lopez	Milwaukee Bucks	C	1988-04-01	4767000
448	Collin Sexton	Cleveland Cavaliers	PG	1999-01-04	4764960
449	Ricky Rubio	Phoenix Suns	PG	1990-10-21	16200000

The `sample` method extracts random rows from the `DataFrame`. Its first parameter specifies the number of rows:

```
In  [29] nba.sample(3)

Out [29]
```

	Name	Team	Position	Birthday	Salary
225	Tomas Satoransky	Chicago Bulls	PG	1991-10-30	10000000
201	Javonte Green	Boston Celtics	SF	1993-07-23	898310
310	Matthew Dellavedova	Cleveland Cavaliers	PG	1990-09-08	9607500

Suppose that we want to find out how many teams, salaries, and positions exist in this data set. In chapter 2, we used the `nunique` method to count the number of unique values in a `Series`. When we invoke the same method on a `DataFrame`, it returns a `Series` object with counts of unique values per column:

```
In  [30] nba.nunique()

Out [30] Name       450
         Team        30
         Position     9
         Birthday   430
         Salary     269
         dtype: int64
```

There are 30 unique teams, 269 unique salaries, and 9 unique positions in `nba`.

You may also recall the `max` and `min` methods. On a `DataFrame`, the `max` method returns a `Series` with the maximum value from each column. The maximum value in a text column is the string closest to the end of the alphabet. The maximum value in a datetime column is the latest date in chronological order:

```
In  [31] nba.max()

Out [31] Name                 Zylan Cheatham
         Team              Washington Wizards
         Position                          SG
         Birthday         2000-12-23 00:00:00
         Salary                      40231758
         dtype: object
```

The min method returns a `Series` with the minimum value from each column (the smallest number, the string closest to the start of the alphabet, the earliest date, and so on):

```
In  [32] nba.min()

Out [32] Name                Aaron Gordon
         Team               Atlanta Hawks
         Position                       C
         Birthday     1977-01-26 00:00:00
         Salary                     79568
         dtype: object
```

What if we want to identify multiple max values, such as the four highest-paid players in the data set? The `nlargest` method retrieves a subset of rows in which a given column has the largest values in the `DataFrame`. We pass the number of rows to extract to its n parameter and the column to use for sorting to its `columns` parameter. The next example extracts the `DataFrame` rows that have the four largest values in the Salary column:

```
In  [33] nba.nlargest(n = 4, columns = "Salary")

Out [33]
```

	Name	Team	Position	Birthday	Salary
205	Stephen Curry	Golden State Warriors	PG	1988-03-14	40231758
38	Chris Paul	Oklahoma City Thunder	PG	1985-05-06	38506482
219	Russell Westbrook	Houston Rockets	PG	1988-11-12	38506482
251	John Wall	Washington Wizards	PG	1990-09-06	38199000

Our next challenge is finding the three oldest players in the league. We can accomplish this task by getting the three earliest dates in the Birthday column. The `nsmallest` method can help us; it returns a subset of rows in which a given column has the smallest values in the data set. The smallest datetime values are those that occur earliest in chronological order. Note that the `nlargest` and `nsmallest` methods can be invoked only on numeric or datetime columns:

```
In  [34] nba.nsmallest(n = 3, columns = ["Birthday"])

Out [34]
```

	Name	Team	Position	Birthday	Salary
98	Vince Carter	Atlanta Hawks	PF	1977-01-26	2564753
196	Udonis Haslem	Miami Heat	C	1980-06-09	2564753
262	Kyle Korver	Milwaukee Bucks	PF	1981-03-17	6004753

What if we want to calculate the sum of all NBA salaries? The `DataFrame` includes a sum method for this purpose:

```
In  [35] nba.sum()

Out [35] Name        Shake MiltonChristian WoodPJ WashingtonDerrick...
         Team        Philadelphia 76ersDetroit PistonsCharlotte Hor...
         Position    SGPFPFPGGPFSGSFCSFPGPGFCPGSGPFCCPFPFSGPFPGSGSF...
         Salary                                           3444112694
         dtype: object
```

We do get the answer we want, but the output is a bit messy. By default, pandas adds the values in each column. For text columns, the library concatenates all strings into one. To limit the addition to numeric volumes, we can pass True to the sum method's numeric_only parameter:

```
In  [36] nba.sum(numeric_only = True)

Out [36] Salary    3444112694
         dtype: int64
```

The total combined salaries of these 450 NBA players is a whopping $3.4 billion. We can calculate the average salary with the mean method. The method accepts the same numeric_only parameter to target only numeric columns:

```
In  [37] nba.mean(numeric_only = True)

Out [37] Salary    7.653584e+06
         dtype: float64
```

A DataFrame also includes methods for statistical calculations such as median, mode, and standard deviation:

```
In  [38] nba.median(numeric_only = True)

Out [38] Salary    3303074.5
         dtype: float64

In  [39] nba.mode(numeric_only = True)

Out [39]

    Salary
  ─────────
0   79568

In  [40] nba.std(numeric_only = True)

Out [40] Salary    9.288810e+06
         dtype: float64
```

For advanced statistical methods, check out the official Series documentation (http://mng.bz/myDa).

4.3   Sorting a DataFrame

Our data set's rows arrived in jumbled, random order, but that's no problem! We can sort a DataFrame by one or more columns by using the sort_values method.

4.3.1   Sorting by a single column

Let's first sort our players in alphabetical order by name. The sort_values method's first parameter, by, accepts the column that pandas should use to sort the DataFrame. Let's pass in the Name column as a string:

```
In  [41] # The two lines below are equivalent
         nba.sort_values("Name")
         nba.sort_values(by = "Name")
```

Out [41]

	Name	Team	Position	Birthday	Salary
52	Aaron Gordon	Orlando Magic	PF	1995-09-16	19863636
101	Aaron Holiday	Indiana Pacers	PG	1996-09-30	2239200
437	Abdel Nader	Oklahoma City Thunder	SF	1993-09-25	1618520
81	Adam Mokoka	Chicago Bulls	G	1998-07-18	79568
399	Admiral Schofield	Washington Wizards	SF	1997-03-30	1000000
...	...	...	...	...	...
159	Zach LaVine	Chicago Bulls	PG	1995-03-10	19500000
302	Zach Norvell	Los Angeles Lakers	SG	1997-12-09	79568
312	Zhaire Smith	Philadelphia 76ers	SG	1999-06-04	3058800
137	Zion Williamson	New Orleans Pelicans	F	2000-07-06	9757440
248	Zylan Cheatham	New Orleans Pelicans	SF	1995-11-17	79568

450 rows × 5 columns

The sort_values method's ascending parameter determines the sort order; it has a default argument of True. By default, pandas will sort a column of numbers in increasing order, a column of strings in alphabetical order, and a column of datetimes in chronological order.

If we wanted to sort the names in reverse alphabetical order, we could pass the ascending parameter a False instead:

```
In  [42] nba.sort_values("Name", ascending = False).head()
```

Out [42]

	Name	Team	Position	Birthday	Salary
248	Zylan Cheatham	New Orleans Pelicans	SF	1995-11-17	79568
137	Zion Williamson	New Orleans Pelicans	F	2000-07-06	9757440
312	Zhaire Smith	Philadelphia 76ers	SG	1999-06-04	3058800
302	Zach Norvell	Los Angeles Lakers	SG	1997-12-09	79568
159	Zach LaVine	Chicago Bulls	PG	1995-03-10	19500000

Here's another example: what if we want to find the five youngest players in nba without using the nsmallest method? We could sort the Birthday column in reverse chronological order by using the sort_values method with ascending set to False and then take five rows off the top with the head method:

```
In  [43] nba.sort_values("Birthday", ascending = False).head()
```

Out [43]

	Name	Team	Position	Birthday	Salary
136	Sekou Doumbouya	Detroit Pistons	SF	2000-12-23	3285120
432	Talen Horton-Tucker	Los Angeles Lakers	GF	2000-11-25	898310
137	Zion Williamson	New Orleans Pelicans	F	2000-07-06	9757440
313	RJ Barrett	New York Knicks	SG	2000-06-14	7839960
392	Jalen Lecque	Phoenix Suns	G	2000-06-13	898310

The youngest player in nba appears first in the output. That player is Sekou Doumbouya, who was born December 23, 2000.

4.3.2   *Sorting by multiple columns*

We can sort multiple columns in a DataFrame by passing a list to the sort_values method's by parameter. Pandas will sort the DataFrame's columns consecutively in the order in which they appear in the list. The next example sorts the nba DataFrame first by the Team column and then by the Name column. Pandas defaults to ascending sorts for all columns:

```
In  [44] nba.sort_values(by = ["Team", "Name"])

Out [44]
```

	Name	Team	Position	Birthday	Salary
359	Alex Len	Atlanta Hawks	C	1993-06-16	4160000
167	Allen Crabbe	Atlanta Hawks	SG	1992-04-09	18500000
276	Brandon Goodwin	Atlanta Hawks	PG	1995-10-02	79568
438	Bruno Fernando	Atlanta Hawks	C	1998-08-15	1400000
194	Cam Reddish	Atlanta Hawks	SF	1999-09-01	4245720
...	...	...	...	...	...
418	Jordan McRae	Washington Wizards	PG	1991-03-28	1645357
273	Justin Robinson	Washington Wizards	PG	1997-10-12	898310
428	Moritz Wagner	Washington Wizards	C	1997-04-26	2063520
21	Rui Hachimura	Washington Wizards	PF	1998-02-08	4469160
36	Thomas Bryant	Washington Wizards	C	1997-07-31	8000000

```
450 rows × 5 columns
```

Here's how you read the output. The Atlanta Hawks are the first team in the data set when we sort teams by alphabetical order. Within the Atlanta Hawks, Alex Len's name comes first, followed by Allen Crabbe and Brandon Goodwin. Pandas repeats this sorting logic for the remaining teams and names.

We can pass a single Boolean to the ascending parameter to apply the same sort order to each column. The next example passes False, so pandas first sorts the Team column in descending order and then the Name column in descending order:

```
In  [45] nba.sort_values(["Team", "Name"], ascending = False)

Out [45]
```

	Name	Team	Position	Birthday	Salary
36	Thomas Bryant	Washington Wizards	C	1997-07-31	8000000
21	Rui Hachimura	Washington Wizards	PF	1998-02-08	4469160
428	Moritz Wagner	Washington Wizards	C	1997-04-26	2063520
273	Justin Robinson	Washington Wizards	PG	1997-10-12	898310
418	Jordan McRae	Washington Wizards	PG	1991-03-28	1645357
...	...	...	...	...	...
194	Cam Reddish	Atlanta Hawks	SF	1999-09-01	4245720
438	Bruno Fernando	Atlanta Hawks	C	1998-08-15	1400000

276	Brandon Goodwin	Atlanta Hawks	PG 1995-10-02	79568
167	Allen Crabbe	Atlanta Hawks	SG 1992-04-09	18500000
359	Alex Len	Atlanta Hawks	C 1993-06-16	4160000

450 rows × 5 columns

What if we want to sort each column in a different order? We might want to sort the teams in ascending order and then sort the salaries within those teams in descending order, for example. To accomplish this task, we can pass the ascending parameter a list of Boolean values. The lists passed to the by and ascending parameters must be equal in length. Pandas will use shared index positions between the two lists to match each column with its associated sort order. In the next example, the Team column occupies index position 0 in the by list; pandas matches it with the True at index position 0 in the ascending list, so it sorts the column in ascending order. Pandas applies the same logic to the Salary column and sorts it in descending order:

```
In  [46] nba.sort_values(
            by = ["Team", "Salary"], ascending = [True, False]
         )
```

Out [46]

	Name	**Team**	**Position**	**Birthday**	**Salary**
111	Chandler Parsons	Atlanta Hawks	SF	1988-10-25	25102512
28	Evan Turner	Atlanta Hawks	PG	1988-10-27	18606556
167	Allen Crabbe	Atlanta Hawks	SG	1992-04-09	18500000
213	De'Andre Hunter	Atlanta Hawks	SF	1997-12-02	7068360
339	Jabari Parker	Atlanta Hawks	PF	1995-03-15	6500000
...	...	...	...	...	...
80	Isaac Bonga	Washington Wizards	PG	1999-11-08	1416852
399	Admiral Schofield	Washington Wizards	SF	1997-03-30	1000000
273	Justin Robinson	Washington Wizards	PG	1997-10-12	898310
283	Garrison Mathews	Washington Wizards	SG	1996-10-24	79568
353	Chris Chiozza	Washington Wizards	PG	1995-11-21	79568

450 rows × 5 columns

The data looks good, so let's make our sort permanent. The sort_values method supports the inplace parameter, but we'll be explicit and reassign the returned DataFrame to the nba variable (see chapter 3 for a discussion of the imperfections of the inplace parameter):

```
In  [47] nba = nba.sort_values(
            by = ["Team", "Salary"],
            ascending = [True, False]
         )
```

Hooray—we've sorted our DataFrame by the values in the Team and Salary columns. Now we can figure out which players on each team get paid the most.

4.4   Sorting by index

With our permanent sort, our DataFrame is in a different order from when it arrived:

```
In  [48] nba.head()
```

```
Out [48]
```

	Name	Team	Position	Birthday	Salary
111	Chandler Parsons	Atlanta Hawks	SF	1988-10-25	25102512
28	Evan Turner	Atlanta Hawks	PG	1988-10-27	18606556
167	Allen Crabbe	Atlanta Hawks	SG	1992-04-09	18500000
213	De'Andre Hunter	Atlanta Hawks	SF	1997-12-02	7068360
339	Jabari Parker	Atlanta Hawks	PF	1995-03-15	6500000

How can we return it to its original form?

4.4.1   Sorting by row index

Our nba DataFrame still has its numeric index. If we could sort the data set by index positions rather than by column values, we could return it to its original shape. The sort_index method does just that:

```
In  [49] # The two lines below are equivalent
         nba.sort_index().head()
         nba.sort_index(ascending = True).head()
```

```
Out [49]
```

	Name	Team	Position	Birthday	Salary
0	Shake Milton	Philadelphia 76ers	SG	1996-09-26	1445697
1	Christian Wood	Detroit Pistons	PF	1995-09-27	1645357
2	PJ Washington	Charlotte Hornets	PF	1998-08-23	3831840
3	Derrick Rose	Detroit Pistons	PG	1988-10-04	7317074
4	Marial Shayok	Philadelphia 76ers	G	1995-07-26	79568

We can also reverse the sort order by passing False to the method's ascending parameter. The next example shows the greatest index positions first:

```
In  [50] nba.sort_index(ascending = False).head()
```

```
Out [50]
```

	Name	Team	Position	Birthday	Salary
449	Ricky Rubio	Phoenix Suns	PG	1990-10-21	16200000
448	Collin Sexton	Cleveland Cavaliers	PG	1999-01-04	4764960
447	Robin Lopez	Milwaukee Bucks	C	1988-04-01	4767000
446	Harry Giles	Sacramento Kings	PF	1998-04-22	2578800
445	Austin Rivers	Houston Rockets	PG	1992-08-01	2174310

We're back where we started, with the DataFrame sorted by index position. Let's assign this DataFrame back to the nba variable:

```
In  [51] nba = nba.sort_index()
```

Next up, let's explore how we can sort our nba on its other axis.

4.4.2   Sorting by column index

A DataFrame is a two-dimensional data structure. We can sort an additional axis: the vertical axis.

To sort the DataFrame columns in order, we'll again rely on the sort_index method. This time, however, we'll need to add an axis parameter and pass it an argument of "columns" or 1. The next example sorts the columns in ascending order:

```
In  [52] # The two lines below are equivalent
         nba.sort_index(axis = "columns").head()
         nba.sort_index(axis = 1).head()

Out [52]
```

	Birthday	Name	Position	Salary	Team
0	1996-09-26	Shake Milton	SG	1445697	Philadelphia 76ers
1	1995-09-27	Christian Wood	PF	1645357	Detroit Pistons
2	1998-08-23	PJ Washington	PF	3831840	Charlotte Hornets
3	1988-10-04	Derrick Rose	PG	7317074	Detroit Pistons
4	1995-07-26	Marial Shayok	G	79568	Philadelphia 76ers

How about sorting the columns in reverse alphabetical order? That task is a simple one: we can pass the ascending parameter an argument of False. The next example invokes the sort_index method, targets the columns with the axis parameter, and sorts in descending order with the ascending parameter:

```
In  [53] nba.sort_index(axis = "columns", ascending = False).head()

Out [53]
```

	Team	Salary	Position	Name	Birthday
0	Philadelphia 76ers	1445697	SG	Shake Milton	1996-09-26
1	Detroit Pistons	1645357	PF	Christian Wood	1995-09-27
2	Charlotte Hornets	3831840	PF	PJ Washington	1998-08-23
3	Detroit Pistons	7317074	PG	Derrick Rose	1988-10-04
4	Philadelphia 76ers	79568	G	Marial Shayok	1995-07-26

Let's take a second to reflect on the power of pandas. With two methods and a few parameters, we were able to sort the DataFrame on both axes, by one column, by multiple columns, in ascending order, in descending order, or in multiple orders. Pandas is remarkably flexible. We only have to combine the right method with the right arguments.

4.5   Setting a new index

At its core, our data set is a collection of players. Therefore, it seems fitting to use the Name column's values as the DataFrame's index labels. Name also has the benefit of being the only column with unique values.

The set_index method returns a new DataFrame with a given column set as the index. Its first parameter, keys, accepts the column name as a string:

```
In  [54] # The two lines below are equivalent
         nba.set_index(keys = "Name")
         nba.set_index("Name")

Out [54]
```

	Team	Position	Birthday	Salary
Name				
Shake Milton	Philadelphia 76ers	SG	1996-09-26	1445697
Christian Wood	Detroit Pistons	PF	1995-09-27	1645357
PJ Washington	Charlotte Hornets	PF	1998-08-23	3831840
Derrick Rose	Detroit Pistons	PG	1988-10-04	7317074
Marial Shayok	Philadelphia 76ers	G	1995-07-26	79568
...	...	...	...	...
Austin Rivers	Houston Rockets	PG	1992-08-01	2174310
Harry Giles	Sacramento Kings	PF	1998-04-22	2578800
Robin Lopez	Milwaukee Bucks	C	1988-04-01	4767000
Collin Sexton	Cleveland Cavaliers	PG	1999-01-04	4764960
Ricky Rubio	Phoenix Suns	PG	1990-10-21	16200000

450 rows × 4 columns

Looks good! Let's overwrite our nba variable:

```
In  [55] nba = nba.set_index(keys = "Name")
```

As a side note, we can set the index when importing a data set. Pass the column name as a string to the read_csv function's index_col parameter. The following code leads to the same DataFrame:

```
In  [56] nba = pd.read_csv(
             "nba.csv", parse_dates = ["Birthday"], index_col = "Name"
         )
```

Next, we'll talk about selecting rows and columns from our DataFrame.

4.6   Selecting columns and rows from a DataFrame

A DataFrame is a collection of Series objects with a common index. Multiple syntax options are available to extract one or more of these Series from the DataFrame.

4.6.1   Selecting a single column from a DataFrame

Each Series column is available as an attribute on the DataFrame. We use dot syntax to access object attributes. We can extract the Salary column with nba.Salary, for example. Notice that the index carries over from the DataFrame to the Series:

```
In  [57] nba.Salary

Out [57] Name
         Shake Milton       1445697
         Christian Wood     1645357
         PJ Washington      3831840
```

```
        Derrick Rose        7317074
        Marial Shayok         79568
                              ...
        Austin Rivers       2174310
        Harry Giles         2578800
        Robin Lopez         4767000
        Collin Sexton       4764960
        Ricky Rubio        16200000
        Name: Salary, Length: 450, dtype: int64
```

We can also extract a column by passing its name in square brackets after the Data-Frame:

```
In  [58] nba["Position"]
```

```
Out [58] Name
        Shake Milton        SG
        Christian Wood      PF
        PJ Washington       PF
        Derrick Rose        PG
        Marial Shayok        G
                            ..
        Austin Rivers       PG
        Harry Giles         PF
        Robin Lopez          C
        Collin Sexton       PG
        Ricky Rubio         PG
        Name: Position, Length: 450, dtype: object
```

The advantage of the square-bracket syntax is that it supports column names with spaces. If our column was named "Player Position", we could extract it only via square brackets:

```
nba["Player Position"]
```

The attribute syntax would raise an exception. Python has no way of knowing the significance of the space and would assume that we're trying to access a Player column:

```
nba.Player Position
```

Although opinions differ, I recommend using the square-bracket syntax for extraction. I like solutions that work 100% of the time, even if they require typing a few extra characters.

4.6.2　*Selecting multiple columns from a DataFrame*

To extract multiple DataFrame columns, declare a pair of opening and closing square brackets; then pass the column names in a list. The result will be a new Data-Frame whose columns are in the same order as the list elements. The next example targets the Salary and Birthday columns:

```
In  [59] nba[["Salary", "Birthday"]]
```

```
Out [59]
```

	Salary	Birthday
Name		
Shake Milton	1445697	1996-09-26
Christian Wood	1645357	1995-09-27
PJ Washington	3831840	1998-08-23
Derrick Rose	7317074	1988-10-04
Marial Shayok	79568	1995-07-26

Pandas will extract the columns based on their order in the list:

```
In  [60] nba[["Birthday", "Salary"]].head()
```

```
Out [60]
```

	Birthday	Salary
Name		
Shake Milton	1996-09-26	1445697
Christian Wood	1995-09-27	1645357
PJ Washington	1998-08-23	3831840
Derrick Rose	1988-10-04	7317074
Marial Shayok	1995-07-26	79568

We can use the `select_dtypes` method to select columns based on their data types. The method accepts two parameters, `include` and `exclude`. The parameters accept a single string or a list, representing the column type(s) that pandas should keep or discard. As a reminder, you can access the `dtypes` attribute if you'd like to see each column's datatype. The next example selects only string columns from `nba`:

```
In  [61] nba.select_dtypes(include = "object")
```

```
Out [61]
```

	Team	Position
Name		
Shake Milton	Philadelphia 76ers	SG
Christian Wood	Detroit Pistons	PF
PJ Washington	Charlotte Hornets	PF
Derrick Rose	Detroit Pistons	PG
Marial Shayok	Philadelphia 76ers	G
...	...	...
Austin Rivers	Houston Rockets	PG
Harry Giles	Sacramento Kings	PF
Robin Lopez	Milwaukee Bucks	C
Collin Sexton	Cleveland Cavaliers	PG
Ricky Rubio	Phoenix Suns	PG

450 rows × 2 columns

The next example selects all columns except string and integer columns:

```
In  [62] nba.select_dtypes(exclude = ["object", "int"])

Out [62]
```

	Birthday
Name	
Shake Milton	1996-09-26
Christian Wood	1995-09-27
PJ Washington	1998-08-23
Derrick Rose	1988-10-04
Marial Shayok	1995-07-26
...	...
Austin Rivers	1992-08-01
Harry Giles	1998-04-22
Robin Lopez	1988-04-01
Collin Sexton	1999-01-04
Ricky Rubio	1990-10-21

```
450 rows × 1 columns
```

The Birthday column is the only column in nba that holds neither string nor integer values. To include or exclude datetime columns, we can pass an argument of "datetime" to the correct parameter.

4.7 *Selecting rows from a DataFrame*

Now that we've practiced extracting columns, let's learn how to extract DataFrame rows by index label or position.

4.7.1 *Extracting rows by index label*

The loc attribute extracts a row by label. We call attributes such as loc *accessors* because they access a piece of data. Type a pair of square brackets immediately after loc and pass in the target index label. The next example extracts the nba row with an index label of "LeBron James". Pandas returns the row's values in a Series. As always, be mindful of case sensitivity:

```
In  [63] nba.loc["LeBron James"]

Out [63] Team              Los Angeles Lakers
         Position                          PF
         Birthday         1984-12-30 00:00:00
         Salary                      37436858
         Name: LeBron James, dtype: object
```

We can pass a list in between the square brackets to extract multiple rows. When the results set includes multiple records, pandas stores the results in a DataFrame:

```
In  [64] nba.loc[["Kawhi Leonard", "Paul George"]]

Out [64]
```

	Team	Position	Birthday	Salary
Name				
Kawhi Leonard	Los Angeles Clippers	SF	1991-06-29	32742000
Paul George	Los Angeles Clippers	SF	1990-05-02	33005556

Pandas organizes the rows in the order in which their index labels appear in the list. The next example swaps the string order from the previous example:

```
In  [65] nba.loc[["Paul George", "Kawhi Leonard"]]

Out [65]
```

	Team	Position	Birthday	Salary
Name				
Paul George	Los Angeles Clippers	SF	1990-05-02	33005556
Kawhi Leonard	Los Angeles Clippers	SF	1991-06-29	32742000

We can use `loc` to extract a sequence of index labels. The syntax mirrors Python's list slicing syntax. We provide the starting value, a colon, and the ending value. For extractions like this one, I strongly recommended sorting the index first, as it accelerates the speed with which pandas finds the value.

Let's say we wanted to target all players between Otto Porter and Patrick Beverley. We can sort the `DataFrame` index to get the player names in alphabetical order and then provide the two player names to the `loc` accessor. `"Otto Porter"` represents our lower bound, and `"Patrick Beverley"` represents the upper bound:

```
In  [66] nba.sort_index().loc["Otto Porter":"Patrick Beverley"]

Out [66]
```

	Team	Position	Birthday	Salary
Name				
Otto Porter	Chicago Bulls	SF	1993-06-03	27250576
PJ Dozier	Denver Nuggets	PG	1996-10-25	79568
PJ Washington	Charlotte Hornets	PF	1998-08-23	3831840
Pascal Siakam	Toronto Raptors	PF	1994-04-02	2351838
Pat Connaughton	Milwaukee Bucks	SG	1993-01-06	1723050
Patrick Beverley	Los Angeles Clippers	PG	1988-07-12	12345680

Note that pandas' `loc` accessor has some differences with Python's list-slicing syntax. For one, the `loc` accessor includes the label at the upper bound, whereas Python's list slicing syntax excludes the value at the upper bound.

Here's a quick example to remind you. The next example uses list-slicing syntax to extract the elements from index 0 to index 2 in a list of three elements. Index 2 (`"PJ Washington"`) is exclusive, so Python leaves it out:

```
In  [67] players = ["Otto Porter", "PJ Dozier", "PJ Washington"]
         players[0:2]

Out [67] ['Otto Porter', 'PJ Dozier']
```

We can use `loc` to pull rows from the middle of the `DataFrame` to its end. Pass the square brackets the starting index label and a colon:

```
In  [68] nba.sort_index().loc["Zach Collins":]
```

```
Out [68]
```

Name	Team	Position	Birthday	Salary
Zach Collins	Portland Trail Blazers	C	1997-11-19	4240200
Zach LaVine	Chicago Bulls	PG	1995-03-10	19500000
Zach Norvell	Los Angeles Lakers	SG	1997-12-09	79568
Zhaire Smith	Philadelphia 76ers	SG	1999-06-04	3058800
Zion Williamson	New Orleans Pelicans	F	2000-07-06	9757440
Zylan Cheatham	New Orleans Pelicans	SF	1995-11-17	79568

Turning in the other direction, we can use `loc` slicing to pull rows from the beginning of the `DataFrame` to a specific index label. Start with a colon and then enter the index label to extract to. The next example returns all players from the start to the data set up to Al Horford:

```
In  [69] nba.sort_index().loc[:"Al Horford"]
```

```
Out [69]
```

Name	Team	Position	Birthday	Salary
Aaron Gordon	Orlando Magic	PF	1995-09-16	19863636
Aaron Holiday	Indiana Pacers	PG	1996-09-30	2239200
Abdel Nader	Oklahoma City Thunder	SF	1993-09-25	1618520
Adam Mokoka	Chicago Bulls	G	1998-07-18	79568
Admiral Schofield	Washington Wizards	SF	1997-03-30	1000000
Al Horford	Philadelphia 76ers	C	1986-06-03	28000000

Pandas will raise an exception if the index label does not exist in the `DataFrame`:

```
In  [70] nba.loc["Bugs Bunny"]
```

```
---------------------------------------------------------------------
KeyError                              Traceback (most recent call last)

KeyError: 'Bugs Bunny'
```

As its name suggests, the `KeyError` exception communicates that a key does not exist in a given data structure.

4.7.2 *Extracting rows by index position*

The `iloc` (index location) accessor extracts rows by index position, which is helpful when the position of our rows has significance in our data set. The syntax is similar to the one we used for `loc`. Enter a pair of square brackets after `iloc`, and pass in an integer. Pandas will extract the row at that index:

```
In  [71] nba.iloc[300]
```

```
Out [71] Team             Denver Nuggets
         Position                     PF
         Birthday      1999-04-03 00:00:00
         Salary                  1416852
         Name: Jarred Vanderbilt, dtype: object
```

The `iloc` accessor also accepts a list of index positions to target multiple records. The next example pulls out the players at index positions 100, 200, 300, and 400:

```
In  [72] nba.iloc[[100, 200, 300, 400]]
```

```
Out [72]
```

	Team	Position	Birthday	Salary
Name				
Brian Bowen	Indiana Pacers	SG	1998-10-02	79568
Marco Belinelli	San Antonio Spurs	SF	1986-03-25	5846154
Jarred Vanderbilt	Denver Nuggets	PF	1999-04-03	1416852
Louis King	Detroit Pistons	F	1999-04-06	79568

We can use list-slicing syntax with the `iloc` accessor as well. Note, however, that pandas excludes the index position after the colon. The next example passes a slice of `400:404`. Pandas includes the rows at index positions 400, 401, 402, and 403, and excludes the row at index 404:

```
In  [73] nba.iloc[400:404]
```

```
Out [73]
```

	Team	Position	Birthday	Salary
Name				
Louis King	Detroit Pistons	F	1999-04-06	79568
Kostas Antetokounmpo	Los Angeles Lakers	PF	1997-11-20	79568
Rodions Kurucs	Brooklyn Nets	PF	1998-02-05	1699236
Spencer Dinwiddie	Brooklyn Nets	PG	1993-04-06	10605600

We can leave out the number before the colon to pull from the start of the Data-Frame. Here, we target rows from the beginning of `nba` up to (but not including) index position 2:

```
In  [74] nba.iloc[:2]
```

```
Out [74]
```

	Team	Position	Birthday	Salary
Name				
Shake Milton	Philadelphia 76ers	SG	1996-09-26	1445697
Christian Wood	Detroit Pistons	PF	1995-09-27	1645357

Similarly, we can remove the number after the colon to pull to the end of the Data-Frame. Here, we target the rows from index position 447 to the end of `nba`:

```
In  [75] nba.iloc[447:]
```

```
Out [75]
```

		Team Position	Birthday	Salary
Name				
Robin Lopez	Milwaukee Bucks	C	1988-04-01	4767000
Collin Sexton	Cleveland Cavaliers	PG	1999-01-04	4764960
Ricky Rubio	Phoenix Suns	PG	1990-10-21	16200000

We can also pass negative numbers for either value or both values. The next example extracts rows from the 10th-to-last row up to (but not including) the sixth-to-last row:

```
In  [76] nba.iloc[-10:-6]
```

```
Out [76]
```

		Team Position	Birthday	Salary
Name				
Jared Dudley	Los Angeles Lakers	PF	1985-07-10	2564753
Max Strus	Chicago Bulls	SG	1996-03-28	79568
Kevon Looney	Golden State Warriors	C	1996-02-06	4464286
Willy Hernangomez	Charlotte Hornets	C	1994-05-27	1557250

We can provide a third number inside the square brackets to create the step sequence, a gap between every two index positions. The next example pulls the first 10 nba rows in increments of 2. The resulting `DataFrame` includes the rows with index positions 0, 2, 4, 6, and 8:

```
In  [77] nba.iloc[0:10:2]
```

```
Out [77]
```

		Team Position	Birthday	Salary
Name				
Shake Milton	Philadelphia 76ers	SG	1996-09-26	1445697
PJ Washington	Charlotte Hornets	PF	1998-08-23	3831840
Marial Shayok	Philadelphia 76ers	G	1995-07-26	79568
Kendrick Nunn	Miami Heat	SG	1995-08-03	1416852
Brook Lopez	Milwaukee Bucks	C	1988-04-01	12093024

This slicing technique is particularly effective when we want to pull out every other row.

4.7.3 *Extracting values from specific columns*

Both the `loc` and `iloc` attributes accept a second argument representing the column(s) to extract. If we're using `loc`, we have to provide the column name. If we're using `iloc`, we have to provide the column position. The next example uses `loc` to pull the value at the intersection of the `"Giannis Antetokounmpo"` row and the Team column:

```
In  [78] nba.loc["Giannis Antetokounmpo", "Team"]
```

```
Out [78] 'Milwaukee Bucks'
```

To specify multiple values, we can pass a list for one or both of the arguments to the `loc` accessor. The next example extracts the row with a `"James Harden"` index label and the values from the Position and Birthday columns. Pandas returns a `Series`:

```
In  [79] nba.loc["James Harden", ["Position", "Birthday"]]

Out [79] Position                    PG
         Birthday     1989-08-26 00:00:00
         Name: James Harden, dtype: object
```

The next example provides multiple row labels and multiple columns:

```
In  [80] nba.loc[
             ["Russell Westbrook", "Anthony Davis"],
             ["Team", "Salary"]
         ]

Out [80]
```

	Team	Salary
Name		
Russell Westbrook	Houston Rockets	38506482
Anthony Davis	Los Angeles Lakers	27093019

We can also use list-slicing syntax to extract multiple columns without explicitly writing out their names. We have four columns in our data set (Team, Position, Birthday, and Salary). Let's extract all columns from Position to Salary. Pandas includes both endpoints in a `loc` slice:

```
In  [81] nba.loc["Joel Embiid", "Position":"Salary"]

Out [81] Position                     C
         Birthday     1994-03-16 00:00:00
         Salary               27504630
         Name: Joel Embiid, dtype: object
```

We must pass the column names in the order in which they appear in the `DataFrame`. The next example yields an empty result because the Salary column comes after the Position column. Pandas is unable to identify which columns to pull out:

```
In  [82] nba.loc["Joel Embiid", "Salary":"Position"]

Out [82] Series([], Name: Joel Embiid, dtype: object)
```

Let's say we wanted to target columns by their order rather than by their name. Remember that pandas assigns an index position to each `DataFrame` column. In nba, the Team column has an index of 0, Position has an index of 1, and so on. We can pass a column's index as the second argument to `iloc`. The next example targets the value at the intersection of the row at index 57 and the column at index 3 (Salary):

```
In  [83] nba.iloc[57, 3]

Out [83] 796806
```

We can use list-slicing syntax here as well. The next example pulls all rows from index position 100 up to but not including index position 104. It also includes all columns from the beginning of the columns up to but not including the column at index position 3 (Salary):

```
In  [84] nba.iloc[100:104, :3]
```

```
Out [84]
```

Name	Team	Position	Birthday
Brian Bowen	Indiana Pacers	SG	1998-10-02
Aaron Holiday	Indiana Pacers	PG	1996-09-30
Troy Daniels	Los Angeles Lakers	SG	1991-07-15
Buddy Hield	Sacramento Kings	SG	1992-12-17

The `iloc` and `loc` accessors are remarkably versatile. Their square brackets can accept a single value, a list of values, a list slice, and more. The disadvantage of this flexibility is that it demands extra overhead; pandas has to figure out what kind of input we've given to `iloc` or `loc`.

We can use two alternative attributes, `at` and `iat`, when we know that we want to extract a single value from a `DataFrame`. The two attributes are speedier because pandas can optimize its searching algorithms when looking for a single value.

The syntax is similar. The `at` attribute accepts row and column labels:

```
In  [85] nba.at["Austin Rivers", "Birthday"]
```

```
Out [85] Timestamp('1992-08-01 00:00:00')
```

The `iat` attribute accepts row and column indices:

```
In  [86] nba.iat[263, 1]
```

```
Out [86] 'PF'
```

Jupyter Notebook includes several magic methods to help enhance our developer experience. We declare magic methods with a `%%` prefix and enter them alongside our regular Python code. One example is `%%timeit`, which runs the code in a cell and calculates the average time it takes to execute. `%%timeit` sometimes runs the cell up to 100,000 times! The next examples use the magic method to compare the speed of the accessors we've explored so far:

```
In  [87] %%timeit
         nba.at["Austin Rivers", "Birthday"]
```

```
6.38 µs ± 53.6 ns per loop (mean ± std. dev. of 7 runs, 100000 loops each)
```

```
In  [88] %%timeit
         nba.loc["Austin Rivers", "Birthday"]
```

```
9.12 µs ± 53.8 ns per loop (mean ± std. dev. of 7 runs, 100000 loops each)
```

```
In  [89] %%timeit
         nba.iat[263, 1]

4.7 µs ± 27.4 ns per loop (mean ± std. dev. of 7 runs, 100000 loops each)

In  [90] %%timeit
         nba.iloc[263, 1]

7.41 µs ± 39.1 ns per loop (mean ± std. dev. of 7 runs, 100000 loops each)
```

The results are subject to some variance between different computers but show the clear speed advantage of at and iat over loc and iloc.

4.8   *Extracting values from Series*

The loc, iloc, at, and iat accessors are available on Series objects as well. We can practice on a sample Series from our DataFrame, such as Salary:

```
In  [91] nba["Salary"].loc["Damian Lillard"]

Out [91] 29802321

In  [92] nba["Salary"].at["Damian Lillard"]

Out [92] 29802321

In  [93] nba["Salary"].iloc[234]

Out [93] 2033160

In  [94] nba["Salary"].iat[234]

Out [94] 2033160
```

Feel free to use whatever accessors work best for you.

4.9   *Renaming columns or rows*

Do you recall the columns attribute? It exposes the Index object that stores the DataFrame's column names:

```
In  [95] nba.columns

Out [95] Index(['Team', 'Position', 'Birthday', 'Salary'], dtype='object')
```

We can rename any or all of a DataFrame's columns by assigning a list of new names to the attribute. The next example changes the name of the Salary column to Pay:

```
In  [96] nba.columns = ["Team", "Position", "Date of Birth", "Pay"]
         nba.head(1)

Out [96]
```

	Team	Position	Date of Birth	Pay
Name				
Shake Milton	Philadelphia 76ers	SG	1996-09-26	1445697

The `rename` method is an alternative option that accomplishes the same result. We can pass to its `columns` parameter a dictionary in which the keys are the existing column names and the values are their new names. The next example alters the Date of Birth column's name to Birthday:

```
In  [97] nba.rename(columns = { "Date of Birth": "Birthday" })

Out [97]
```

Name		Team	Position	Birthday	Pay
Shake Milton	Philadelphia 76ers		SG	1996-09-26	1445697
Christian Wood	Detroit Pistons		PF	1995-09-27	1645357
PJ Washington	Charlotte Hornets		PF	1998-08-23	3831840
Derrick Rose	Detroit Pistons		PG	1988-10-04	7317074
Marial Shayok	Philadelphia 76ers		G	1995-07-26	79568
...	...		...	...	...
Austin Rivers	Houston Rockets		PG	1992-08-01	2174310
Harry Giles	Sacramento Kings		PF	1998-04-22	2578800
Robin Lopez	Milwaukee Bucks		C	1988-04-01	4767000
Collin Sexton	Cleveland Cavaliers		PG	1999-01-04	4764960
Ricky Rubio	Phoenix Suns		PG	1990-10-21	16200000

```
450 rows × 4 columns
```

Let's make the operation permanent by assigning the returned `DataFrame` to the `nba` variable:

```
In  [98] nba = nba.rename(columns = { "Date of Birth": "Birthday" })
```

We can also rename index labels by passing a dictionary to the method's `index` parameter. The same logic applies; the keys are the old labels, and the values are the new ones. The following example swaps `"Giannis Antetokounmpo"` with his popular nickname `"Greek Freak"`:

```
In  [99] nba.loc["Giannis Antetokounmpo"]

Out [99] Team                Milwaukee Bucks
         Position                         PF
         Birthday        1994-12-06 00:00:00
         Pay                        25842697

         Name: Giannis Antetokounmpo, dtype: object

In  [100] nba = nba.rename(
              index = { "Giannis Antetokounmpo": "Greek Freak" }
          )
```

Let's try looking up the row by its new label:

```
In  [101] nba.loc["Greek Freak"]

Out [101] Team                Milwaukee Bucks
          Position                         PF
          Birthday        1994-12-06 00:00:00
          Pay                        25842697
          Name: Greek Freak, dtype: object
```

We've successfully changed the row label!

4.10   *Resetting an index*

Sometimes, we want to set another column as the index of our DataFrame. Let's say we wanted to make Team the index of nba. We could invoke the set_index method we introduced earlier in the chapter with a different column, but we would lose our current index of player names. Take a look at this example:

```
In  [102] nba.set_index("Team").head()
```

```
Out [102]
```

Team	Position	Birthday	Salary
Philadelphia 76ers	SG	1996-09-26	1445697
Detroit Pistons	PF	1995-09-27	1645357
Charlotte Hornets	PF	1998-08-23	3831840
Detroit Pistons	PG	1988-10-04	7317074
Philadelphia 76ers	G	1995-07-26	79568

To preserve the players' names, we must first reintegrate the existing index as a regular column in the DataFrame. The reset_index method moves the current index to a DataFrame column and replaces the former index with pandas' numeric index:

```
In  [103] nba.reset_index().head()
```

```
Out [103]
```

	Name	Team	Position	Birthday	Salary
0	Shake Milton	Philadelphia 76ers	SG	1996-09-26	1445697
1	Christian Wood	Detroit Pistons	PF	1995-09-27	1645357
2	PJ Washington	Charlotte Hornets	PF	1998-08-23	3831840
3	Derrick Rose	Detroit Pistons	PG	1988-10-04	7317074
4	Marial Shayok	Philadelphia 76ers	G	1995-07-26	79568

Now we can use the set_index method to move the Team column to the index with no data loss:

```
In  [104] nba.reset_index().set_index("Team").head()
```

```
Out [104]
```

Team	Name	Position	Birthday	Salary
Philadelphia 76ers	Shake Milton	SG	1996-09-26	1445697
Detroit Pistons	Christian Wood	PF	1995-09-27	1645357
Charlotte Hornets	PJ Washington	PF	1998-08-23	3831840
Detroit Pistons	Derrick Rose	PG	1988-10-04	7317074
Philadelphia 76ers	Marial Shayok	G	1995-07-26	79568

One advantage of avoiding the inplace parameter is that we can chain multiple method calls. Let's chain the reset_index and set_index method calls and overwrite the nba variable with the result:

```
In  [105] nba = nba.reset_index().set_index("Team")
```

That's all there is to cover. You're now acquainted with the `DataFrame`, the core work-horse of the pandas library.

4.11 Coding challenge

Now that we've explored the NBA's financials, let's apply the chapter's concepts in a different sports league.

4.11.1 Problems

The nfl.csv file contains a list of players in the National Football League with similar Name, Team, Position, Birthday, and Salary columns. See whether you can answer these questions:

1. How can we import the nfl.csv file? What's an effective way to convert the values in its Birthday column to datetimes?
2. What are the two ways we can set the `DataFrame` index to store the player names?
3. How can we count the number of players per team in this data set?
4. Who are the five highest-paid players?
5. How can we sort the data set first by teams in alphabetical order and then by salary in descending order?
6. Who is the oldest player on the New York Jets roster, and what is his birthday?

4.11.2 Solutions

Let's walk through the challenges step by step:

1. We can import the CSV with the `read_csv` function. To store the Birthday column values as datetimes, we'll pass the column to the `parse_dates` parameter in a list:

```
In  [106] nfl = pd.read_csv("nfl.csv", parse_dates = ["Birthday"])
         nfl
```

```
Out [106]
```

	Name	Team	Position	Birthday	Salary
0	Tremon Smith	Philadelphia Eagles	RB	1996-07-20	570000
1	Shawn Williams	Cincinnati Bengals	SS	1991-05-13	3500000
2	Adam Butler	New England Patriots	DT	1994-04-12	645000
3	Derek Wolfe	Denver Broncos	DE	1990-02-24	8000000
4	Jake Ryan	Jacksonville Jaguars	OLB	1992-02-27	1000000
...	...	...	...	...	...
1650	Bashaud Breeland	Kansas City Chiefs	CB	1992-01-30	805000
1651	Craig James	Philadelphia Eagles	CB	1996-04-29	570000
1652	Jonotthan Harrison	New York Jets	C	1991-08-25	1500000
1653	Chuma Edoga	New York Jets	OT	1997-05-25	495000
1654	Tajae Sharpe	Tennessee Titans	WR	1994-12-23	2025000

1655 rows × 5 columns

2 Our next challenge is setting the player names as the index labels. Our option is to invoke the `set_index` method and assign the new `DataFrame` to the `nfl` variable:

```
In  [107] nfl = nfl.set_index("Name")
```

Another option is to provide the `index_col` parameter to the `read_csv` function when importing the data set:

```
In  [108] nfl = pd.read_csv(
              "nfl.csv", index_col = "Name", parse_dates = ["Birthday"]
          )
```

The result will be the same either way:

```
In  [109] nfl.head()

Out [109]
```

	Team	Position	Birthday	Salary
Name				
Tremon Smith	Philadelphia Eagles	RB	1996-07-20	570000
Shawn Williams	Cincinnati Bengals	SS	1991-05-13	3500000
Adam Butler	New England Patriots	DT	1994-04-12	645000
Derek Wolfe	Denver Broncos	DE	1990-02-24	8000000
Jake Ryan	Jacksonville Jaguars	OLB	1992-02-27	1000000

3 To count the number of players per team, we can invoke the `value_counts` method on the Team column. First, we need to extract the Team `Series` with dot syntax or square brackets:

```
In  [110] # The two lines below are equivalent
          nfl.Team.value_counts().head()
          nfl["Team"].value_counts().head()

Out [110] New York Jets          58
          Washington Redskins    56
          Kansas City Chiefs     56
          San Francisco 49Ers    55
          New Orleans Saints     55
```

4 To identify the five highest-paid players, we can use the `sort_values` method to sort the Salary column. To tell pandas to sort in descending order, we can pass the `ascending` parameter an argument of `False`. Another option is the `nlargest` method:

```
In  [111] nfl.sort_values("Salary", ascending = False).head()

Out [111]
```

	Team	Position	Birthday	Salary
Name				
Kirk Cousins	Minnesota Vikings	QB	1988-08-19	27500000
Jameis Winston	Tampa Bay Buccaneers	QB	1994-01-06	20922000

```
Marcus Mariota        Tennessee Titans     QB 1993-10-30  20922000
Derek Carr             Oakland Raiders      QB 1991-03-28  19900000
Jimmy Garoppolo    San Francisco 49Ers     QB 1991-11-02  17200000
```

5 To sort by multiple columns, we'll have to pass arguments to both the `by` and `ascending` parameters of the `sort_values` method. The following code sorts the Team column in ascending order followed by the Salary column in descending order:

```
In  [112] nfl.sort_values(
              by = ["Team", "Salary"],
              ascending = [True, False]
          )
```

Out [112]

Name	Team	Position	Birthday	Salary
Chandler Jones	Arizona Cardinals	OLB	1990-02-27	16500000
Patrick Peterson	Arizona Cardinals	CB	1990-07-11	11000000
Larry Fitzgerald	Arizona Cardinals	WR	1983-08-31	11000000
David Johnson	Arizona Cardinals	RB	1991-12-16	5700000
Justin Pugh	Arizona Cardinals	G	1990-08-15	5000000
...	...	...	...	...
Ross Pierschbacher	Washington Redskins	C	1995-05-05	495000
Kelvin Harmon	Washington Redskins	WR	1996-12-15	495000
Wes Martin	Washington Redskins	G	1996-05-09	495000
Jimmy Moreland	Washington Redskins	CB	1995-08-26	495000
Jeremy Reaves	Washington Redskins	SS	1996-08-29	495000

```
1655 rows × 4 columns
```

6 The final challenge is a tricky one: we have to find the oldest player on the New York Jets roster. Given the current tools at our disposal, we can set the Team column as the `DataFrame` index to allow for easy extraction of all Jets players. To preserve the player names currently in our index, we'll first use the `reset_index` method to move them back into the `DataFrame` as a regular column:

```
In  [113] nfl = nfl.reset_index().set_index(keys = "Team")
          nfl.head(3)
```

Out [113]

Team	Name	Position	Birthday	Salary
Philadelphia Eagles	Tremon Smith	RB	1996-07-20	570000
Cincinnati Bengals	Shawn Williams	SS	1991-05-13	3500000
New England Patriots	Adam Butler	DT	1994-04-12	645000

Next, we can use the `loc` attribute to isolate all players on the New York Jets:

```
In  [114] nfl.loc["New York Jets"].head()
```

Out [114]

Team	Name	Position	Birthday	Salary
New York Jets	Bronson Kaufusi	DE	1991-07-06	645000
New York Jets	Darryl Roberts	CB	1990-11-26	1000000
New York Jets	Jordan Willis	DE	1995-05-02	754750
New York Jets	Quinnen Williams	DE	1997-12-21	495000
New York Jets	Sam Ficken	K	1992-12-14	495000

The last step is to sort the Birthday column and extract the top record. This sort is possible only because we converted the column's values to datetimes:

```
In  [115] nfl.loc["New York Jets"].sort_values("Birthday").head(1)

Out [115]
```

Team	Name	Position	Birthday	Salary
New York Jets	Ryan Kalil	C	1985-03-29	2400000

The oldest player on the New York Jets in this data set is Ryan Kalil. His birthday was March 29, 1985.

Congratulations on completing the coding challenge!

Summary

- The `DataFrame` is a two-dimensional data structure consisting of rows and columns.
- The `DataFrame` shares attributes and methods with the `Series`. Many of the attributes and methods operate differently due to the dimensional differences between the two objects.
- The `sort_values` method sorts one or more `DataFrame` columns. We can assign each column a different sort order (ascending or descending).
- The `loc` attribute extracts rows or columns by index label. The `at` attribute is a convenient shortcut for targeting only one value.
- The `iloc` attribute extracts rows or columns by index position. The `iat` attribute is a convenient shortcut for targeting only one value.
- The `reset_index` method restores an index as a regular column in the Data-Frame.
- The `rename` method sets a different name for one or more columns or rows.

Filtering a DataFrame 5

This chapter covers

- Reducing a DataFrame's memory use
- Extracting DataFrame rows by one or more conditions
- Filtering a DataFrame for rows that include or exclude null values
- Selecting column values that fall between a range
- Removing duplicate and null values from a DataFrame

In chapter 4, we learned how to extract rows, columns, and cell values from a DataFrame by using the loc and iloc accessors. These accessors work well when we know the index labels and positions of the rows/columns we want to target. Sometimes, we may want to target rows not by an identifier but by a condition or a criterion. We may want to extract a subset of rows in which a column holds a specific value, for example.

In this chapter, we'll learn how to declare logical conditions that include and exclude rows from a `DataFrame`. We'll see how to combine multiple conditions by using `AND` and `OR` logic. Finally, we'll introduce some pandas utility methods that simplify the filtering process. Lots of fun lies ahead, so let's jump in.

5.1   *Optimizing a data set for memory use*

Before we segue into filtering, let's quickly talk about reducing memory in pandas. Whenever importing a data set, it's important to consider whether each column stores its data in the most optimal type. The "best" data type is the one that consumes the least memory or provides the most utility. Integers occupy less memory than floating-point numbers on most computers, for example, so if your data set includes whole numbers, it's ideal to import them as integers rather than floating-points. As another example, if your data set includes dates, it's ideal to import them as datetimes rather than as strings, which allows for datetime-specific operations. In this section, we'll learn some tips and tricks to shrink memory consumption by converting column data to different types, which will facilitate faster filtering later. Let's begin with the usual import of our favorite data analysis library:

```
In  [1] import pandas as pd
```

This chapter's employees.csv data set is a fictional collection of workers at a company. Each record includes the employee's first name, gender, start date at the firm, salary, manager status (`True` or `False`), and team. Let's take a peek at the data set with the `read_csv` function:

```
In  [2] pd.read_csv("employees.csv")
```

```
Out [2]
```

	First Name	Gender	Start Date	Salary	Mgmt	Team
0	Douglas	Male	8/6/93	NaN	True	Marketing
1	Thomas	Male	3/31/96	61933.0	True	NaN
2	Maria	Female	NaN	130590.0	False	Finance
3	Jerry	NaN	3/4/05	138705.0	True	Finance
4	Larry	Male	1/24/98	101004.0	True	IT
...	...	...	...	...	...	...
996	Phillip	Male	1/31/84	42392.0	False	Finance
997	Russell	Male	5/20/13	96914.0	False	Product
998	Larry	Male	4/20/13	60500.0	False	Business Dev
999	Albert	Male	5/15/12	129949.0	True	Sales
1000	NaN	NaN	NaN	NaN	NaN	NaN

1001 rows × 6 columns

Take a second to notice the NaNs scattered throughout the output. Every column has missing values. In fact, the last row consists only of NaNs. Imperfect data like this is common in the real world. Data sets can arrive with blank rows, blank columns, and more.

How can we increase the utility of our data set? Our first optimization is one that we should feel comfortable with by now. We can convert the text values in the Start Date column to datetimes with the `parse_dates` parameter:

```
In  [3] pd.read_csv("employees.csv", parse_dates = ["Start Date"]).head()

Out [3]
```

	First Name	Gender	Start Date	Salary	Mgmt	Team
0	Douglas	Male	1993-08-06	NaN	True	Marketing
1	Thomas	Male	1996-03-31	61933.0	True	NaN
2	Maria	Female	NaT	130590.0	False	Finance
3	Jerry	NaN	2005-03-04	138705.0	True	Finance
4	Larry	Male	1998-01-24	101004.0	True	IT

We're in a good place with the CSV import, so let's assign the `DataFrame` object to a descriptive variable such as `employees`:

```
In  [4] employees = pd.read_csv(
            "employees.csv", parse_dates = ["Start Date"]
        )
```

A few options are available for improving the speed and efficiency of `DataFrame` operations. First, let's summarize the data set as it currently stands. We can invoke the `info` method to see a list of the columns, their data types, a count of missing values, and the `DataFrame`'s total memory consumption:

```
In  [5] employees.info()

Out [5]

<class 'pandas.core.frame.DataFrame'>
RangeIndex: 1001 entries, 0 to 1000
Data columns (total 6 columns):
 #   Column      Non-Null Count  Dtype
---  ------      --------------  -----
 0   First Name  933 non-null    object
 1   Gender      854 non-null    object
 2   Start Date  999 non-null    datetime64[ns]
 3   Salary      999 non-null    float64
 4   Mgmt        933 non-null    object
 5   Team        957 non-null    object
dtypes: datetime64[ns](1), float64(1), object(4)
message usage: 47.0+ KB
```

Let's walk through the output from top to bottom. We have a `DataFrame` with 1,001 rows, starting at index 0 and proceeding to index 1000. There are four string columns, one datetime column, and one floating-point column. All six columns have missing data.

Memory use currently is ~47 KB—a small amount for modern computers, but let's try to whittle the number down. As you read the following examples, focus more on the percentage reductions than on the numeric reductions. The larger your data sets grow, the more significant the performance improvement will be.

5.1.1   *Converting data types with the astype method*

Did you notice that pandas imported the Mgmt column's values as strings? The column stores only two values: `True` and `False`. We can reduce memory use by converting the values to the more lightweight Boolean data type.

The `astype` method converts a `Series`' values to a different data type. It accepts a single argument: the new data type. We can pass either the data type or a string with its name.

The next example extracts the Mgmt `Series` from `employees` and invokes its `astype` method with an argument of `bool`. Pandas returns a new `Series` object of Booleans. Note that the library converts `NaN`s to `True` values. We'll discuss removing missing values in section 5.5.4.

```
In   [6] employees["Mgmt"].astype(bool)

Out [6] 0          True
        1          True
        2          False
        3          True
        4          True
                   ...
        996        False
        997        False
        998        False
        999        True
        1000       True
        Name: Mgmt, Length: 1001, dtype: bool
```

Looks good! Now that we've previewed what the `Series` will look like, we can overwrite the existing Mgmt column in `employees`. Updating a `DataFrame` column works similarly to setting a key-value pair in a dictionary. If a column with the specified name exists, pandas overwrites it with the new `Series`. If the column with the name does not exist, pandas creates a new `Series` and appends it to the right of the `DataFrame`. The library matches rows in the `Series` and `DataFrame` by shared index labels.

The next code sample overwrites the Mgmt column with our new `Series` of Booleans. As a reminder, Python evaluates the right side of the assignment operator (=) first. First, we create a new `Series`, then we overwrite our existing Mgmt column:

```
In   [7] employees["Mgmt"] = employees["Mgmt"].astype(bool)
```

A column assignment does not produce a return value, so the code does not output anything in Jupyter Notebook. Let's take a look at the `DataFrame` again to see the results:

```
In  [8] employees.tail()

Out [8]
```

	First Name	Gender	Start Date	Salary	Mgmt	Team
996	Phillip	Male	1984-01-31	42392.0	False	Finance
997	Russell	Male	2013-05-20	96914.0	False	Product
998	Larry	Male	2013-04-20	60500.0	False	Business Dev
999	Albert	Male	2012-05-15	129949.0	True	Sales
1000	NaN	NaN	NaT	NaN	True	NaN

Except for the `True` in the last row of missing values, the `DataFrame` looks no different. But what about our memory use? Let's invoke the `info` method again to see the difference:

```
In  [9] employees.info()

Out [9]

<class 'pandas.core.frame.DataFrame'>
RangeIndex: 1001 entries, 0 to 1000
Data columns (total 6 columns):
 #   Column      Non-Null Count  Dtype
---  ------      --------------  -----
 0   First Name  933 non-null    object
 1   Gender      854 non-null    object
 2   Start Date  999 non-null    datetime64[ns]
 3   Salary      999 non-null    float64
 4   Mgmt        1001 non-null   bool
 5   Team        957 non-null    object
dtypes: bool(1), datetime64[ns](1), float64(1), object(3)
memory usage: 40.2+ KB
```

We've reduced `employees`' memory use by almost 15%, from 47 KB to 40.2 KB. That's a pretty good start!

Next, let's transition to the Salary column. If we open the raw CSV file, we can see that its values are stored as whole numbers:

```
First Name,Gender,Start Date,Salary,Mgmt,Team
Douglas,Male,8/6/93,,True,Marketing
Thomas,Male,3/31/96,61933,True,
Maria,Female,,130590,False,Finance
Jerry,,3/4/05,138705,True,Finance
```

In `employees`, however, pandas stores the Salary values at floats. To support the `NaN`s throughout the column, pandas converts the integers to floating-point numbers—a technical requirement of the library that we observed in earlier chapters.

Following our previous Boolean example, we might try to coerce the column's values to integers with the `astype` method. Unfortunately, pandas raises a `ValueError` exception:

```
In  [10] employees["Salary"].astype(int)

---------------------------------------------------------------------------
ValueError                                Traceback (most recent call last)
<ipython-input-99-b148c8b8be90> in <module>
----> 1 employees["Salary"].astype(int)

ValueError: Cannot convert non-finite values (NA or inf) to integer
```

Pandas is unable to convert the NaN values to integers. We can solve this problem by replacing the NaN values with a constant value. The `fillna` method replaces a `Series`' null values with the argument we pass in. The next example provides a fill value of 0. Note that your choice of value can distort the data; 0 is passed solely for the sake of example.

We know that the original Salary column has a missing value in its last row. Let's take a look at the last row after we invoke the `fillna` method:

```
In  [11] employees["Salary"].fillna(0).tail()

Out [11] 996       42392.0
         997       96914.0
         998       60500.0
         999      129949.0
         1000          0.0
         Name: Salary, dtype: float64
```

Excellent. Now that the Salary column has no missing values, we can convert its values to integers with the `astype` method:

```
In  [12] employees["Salary"].fillna(0).astype(int).tail()

Out [12] 996       42392
         997       96914
         998       60500
         999      129949
         1000          0
         Name: Salary, dtype: int64
```

Next, we can overwrite the existing Salary `Series` in `employees`:

```
In  [13] employees["Salary"] = employees["Salary"].fillna(0).astype(int)
```

We can make one additional optimization. Pandas includes a special data type called a *category*, which is ideal for a column consisting of a small number of unique values relative to its total size. Some everyday examples of data points with a limited number of values include gender, weekdays, blood types, planets, and income groups. Behind the scenes, pandas stores only one copy of each categorical value rather than storing duplicates across rows.

The `nunique` method can reveal the number of unique values in each `DataFrame` column. Note that it excludes missing values (NaN) from the count by default:

```
In  [14] employees.nunique()

Out [14] First Name  200
         Gender        2
         Start Date  971
         Salary      995
         Mgmt          2
         Team         10
         dtype: int64
```

The Gender and Team columns stand out as good candidates to store categorical values. In 1,001 rows of data, Gender has only two unique values, and Team has only ten unique values.

Let's use the `astype` method again. First, we'll convert the Gender column's values to categories by passing an argument of `"category"` to the method:

```
In  [15] employees["Gender"].astype("category")

Out [15] 0          Male
         1          Male
         2        Female
         3           NaN
         4          Male
                   ...
         996        Male
         997        Male
         998        Male
         999        Male
         1000        NaN
         Name: Gender, Length: 1001, dtype: category
         Categories (2, object): [Female, Male]
```

Pandas has identified two unique categories: `"Female"` and `"Male"`. We're good to overwrite our existing Gender column:

```
In  [16] employees["Gender"] = employees["Gender"].astype("category")
```

Let's check in on the memory use by invoking the `info` method. Memory use has dropped significantly once again because pandas has to keep track of only two values instead of 1,001:

```
In  [17] employees.info()

Out [17]

<class 'pandas.core.frame.DataFrame'>
RangeIndex: 1001 entries, 0 to 1000
Data columns (total 6 columns):
 #   Column      Non-Null Count  Dtype
---  ------      --------------  -----
 0   First Name  933 non-null    object
 1   Gender      854 non-null    category
 2   Start Date  999 non-null    datetime64[ns]
```

```
 3    Salary      1001 non-null    int64
 4    Mgmt        1001 non-null    bool
 5    Team         957 non-null    object
dtypes: bool(1), category(1), datetime64[ns](1), int64(1), object(2)
memory usage: 33.5+ KB
```

Let's repeat the same process for the Team column, which has only ten unique values:

```
In  [18] employees["Team"] = employees["Team"].astype("category")

In  [19] employees.info()

Out [19]


<class 'pandas.core.frame.DataFrame'>
RangeIndex: 1001 entries, 0 to 1000
Data columns (total 6 columns):
 #    Column      Non-Null Count   Dtype
---   ------      --------------   -----
 0    First Name  933 non-null     object
 1    Gender      854 non-null     category
 2    Start Date  999 non-null     datetime64[ns]
 3    Salary      1001 non-null    int64
 4    Mgmt        1001 non-null    bool
 5    Team         957 non-null    category
dtypes: bool(1), category(2)
memory usage: 27.0+ KB
```

With fewer than ten lines of code, we've reduced the DataFrame's memory consumption by more than 40%. Imagine that impact on data sets with millions of rows!

5.2   *Filtering by a single condition*

Extracting a subset of data is perhaps the most common operation in data analysis. A *subset* is a portion of a larger data set that fits some kind of condition.

Suppose that we want to generate a list of all employees named "Maria". To accomplish this task, we need to filter our employees data set based on the values in the First Name column. The list of employees named Maria is a subset of all employees.

First, a quick reminder of how equality works in Python. The equality operator (==) compares the equality of two objects in Python, returning True if the objects are equal and False if they are unequal. (See appendix B for a detailed explanation.) Here's a simple example:

```
In  [20] "Maria" == "Maria"

Out [20] True

In  [21] "Maria" == "Taylor"

Out [21] False
```

To compare every `Series` entry with a constant value, we place the `Series` on one side of the equality operator and the value on the other:

```
Series == value
```

One might think that this syntax would lead to an error, but pandas is smart enough to recognize that we want to compare the equality of each `Series` value with the specified string, not with the `Series` itself. We explored similar ideas in chapter 2 when we paired a `Series` with mathematical operators such as the addition sign.

When we combine a `Series` with an equality operator, pandas returns a `Series` of Booleans. The next example compares each First Name column value with `"Maria"`. A `True` value indicates that the string `"Maria"` does occur at that index, and a `False` value indicates that it does not. The following output communicates that index 2 stores the value `"Maria"`:

```
In  [22] employees["First Name"] == "Maria"

Out [22] 0       False
         1       False
         2       True
         3       False
         4       False
               ...
         996     False
         997     False
         998     False
         999     False
         1000    False
         Name: First Name, Length: 1001, dtype: bool
```

If we could extract only the rows with a `True` value above from our employees Data-Frame, we would have all the `"Maria"` records in the data set. Luckily, pandas offers a convenient syntax for extracting rows by using a Boolean `Series`. To filter rows, we provide the Boolean `Series` between square brackets following the `DataFrame`:

```
In  [23] employees[employees["First Name"] == "Maria"]

Out [23]
```

	First Name	Gender	Start Date	Salary	Mgmt	Team
2	Maria	Female	NaT	130590	False	Finance
198	Maria	Female	1990-12-27	36067	True	Product
815	Maria	NaN	1986-01-18	106562	False	HR
844	Maria	NaN	1985-06-19	148857	False	Legal
936	Maria	Female	2003-03-14	96250	False	Business Dev
984	Maria	Female	2011-10-15	43455	False	Engineering

Great success! We've used our Boolean `Series` to filter rows with a value of `"Maria"` in the First Name column.

If the use of multiple square brackets is confusing, you can assign the Boolean `Series` to a descriptive variable and then pass the variable into the square brackets instead. The following code yields the same subset of rows as the preceding code:

```
In  [24] marias = employees["First Name"] == "Maria"
         employees[marias]

Out [24]
```

	First Name	Gender	Start Date	Salary	Mgmt	Team
2	Maria	Female	NaT	130590	False	Finance
198	Maria	Female	1990-12-27	36067	True	Product
815	Maria	NaN	1986-01-18	106562	False	HR
844	Maria	NaN	1985-06-19	148857	False	Legal
936	Maria	Female	2003-03-14	96250	False	Business Dev
984	Maria	Female	2011-10-15	43455	False	Engineering

The most common mistake beginners make when comparing the equality of values is using one equal sign instead of two. Remember that a single equal sign assigns an object to a variable, and two equal signs check for equality between objects. If we accidentally used a single equal sign in this example, we would overwrite all the First Name column's values with the string `"Maria"`. No good.

Let's try another example. What if we want to extract a subset of employees who are not on the Finance team? The protocol remains the same, but with a slight twist. We need to generate a Boolean `Series` that checks which of the Team column's values are not equal to `"Finance"`. Then we can use the Boolean `Series` to filter employees. Python's inequality operator returns `True` if two values are not equal and `False` if they are equal:

```
In  [25] "Finance" != "Engineering"

Out [25] True
```

The `Series` object plays friendly with the inequality operator as well. The next example compares the values in the Team column with the string `"Finance"`. `True` denotes that the Team value for a given index is not `"Finance"`, and `False` indicates the Team value is `"Finance"`:

```
In  [26] employees["Team"] != "Finance"

Out [26] 0        True
         1        True
         2        False
         3        False
         4        True
                 ...
         996      False
         997      True
         998      True
         999      True
         1000     True
         Name: Team, Length: 1001, dtype: bool
```

Now that we have our Boolean `Series`, we can pass it inside square brackets to extract the `DataFrame` rows with a value of `True`. In the following output, we see that pandas has excluded the rows at indexes 2 and 3 because the Team value there is `"Finance"`:

```
In  [27] employees[employees["Team"] != "Finance"]

Out [27]
```

	First Name	Gender	Start Date	Salary	Mgmt	Team
0	Douglas	Male	1993-08-06	0	True	Marketing
1	Thomas	Male	1996-03-31	61933	True	NaN
4	Larry	Male	1998-01-24	101004	True	IT
5	Dennis	Male	1987-04-18	115163	False	Legal
6	Ruby	Female	1987-08-17	65476	True	Product
...	...	...	...	...	...	...
995	Henry	NaN	2014-11-23	132483	False	Distribution
997	Russell	Male	2013-05-20	96914	False	Product
998	Larry	Male	2013-04-20	60500	False	Business Dev
999	Albert	Male	2012-05-15	129949	True	Sales
1000	NaN	NaN	NaT	0	True	NaN

```
899 rows × 6 columns
```

Note that the results include rows with missing values. We can see an example at index 1000. In this scenario, pandas considers a `NaN` to be unequal to the string `"Finance"`.

What if we want to retrieve all the managers in the company? Managers have a value of `True` in the Mgmt column. We could execute `employees["Mgmt"] == True`, but we don't need to because Mgmt is already a `Series` of Booleans. The `True` values and `False` values already indicate whether pandas should keep or discard a row. Therefore, we can pass the Mgmt column by itself inside the square brackets:

```
In  [28] employees[employees["Mgmt"]].head()

Out [28]
```

	First Name	Gender	Start Date	Salary	Mgmt	Team
0	Douglas	Male	1993-08-06	0	True	Marketing
1	Thomas	Male	1996-03-31	61933	True	NaN
3	Jerry	NaN	2005-03-04	138705	True	Finance
4	Larry	Male	1998-01-24	101004	True	IT
6	Ruby	Female	1987-08-17	65476	True	Product

We can also use arithmetic operands to filter columns based on mathematical conditions. The next example generates a Boolean `Series` for Salary values greater than $100,000 (see chapter 2 for more on this syntax):

```
In  [29] high_earners = employees["Salary"] > 100000
         high_earners.head()

Out [29] 0    False
         1    False
         2     True
         3     True
         4     True
         Name: Salary, dtype: bool
```

Let's see which employees earn a salary above $100,000:

```
In  [30] employees[high_earners].head()
```

```
Out [30]
```

	First Name	Gender	Start Date	Salary	Mgmt	Team
2	Maria	Female	NaT	130590	False	Finance
3	Jerry	NaN	2005-03-04	138705	True	Finance
4	Larry	Male	1998-01-24	101004	True	IT
5	Dennis	Male	1987-04-18	115163	False	Legal
9	Frances	Female	2002-08-08	139852	True	Business Dev

Try practicing the syntax on some of the other columns in employees. As long as you provide a Boolean Series, pandas will be able to filter the DataFrame.

5.3   *Filtering by multiple conditions*

We can filter a DataFrame with multiple conditions by creating two independent Boolean Series and then declaring the logical criterion that pandas should apply between them.

5.3.1   *The AND condition*

Suppose that we want to find all female employees who work on the business development team. Now pandas must look for two conditions to select a row: a value of "Female" in the Gender column and a value of "Business Dev" in the Team column. The two criteria are independent, but both must be met. Here's a quick reminder of how AND logic works with two conditions:

Condition 1	Condition 2	Evaluation
True	True	True
True	False	False
False	True	False
False	False	False

Let's construct one Boolean Series at a time. We can begin by isolating the "Female" values in the Gender column:

```
In  [31] is_female = employees["Gender"] == "Female"
```

Next, we'll target all employees who work on the "Business Dev" team:

```
In  [32] in_biz_dev = employees["Team"] == "Business Dev"
```

Finally, we need to calculate the intersection of the two Series, the rows in which both the is_female and in_biz_dev Series have True values. Pass both Series into the square brackets, and place an ampersand symbol (&) between them. The ampersand declares an AND logical criterion. The `is_female` Series must have True *and* the `in_biz_dev` Series must have True:

```
In  [33] employees[is_female & in_biz_dev].head()
```

```
Out [33]
```

	First Name	Gender	Start Date	Salary	Mgmt	Team
9	Frances	Female	2002-08-08	139852	True	Business Dev
33	Jean	Female	1993-12-18	119082	False	Business Dev
36	Rachel	Female	2009-02-16	142032	False	Business Dev
38	Stephanie	Female	1986-09-13	36844	True	Business Dev
61	Denise	Female	2001-11-06	106862	False	Business Dev

We can include any amount of Series within the square brackets as long as we separate every subsequent two with a & symbol. The next example adds a third criterion to identify the female managers on the business development team:

```
In  [34] is_manager = employees["Mgmt"]
         employees[is_female & in_biz_dev & is_manager].head()
```

```
Out [34]
```

	First Name	Gender	Start Date	Salary	Mgmt	Team
9	Frances	Female	2002-08-08	139852	True	Business Dev
38	Stephanie	Female	1986-09-13	36844	True	Business Dev
66	Nancy	Female	2012-12-15	125250	True	Business Dev
92	Linda	Female	2000-05-25	119009	True	Business Dev
111	Bonnie	Female	1999-12-17	42153	True	Business Dev

In summary, the & symbol selects rows that fit all conditions. Declare two or more Boolean Series and then use the ampersand to weave them together.

5.3.2 The OR condition

We can also extract rows if they fit one of several conditions. Not all conditions have to be true, but at least one does. Here's a quick reminder of how OR logic works with two conditions:

Condition 1	Condition 2	Evaluation
True	True	True
True	False	True
False	True	True
False	False	False

Suppose that we want to identify all employees with a Salary below $40,000 or a Start Date after January 1, 2015. We can use mathematical operators such as < and > to arrive at two separate Boolean Series for these conditions:

```
In  [35] earning_below_40k = employees["Salary"] < 40000
         started_after_2015 = employees["Start Date"] > "2015-01-01"
```

We use a pipe symbol (|) between Boolean `Series` to declare `OR` criteria. The next example selects the rows in which either of the Boolean `Series` holds a `True` value:

```
In  [36] employees[earning_below_40k | started_after_2015].tail()
```

Out [36]

	First Name	Gender	Start Date	Salary	Mgmt	Team
958	Gloria	Female	1987-10-24	39833	False	Engineering
964	Bruce	Male	1980-05-07	35802	True	Sales
967	Thomas	Male	2016-03-12	105681	False	Engineering
989	Justin	NaN	1991-02-10	38344	False	Legal
1000	NaN	NaN	NaT	0	True	NaN

The rows at index positions 958, 964, 989, and 1000 fit the Salary condition, and the row at index 967 fits the Start Date condition. Pandas will also include rows that fit both conditions.

5.3.3   *Inversion with ~*

The tilde symbol (~) inverts the values in a Boolean `Series`. All `True` values become `False`, and all `False` values become `True`. Here's a simple example with a small `Series`:

```
In  [37] my_series = pd.Series([True, False, True])
         my_series
```

```
Out [37] 0    True
         1    False
         2    True
         dtype: bool
```

```
In  [38] ~my_series
```

```
Out [38] 0    False
         1    True
         2    False
         dtype: bool
```

Inversion is helpful when we'd like to reverse a condition. Let's say we want to identify employees with a Salary of less than $100,000. We could use two approaches, the first of which is to write `employees["Salary"] < 100000`:

```
In  [39] employees[employees["Salary"] < 100000].head()
```

Out [39]

	First Name	Gender	Start Date	Salary	Mgmt	Team
0	Douglas	Male	1993-08-06	0	True	Marketing
1	Thomas	Male	1996-03-31	61933	True	NaN
6	Ruby	Female	1987-08-17	65476	True	Product
7	NaN	Female	2015-07-20	45906	True	Finance
8	Angela	Female	2005-11-22	95570	True	Engineering

Alternatively, we could invert the results set of employees earning more than or equal to $100,000. The resulting `DataFrames` will be identical. In the next example, we wrap our greater-than operation inside a parenthesis. The syntax ensures that pandas generates the Boolean `Series` before inverting its values. In general, you should use parentheses whenever the order of evaluation may be unclear to pandas:

```
In  [40] employees[~(employees["Salary"] >= 100000)].head()
```

```
Out [40]
```

	First Name	Gender	Start Date	Salary	Mgmt	Team
0	Douglas	Male	1993-08-06	0	True	Marketing
1	Thomas	Male	1996-03-31	61933	True	NaN
6	Ruby	Female	1987-08-17	65476	True	Product
7	NaN	Female	2015-07-20	45906	True	Finance
8	Angela	Female	2005-11-22	95570	True	Engineering

TIP For complex extractions like this one, consider assigning the Boolean `Series` to a descriptive variable.

5.3.4 *Methods for Booleans*

Pandas provides an alternative syntax for analysts who prefer methods over operators. The following table displays the method alternatives for equality, inequality, and other arithmetic operations:

Operation	Arithmetic syntax	Method syntax
Equality	`employees["Team"] == "Marketing"`	`employees["Team"].eq("Marketing")`
Inequality	`employees["Team"] != "Marketing"`	`employees["Team"].ne("Marketing")`
Less than	`employees["Salary"] < 100000`	`employees["Salary"].lt(100000)`
Less than or equal to	`employees["Salary"] <= 100000`	`employees["Salary"].le(100000)`
Greater than	`employees["Salary"] > 100000`	`employees["Salary"].gt(100000)`
Greater than or equal to	`employees["Salary"] >= 100000`	`employees["Salary"].ge(100000)`

The same rules apply regarding the use of & and | symbols for AND/OR logic.

5.4 *Filtering by condition*

Some filtering operations are more complex than simple equality or inequality checks. Luckily, pandas ships with many helper methods that generate Boolean Series for these types of extractions.

5.4.1 *The isin method*

What if we want to isolate the employees who belong to either the Sales, Legal, or Marketing team? We could provide three separate Boolean `Series` inside the square brackets and add the | symbol to declare OR criteria:

```
In  [41] sales = employees["Team"] == "Sales"
         legal = employees["Team"] == "Legal"
         mktg  = employees["Team"] == "Marketing"
         employees[sales | legal | mktg].head()
```

Out [41]

	First Name	Gender	Start Date	Salary	Mgmt	Team
0	Douglas	Male	1993-08-06	0	True	Marketing
5	Dennis	Male	1987-04-18	115163	False	Legal
11	Julie	Female	1997-10-26	102508	True	Legal
13	Gary	Male	2008-01-27	109831	False	Sales
20	Lois	NaN	1995-04-22	64714	True	Legal

Although this solution works, it isn't scalable. What if our next report asked for employees from 15 teams instead of three? Declaring a Series for each condition is laborious.

A better solution is the isin method, which accepts an iterable of elements (list, tuple, Series, and so on) and returns a Boolean Series. True denotes that pandas found the row's value among the iterable's values, and False denotes that it did not. When we have the Series, we can use it to filter the DataFrame in the usual manner. The next example achieves the same result set:

```
In  [42] all_star_teams = ["Sales", "Legal", "Marketing"]
         on_all_star_teams = employees["Team"].isin(all_star_teams)
         employees[on_all_star_teams].head()
```

Out [42]

	First Name	Gender	Start Date	Salary	Mgmt	Team
0	Douglas	Male	1993-08-06	0	True	Marketing
5	Dennis	Male	1987-04-18	115163	False	Legal
11	Julie	Female	1997-10-26	102508	True	Legal
13	Gary	Male	2008-01-27	109831	False	Sales
20	Lois	NaN	1995-04-22	64714	True	Legal

An optimal situation for using the isin method is when we do not know the comparison collection in advance, such as when it is generated dynamically.

5.4.2   *The between method*

When working with numbers or dates, we often want to extract values that fall within a range. Suppose that we want to identify all employees with a salary between $80,000 and $90,000. We could create two Boolean Series, one to declare the lower bound and one to declare the upper bound. Then we could use the & operator to mandate that both conditions are True:

```
In  [43] higher_than_80 = employees["Salary"] >= 80000
         lower_than_90 = employees["Salary"] < 90000
         employees[higher_than_80 & lower_than_90].head()
```

Out [43]

	First Name	Gender	Start Date	Salary	Mgmt	Team
19	Donna	Female	2010-07-22	81014	False	Product
31	Joyce	NaN	2005-02-20	88657	False	Product
35	Theresa	Female	2006-10-10	85182	False	Sales
45	Roger	Male	1980-04-17	88010	True	Sales
54	Sara	Female	2007-08-15	83677	False	Engineering

A slightly cleaner solution is to use a method called `between`, which accepts a lower bound and an upper bound; it returns a Boolean `Series` where `True` denotes that a row's value falls between the specified interval. Note that the first argument, the lower bound, is inclusive, and the second argument, the upper bound, is exclusive. The following code returns the same `DataFrame` as the preceding code, filtering for salaries between $80,000 and $90,000:

```
In [44] between_80k_and_90k = employees["Salary"].between(80000, 90000)
        employees[between_80k_and_90k].head()
```

Out [44]

	First Name	Gender	Start Date	Salary	Mgmt	Team
19	Donna	Female	2010-07-22	81014	False	Product
31	Joyce	NaN	2005-02-20	88657	False	Product
35	Theresa	Female	2006-10-10	85182	False	Sales
45	Roger	Male	1980-04-17	88010	True	Sales
54	Sara	Female	2007-08-15	83677	False	Engineering

The `between` method also works on columns of other data types. To filter datetimes, we can pass strings for the start and end dates of our time range. The keyword parameters for the first and second arguments of the method are `left` and `right`. Here, we find all employees who started with the company in the 1980s:

```
In [45] eighties_folk = employees["Start Date"].between(
            left = "1980-01-01",
            right = "1990-01-01"
        )

        employees[eighties_folk].head()
```

Out [45]

	First Name	Gender	Start Date	Salary	Mgmt	Team
5	Dennis	Male	1987-04-18	115163	False	Legal
6	Ruby	Female	1987-08-17	65476	True	Product
10	Louise	Female	1980-08-12	63241	True	NaN
12	Brandon	Male	1980-12-01	112807	True	HR
17	Shawn	Male	1986-12-07	111737	False	Product

We can also apply the `between` method to string columns. Let's extract all employees whose first names starts with the letter `"R"`. We'll start with a capital `"R"` as our inclusive lower bound and go up to the noninclusive upper bound of `"S"`:

```
In  [46] name_starts_with_r = employees["First Name"].between("R", "S")
         employees[name_starts_with_r].head()

Out [46]
```

	First Name	Gender	Start Date	Salary	Mgmt	Team
6	Ruby	Female	1987-08-17	65476	True	Product
36	Rachel	Female	2009-02-16	142032	False	Business Dev
45	Roger	Male	1980-04-17	88010	True	Sales
67	Rachel	Female	1999-08-16	51178	True	Finance
78	Robin	Female	1983-06-04	114797	True	Sales

As always, be mindful of case sensitivity when working with characters and strings.

5.4.3 *The isnull and notnull methods*

The employees data set includes plenty of missing values. We can see a few missing values in our first five rows:

```
In  [47] employees.head()

Out [47]
```

	First Name	Gender	Start Date	Salary	Mgmt	Team
0	Douglas	Male	1993-08-06	0	True	Marketing
1	Thomas	Male	1996-03-31	61933	True	NaN
2	Maria	Female	NaT	130590	False	Finance
3	Jerry	NaN	2005-03-04	138705	True	Finance
4	Larry	Male	1998-01-24	101004	True	IT

Pandas marks missing text values and missing numeric values with a NaN (not a number) designation, and it marks missing datetime values with a NaT (not a time) designation. We can see an example in the Start Date column at index position 2.

We can use several pandas methods to isolate rows with either null or present values in a given column. The isnull method returns a Boolean Series in which True denotes that a row's value is missing:

```
In  [48] employees["Team"].isnull().head()

Out [48] 0    False
         1     True
         2    False
         3    False
         4    False
         Name: Team, dtype: bool
```

Pandas considers the NaT and None values to be null as well. The next example invokes the isnull method on the Start Date column:

```
In  [49] employees["Start Date"].isnull().head()

Out [49] 0    False
         1    False
         2     True
         3    False
         4    False
         Name: Start Date, dtype: bool
```

The `notnull` method returns the inverse `Series`, one in which `True` indicates that a row's value is present. The following output communicates that indices 0, 2, 3, and 4 do not have missing values:

```
In  [50] employees["Team"].notnull().head()

Out [50] 0    True
         1    False
         2    True
         3    True
         4    True
         Name: Team, dtype: bool
```

We can produce the same result set by inverting the `Series` returned by the `isnull` method. As a reminder, we use the tilde symbol (~) to invert a Boolean `Series`:

```
In  [51] (~employees["Team"].isnull()).head()

Out [51] 0    True
         1    False
         2    True
         3    True
         4    True
         Name: Team, dtype: bool
```

Either approach works, but `notnull` is a bit more descriptive and thus is recommended.

As always, we can use these Boolean `Series` to extract specific `DataFrame` rows. Here, we extract all employees with a missing Team value:

```
In  [52] no_team = employees["Team"].isnull()
         employees[no_team].head()

Out [52]
```

	First Name	Gender	Start Date	Salary	Mgmt	Team
1	Thomas	Male	1996-03-31	61933	True	NaN
10	Louise	Female	1980-08-12	63241	True	NaN
23	NaN	Male	2012-06-14	125792	True	NaN
32	NaN	Male	1998-08-21	122340	True	NaN
91	James	NaN	2005-01-26	128771	False	NaN

The next example pulls out employees with a present First Name value:

```
In  [53] has_name = employees["First Name"].notnull()
         employees[has_name].tail()

Out [53]
```

	First Name	Gender	Start Date	Salary	Mgmt	Team
995	Henry	NaN	2014-11-23	132483	False	Distribution
996	Phillip	Male	1984-01-31	42392	False	Finance
997	Russell	Male	2013-05-20	96914	False	Product
998	Larry	Male	2013-04-20	60500	False	Business Dev
999	Albert	Male	2012-05-15	129949	True	Sales

The `isnull` and `notnull` methods are the best way to quickly filter for present and missing values in one or more rows.

5.4.4   *Dealing with null values*

While we're on the topic of missing values, let's discuss some options for dealing with them. In section 5.2, we learned how to use the `fillna` method to replace `NaN`s with a constant value. We could also remove them.

Let's kick off this section by bringing our data set back to its original shape. We'll reimport the CSV by using the `read_csv` function:

```
In  [54] employees = pd.read_csv(
             "employees.csv", parse_dates = ["Start Date"]
         )
```

Here's a reminder of what it looks like:

```
In  [55] employees

Out [55]
```

	First Name	Gender	Start Date	Salary	Mgmt	Team
0	Douglas	Male	1993-08-06	NaN	True	Marketing
1	Thomas	Male	1996-03-31	61933.0	True	NaN
2	Maria	Female	NaT	130590.0	False	Finance
3	Jerry	NaN	2005-03-04	138705.0	True	Finance
4	Larry	Male	1998-01-24	101004.0	True	IT
...	...	...	...	...	...	...
996	Phillip	Male	1984-01-31	42392.0	False	Finance
997	Russell	Male	2013-05-20	96914.0	False	Product
998	Larry	Male	2013-04-20	60500.0	False	Business Dev
999	Albert	Male	2012-05-15	129949.0	True	Sales
1000	NaN	NaN	NaT	NaN	NaN	NaN

```
1001 rows × 6 columns
```

The `dropna` method removes `DataFrame` rows that hold any `NaN` values. It doesn't matter how many values a row is missing; the method excludes the row if a single `NaN` is present. The employees `DataFrame` has a missing value at index 0 of the Salary column, index 1 of the Team column, index 2 of the Start Date column, and index 3 of the Gender column. Notice that pandas excludes all these rows in the following output:

```
In  [56] employees.dropna()

Out [56]
```

	First Name	Gender	Start Date	Salary	Mgmt	Team
4	Larry	Male	1998-01-24	101004.0	True	IT
5	Dennis	Male	1987-04-18	115163.0	False	Legal
6	Ruby	Female	1987-08-17	65476.0	True	Product
8	Angela	Female	2005-11-22	95570.0	True	Engineering
9	Frances	Female	2002-08-08	139852.0	True	Business Dev
...	...	...	...	...	...	...

```
994     George    Male 2013-06-21    98874.0    True      Marketing
996    Phillip    Male 1984-01-31    42392.0   False        Finance
997    Russell    Male 2013-05-20    96914.0   False        Product
998      Larry    Male 2013-04-20    60500.0   False   Business Dev
999     Albert    Male 2012-05-15   129949.0    True          Sales
```

761 rows × 6 columns

We can pass the how parameter an argument of `"all"` to remove rows in which all values are missing. Only one row in the data set, the last one, satisfies this condition:

```
In  [57] employees.dropna(how = "all").tail()
```

Out [57]

	First Name	Gender	Start Date	Salary	Mgmt	Team
995	Henry	NaN	2014-11-23	132483.0	False	Distribution
996	Phillip	Male	1984-01-31	42392.0	False	Finance
997	Russell	Male	2013-05-20	96914.0	False	Product
998	Larry	Male	2013-04-20	60500.0	False	Business Dev
999	Albert	Male	2012-05-15	129949.0	True	Sales

The how parameter's default argument is `"any"`. An argument of `"any"` removes a row if any of its values is absent. Notice that the row at index label 995 has NaN in the Gender column of the preceding output. Compare that output with the following output, in which row 995 is not present; pandas still removes the last row because it has at least one NaN value:

```
In  [58] employees.dropna(how = "any").tail()
```

Out [58]

	First Name	Gender	Start Date	Salary	Mgmt	Team
994	George	Male	2013-06-21	98874.0	True	Marketing
996	Phillip	Male	1984-01-31	42392.0	False	Finance
997	Russell	Male	2013-05-20	96914.0	False	Product
998	Larry	Male	2013-04-20	60500.0	False	Business Dev
999	Albert	Male	2012-05-15	129949.0	True	Sales

We can use the subset parameter to target rows with a missing value in a specific column. The next example removes rows that have a missing value in the Gender column:

```
In  [59] employees.dropna(subset = ["Gender"]).tail()
```

Out [59]

	First Name	Gender	Start Date	Salary	Mgmt	Team
994	George	Male	2013-06-21	98874.0	True	Marketing
996	Phillip	Male	1984-01-31	42392.0	False	Finance
997	Russell	Male	2013-05-20	96914.0	False	Product
998	Larry	Male	2013-04-20	60500.0	False	Business Dev
999	Albert	Male	2012-05-15	129949.0	True	Sales

We can also pass the `subset` parameter a list of columns. Pandas will remove a row if it has a missing value in any of the specified columns. The next example removes rows with missing values in the Start Date column, the Salary column, or both:

```
In [60] employees.dropna(subset = ["Start Date", "Salary"]).head()

Out [60]
```

	First Name	Gender	Start Date	Salary	Mgmt	Team
1	Thomas	Male	1996-03-31	61933.0	True	NaN
3	Jerry	NaN	2005-03-04	138705.0	True	Finance
4	Larry	Male	1998-01-24	101004.0	True	IT
5	Dennis	Male	1987-04-18	115163.0	False	Legal
6	Ruby	Female	1987-08-17	65476.0	True	Product

The `thresh` parameter specifies a minimum threshold of non-null values that a row must have for pandas to keep it. The next example filters `employees` for rows with at least four present values:

```
In [61] employees.dropna(how = "any", thresh = 4).head()

Out [61]
```

	First Name	Gender	Start Date	Salary	Mgmt	Team
0	Douglas	Male	1993-08-06	NaN	True	Marketing
1	Thomas	Male	1996-03-31	61933.0	True	NaN
2	Maria	Female	NaT	130590.0	False	Finance
3	Jerry	NaN	2005-03-04	138705.0	True	Finance
4	Larry	Male	1998-01-24	101004.0	True	IT

The `thresh` parameter is great when a certain number of missing values renders a row useless for analysis.

5.5 Dealing with duplicates

Missing values are a common occurrence in messy data sets, and so are duplicate values. Luckily, pandas includes several methods for identifying and excluding duplicate values.

5.5.1 The duplicated method

First up, here's a quick reminder of the first five rows of the Team column. Notice that the value `"Finance"` appears at index positions 2 and 3:

```
In [62] employees["Team"].head()

Out [62] 0      Marketing
         1            NaN
         2        Finance
         3        Finance
         4             IT
         Name: Team, dtype: object
```

The `duplicated` method returns a Boolean `Series` that identifies duplicates in a column. Pandas returns `True` any time it sees a value that it previously encountered in the `Series`. Consider the next example. The `duplicated` method marks the first occurrence of `"Finance"` in the Team column as a nonduplicate with `False`. It marks all subsequent occurrences of `"Finance"` as duplicates (with `True`). The same logic applies to all other Team values:

```
In  [63] employees["Team"].duplicated().head()

Out [63] 0     False
         1     False
         2     False
         3      True
         4     False
         Name: Team, dtype: bool
```

The `duplicated` method's `keep` parameter informs pandas which duplicate occurrence to keep. Its default argument, `"first"`, keeps the first occurrence of each duplicate value. The following code is equivalent to the preceding code:

```
In  [64] employees["Team"].duplicated(keep = "first").head()

Out [64] 0     False
         1     False
         2     False
         3      True
         4     False
         Name: Team, dtype: bool
```

We can also ask pandas to mark the last occurrence of a value in a column as the nonduplicate. Pass a string of `"last"` to the `keep` parameter:

```
In  [65] employees["Team"].duplicated(keep = "last")

Out [65] 0         True
         1         True
         2         True
         3         True
         4         True
                  ...
         996      False
         997      False
         998      False
         999      False
         1000     False
         Name: Team, Length: 1001, dtype: bool
```

Let's say we want to extract one employee from each team. One strategy we could use is pulling out the first row for each unique team in the Team column. Our existing `duplicated` method returns a Boolean `Series`; `True` identifies all duplicate values after the first encounter. If we invert that `Series`, we'll get a `Series` in which `True` denotes the first time pandas encounters a value:

```
In  [66] (~employees["Team"].duplicated()).head()
```

```
Out [66] 0     True
         1     True
         2     True
         3     False
         4     True
         Name: Team, dtype: bool
```

Now we can extract one employee per team by passing the Boolean `Series` inside square brackets. Pandas will include the rows with the first occurrences of a value in the Team column. Note that the library considers `NaN`s to be a unique value:

```
In  [67] first_one_in_team = ~employees["Team"].duplicated()
         employees[first_one_in_team]
```

```
Out [67]
```

	First Name	Gender	Start Date	Salary	Mgmt	Team
0	Douglas	Male	1993-08-06	NaN	True	Marketing
1	Thomas	Male	1996-03-31	61933.0	True	NaN
2	Maria	Female	NaT	130590.0	False	Finance
4	Larry	Male	1998-01-24	101004.0	True	IT
5	Dennis	Male	1987-04-18	115163.0	False	Legal
6	Ruby	Female	1987-08-17	65476.0	True	Product
8	Angela	Female	2005-11-22	95570.0	True	Engineering
9	Frances	Female	2002-08-08	139852.0	True	Business Dev
12	Brandon	Male	1980-12-01	112807.0	True	HR
13	Gary	Male	2008-01-27	109831.0	False	Sales
40	Michael	Male	2008-10-10	99283.0	True	Distribution

This output tells us that Douglas is the first employee on the Marketing team in the data set, Thomas is the first one with a missing team, Maria is the first one on the Finance team, and so on.

5.5.2   The drop_duplicates method

A `DataFrame`'s `drop_duplicates` method provides a convenient shortcut for accomplishing the operation in section 5.5.1. By default, the method removes rows in which all values are equal to those in a previously encountered row. There are no `employees` rows in which all six row values are equal, so the method doesn't accomplish much for us with a standard invocation:

```
In  [68] employees.drop_duplicates()
```

```
Out [68]
```

	First Name	Gender	Start Date	Salary	Mgmt	Team
0	Douglas	Male	1993-08-06	NaN	True	Marketing
1	Thomas	Male	1996-03-31	61933.0	True	NaN
2	Maria	Female	NaT	130590.0	False	Finance
3	Jerry	NaN	2005-03-04	138705.0	True	Finance
4	Larry	Male	1998-01-24	101004.0	True	IT
...	...	...	...	...	...	...

```
996       Phillip    Male 1984-01-31     42392.0   False        Finance
997       Russell    Male 2013-05-20     96914.0   False        Product
998         Larry    Male 2013-04-20     60500.0   False   Business Dev
999        Albert    Male 2012-05-15    129949.0    True          Sales
1000          NaN     NaN        NaT         NaN     NaN            NaN
```

1001 rows × 6 columns

But we can pass the method a subset parameter with a list of columns that pandas should use to determine a row's uniqueness. The next example finds the first occurrence of each unique value in the Team column. In other words, pandas keeps a row only if it has the first occurrence of a Team value (such as "Marketing"). It excludes all rows with duplicate Team values after the first one:

```
In   [69] employees.drop_duplicates(subset = ["Team"])
```

Out [69]

	First Name	Gender	Start Date	Salary	Mgmt	Team
0	Douglas	Male	1993-08-06	NaN	True	Marketing
1	Thomas	Male	1996-03-31	61933.0	True	NaN
2	Maria	Female	NaT	130590.0	False	Finance
4	Larry	Male	1998-01-24	101004.0	True	IT
5	Dennis	Male	1987-04-18	115163.0	False	Legal
6	Ruby	Female	1987-08-17	65476.0	True	Product
8	Angela	Female	2005-11-22	95570.0	True	Engineering
9	Frances	Female	2002-08-08	139852.0	True	Business Dev
12	Brandon	Male	1980-12-01	112807.0	True	HR
13	Gary	Male	2008-01-27	109831.0	False	Sales
40	Michael	Male	2008-10-10	99283.0	True	Distribution

The drop_duplicates method also accepts a keep parameter. We can pass it an argument of "last" to keep the rows with each duplicate value's last occurrence. These rows are likely to be closer to the end of the data set. In the following example, Alice is the last employee in the data set on the HR team, Justin is the last employee on the Legal team, and so on:

```
In   [70] employees.drop_duplicates(subset = ["Team"], keep = "last")
```

Out [70]

	First Name	Gender	Start Date	Salary	Mgmt	Team
988	Alice	Female	2004-10-05	47638.0	False	HR
989	Justin	NaN	1991-02-10	38344.0	False	Legal
990	Robin	Female	1987-07-24	100765.0	True	IT
993	Tina	Female	1997-05-15	56450.0	True	Engineering
994	George	Male	2013-06-21	98874.0	True	Marketing
995	Henry	NaN	2014-11-23	132483.0	False	Distribution
996	Phillip	Male	1984-01-31	42392.0	False	Finance
997	Russell	Male	2013-05-20	96914.0	False	Product
998	Larry	Male	2013-04-20	60500.0	False	Business Dev
999	Albert	Male	2012-05-15	129949.0	True	Sales
1000	NaN	NaN	NaT	NaN	NaN	NaN

One additional option is available for the `keep` parameter. We can pass an argument of `False` to exclude all rows with duplicate values. Pandas will reject a row if there are any other rows with the same value. The next example filters for rows in `employees` with a unique value in the First Name column. In other words, these first names occur only once in the `DataFrame`:

```
In  [71] employees.drop_duplicates(subset = ["First Name"], keep = False)

Out [71]
```

	First Name	Gender	Start Date	Salary	Mgmt	Team
5	Dennis	Male	1987-04-18	115163.0	False	Legal
8	Angela	Female	2005-11-22	95570.0	True	Engineering
33	Jean	Female	1993-12-18	119082.0	False	Business Dev
190	Carol	Female	1996-03-19	57783.0	False	Finance
291	Tammy	Female	1984-11-11	132839.0	True	IT
495	Eugene	Male	1984-05-24	81077.0	False	Sales
688	Brian	Male	2007-04-07	93901.0	True	Legal
832	Keith	Male	2003-02-12	120672.0	False	Legal
887	David	Male	2009-12-05	92242.0	False	Legal

Let's say we want to identify duplicates by a combination of values across multiple columns. We may want the first occurrence of each employee with a unique combination of First Name and Gender in the data set, for example. For reference, here's a subset of all employees with a First Name of `"Douglas"` and a Gender of `"Male"`:

```
In  [72] name_is_douglas = employees["First Name"] == "Douglas"
         is_male = employees["Gender"] == "Male"
         employees[name_is_douglas & is_male]

Out [72]
```

	First Name	Gender	Start Date	Salary	Mgmt	Team
0	Douglas	Male	1993-08-06	NaN	True	Marketing
217	Douglas	Male	1999-09-03	83341.0	True	IT
322	Douglas	Male	2002-01-08	41428.0	False	Product
835	Douglas	Male	2007-08-04	132175.0	False	Engineering

We can pass a list of columns to the `drop_duplicates` method's `subset` parameter. Pandas will use the columns to determine the presence of duplicates. The next example uses a combination of values across the Gender and Team columns to identify duplicates:

```
In  [73] employees.drop_duplicates(subset = ["Gender", "Team"]).head()

Out [73]
```

	First Name	Gender	Start Date	Salary	Mgmt	Team
0	Douglas	Male	1993-08-06	NaN	True	Marketing
1	Thomas	Male	1996-03-31	61933.0	True	NaN
2	Maria	Female	NaT	130590.0	False	Finance
3	Jerry	NaN	2005-03-04	138705.0	True	Finance
4	Larry	Male	1998-01-24	101004.0	True	IT

Let's walk through the output. The row at index 0 holds the first occurrence of the name `"Douglas"` and the gender `"Male"` in the employees data set. Pandas will exclude any other rows with the same two values from the results set. To clarify, the library will still include a row if it has a First Name of `"Douglas"` and a Gender not equal to `"Male"`. Similarly, it will include rows with Gender of `"Male"` and a First Name not equal to `"Douglas"`. Pandas uses the combination of values across the two columns to identify the duplicates.

5.6 Coding challenge

Here's your chance to practice the concepts introduced in this chapter.

5.6.1 Problems

The netflix.csv data set is a collection of almost 6,000 titles that were available to watch in November 2019 on the video streaming service Netflix. It includes four columns: the video's title, director, the date Netflix added it, and its type/category. The director and date_added columns contain missing values. We can see examples at index positions 0, 2, and 5836 of the following output:

```
In  [74] pd.read_csv("netflix.csv")

Out [74]
```

	title	director	date_added	type
0	Alias Grace	NaN	3-Nov-17	TV Show
1	A Patch of Fog	Michael Lennox	15-Apr-17	Movie
2	Lunatics	NaN	19-Apr-19	TV Show
3	Uriyadi 2	Vijay Kumar	2-Aug-19	Movie
4	Shrek the Musical	Jason Moore	29-Dec-13	Movie
...	...	...	...	...
5832	The Pursuit	John Papola	7-Aug-19	Movie
5833	Hurricane Bianca	Matt Kugelman	1-Jan-17	Movie
5834	Amar's Hands	Khaled Youssef	26-Apr-19	Movie
5835	Bill Nye: Science Guy	Jason Sussberg	25-Apr-18	Movie
5836	Age of Glory	NaN	NaN	TV Show

5837 rows × 4 columns

Using the skills you learned in this chapter, solve the following challenges:

1 Optimize the data set for limited memory use and maximum utility.
2 Find all rows with a title of `"Limitless"`.
3 Find all rows with a director of `"Robert Rodriguez"` and a type of `"Movie"`.
4 Find all rows with either a date_added of `"2019-07-31"` or a director of `"Robert Altman"`.
5 Find all rows with a director of `"Orson Welles"`, `"Aditya Kripalani"`, or `"Sam Raimi"`.
6 Find all rows with a date_added value between May 1, 2019 and June 1, 2019.
7 Drop all rows with a `NaN` value in the director column.
8 Identify the days when Netflix added only one movie to its catalog.

5.6.2   *Solutions*

Let's tackle the questions!

1 To optimize the data set for memory and utility, we can first convert the date_
added column's values to datetimes. We can force the type coercion during the
import with the `parse_dates` parameter to the `read_csv` function:

```
In  [75] netflix = pd.read_csv("netflix.csv", parse_dates = ["date_added"])
```

It's important to keep benchmarks, so let's take a look at current memory use:

```
In  [76] netflix.info()

Out [76]

<class 'pandas.core.frame.DataFrame'>
RangeIndex: 5837 entries, 0 to 5836
Data columns (total 4 columns):
 #   Column       Non-Null Count   Dtype
---  ------       --------------   -----
 0   title        5837 non-null    object
 1   director     3936 non-null    object
 2   date_added   5195 non-null    datetime64[ns]
 3   type         5837 non-null    object
dtypes: datetime64[ns](1), object(3)
memory usage: 182.5+ KB
```

Can we convert any column's values to a different data type? How about categorical values? Let's use the `nunique` method to count the number of unique
values per column:

```
In  [77] netflix.nunique()

Out [77] title        5780
         director     3024
         date_added   1092
         type            2
         dtype: int64
```

The type column is a perfect candidate for categorical values. In a data set of
5,837 rows, it has only two unique values: `"Movie"` and `"TV Show"`. We can
convert its values by using the `astype` method. Remember to overwrite the
original `Series`:

```
In  [78] netflix["type"] = netflix["type"].astype("category")
```

How much has the conversion to categorical data reduced our memory use? A
whopping 22%:

```
In  [79] netflix.info()

Out [79]

<class 'pandas.core.frame.DataFrame'>
RangeIndex: 5837 entries, 0 to 5836
```

```
Data columns (total 4 columns):
 #   Column      Non-Null Count  Dtype
---  ------      --------------  -----
 0   title       5837 non-null   object
 1   director    3936 non-null   object
 2   date_added  5195 non-null   datetime64[ns]
 3   type        5837 non-null   category
dtypes: category(1), datetime64[ns](1), object(2)
memory usage: 142.8+ KB
```

2   We'll need to use the equality operator to compare each title column value with the string `"Limitless"`. Afterward, we can use the Boolean `Series` to extract rows from `netflix` for which the evaluation returns `True`:

```
In  [80] netflix[netflix["title"] == "Limitless"]
```

Out [80]

	title	director	date_added	type
1559	Limitless	Neil Burger	2019-05-16	Movie
2564	Limitless	NaN	2016-07-01	TV Show
4579	Limitless	Vrinda Samartha	2019-10-01	Movie

3   To extract movies directed by Robert Rodriguez, we'll need two Boolean `Series`, one comparing the director column's values with `"Robert Rodri-guez"` and the other comparing the type column's values with `"Movie"`. The `&` symbol applies AND logic for two Boolean `Series`:

```
In  [81] directed_by_robert_rodriguez = (
             netflix["director"] == "Robert Rodriguez"
         )
         is_movie = netflix["type"] == "Movie"
         netflix[directed_by_robert_rodriguez & is_movie]
```

Out [81]

	title	director	date_added	type
1384	Spy Kids: All the Time in the …	Robert Rodriguez	2019-02-19	Movie
1416	Spy Kids 3: Game…	Robert Rodriguez	2019-04-01	Movie
1460	Spy Kids 2: The Island of Lost D…	Robert Rodriguez	2019-03-08	Movie
2890	Sin City	Robert Rodriguez	2019-10-01	Movie
3836	Shorts	Robert Rodriguez	2019-07-01	Movie
3883	Spy Kids	Robert Rodriguez	2019-04-01	Movie

4   The next question asks all for all titles with a date_added of `"2019-07-31"` or a director of `"Robert Altman"`. This problem is similar to the preceding one but requires a `|` symbol for OR logic:

```
In  [82] added_on_july_31 = netflix["date_added"] == "2019-07-31"
         directed_by_altman = netflix["director"] == "Robert Altman"
         netflix[added_on_july_31 | directed_by_altman]
```

Out [82]

	title	director	date_added	type
611	Popeye	Robert Altman	2019-11-24	Movie
1028	The Red Sea Diving Resort	Gideon Raff	2019-07-31	Movie
1092	Gosford Park	Robert Altman	2019-11-01	Movie
3473	Bangkok Love Stories: Innocence	NaN	2019-07-31	TV Show
5117	Ramen Shop	Eric Khoo	2019-07-31	Movie

5   The next challenge asks for entries with a director of `"Orson Welles"`, `"Aditya Kripalani"`, or `"Sam Raimi"`. One option is to create three Boolean `Series`, one for each of the three directors, and then use the `|` operator. But a more concise and scalable way to generate the Boolean `Series` is to invoke the `isin` method on the director column and pass in the list of directors:

```
In  [83] directors = ["Orson Welles", "Aditya Kripalani", "Sam Raimi"]
         target_directors = netflix["director"].isin(directors)
         netflix[target_directors]
```

Out [83]

	title	director	date_added	type
946	The Stranger	Orson Welles	2018-07-19	Movie
1870	The Gift	Sam Raimi	2019-11-20	Movie
3706	Spider-Man 3	Sam Raimi	2019-11-01	Movie
4243	Tikli and Laxmi Bomb	Aditya Kripalani	2018-08-01	Movie
4475	The Other Side of the Wind	Orson Welles	2018-11-02	Movie
5115	Tottaa Pataaka Item Maal	Aditya Kripalani	2019-06-25	Movie

6   The most concise way to find all rows with a date_added value between May 1, 2019 and June 1, 2019, is to use the `between` method. We can provide the two dates as the lower and upper bounds. This approach eliminates the need for two separate Boolean `Series`:

```
In  [84] may_movies = netflix["date_added"].between(
             "2019-05-01", "2019-06-01"
         )

         netflix[may_movies].head()
```

Out [84]

	title	director	date_added	type
29	Chopsticks	Sachin Yardi	2019-05-31	Movie
60	Away From Home	NaN	2019-05-08	TV Show
82	III Smoking Barrels	Sanjib Dey	2019-06-01	Movie
108	Jailbirds	NaN	2019-05-10	TV Show
124	Pegasus	Han Han	2019-05-31	Movie

7   The `dropna` method removes `DataFrame` rows with missing values. We have to include the `subset` parameter to limit the columns in which pandas should look for null values. For this question, we'll target `NaN` values in the director column:

```
In  [85] netflix.dropna(subset = ["director"]).head()

Out [85]
```

	title	director	date_added	type
1	A Patch of Fog	Michael Lennox	2017-04-15	Movie
3	Uriyadi 2	Vijay Kumar	2019-08-02	Movie
4	Shrek the Musical	Jason Moore	2013-12-29	Movie
5	Schubert In Love	Lars Büchel	2018-03-01	Movie
6	We Have Always Lived in the Castle	Stacie Passon	2019-09-14	Movie

8 The final challenge asks to identify the days when Netflix added only one movie to the service. One solution is to recognize that the date_added column holds duplicate date values for titles added on the same day. We can invoke the drop_duplicates method with a subset of date_added and the keep parameter set to False. Pandas will remove any rows with duplicate entries in the date_added column. The resulting DataFrame will have the titles that were the only ones added on their respective dates:

```
In  [86] netflix.drop_duplicates(subset = ["date_added"], keep = False)

Out [86]
```

	title	director	date_added	type
4	Shrek the Musical	Jason Moore	2013-12-29	Movie
12	Without Gorky	Cosima Spender	2017-05-31	Movie
30	Anjelah Johnson: Not Fancy	Jay Karas	2015-10-02	Movie
38	One Last Thing	Tim Rouhana	2019-08-25	Movie
70	Marvel's Iron Man & Hulk: Heroes …	Leo Riley	2014-02-16	Movie
...	...	...	...	...
5748	Menorca	John Barnard	2017-08-27	Movie
5749	Green Room	Jeremy Saulnier	2018-11-12	Movie
5788	Chris Brown: Welcome to My Life	Andrew Sandler	2017-10-07	Movie
5789	A Very Murray Christmas	Sofia Coppola	2015-12-04	Movie
5812	Little Singham in London	Prakash Satam	2019-04-22	Movie

391 rows × 4 columns

Congratulations on completing the coding challenge!

Summary

- The astype method converts a Series' values to another data type.
- The category data type is ideal when a Series has a small number of unique values.
- Pandas can extract subsets of data from a DataFrame based on one or more conditions.
- Pass a Boolean Series inside square brackets to extract a subset of a DataFrame.
- Use the equality, inequality, and mathematical operators to compare each Series entry with a constant value.

- The `&` symbol mandates that multiple conditions be met to extract a row.
- The `|` symbol mandates that either condition be met to extract a row.
- Helper methods such as `isnull`, `notnull`, `between`, and `duplicated` return Boolean `Series` that we can use to filter data sets.
- The `fillna` method replaces NaNs with a constant value.
- The `dropna` method removes rows with null values. We can customize its arguments to target missing values in all or some columns.

Part 2

Applied pandas

In part 1, we laid the groundwork for our mastery of pandas. Now that we're comfortable working with `Series` and `DataFrames`, we can expand our horizons and learn how to tackle common problems in data analysis. Chapter 6 dives right into working with messy text data, including dealing with whitespace and inconsistent character casing. In chapter 7, we learn how to use the powerful `MultiIndex` to store and extract hierarchical data. Chapters 8 and 9 focus on aggregation: pivoting our `DataFrames`, grouping data into buckets, summarizing data, and more. In chapter 10, we explore how to merge datasets by using a variety of joins. Immediately afterward, we learn the ins and outs of working with another common data type, datetimes, in chapter 11. In chapter 12, we look at importing and exporting data sets to and from pandas. Chapter 13 covers how to adjust the library's configuration settings. Finally, chapter 14 provides a tutorial on creating visualizations from our `DataFrames`.

Along the way, we'll practice pandas concepts on more than 30 datasets that cover everything from baby names to breakfast cereals, from Fortune 1000 companies to Nobel Prize winners. You are welcome to proceed through the chapters linearly or explore whichever topic piques your interest most. Consider each chapter here to be a new specialization to add to your pandas toolbox. Good luck!

Working with text data

This chapter covers

- Removing whitespace from strings
- Uppercasing and lowercasing strings
- Finding and replacing characters in strings
- Slicing a string by character index positions
- Splitting text by a delimiter

Text data can get quite messy. Real-world data sets are riddled with incorrect characters, improper letter casings, whitespace, and more. The process of cleaning data is called *wrangling* or *munging*. Often, the majority of our data analysis is dedicated to munging. We may know the insight we want to derive early on, but the difficulty lies in arranging the data in a suitable shape for the manipulation. Luckily for us, one of the primary motivations behind pandas was easing the difficulty of cleaning up improperly formatted text values. The library is battle-tested and flexible. In this chapter, we'll learn how to use pandas to fix all sorts of imperfections in our text data sets. There's a lot of ground to cover, so let's dive right in.

147

6.1   *Letter casing and whitespace*

We'll begin by importing pandas in a new Jupyter Notebook:

```
In  [1] import pandas as pd
```

This chapter's first data set, chicago_food_inspections.csv, is a listing of more than 150,000 food inspections conducted across the city of Chicago. The CSV includes only two columns: one with an establishment's name and the other with its risk ranking. The four risk levels are Risk 1 (High), Risk 2 (Medium), Risk 3 (Low), and a special All for the worst offenders:

```
In  [2] inspections = pd.read_csv("chicago_food_inspections.csv")
        inspections
```

```
Out [2]
```

	Name	Risk
0	MARRIOT MARQUIS CHICAGO	Risk 1 (High)
1	JETS PIZZA	Risk 2 (Medium)
2	ROOM 1520	Risk 3 (Low)
3	MARRIOT MARQUIS CHICAGO	Risk 1 (High)
4	CHARTWELLS	Risk 1 (High)
...	...	...
153805	WOLCOTT'S	Risk 1 (High)
153806	DUNKIN DONUTS/BASKIN-ROBBINS	Risk 2 (Medium)
153807	Cafe 608	Risk 1 (High)
153808	mr.daniel's	Risk 1 (High)
153809	TEMPO CAFE	Risk 1 (High)

153810 rows × 2 columns

> **NOTE** chicago_food_inspections.csv is a modified version of a data set available from the city of Chicago (http://mng.bz/9N60). There are typos and inconsistencies within the data; we have preserved them so that you can see the data irregularities that appear in the real world. I encourage you to consider how you can optimize this data with the techniques you'll learn in this chapter.

We immediately see an issue in the Name column: inconsistency in letter casing. Most row values are uppercase, some are lowercase (`"mr.daniel's"`), and some are normal case (`"Café 608"`).

The preceding output does not show another problem hiding in `inspections`: the Name column's values are surrounded by whitespace. We can spot the extra spacing more easily if we isolate the Name `Series` with square-bracket syntax. Notice that the ends of the rows do not align:

```
In  [3] inspections["Name"].head()
```

```
Out [3] 0       MARRIOT MARQUIS CHICAGO
        1                   JETS PIZZA
        2                    ROOM 1520
        3       MARRIOT MARQUIS CHICAGO
        4                   CHARTWELLS
        Name: Name, dtype: object
```

We can use the `values` attribute on the `Series` to get the underlying NumPy `ndarray` storing the values. The whitespace is present at the ends and the beginnings of the values:

```
In  [4] inspections["Name"].head().values

Out [4] array([' MARRIOT MARQUIS CHICAGO    ', ' JETS PIZZA ',
               '   ROOM 1520 ', '  MARRIOT MARQUIS CHICAGO  ',
               ' CHARTWELLS   '], dtype=object)
```

Let's focus on the whitespace first. We'll deal with the letter casings a little later.

The `Series` object's `str` attribute exposes a `StringMethods` object, a powerful toolbox of methods for working with strings:

```
In  [5] inspections["Name"].str

Out [5] <pandas.core.strings.StringMethods at 0x122ad8510>
```

Any time we'd like to perform string manipulations, we invoke a method on the `StringMethods` object rather than the `Series` itself. Some methods work like Python's native string methods, whereas other methods are exclusive to pandas. For a comprehensive review of Python's string methods, see appendix B.

We can use the `strip` family of methods to remove whitespace from a string. The `lstrip` (left strip) method removes whitespace from the beginning of a string. Here's a basic example:

```
In  [6] dessert = "  cheesecake  "
        dessert.lstrip()

Out [6] 'cheesecake  '
```

The `rstrip` (right strip) method removes whitespace from the end of a string:

```
In  [7] dessert.rstrip()

Out [7] '  cheesecake'
```

The `strip` method removes whitespace from both ends of a string:

```
In  [8] dessert.strip()

Out [8] 'cheesecake'
```

These three `strip` methods are available on the `StringMethods` object. Each one returns a new `Series` object with the operation applied to every column value. Let's invoke each of them:

```
In  [9] inspections["Name"].str.lstrip().head()

Out [9] 0      MARRIOT MARQUIS CHICAGO
        1                   JETS PIZZA
        2                    ROOM 1520
        3      MARRIOT MARQUIS CHICAGO
        4                   CHARTWELLS
        Name: Name, dtype: object
```

```
In  [10] inspections["Name"].str.rstrip().head()
```

```
Out [10] 0       MARRIOT MARQUIS CHICAGO
         1                   JETS PIZZA
         2                    ROOM 1520
         3       MARRIOT MARQUIS CHICAGO
         4                   CHARTWELLS
         Name: Name, dtype: object
```

```
In  [11] inspections["Name"].str.strip().head()
```

```
Out [11] 0       MARRIOT MARQUIS CHICAGO
         1                   JETS PIZZA
         2                    ROOM 1520
         3       MARRIOT MARQUIS CHICAGO
         4                   CHARTWELLS
         Name: Name, dtype: object
```

Now we can overwrite our existing `Series` with the new one that has no extra whitespace. On the right side of an equal sign, we'll use the `strip` code to create the new `Series`. On the left side, we'll use square-bracket syntax to denote the column we'd like to overwrite. Python processes the right side of the equal sign first. In summary, we use the Name column to create a new `Series` without whitespace and then overwrite the Name column with that new `Series`:

```
In  [12] inspections["Name"] = inspections["Name"].str.strip()
```

This one-line solution is suitable for a small data set, but it may quickly become tedious for one with a large number of columns. How can we quickly apply the same logic to all `DataFrame` columns? You may recall the `columns` attribute, which exposes the iterable `Index` object that holds the `DataFrame`'s column names:

```
In  [13] inspections.columns
```

```
Out [13] Index(['Name', 'Risk'], dtype='object')
```

We can use Python's `for` loop to iterate over each column, extract it dynamically from the `DataFrame`, invoke the `str.strip` method to return a new `Series`, and overwrite the original column. The logic requires only two lines:

```
In  [14] for column in inspections.columns:
             inspections[column] = inspections[column].str.strip()
```

All of Python's character casing methods are available on the `StringMethods` object. The `lower` method, for example, lowercases all string characters:

```
In  [15] inspections["Name"].str.lower().head()
```

```
Out [15] 0       marriot marquis chicago
         1                   jets pizza
         2                    room 1520
         3       marriot marquis chicago
         4                   chartwells
         Name: Name, dtype: object
```

The complementary `str.upper` method returns a `Series` with uppercase strings. The next example invokes the method on a different `Series` because the Name column is mostly uppercase already:

```
In  [16] steaks = pd.Series(["porterhouse", "filet mignon", "ribeye"])
         steaks

Out [16] 0      porterhouse
         1    filet mignon
         2           ribeye
         dtype: object

In  [17] steaks.str.upper()

Out [17] 0      PORTERHOUSE
         1    FILET MIGNON
         2           RIBEYE
         dtype: object
```

Suppose that we want to get the establishments' names in a more standardized, readable format. We can use the `str.capitalize` method to capitalize the first letter of each string in the `Series`:

```
In  [18] inspections["Name"].str.capitalize().head()

Out [18] 0    Marriot marquis chicago
         1                Jets pizza
         2                 Room 1520
         3    Marriot marquis chicago
         4                Chartwells
         Name: Name, dtype: object
```

That's a step in the right direction, but perhaps the best method available is `str.title`, which capitalizes each word's first letter. Pandas uses spaces to identify where one word ends and the next begins:

```
In  [19] inspections["Name"].str.title().head()

Out [19] 0    Marriot Marquis Chicago
         1                Jets Pizza
         2                 Room 1520
         3    Marriot Marquis Chicago
         4                Chartwells
         Name: Name, dtype: object
```

The `title` method is a fantastic option for dealing with locations, countries, cities, and people's full names.

6.2 String slicing

Let's turn our focus to the Risk column. Each row's value includes both a numeric and categorical representation of the risk (such as 1 and `"High"`). Here's a reminder of what the column looks like:

```
In  [20] inspections["Risk"].head()
```

```
Out [20]
```

```
0       Risk 1 (High)
1     Risk 2 (Medium)
2        Risk 3 (Low)
3       Risk 1 (High)
4       Risk 1 (High)
Name: Risk, dtype: object
```

Let's say we want to extract the numeric risk value from each row. This operation may appear simple, given the seemingly consistent format of each row, but we have to tread carefully. There is always room for deception in a data set this large:

```
In  [21] len(inspections)
```

```
Out [21] 153810
```

Do all rows follow a `"Risk Number (Risk Level)"` format? We can find out by invoking the `unique` method, which returns a NumPy `ndarray` consisting of the column's unique values:

```
In  [22] inspections["Risk"].unique()
```

```
Out [22] array(['Risk 1 (High)', 'Risk 2 (Medium)', 'Risk 3 (Low)', 'All',
               nan], dtype=object)
```

We have to account for two additional values: missing `NaNs` and the `'All'` string. How we deal with these values is ultimately up to the analyst and the business. Are the values significant, or can they be discarded? In this scenario, let's propose a compromise: we'll remove the missing `NaN` values and replace the `"All"` values with `"Risk 4 (Extreme)"`. We'll pick this approach to ensure that all Risk values have a consistent format.

We can remove missing values from a `Series` with the `dropna` method introduced in chapter 5. We'll pass its `subset` parameter a list of the `DataFrame` columns in which pandas should look for `NaNs`. The next example removes rows in `inspections` with a `NaN` value in the Risk column:

```
In  [23] inspections = inspections.dropna(subset = ["Risk"])
```

Let's check in on unique values in the Risk column:

```
In  [24] inspections["Risk"].unique()
```

```
Out [24] array(['Risk 1 (High)', 'Risk 2 (Medium)', 'Risk 3 (Low)', 'All'],
               dtype=object)
```

We can use the `DataFrame`'s helpful `replace` method to replace all occurrences of one value with another. The method's first parameter, `to_replace`, sets the value to search for, and its second parameter, `value`, specifies what to replace each occurrence of it with. The next example replaces the `"All"` string values with `"Risk 4 (Extreme)"`:

```
In  [25] inspections = inspections.replace(
             to_replace = "All", value = "Risk 4 (Extreme)"
         )
```

Now we have a consistent format for all values in the Risk column:

```
In  [26] inspections["Risk"].unique()

Out [26] array(['Risk 1 (High)', 'Risk 2 (Medium)', 'Risk 3 (Low)',
                 'Risk 4 (Extreme)'], dtype=object)
```

Next, let's continue with our original goal of extracting each row's risk number.

6.3 *String slicing and character replacement*

We can use the `slice` method on the `StringMethods` object to extract a substring from a string by index position. The method accepts a starting index and an ending index as arguments. The lower bound (the starting point) is inclusive, whereas the upper bound (the endpoint) is exclusive.

Our risk number starts at index position 5 in each string. The next example pulls the characters from index position 5 up to (but not including) index position 6:

```
In  [27] inspections["Risk"].str.slice(5, 6).head()

Out [27] 0    1
         1    2
         2    3
         3    1
         4    1
         Name: Risk, dtype: object
```

We can also replace the `slice` method with Python's list-slicing syntax (see appendix B). The following code returns the same result as the preceding code:

```
In  [28] inspections["Risk"].str[5:6].head()

Out [28] 0    1
         1    2
         2    3
         3    1
         4    1
         Name: Risk, dtype: object
```

What if we want to extract the categorical ranking (`"High"`, `"Medium"`, `"Low"`, and `"All"`) from each row? This challenge is made difficult by the different lengths of the words; we cannot extract the same number of characters from a starting index position. A few solutions are available. We'll discuss the most resilient option, regular expressions, in section 6.7.

For now, let's attack the problem step by step. We can start by using the `slice` method to extract each row's risk category. If we pass the `slice` method a single value, pandas will use it as the lower bound and extract until the end of the string.

The next example pulls the characters from index position 8 to the end of each string. The character at index position 8 is the first letter in each risk type (the `"H"` in `"High"`, the `"M"` in `"Medium"`, the `"L"` in `"Low"`, and the `"E"` in `"Extreme"`):

```
In  [29] inspections["Risk"].str.slice(8).head()

Out [29] 0       High)
         1     Medium)
         2        Low)
         3       High)
         4       High)
         Name: Risk, dtype: object
```

We can use Python's list-slicing syntax, too. Inside the square brackets, provide a starting index position followed by a single colon. The result is identical:

```
In  [30] inspections["Risk"].str[8:].head()

Out [30] 0       High)
         1     Medium)
         2        Low)
         3       High)
         4       High)
         Name: Risk, dtype: object
```

We still have to deal with the pesky closing parentheses. Here's a cool solution: pass a negative argument to the `str.slice` method. A negative argument sets the index bound relative to the end of the string: -1 extracts up to the last character, -2 extracts up to the second-to-last character, and so on. Let's extract a substring from index position 8 up until the last character in each string:

```
In  [31] inspections["Risk"].str.slice(8, -1).head()

Out [31] 0       High
         1     Medium
         2        Low
         3       High
         4       High
         Name: Risk, dtype: object
```

We've got it! If you prefer list-slicing syntax, you can pass the -1 after the colon inside the square brackets:

```
In  [32] inspections["Risk"].str[8:-1].head()

Out [32] 0       High
         1     Medium
         2        Low
         3       High
         4       High
         Name: Risk, dtype: object
```

Another strategy we can use to remove the closing parentheses is the `str.replace` method. We can replace each closing parentheses with an empty string—a string without characters.

Each `str` method returns a new `Series` object with its own `str` attribute. This aspect allows us to chain multiple string methods in sequence, as long as we reference the `str` attribute in each method invocation. The next example chains the `slice` and `replace` methods:

```
In  [33] inspections["Risk"].str.slice(8).str.replace(")", "").head()

Out [33] 0        High
         1      Medium
         2         Low
         3        High
         4        High
         Name: Risk, dtype: object
```

By slicing from a middle index position and removing the ending parenthesis, we were able to isolate the Risk level for each row.

6.4 *Boolean methods*

Section 6.3 introduced methods such as `upper` and `slice` that return a `Series` of strings. Other methods available on the `StringMethods` object return a `Series` of Booleans. These methods can prove to be particularly helpful for filtering a DataFrame.

Suppose that we want to isolate all establishments with the word `"Pizza"` in their names. In vanilla Python, we use the `in` operator to search for a substring with a string:

```
In  [34] "Pizza" in "Jets Pizza"

Out [34] True
```

The biggest challenge in string matching is case sensitivity. Python will not find the string `"pizza"` in `"Jets Pizza"`, for example, because of the mismatch in casing of the `"p"` character:

```
In  [35] "pizza" in "Jets Pizza"

Out [35] False
```

To solve this problem, we need to ensure consistent casing across all column values before we check for the presence of a substring. We can look for a lowercase `"pizza"` in an all-lowercase `Series` or an uppercase `"PIZZA"` in an all-uppercase `Series`. Let's go with the former approach.

The `contains` method checks for a substring's inclusion in each `Series` value. The method returns `True` when pandas finds the method's argument within the row's string and `False` when it does not. The next example first lowercases the Name column with the `lower` method and then searches for `"pizza"` within each row:

```
In  [36]  inspections["Name"].str.lower().str.contains("pizza").head()
```

```
Out [36] 0     False
         1      True
         2     False
         3     False
         4     False
         Name: Name, dtype: bool
```

We have a Boolean `Series`, which we can use to extract all establishments with `"Pizza"` in their name:

```
In  [37]  has_pizza = inspections["Name"].str.lower().str.contains("pizza")
          inspections[has_pizza]
```

```
Out [37]
```

	Name	Risk
1	JETS PIZZA	Risk 2 (Medium)
19	NANCY'S HOME OF STUFFED PIZZA	Risk 1 (High)
27	NARY'S GRILL & PIZZA ,INC.	Risk 1 (High)
29	NARYS GRILL & PIZZA	Risk 1 (High)
68	COLUTAS PIZZA	Risk 1 (High)
...	...	...
153756	ANGELO'S STUFFED PIZZA CORP	Risk 1 (High)
153764	COCHIAROS PIZZA #2	Risk 1 (High)
153772	FERNANDO'S MEXICAN GRILL & PIZZA	Risk 1 (High)
153788	REGGIO'S PIZZA EXPRESS	Risk 1 (High)
153801	State Street Pizza Company	Risk 1 (High)

```
3992 rows × 2 columns
```

Notice that pandas preserves the original letter casing of the values in Name. The `inspections` DataFrame is never mutated. The `lower` method returns a new `Series`, and the `contains` method we invoke on it returns another new `Series`, which pandas uses to filter rows from the original `DataFrame`.

What if we want to be more precise in our targeting, perhaps extracting all establishments beginning with the string `"tacos"`? Now we care about the position of the substring within each string. The `str.startswith` method solves the problem, returning `True` if a string begins with its argument:

```
In  [38]  inspections["Name"].str.lower().str.startswith("tacos").head()
```

```
Out [38] 0     False
         1     False
         2     False
         3     False
         4     False
         Name: Name, dtype: bool
```

```
In  [39]  starts_with_tacos = (
              inspections["Name"].str.lower().str.startswith("tacos")
          )

          inspections[starts_with_tacos]
```

Out [39]

	Name	Risk
69	TACOS NIETOS	Risk 1 (High)
556	TACOS EL TIO 2 INC.	Risk 1 (High)
675	TACOS DON GABINO	Risk 1 (High)
958	TACOS EL TIO 2 INC.	Risk 1 (High)
1036	TACOS EL TIO 2 INC.	Risk 1 (High)
...	...	...
143587	TACOS DE LUNA	Risk 1 (High)
144026	TACOS GARCIA	Risk 1 (High)
146174	Tacos Place's 1	Risk 1 (High)
147810	TACOS MARIO'S LIMITED	Risk 1 (High)
151191	TACOS REYNA	Risk 1 (High)

105 rows × 2 columns

The complementary `str.endswith` method checks for a substring at the end of each Series string:

```
In  [40] ends_with_tacos = (
             inspections["Name"].str.lower().str.endswith("tacos")
         )

         inspections[ends_with_tacos]
```

Out [40]

	Name	Risk
382	LAZO'S TACOS	Risk 1 (High)
569	LAZO'S TACOS	Risk 1 (High)
2652	FLYING TACOS	Risk 3 (Low)
3250	JONY'S TACOS	Risk 1 (High)
3812	PACO'S TACOS	Risk 1 (High)
...	...	...
151121	REYES TACOS	Risk 1 (High)
151318	EL MACHO TACOS	Risk 1 (High)
151801	EL MACHO TACOS	Risk 1 (High)
153087	RAYMOND'S TACOS	Risk 1 (High)
153504	MIS TACOS	Risk 1 (High)

304 rows × 2 columns

Whether you're looking for text at the beginning, middle, or end of a string, the `StringMethods` object has a helper method to assist you.

6.5 *Splitting strings*

Our next data set is a collection of fictional customers. Each row includes the customer's Name and Address. Let's import the customers.csv file with the `read_csv` function and assign the `DataFrame` to a `customers` variable:

```
In  [41] customers = pd.read_csv("customers.csv")
         customers.head()
```

Out [41]

Name	Address
0 Frank Manning	6461 Quinn Groves, East Matthew, New Hampshire,166...
1 Elizabeth Johnson	1360 Tracey Ports Apt. 419, Kyleport, Vermont,319...
2 Donald Stephens	19120 Fleming Manors, Prestonstad, Montana, 23495
3 Michael Vincent III	441 Olivia Creek, Jimmymouth, Georgia, 82991
4 Jasmine Zamora	4246 Chelsey Ford Apt. 310, Karamouth, Utah, 76...

We can use the `str.len` method to return the length of each row's string. Row 0's value of `"Frank Manning"`, for example, has a length of 13 characters:

```
In  [42] customers["Name"].str.len().head()

Out [42] 0    13
         1    17
         2    15
         3    19
         4    14
         Name: Name, dtype: int64
```

Suppose that we want to isolate each customer's first and last names in two separate columns. You may be familiar with Python's `split` method, which separates a string by using a specified delimiter. The method returns a list consisting of all the substrings after the split. The next example splits a phone number into a list of three strings by using a hyphen delimiter:

```
In  [43] phone_number = "555-123-4567"
         phone_number.split("-")

Out [43] ['555', '123', '4567']
```

The `str.split` method performs the same operation on each row in a `Series`; its return value is a `Series` of lists. We pass the delimiter to the method's first parameter, `pat` (short for *pattern*). The next example splits the values in Name by the presence of a space:

```
In  [44] # The two lines below are equivalent
         customers["Name"].str.split(pat = " ").head()
         customers["Name"].str.split(" ").head()

Out [44] 0             [Frank, Manning]
         1         [Elizabeth, Johnson]
         2          [Donald, Stephens]
         3     [Michael, Vincent, III]
         4            [Jasmine, Zamora]
         Name: Name, dtype: object
```

Next, let's reinvoke the `str.len` method on this new `Series` of lists to get the length of each list. Pandas reacts dynamically to whatever data type a `Series` is storing:

```
In  [45] customers["Name"].str.split(" ").str.len().head()

Out [45] 0    2
         1    2
         2    2
```

```
3      3
4      2
Name: Name, dtype: int64
```

We have a small issue. Due to suffixes such as `"MD"` and `"Jr"`, some names have more than two words. We can see an example at index position 3: Michael Vincent III, which pandas splits into a list of three elements. To ensure an equal number of elements per list, we can limit the number of splits. If we set a maximum threshold of one split, pandas will split a string at the first space and stop. Then we'll have a `Series` consisting of two-element lists. Each list will hold the customer's first name and anything that follows it.

The next example passes an argument of 1 to the `split` method's n parameter, which sets the maximum number of splits. Take a look at how pandas deals with `"Michael Vincent III"` at index 3:

```
In  [46] customers["Name"].str.split(pat = " ", n = 1).head()

Out [46] 0          [Frank, Manning]
         1       [Elizabeth, Johnson]
         2         [Donald, Stephens]
         3     [Michael, Vincent III]
         4         [Jasmine, Zamora]
         Name: Name, dtype: object
```

Now all our lists have equal lengths. We can use `str.get` to pull out a value from *each* row's list based on its index position. We can target index 0, for example, to pull out the first element of each list, which is the customer's first name:

```
In  [47] customers["Name"].str.split(pat = " ", n = 1).str.get(0).head()

Out [47] 0          Frank
         1      Elizabeth
         2         Donald
         3        Michael
         4        Jasmine
         Name: Name, dtype: object
```

To pull the last name from each list, we could pass the `get` method an index position of 1:

```
In  [48] customers["Name"].str.split(pat = " ", n = 1).str.get(1).head()

Out [48] 0         Manning
         1         Johnson
         2        Stephens
         3     Vincent III
         4          Zamora
         Name: Name, dtype: object
```

The `get` method also supports negative arguments. An argument of `-1` extracts the last element from each row's list, regardless of how many elements the list holds. The following code produces the same result as the preceding code and is a bit more versa-tile in scenarios in which the lists have different lengths:

```
In   [49] customers["Name"].str.split(pat = " ", n = 1).str.get(-1).head()

Out  [49] 0          Manning
          1          Johnson
          2          Stephens
          3      Vincent III
          4          Zamora
          Name: Name, dtype: object
```

So far, so good. We've used two separate `get` method calls to extract the first and last names in two separate `Series`. Wouldn't it be nice to perform the same logic in a sin-gle method call? Luckily, the `str.split` method accepts an `expand` parameter, and when we pass it an argument of `True`, the method returns a new `DataFrame` instead of a `Series` of lists:

```
In   [50] customers["Name"].str.split(
              pat = " ", n = 1, expand = True
          ).head()

Out  [50]
```

	0	1
0	Frank	Manning
1	Elizabeth	Johnson
2	Donald	Stephens
3	Michael	Vincent III
4	Jasmine	Zamora

We've got a new `DataFrame`! Because we did not provide custom names for the col-umns, pandas defaulted to a numeric index on the column axis.

Be careful in these scenarios. If we do not limit the number of splits with the n parameter, pandas will place `None` values in rows that do not have sufficient elements:

```
In   [51] customers["Name"].str.split(pat = " ", expand = True).head()

Out  [51]
```

	0	1	2
0	Frank	Manning	None
1	Elizabeth	Johnson	None
2	Donald	Stephens	None
3	Michael	Vincent	III
4	Jasmine	Zamora	None

Now that we've isolated the customers' names, let's attach the new two-column Data-Frame to the existing customers `DataFrame`. On the right side of an equal sign, we'll use the `split` code to create the `DataFrame`. On the left side of the equal sign, we'll provide a list of column names inside a pair of square brackets. Pandas will append these columns to customers. The next example adds two new columns, First Name and Last Name, and populates them with the `DataFrame` returned by the `split` method:

```
In  [52] customers[["First Name", "Last Name"]] = customers[
             "Name"
         ].str.split(pat = " ", n = 1, expand = True)
```

Let's take a look at the result:

```
In  [53] customers
```

```
Out [53]
```

	Name	Address	First Name	Last Name
0	Frank Manning	6461 Quinn Groves, E…	Frank	Manning
1	Elizabeth Johnson	1360 Tracey Ports Ap…	Elizabeth	Johnson
2	Donald Stephens	19120 Fleming Manors…	Donald	Stephens
3	Michael Vincent III	441 Olivia Creek, Ji…	Michael	Vincent III
4	Jasmine Zamora	4246 Chelsey Ford Ap…	Jasmine	Zamora
...	...		...	...
9956	Dana Browning	762 Andrew Views Apt…	Dana	Browning
9957	Amanda Anderson	44188 Day Crest Apt …	Amanda	Anderson
9958	Eric Davis	73015 Michelle Squar…	Eric	Davis
9959	Taylor Hernandez	129 Keith Greens, Ha…	Taylor	Hernandez
9960	Sherry Nicholson	355 Griffin Valley, …	Sherry	Nicholson

9961 rows × 4 columns

Excellent! Now that we've extracted the customers' names to separate columns, we can delete the original Name column. One way is to use the `drop` method on our customers `DataFrame`. We'll pass the column's name to the `labels` parameter and an argument of `"columns"` to the `axis` parameter. We need to include the `axis` parameter to tell pandas to look for the Name label in the columns instead of the rows:

```
In  [54] customers = customers.drop(labels = "Name", axis = "columns")
```

Remember that mutational operations do not produce output in Jupyter Notebook. We must print the `DataFrame` to see the result:

```
In  [55] customers.head()
```

```
Out [55]
```

	Address	First Name	Last Name
0	6461 Quinn Groves, East Matthew, New Hampshire…	Frank	Manning
1	1360 Tracey Ports Apt. 419, Kyleport, Vermont…	Elizabeth	Johnson
2	19120 Fleming Manors, Prestonstad, Montana…	Donald	Stephens
3	441 Olivia Creek, Jimmymouth, Georgia…	Michael	Vincent III
4	4246 Chelsey Ford Apt. 310, Karamouth, Utah…	Jasmine	Zamora

There we go. The Name column is gone, and we have split its contents across two new columns.

6.6   *Coding challenge*

Here's your chance to practice the concepts introduced in this chapter.

6.6.1   *Problems*

Our customers data set includes an Address column. Each address consists of a street, a city, a state, and a zip code. Your challenge is to separate these four values; assign them to new Street, City, State, and Zip columns; and then remove the Address column. Give the problem a shot, and then review the solution.

6.6.2   *Solutions*

Our first step is splitting the address strings with a delimiter, using the `split` method. A comma by itself seems to be a good argument:

```
In  [56] customers["Address"].str.split(",").head()

Out [56] 0    [6461 Quinn Groves,  East Matthew,  New Hampsh...
         1    [1360 Tracey Ports Apt. 419,  Kyleport,  Vermo...
         2    [19120 Fleming Manors,  Prestonstad,  Montana,...
         3    [441 Olivia Creek,  Jimmymouth,  Georgia,  82991]
         4    [4246 Chelsey Ford Apt. 310,  Karamouth,  Utah...
         Name: Address, dtype: object
```

Unfortunately, this split keeps the spaces after the commas. We could perform additional cleanup by using a method such as `strip`, but a better solution is available. If we think about it, each portion of the address is separated by a comma and a space. Therefore, we can pass the `split` method a delimiter of both characters:

```
In  [57] customers["Address"].str.split(", ").head()

Out [57] 0    [6461 Quinn Groves, East Matthew, New Hampshir...
         1    [1360 Tracey Ports Apt. 419, Kyleport, Vermont...
         2    [19120 Fleming Manors, Prestonstad, Montana, 2...
         3    [441 Olivia Creek, Jimmymouth, Georgia, 82991]
         4    [4246 Chelsey Ford Apt. 310, Karamouth, Utah, ...
         Name: Address, dtype: object
```

Now there is no extra whitespace at the start of each substring within the lists.

By default, the `split` method returns a `Series` of lists. We can make the method return a `DataFrame` by passing the `expand` parameter an argument of `True`:

```
In  [58] customers["Address"].str.split(", ", expand = True).head()

Out [58]
```

	0	1	2	3
0	6461 Quinn Groves	East Matthew	New Hampshire	16656
1	1360 Tracey Ports Apt. 419	Kyleport	Vermont	31924
2	19120 Fleming Manors	Prestonstad	Montana	23495
3	441 Olivia Creek	Jimmymouth	Georgia	82991
4	4246 Chelsey Ford Apt. 310	Karamouth	Utah	76252

We have a couple more steps left. Let's add the new four-column `DataFrame` to our existing customers `DataFrame`. We'll define a list with the new column names. This time around, let's assign the list to a variable to simplify readability. Next, we'll pass the list in square brackets before an equal sign. On the right side of the equal sign, we'll use the preceding code to create the new `DataFrame`:

```
In [59] new_cols = ["Street", "City", "State", "Zip"]

        customers[new_cols] = customers["Address"].str.split(
            pat = ", ", expand = True
        )
```

The last step is deleting the original Address column. The `drop` method is a good solution here. To alter the `DataFrame` permanently, make sure to overwrite customers with the returned `DataFrame`:

```
In [60] customers.drop(labels = "Address", axis = "columns").head()
```

```
Out [60]
```

	First Name	Last Name	Street	City	State	Zip
0	Frank	Manning	6461 Quin...	East Matthew	New Hamps...	16656
1	Elizabeth	Johnson	1360 Trac...	Kyleport	Vermont	31924
2	Donald	Stephens	19120 Fle...	Prestonstad	Montana	23495
3	Michael	Vincent III	441 Olivi...	Jimmymouth	Georgia	82991
4	Jasmine	Zamora	4246 Chel...	Karamouth	Utah	76252

Another option is to use Python's built-in `del` keyword before the target column. This syntax mutates the `DataFrame`:

```
In [61] del customers["Address"]
```

Let's take a look at the final product:

```
In [62] customers.tail()
```

```
Out [62]
```

	First Name	Last Name	Street	City	State	Zip
9956	Dana	Browning	762 Andrew …	North Paul	New Mexico	28889
9957	Amanda	Anderson	44188 Day C…	Lake Marcia	Maine	37378
9958	Eric	Davis	73015 Miche…	Watsonville	West Virginia	03933
9959	Taylor	Hernandez	129 Keith G…	Haleyfurt	Oklahoma	98916
9960	Sherry	Nicholson	355 Griffin…	Davidtown	New Mexico	17581

We've successfully extracted the contents of the Address column to four new columns. Congratulations on completing the coding challenge!

6.7 *A note on regular expressions*

Any discussion of working with text data is incomplete without mentioning regular expressions, also known as RegEx. A *regular expression* is a search pattern that looks for a sequence of characters within a string.

We declare regular expressions with a special syntax consisting of symbols and characters. \d, for example, matches any numeric digit between 0 and 9. With regular expressions, we can define complex search patterns by targeting lowercase characters, uppercase characters, digits, slashes, whitespace, string boundaries, and more.

Suppose that a phone number like 555-555-5555 is hidden in a larger string. We can use regular expressions to define a search algorithm that extracts sequences of three sequential digits, a dash, three sequential digits, another dash, and four more sequential digits. That level of granularity grants regular expressions their power.

Here's a quick example that shows the syntax in action. The next code sample uses the `replace` method on the Street column to swap all occurrences of four sequential digits with an asterisk character:

```
In  [63] customers["Street"].head()

Out [63]  0              6461 Quinn Groves
          1    1360 Tracey Ports Apt. 419
          2           19120 Fleming Manors
          3              441 Olivia Creek
          4    4246 Chelsey Ford Apt. 310
          Name: Street, dtype: object

In  [64] customers["Street"].str.replace(
            "\d{4,}", "*", regex = True
         ).head()

Out [64] 0              * Quinn Groves
         1    * Tracey Ports Apt. 419
         2           * Fleming Manors
         3              441 Olivia Creek
         4    * Chelsey Ford Apt. 310
         Name: Street, dtype: object
```

Regular expressions are a highly specialized technical topic. Whole books are written on the complexities of RegEx. For now, it's important to note that pandas supports RegEx arguments for most of its string methods. You can check out appendix E for a more comprehensive introduction to the domain.

Summary

- The `str` attribute holds a `StringMethods` object with methods for performing string manipulations on `Series` values.
- The `strip` family of methods removes whitespace from the start of a string, the end of a string, or both sides.
- Methods such as `upper`, `lower`, `capitalize`, and `title` modify the letter casing of string characters.
- The `contains` method checks for the presence of a substring within another string.
- The `startswith` method checks for a substring at the beginning of a string.
- The complementary `endswith` method checks for a substring at the end of a string.
- The `split` method splits a string into a list by using a specified delimiter. We can use it to split a `DataFrame` column's text across several `Series`.

MultiIndex DataFrames

7

This chapter covers

- Creating a `MultiIndex`
- Selecting rows and columns from a `MultiIndex` `DataFrame`
- Extracting a cross-section from a `MultiIndex` `DataFrame`
- Swapping `MultiIndex` levels

So far on our pandas journey, we've explored the one-dimensional `Series` and the two-dimensional `DataFrame`. The number of dimensions is the number of reference points we need to extract a value from a data structure. We need only one label or one index position to locate a value in a `Series`. We need two reference points to locate a value in a `DataFrame`: a label/index for the rows and a label/index for the columns. Can we expand beyond two dimensions? Absolutely! Pandas supports data sets with any number of dimensions through the use of a `MultiIndex`.

A `MultiIndex` is an index object that holds multiple levels. Each level stores a value for the row. It is optimal to use a `MultiIndex` when a combination of values

Stock	Date	Price
MSFT	02/08/2021	793.60
MSFT	02/09/2021	1,408.38
GOOG	02/08/2021	565.81
GOOG	02/09/2021	17.62

Figure 7.1   Sample data set with Stock, Date, and Price columns

provides the best identifier for a row of data. Consider the data set in figure 7.1, which stores stock prices across multiple dates.

Suppose that we want to find a unique identifier for each price. Neither a stock's name nor its date is sufficient by itself, but the combination of both values is a good fit. The stock "MSFT" appears twice, the date "02/08/2021" appears twice, but the combination of "MSFT" and "02/08/2021" appears only once. A MultiIndex storing the values of the Stock and Date columns would suit this data set well.

A MultiIndex is also ideal for *hierarchical* data—data in which one column's values are a subcategory of another column's values. Consider the data set in figure 7.2.

Group	Item	Calories
Fruit	Apple	95
Fruit	Banana	105
Vegetable	Broccoli	50
Vegetable	Tomato	22

Figure 7.2   Sample data set with Group, Item, and Calories columns

The Item column's values are subcategories of the Group column's values. An Apple is a type of Fruit, and Broccoli is a type of Vegetable. Thus, the Group and Item columns could serve as a MultiIndex combo.

The MultiIndex is an obscure feature in pandas but one that's worth taking the time to learn. The introduction of multiple index levels adds a lot of versatility to how we slice and dice data sets.

7.1   *The MultiIndex object*

Let's open a new Jupyter Notebook, import the pandas library, and assign it the alias pd:

```
In  [1] import pandas as pd
```

To keep things simple, we'll start by creating a MultiIndex object from scratch. In section 7.2, we'll practice these concepts on an imported data set.

Do you recall Python's built-in tuple object? The tuple is an immutable data structure that holds a sequence of values in order. A tuple is effectively a list that cannot be modified after creation. For a deeper dive into this data structure, see appendix B.

Let's say we want to model a street address. An address typically includes a street name, city, town, and zip code. We could store these four elements in a tuple:

```
In  [2] address = ("8809 Flair Square", "Toddside", "IL", "37206")
        address

Out [2] ('8809 Underwood Squares', 'Toddside', 'IL', '37206')
```

`Series` and `DataFrame` indices can hold various data types: strings, numbers, datetimes, and more. But all these objects can store only one value per index position, one label per row. A tuple doesn't have that limitation.

What if we gathered multiple tuples in a list? The list would look like this:

```
In  [3] addresses = [
            ("8809 Flair Square", "Toddside", "IL", "37206"),
            ("9901 Austin Street", "Toddside", "IL", "37206"),
            ("905 Hogan Quarter", "Franklin", "IL", "37206"),
        ]
```

Now imagine these tuples serving as a `DataFrame`'s index labels. I hope that the idea is not too confusing. All operations remain the same. We would still be able to reference a row by its index label, but each index label would be a container holding multiple elements. That's a good way to start thinking about the `MultiIndex` object—as an index in which each label can store multiple pieces of data.

We can create a `MultiIndex` object independently of a `Series` or `DataFrame`. The `MultiIndex` class is available as a top-level attribute on the pandas library. It includes a `from_tuples` class method that instantiates a `MultiIndex` from a list of tuples. A *class method* is a method we invoke on a class rather than an instance. The next example invokes the `from_tuples` class method and passes it the `addresses` list:

```
In  [4] # The two lines below are equivalent
        pd.MultiIndex.from_tuples(addresses)
        pd.MultiIndex.from_tuples(tuples = addresses)

Out [4] MultiIndex([( '8809 Flair Square',   'Toddside', 'IL', '37206'),
                     ('9901 Austin Street',   'Toddside', 'IL', '37206'),
                     ( '905 Hogan Quarter',   'Franklin', 'IL', '37206')],
                    )
```

We have our first `MultiIndex`, which stores three tuples of four elements each. There is a consistent pattern to each tuple's elements:

- The first value is the address.
- The second value is the city.
- The third value is the state.
- The fourth value is the zip code.

In pandas terminology, the collection of tuple values at the same position forms a *level* of the `MultiIndex`. In the previous example, the first `MultiIndex` level consists of the values `"8809 Flair Square"`, `"9901 Austin Street"`, and `"905 Hogan`

Quarter". Similarly, the second `MultiIndex` level consists of "Toddside", "Toddside", and "Franklin".

We can assign each `MultiIndex` level a name by passing a list to the `from_tuples` method's names parameter. Here, we assign the names "Street", "City", "State", and "Zip":

```
In  [5] row_index = pd.MultiIndex.from_tuples(
            tuples = addresses,
            names = ["Street", "City", "State", "Zip"]
        )

        row_index

Out [5] MultiIndex([( '8809 Flair Square',    'Toddside', 'IL', '37206'),
                    ('9901 Austin Street',    'Toddside', 'IL', '37206'),
                    ( '905 Hogan Quarter',    'Franklin', 'IL', '37206')],
                    names=['Street', 'City', 'State', 'Zip'])
```

To summarize, a `MultiIndex` is a storage container in which each label holds multiple values. A level consists of the values at the same position across the labels.

Now that we have a `MultiIndex`, let's attach it to a `DataFrame`. The easiest way is to use the `DataFrame` constructor's index parameter. We passed this parameter a list of strings in earlier chapters, but it also accepts any valid index object. Let's pass it the `MultiIndex` we assigned to the row_index variable. Because our `MultiIndex` has three tuples (or, equivalently, three labels), we'll need to provide three rows of data:

```
In  [6] data = [
            ["A", "B+"],
            ["C+", "C"],
            ["D-", "A"],
        ]

        columns = ["Schools", "Cost of Living"]

        area_grades = pd.DataFrame(
            data = data, index = row_index, columns = columns
        )

        area_grades

Out [6]
```

Street	City	State	Zip	Schools	Cost of Living
8809 Flair Square	Toddside	IL	37206	A	B+
9901 Austin Street	Toddside	IL	37206	C+	C
905 Hogan Quarter	Franklin	IL	37206	D-	A

We have a `DataFrame` with a `MultiIndex` on its row axis. Each row's label holds four values: a street, a city, a state, and a zip code.

Let's turn our focus to the column axis. Pandas stores a `DataFrame`'s column headers in an index object as well. We can access that index via the `columns` attribute:

```
In  [7] area_grades.columns

Out [7] Index(['Schools', 'Cost of Living'], dtype='object')
```

Pandas currently stores the two column names in a single-level `Index` object. Let's create a second `MultiIndex` and attach it to the column axis. The next example invokes the `from_tuples` class method again, passing it a list of four tuples. Each tuple holds two strings:

```
In  [8] column_index = pd.MultiIndex.from_tuples(
            [
                ("Culture", "Restaurants"),
                ("Culture", "Museums"),
                ("Services", "Police"),
                ("Services", "Schools"),
            ]
        )

        column_index

Out [8] MultiIndex([( 'Culture', 'Restaurants'),
                    ( 'Culture',     'Museums'),
                    ('Services',      'Police'),
                    ('Services',     'Schools')],
                    )
```

Let's attach both of our `MultiIndexes` to a `DataFrame`. The `MultiIndex` for the row axis (`row_index`) requires the data set to hold three rows. The `MultiIndex` for the column axis (`column_index`) requires the data set to hold four columns. Therefore, our data set must have a 3 x 4 shape. Let's create that sample data. The next example declares a list of three lists. Each nested list stores four strings:

```
In  [9] data = [
            ["C-", "B+", "B-", "A"],
            ["D+", "C", "A", "C+"],
            ["A-", "A", "D+", "F"]
        ]
```

We're ready to put the pieces together and create a `DataFrame` with a `MultiIndex` on both the row and column axes. In the `DataFrame` constructor, let's pass our respective `MultiIndex` variables to the `index` and `columns` parameters:

```
In  [10] pd.DataFrame(
            data = data, index = row_index, columns = column_index
         )

Out [10]
```

| | | | | Culture | | Services | |
				Restaurants	Museums	Police	Schools
Street	City	State	Zip				
8809 Flai...	Toddside	IL	37206	C-	B+	B-	A
9901 Aust...	Toddside	IL	37206	D+	C	A	C+
905 Hogan...	Franklin	IL	37206	A-	A	D+	F

Hooray! We've successfully created a `DataFrame` with a four-level row `MultiIndex` and a two-level column `MultiIndex`. A `MultiIndex` is an index that can store multiple levels, multiple tiers. Each index label is made of multiple components. That's all there is to it.

7.2   *MultiIndex DataFrames*

Let's scale things up a bit. The neighborhoods.csv data set is similar to the one we created in section 7.1; it's a listing of ~250 fictional addresses in cities across the United States. Each address is graded on four characteristics of livability: Restaurants, Museums, Police, and Schools. The four grades are grouped in two parent categories: Culture and Services.

Here's a preview of the first couple of rows of the raw CSV file. In a CSV, a comma separates every two subsequent values in a row of data. Thus, the presence of sequential commas with nothing between them indicates missing values:

```
,,,Culture,Culture,Services,Services
,,,Restaurants,Museums,Police,Schools
State,City,Street,,,,
MO,Fisherborough,244 Tracy View,C+,F,D-,A+
```

How will pandas import this CSV file's data? Let's find out with the `read_csv` function:

```
In  [11] neighborhoods = pd.read_csv("neighborhoods.csv")
         neighborhoods.head()
```

Out [11]

	Unnamed: 0	Unnamed: 1	Unnamed: 2	Culture	Culture.1	Services	Services.1
0	NaN	NaN	NaN	Restau...	Museums	Police	Schools
1	State	City	Street	NaN	NaN	NaN	NaN
2	MO	Fisher...	244 Tr...	C+	F	D-	A+
3	SD	Port C...	446 Cy...	C-	B	B	D+
4	WV	Jimene...	432 Jo...	A	A+	F	B

Something is off here! First, we have three Unnamed columns, each one ending in a different number. When importing a CSV, pandas assumes that the file's first row holds the column names, also known as the headers. If a header slot does not have a value, pandas assigns a title of "Unnamed" to the column. Simultaneously, the library tries to avoid duplicate column names. To distinguish between multiple missing headers, the library adds a numerical index to each. Thus, we have three Unnamed columns: Unnamed: 0, Unnamed: 1, and Unnamed: 2.

The four columns to the right have the same naming issue. Notice that pandas assigns a title of Culture to the column at index 3 and Culture 1 to the one after it. The CSV file has the same value of "Culture" for two header cells in a row, followed by the same value of "Services" for two header cells in a row.

Unfortunately, that's not the end of our problems. In row 0, each of the first three columns holds a NaN value. In row 1, we have NaN values present in the last four columns. The issue is that the CSV is trying to model a multilevel row index and a multilevel column index, but the default arguments to the `read_csv` function's parameters don't recognize it. Luckily, we can solve this problem by altering the arguments to a couple of `read_csv` parameters.

First, we have to tell pandas that the three leftmost columns should serve as the index of the `DataFrame`. We can do this by passing the `index_col` parameter a list of numbers, each one representing the index (or numeric position) of a column that should be in the `DataFrame`'s index. The index starts counting from 0. Thus, the first three columns (the Unnamed ones) will have index positions 0, 1, and 2. When we pass `index_col` a list with multiple values, pandas automatically creates a Multi-Index for the `DataFrame`:

```
In  [12] neighborhoods = pd.read_csv(
             "neighborhoods.csv",
             index_col = [0, 1, 2]
         )

         neighborhoods.head()
```

```
Out [12]
```

			Culture	Culture.1	Services	Services.1
NaN	NaN	NaN	Restaurants	Museums	Police	Schools
State	City	Street	NaN	NaN	NaN	NaN
MO	Fisherbor...	244 Tracy...	C+	F	D-	A+
SD	Port Curt...	446 Cynth...	C-	B	B	D+
WV	Jimenezview	432 John ...	A	A+	F	B

We're halfway there. Next, we need to tell pandas which data set rows we'd like to use for our `DataFrame`'s headers. The `read_csv` function assumes that only the first row will hold the headers. In this data set, the first two rows will hold the headers. We can customize the `DataFrame` headers with the `read_csv` function's `header` parameter, which accepts a list of integers representing the *rows* that pandas should set as column headers. If we provide a list with more than one element, pandas will assign a Multi-Index to the columns. The next example sets the first two rows (indexes 0 and 1) as column headers:

```
In  [13] neighborhoods = pd.read_csv(
             "neighborhoods.csv",
             index_col = [0, 1, 2],
             header = [0, 1]
         )

         neighborhoods.head()
```

```
Out [13]
```

			Culture		Services	
State	City	Street	Restaurants	Museums	Police	Schools
MO	Fisherborough	244 Tracy View	C+	F	D-	A+
SD	Port Curtisv...	446 Cynthia ...	C-	B	B	D+
WV	Jimenezview	432 John Common	A	A+	F	B
AK	Stevenshire	238 Andrew Rue	D-	A	A-	A-
ND	New Joshuaport	877 Walter Neck	D+	C-	B	B

Now we have something we can work with!

As mentioned earlier, the data set groups four characteristics of livability (Restaurants, Museums, Police, and Schools) in two categories (Culture and Services). When we have a parent category encompassing smaller child categories, creating a `Multi-Index` is an optimal way to enable quick slicing.

Let's invoke some familiar methods to observe how the output changes with a `MultiIndex` DataFrame. The `info` method is a good place to start:

```
In  [14] neighborhoods.info()

Out [14]

<class 'pandas.core.frame.DataFrame'>
MultiIndex: 251 entries, ('MO', 'Fisherborough', '244 Tracy View') to ('NE',
    'South Kennethmouth', '346 Wallace Pass')
Data columns (total 4 columns):
 #   Column                 Non-Null Count  Dtype
---  ------                 --------------  -----
 0   (Culture, Restaurants)  251 non-null   object
 1   (Culture, Museums)      251 non-null   object
 2   (Services, Police)      251 non-null   object
 3   (Services, Schools)     251 non-null   object
dtypes: object(4)
memory use: 27.2+ KB
```

Notice that pandas prints each column's name as a two-element tuple, such as `(Culture, Restaurants)`. Similarly, the library stores each row's label as a three-element tuple, such as `('MO', 'Fisherborough', '244 Tracy View')`.

We can access the rows' `MultiIndex` object with the familiar `index` attribute. The output allows us to see the tuples that hold each row's values:

```
In  [15] neighborhoods.index

Out [15] MultiIndex([
             ('MO',        'Fisherborough',        '244 Tracy View'),
             ('SD',      'Port Curtisville',      '446 Cynthia Inlet'),
             ('WV',         'Jimenezview',         '432 John Common'),
             ('AK',         'Stevenshire',         '238 Andrew Rue'),
             ('ND',      'New Joshuaport',         '877 Walter Neck'),
             ('ID',         'Wellsville',     '696 Weber Stravenue'),
             ('TN',          'Jodiburgh',       '285 Justin Corners'),
             ('DC',    'Lake Christopher',       '607 Montoya Harbors'),
             ('OH',           'Port Mike',        '041 Michael Neck'),
             ('ND',          'Hardyburgh',  '550 Gilmore Mountains'),
             ...
             ('AK', 'South Nicholasshire',         '114 Jones Garden'),
             ('IA',      'Port Willieport',  '320 Jennifer Mission'),
             ('ME',           'Port Linda',         '692 Hill Glens'),
             ('KS',           'Kaylamouth',        '483 Freeman Via'),
             ('WA',       'Port Shawnfort',     '691 Winters Bridge'),
             ('MI',        'North Matthew',        '055 Clayton Isle'),
             ('MT',             'Chadton',       '601 Richards Road'),
             ('SC',            'Diazmouth',        '385 Robin Harbors'),
             ('VA',           'Laurentown',       '255 Gonzalez Land'),
             ('NE',  'South Kennethmouth',        '346 Wallace Pass')],
           names=['State', 'City', 'Street'], length=251)
```

We can access the columns' `MultiIndex` object with the `columns` attribute, which also uses tuples to store the nested column labels:

```
In  [16] neighborhoods.columns

Out [16] MultiIndex([( 'Culture', 'Restaurants'),
            ( 'Culture',      'Museums'),
            ('Services',       'Police'),
            ('Services',      'Schools')],
           )
```

Under its hood, pandas composes a `MultiIndex` from multiple `Index` objects. When importing the data set, the library assigned a name to each `Index` from a CSV header. We can access the list of index names with the `names` attribute on the `MultiIndex` object. State, City, and Street are the names of the three CSV columns that became our index:

```
In  [17] neighborhoods.index.names

Out [17] FrozenList(['State', 'City', 'Street'])
```

Pandas assigns an order to each nested level within the `MultiIndex`. In our current neighborhoods `DataFrame`,

- The State level has an index position of 0.
- The City level has an index position of 1.
- The Street level has an index position of 2.

The `get_level_values` method extracts the `Index` object at a given level of the `MultiIndex`. We can pass either the level's index position or the level's name to the method's first and only parameter, `level`:

```
In  [18] # The two lines below are equivalent
         neighborhoods.index.get_level_values(1)
         neighborhoods.index.get_level_values("City")

Out [18] Index(['Fisherborough', 'Port Curtisville', 'Jimenezview',
               'Stevenshire', 'New Joshuaport', 'Wellsville', 'Jodiburgh',
               'Lake Christopher', 'Port Mike', 'Hardyburgh',
               ...
               'South Nicholasshire', 'Port Willieport', 'Port Linda',
               'Kaylamouth', 'Port Shawnfort', 'North Matthew', 'Chadton',
               'Diazmouth', 'Laurentown', 'South Kennethmouth'],
              dtype='object', name='City', length=251)
```

The columns' `MultiIndex` levels do not have any names because the CSV did not provide any:

```
In  [19] neighborhoods.columns.names

Out [19] FrozenList([None, None])
```

Let's fix this problem. We can access the columns' `MultiIndex` with the `columns` attribute. Then we can assign a new list of column names to the `names` attribute of the

MultiIndex object. The names "Category" and "Subcategory" seem to be fitting here:

```
In  [20] neighborhoods.columns.names = ["Category", "Subcategory"]
         neighborhoods.columns.names

Out [20] FrozenList(['Category', 'Subcategory'])
```

The level names will appear to the left of the column headers in the output. Let's invoke the head method to see the difference:

```
In  [21] neighborhoods.head(3)

Out [21]
```

Category			Culture		Services	
Subcategory			Restaurants	Museums	Police	Schools
State	City	Street				
MO	Fisherbor...	244 Tracy...	C+	F	D-	A+
SD	Port Curt...	446 Cynth...	C-	B	B	D+
WV	Jimenezview	432 John ...	A	A+	F	B

Now that we've assigned names to the levels, we can use the get_level_values method to retrieve any Index from the columns' MultiIndex. Remember that we can pass either the column's index position or its name to the method:

```
In  [22] # The two lines below are equivalent
         neighborhoods.columns.get_level_values(0)
         neighborhoods.columns.get_level_values("Category")

Out [22] Index(['Culture', 'Culture', 'Services', 'Services'],
         dtype='object', name='Category')
```

A MultiIndex will carry over to new objects derived from a data set. The index can switch axes depending on the operation. Consider a DataFrame's nunique method, which returns a Series with a count of unique values per column. If we invoke nunique on neighborhoods, the DataFrame's column MultiIndex will swap axes and serve as the row's MultiIndex in the resulting Series:

```
In  [23] neighborhoods.head(1)

Out [23]
```

Category			Culture		Services	
Subcategory			Restaurants	Museums	Police	Schools
State	City	Street				
AK	Rowlandchester	386 Rebecca ...	C-	A-	A+	C

```
In  [24] neighborhoods.nunique()

Out [24] Culture   Restaurants   13
                   Museums       13
```

```
      Services  Police        13
                Schools       13
      dtype: int64
```

The `MultiIndex Series` tells us how many unique values pandas found in each of the four columns. The values are equal in this case because all four columns hold the 13 possible grades (A+ to F).

7.3 **Sorting a MultiIndex**

Pandas can find a value in an ordered collection much quicker than in a jumbled one. A good analogous example is searching for a word in a dictionary. It's easier to locate a word when words are in alphabetical order rather than a random sequence. Thus, it's optimal to sort an index before selecting any rows and columns from a `DataFrame`.

Chapter 4 introduced the `sort_index` method for sorting a `DataFrame`. When we invoke the method on a `MultiIndex DataFrame`, pandas sorts all levels in ascending order and proceeds from the outside in. In the next example, pandas sorts the State-level values first, then the City-level values, and finally the Street-level values:

```
In  [25] neighborhoods.sort_index()

Out [25]
```

Category				Culture		Services	
Subcategory				Restaurants	Museums	Police	Schools
State	City		Street				
AK	Rowlandchester	386	Rebecca ...	C-	A-	A+	C
	Scottstad	082	Leblanc ...	D	C-	D	B+
		114	Jones Ga...	D-	D-	D	D
	Stevenshire	238	Andrew Rue	D-	A	A-	A-
AL	Clarkland	430	Douglas ...	A	F	C+	B+
...	...		...	...	...	...	...
WY	Lake Nicole	754	Weaver T...	B	D-	B	D
		933	Jennifer...	C	A+	A-	C
	Martintown	013	Bell Mills	C-	D	A-	B-
	Port Jason	624	Faulkner...	A-	F	C+	C+
	Reneeshire	717	Patel Sq...	B	B+	D	A

251 rows × 4 columns

Let's make sure that we understand the output. First, pandas targets the State level and sorts the value `"AK"` before `"AL"`. Then, within the state of `"AK"`, pandas sorts the city of `"Rowlandchester"` before `"Scottstad"`. It applies the same logic to the final level, Street.

The `sort_values` method includes an `ascending` parameter. We can pass the parameter a Boolean to apply a consistent sort order to all `MultiIndex` levels. The next example provides an argument of `False`. Pandas sorts the State values in reverse alphabetical order, then the City values in reverse alphabetical order, and finally the Street values in reverse alphabetical order:

```
In  [26] neighborhoods.sort_index(ascending = False).head()
```

Out [26]

Category			Culture		Services	
Subcategory			Restaurants	Museums	Police	Schools
State	City	Street				
WY	Reneeshire	717 Patel Sq...	B	B+	D	A
	Port Jason	624 Faulkner...	A-	F	C+	C+
	Martintown	013 Bell Mills	C-	D	A-	B-
	Lake Nicole	933 Jennifer...	C	A+	A-	C
		754 Weaver T...	B	D-	B	D

Suppose that we want to vary the sort order for different levels. We can pass the ascending parameter a list of Booleans. Each Boolean sets the sort order for the next MultiIndex level, starting with the outermost one and proceeding inward. An argument of [True, False, True], for example, will sort the State level in ascending order, the City level in descending order, and the Street level in ascending order:

```
In  [27] neighborhoods.sort_index(ascending = [True, False, True]).head()
```

Out [27]

Category			Culture		Services	
Subcategory			Restaurants	Museums	Police	Schools
State	City	Street				
AK	Stevenshire	238 Andrew Rue	D-	A	A-	A-
	Scottstad	082 Leblanc ...	D	C-	D	B+
		114 Jones Ga...	D-	D-	D	D
	Rowlandchester	386 Rebecca ...	C-	A-	A+	C
AL	Vegaside	191 Mindy Me...	B+	A-	A+	D+

We can also sort a MultiIndex level by itself. Let's say we want to sort the rows by the values in the second MultiIndex level, City. We can pass the level's index position or its name to the level parameter of the sort_index method. Pandas will ignore the remaining levels when sorting:

```
In  [28] # The two lines below are equivalent
         neighborhoods.sort_index(level = 1)
         neighborhoods.sort_index(level = "City")
```

Out [28]

Category			Culture		Services	
Subcategory			Restaurants	Museums	Police	Schools
State	City	Street				
AR	Allisonland	124 Diaz Brooks	C-	A+	F	C+
GA	Amyburgh	941 Brian Ex...	B	B	D-	C+
IA	Amyburgh	163 Heather ...	F	D	A+	A-
ID	Andrewshire	952 Ellis Drive	C+	A-	C+	A
UT	Baileyfort	919 Stewart ...	D+	C+	A	C
...	...	...	...	...	...	...
NC	West Scott	348 Jack Branch	A-	D-	A-	A

			C+	A-	D+	B-
SD	West Scott	139 Hardy Vista	C+	A-	D+	B-
IN	Wilsonborough	066 Carr Road	A+	C-	B	F
NC	Wilsonshire	871 Christop...	B+	B	D+	F
NV	Wilsonshire	542 Jessica ...	A	A+	C-	C+

251 rows × 4 columns

The `level` parameter also accepts a list of levels. The next example sorts the City level's values first, followed by the Street level's values. The State level's values do not influence the sort at all:

```
In  [29] # The two lines below are equivalent
         neighborhoods.sort_index(level = [1, 2]).head()
         neighborhoods.sort_index(level = ["City", "Street"]).head()
```

Out [29]

Category			Culture		Services	
Subcategory			Restaurants	Museums	Police	Schools
State	City	Street				
AR	Allisonland	124 Diaz Brooks	C-	A+	F	C+
IA	Amyburgh	163 Heather ...	F	D	A+	A-
GA	Amyburgh	941 Brian Ex...	B	B	D-	C+
ID	Andrewshire	952 Ellis Drive	C+	A-	C+	A
VT	Baileyfort	831 Norma Cove	B	D+	A+	D+

We can also combine the `ascending` and `level` parameters. Notice in the preceding example that pandas sorted the two Street values for the city of Amyburgh (`"163 Heather Neck"` and `"941 Brian Expressway"`) in alphabetical/ascending order. The next example sorts the City level in ascending order and the Street level in descending order, thus swapping the positions of the two Amyburgh Street values:

```
In  [30] neighborhoods.sort_index(
             level = ["City", "Street"], ascending = [True, False]
         ).head()
```

Out [30]

Category			Culture		Services	
Subcategory			Restaurants	Museums	Police	Schools
State	City	Street				
AR	Allisonland	124 Diaz Brooks	C-	A+	F	C+
GA	Amyburgh	941 Brian Ex...	B	B	D-	C+
IA	Amyburgh	163 Heather ...	F	D	A+	A-
ID	Andrewshire	952 Ellis Drive	C+	A-	C+	A
UT	Baileyfort	919 Stewart ...	D+	C+	A	C

We can sort the columns' `MultiIndex` as well by supplying an `axis` parameter to the `sort_index` method. The parameter's default argument is 0, which represents the row index. To sort the columns, we can pass either the number 1 or the string `"columns"`. In the next example, pandas sorts the Category level first and the Subcategory level second. The value Culture comes before Services. Within the Culture level, the value Museums comes before Restaurants. Within Services, the value Police comes before Schools:

```
In  [31] # The two lines below are equivalent
         neighborhoods.sort_index(axis = 1).head(3)
         neighborhoods.sort_index(axis = "columns").head(3)

Out [31]
```

Category			Culture		Services	
Subcategory			Museums	Restaurants	Police	Schools
State	City	Street				
MO	Fisherborough	244 Tracy View	F	C+	D-	A+
SD	Port Curtisv...	446 Cynthia ...	B	C-	B	D+
WV	Jimenezview	432 John Common	A+	A	F	B

We can combine the level and ascending parameters with the axis parameter to further customize the columns' sort orders. The next example sorts the Subcategory level values in descending order. Pandas ignores the values in the Category level. The reverse alphabetical order of the subcategories ("Schools", "Restaurants", "Police", and "Museums") forces a visual breakup of the Category group. Thus, the output prints the Services and Culture column headers multiple times:

```
In  [32] neighborhoods.sort_index(
             axis = 1, level = "Subcategory", ascending = False
         ).head(3)

Out [32]
```

Category			Services	Culture	Services	Culture
Subcategory			Schools	Restaurants	Police	Museums
State	City	Street				
MO	Fisherborough	244 Tracy View	A+	C+	D-	F
SD	Port Curtisv...	446 Cynthia ...	D+	C-	B	B
WV	Jimenezview	432 John Common	B	A	F	A+

In section 7.4, we'll learn how to extract rows and columns from a MultiIndex DataFrame with familiar accessor attributes such as loc and iloc. As mentioned earlier, it's optimal to sort our index before we look up any row. Let's sort the Multi-Index levels in ascending order and overwrite our neighborhoods DataFrame:

```
In  [33] neighborhoods = neighborhoods.sort_index(ascending = True)
```

Here's the result:

```
In  [34] neighborhoods.head(3)

Out [34]
```

Category			Culture		Services	
Subcategory			Restaurants	Museums	Police	Schools
State	City	Street				
AK	Rowlandchester	386 Rebecca ...	C-	A-	A+	C
	Scottstad	082 Leblanc ...	D	C-	D	B+
		114 Jones Ga...	D-	D-	D	D

Looks good. We've sorted each level in the `MultiIndex` and are clear to proceed.

7.4 Selecting with a MultiIndex

Extracting `DataFrame` rows and columns gets tricky when multiple levels are involved. The key question to ask before writing any code is what we want to pull out.

Chapter 4 introduced the square-bracket syntax for selecting a column from a `DataFrame`. Here's a quick reminder. The following code creates a `DataFrame` with two rows and two columns:

```
In  [35] data = [
            [1, 2],
            [3, 4]
        ]

        df = pd.DataFrame(
            data = data, index = ["A", "B"], columns = ["X", "Y"]
        )

        df

Out [35]
```

	X	Y
A	1	2
B	3	4

The square-bracket syntax extracts a column from the `DataFrame` as a `Series`:

```
In  [36] df["X"]

Out [36] A    1
         B    3
         Name: X, dtype: int64
```

Suppose that we want to pull out a column from neighborhoods. Each of the four columns in the `DataFrame` requires a combination of two identifiers: a Category and a Subcategory. What happens if we pass only one?

7.4.1 Extracting one or more columns

If we pass a single value in square brackets, pandas will look for it in the outermost level of the columns' `MultiIndex`. The following example searches for `"Services"`, which is a valid value in the Category level:

```
In  [37] neighborhoods["Services"]

Out [37]
```

Subcategory			Police	Schools
State	City	Street		
AK	Rowlandchester	386 Rebecca Cove	A+	C
	Scottstad	082 Leblanc Freeway	D	B+
		114 Jones Garden	D	D
	Stevenshire	238 Andrew Rue	A-	A-

```
AL      Clarkland       430 Douglas Mission       C+      B+
...                ...  ...                 ...    ...     ...
WY      Lake Nicole     754 Weaver Turnpike       B       D
                        933 Jennifer Burg         A-      C
        Martintown      013 Bell Mills            A-      B-
        Port Jason      624 Faulkner Orchard      C+      C+
        Reneeshire      717 Patel Square          D       A
```

251 rows × 2 columns

Notice that the new `DataFrame` does not have a Category level. It has a plain `Index` with two values: `"Police"` and `"Schools"`. There is no longer a need for a `MultiIndex`; the two columns in this `DataFrame` are the subcategories that fall under the Services value. The Category level no longer has any variation that merits listing.

Pandas will raise a `KeyError` exception if the value does not exist in the outermost level of the columns' `MultiIndex`:

```
In  [38] neighborhoods["Schools"]
```

```
---------------------------------------------------------------------

KeyError                             Traceback (most recent call last)

KeyError: 'Schools'
```

What if we want to target a specific Category and then a Subcategory within it? To specify values across multiple levels in the column's `MultiIndex`, we can pass them inside a tuple. The next example targets the column with a value of `"Services"` in the Category level and a value of `"Schools"` in the Subcategory level:

```
In  [39] neighborhoods[("Services", "Schools")]
```

```
Out [39] State  City
         AK     Rowlandchester  386 Rebecca Cove         C
                Scottstad       082 Leblanc Freeway      B+
                                114 Jones Garden         D
                Stevenshire     238 Andrew Rue           A-
         AL     Clarkland       430 Douglas Mission      B+
                                                         ..
         WY     Lake Nicole     754 Weaver Turnpike      D
                                933 Jennifer Burg        C
                Martintown      013 Bell Mills           B-
                Port Jason      624 Faulkner Orchard     C+
                Reneeshire      717 Patel Square         A
         Name: (Services, Schools), Length: 251, dtype: object
```

The method returns a `Series` without a column index! Once again, when we provide a value for a `MultiIndex` level, we remove the need for that level to exist. We explicitly told pandas what values to target in the Category and Subcategory levels, so the library removed the two levels from the column index. Because the `("Services", "Schools")` combination yielded a single column of data, pandas returned a `Series` object.

To extract multiple `DataFrame` columns, we need to pass the square brackets a list of tuples. Each tuple should specify the level values for one column. The order of tuples within the list sets the order of columns in the resulting `DataFrame`. The next example pulls out two columns from neighborhoods:

```
In  [40] neighborhoods[[("Services", "Schools"), ("Culture", "Museums")]]
```

```
Out [40]
```

Category			Services	Culture
Subcategory			Schools	Museums
State	City	Street		
AK	Rowlandchester	386 Rebecca Cove	C	A-
	Scottstad	082 Leblanc Freeway	B+	C-
		114 Jones Garden	D	D-
	Stevenshire	238 Andrew Rue	A-	A
AL	Clarkland	430 Douglas Mission	B+	F
...	...	...	...	...
WY	Lake Nicole	754 Weaver Turnpike	D	D-
		933 Jennifer Burg	C	A+
	Martintown	013 Bell Mills	B-	D
	Port Jason	624 Faulkner Orchard	C+	F
	Reneeshire	717 Patel Square	A	B+

251 rows × 2 columns

Syntax tends to become confusing and error-prone when it involves multiple parentheses and brackets. We can simplify the preceding code by assigning the list to a variable and breaking its tuples across several lines:

```
In  [41] columns = [
            ("Services", "Schools"),
            ("Culture", "Museums")
         ]

         neighborhoods[columns]
```

```
Out [41]
```

Category			Services	Culture
Subcategory			Schools	Museums
State	City	Street		
AK	Rowlandchester	386 Rebecca Cove	C	A-
	Scottstad	082 Leblanc Freeway	B+	C-
		114 Jones Garden	D	D-
	Stevenshire	238 Andrew Rue	A-	A
AL	Clarkland	430 Douglas Mission	B+	F
...	...	...	...	...
WY	Lake Nicole	754 Weaver Turnpike	D	D-
		933 Jennifer Burg	C	A+
	Martintown	013 Bell Mills	B-	D
	Port Jason	624 Faulkner Orchard	C+	F
	Reneeshire	717 Patel Square	A	B+

251 rows × 2 columns

The previous two examples accomplish the same result, but this code is significantly easier to read; its syntax clearly identifies where each tuple begins and ends.

7.4.2   *Extracting one or more rows with loc*

Chapter 4 introduced the `loc` and `iloc` accessors for selecting rows and columns from a `DataFrame`. The `loc` accessor extracts by index label, and the `iloc` accessor extracts by index position. Here's a quick review, using the `df` DataFrame we declared in section 7.4.1:

```
In  [42] df

Out [42]

      X  Y

A     1  2
B     3  4
```

The next example uses `loc` to select the row with an index label of `"A"`:

```
In  [43] df.loc["A"]

Out [43] X    1
         Y    2
         Name: A, dtype: int64
```

The next example uses `iloc` to select the row at index position 1:

```
In  [44] df.iloc[1]

Out [44] X    3
         Y    4
         Name: B, dtype: int64
```

We can use the `loc` and `iloc` accessors to pull rows from a `MultiIndex` DataFrame. Let's start slow and work our way up.

The neighborhoods DataFrame's `MultiIndex` has three levels: State, City, and Address. If we know the values to target in each level, we can pass them in a tuple within the square brackets. When we provide a value for a level, we remove the need for the level to exist in the result. The next example provides `"TX"` for the State level, `"Kingchester"` for the City level, and `"534 Gordon Falls"` for the Address level. Pandas returns a `Series` object with an index constructed from the column headers in neighborhoods:

```
In  [45] neighborhoods.loc[("TX", "Kingchester", "534 Gordon Falls")]

Out [45] Category   Subcategory
         Culture    Restaurants    C
                    Museums        D+
         Services   Police         B
                    Schools        B
         Name: (TX, Kingchester, 534 Gordon Falls), dtype: object
```

If we pass a single label in the square brackets, pandas looks for it in the outermost `MultiIndex` level. The next example selects the rows with a State value of `"CA"`. State is the first level of the rows' `MultiIndex`:

```
In  [46] neighborhoods.loc["CA"]
```

```
Out [46]
```

Category		Culture		Services	
Subcategory		Restaurants	Museums	Police	Schools
City	Street				
Dustinmouth	793 Cynthia ...	A-	A+	C-	A
North Jennifer	303 Alisha Road	D-	C+	C+	A+
Ryanfort	934 David Run	F	B+	F	D-

Pandas returns a `DataFrame` with a two-level `MultiIndex`. Notice that the State level is not present. There is no longer a need for it because all three rows belong to that level; there is no longer any variation to display.

Usually, the second argument to the square brackets denotes the column(s) we'd like to extract, but we can also provide the value to look for in the next `MultiIndex` level. The next example targets rows with a State value of `"CA"` and a City value of `"Dustinmouth"`. Once again, pandas returns a `DataFrame` with one fewer level. Because only one level is left, pandas falls back to a plain `Index` object to store the row labels from the Street level:

```
In  [47] neighborhoods.loc["CA", "Dustinmouth"]
```

```
Out [47]
```

Category	Culture		Services	
Subcategory	Restaurants	Museums	Police	Schools
Street				
793 Cynthia Square	A-	A+	C-	A

We can still use the second argument to `loc` to declare the column(s) to extract. The next example extracts rows with a State value of `"CA"` in the row `MultiIndex` and a Category value of `"Culture"` in the column `MultiIndex`:

```
In  [48] neighborhoods.loc["CA", "Culture"]
```

```
Out [48]
```

Subcategory		Restaurants	Museums
City	Street		
Dustinmouth	793 Cynthia Square	A-	A+
North Jennifer	303 Alisha Road	D-	C+
Ryanfort	934 David Run	F	B+

The syntax in the previous two examples is not ideal because of its ambiguity. The second argument to `loc` can represent either a value from the second level of the rows' `MultiIndex` or a value from the first level of the columns' `MultiIndex`.

The pandas documentation[1] recommends the following indexing strategy to avoid uncertainty. Use the first argument to `loc` for row index labels and the second argument for column index labels. Wrap all arguments for a given index inside a tuple. Following this standard, we should place our row levels' values inside a tuple and our column levels' values inside a tuple as well. The recommended way to access rows with a State value of `"CA"` and a City value of `"Dustinmouth"` looks like this:

```
In  [49] neighborhoods.loc[("CA", "Dustinmouth")]

Out [49]
```

Category		Culture		Services	
Subcategory		Restaurants	Museums	Police	Schools
Street					
793 Cynthia Square		A-	A+	C-	A

This syntax is more straightforward and more consistent; it allows `loc`'s second argument to always represent the columns' index labels to target. The next example pulls out the Services columns for the same state of `"CA"` and city of `"Dustinmouth"`. We pass `"Services"` inside a tuple. A one-element tuple requires a comma for Python to recognize it as a tuple:

```
In  [50] neighborhoods.loc[("CA", "Dustinmouth"), ("Services",)]

Out [50]
```

Subcategory	Police	Schools
Street		
793 Cynthia Square	C-	A

Here's another helpful hint: pandas distinguishes between list and tuple arguments to accessors. Use a list to store multiple keys. Use a tuple to store the components of one multilevel key.

We can pass a tuple as the second argument to `loc` to provide values for levels in the columns' `MultiIndex`. The next example targets

- `"CA"` and `"Dustinmouth"` in the rows' `MultiIndex` levels
- `"Services"` and `"Schools"` in the columns' `MultiIndex` levels

The placement of `"Services"` and `"Schools"` in a single tuple tells pandas to view them as components that make up a single label. `"Services"` is the value for the Category level, and `"Schools"` is the value for the Subcategory level:

```
In  [51] neighborhoods.loc[("CA", "Dustinmouth"), ("Services", "Schools")]

Out [51] Street
         793 Cynthia Square    A
         Name: (Services, Schools), dtype: object
```

---

[1] See "Advanced indexing with hierarchical index," http://mng.bz/5WJO.

What about selecting sequential rows? We can use Python's list-slicing syntax. We place a colon between our starting point and our ending point. The next code sample pulls all consecutive rows with a State value between `"NE"` and `"NH"`. In pandas slicing, the endpoint (the value after the colon) is inclusive:

```
In  [52] neighborhoods["NE":"NH"]

Out [52]
```

Category Subcategory State City	Street	Culture Restaurants	Museums	Services Police	Schools
NE Barryborough	460 Anna Tunnel	A+	A+	B	A
Shawnchester	802 Cook Cliff	D-	D+	D	A
South Kennet...	346 Wallace ...	C-	B-	A	A-
South Nathan	821 Jake Fork	C+	D	D+	A
NH Courtneyfort	697 Spencer ...	A+	A+	C+	A+
East Deborah...	271 Ryan Mount	B	C	D+	B-
Ingramton	430 Calvin U...	C+	D+	C	C-
North Latoya	603 Clark Mount	D-	A-	B+	B-
South Tara	559 Michael ...	C-	C-	F	B

We can combine list-slicing syntax with tuple arguments. The next example extracts all rows that

- Start from a value of `"NE"` in the State level and `"Shawnchester"` in the City level
- End with a value of `"NH"` in the State level and `"North Latoya"` in the City level

```
In  [53] neighborhoods.loc[("NE", "Shawnchester"):("NH", "North Latoya")]

Out [53]
```

Category Subcategory State City	Street	Culture Restaurants	Museums	Services Police	Schools
NE Shawnchester	802 Cook Cliff	D-	D+	D	A
South Kennet...	346 Wallace ...	C-	B-	A	A-
South Nathan	821 Jake Fork	C+	D	D+	A
NH Courtneyfort	697 Spencer ...	A+	A+	C+	A+
East Deborah...	271 Ryan Mount	B	C	D+	B-
Ingramton	430 Calvin U...	C+	D+	C	C-
North Latoya	603 Clark Mount	D-	A-	B+	B-

Be careful with this syntax; a single missing parenthesis or comma can raise an exception. We can simplify the code by assigning the tuples to descriptive variables and breaking the extraction into smaller pieces. The next example returns the same result set but is significantly easier to read:

```
In  [54] start = ("NE", "Shawnchester")
         end   = ("NH", "North Latoya")
         neighborhoods.loc[start:end]

Out [54]
```

Category			Culture		Services	
Subcategory			Restaurants	Museums	Police	Schools
State	City	Street				
NE	Shawnchester	802 Cook Cliff	D-	D+	D	A
	South Kennet...	346 Wallace ...	C-	B-	A	A-
	South Nathan	821 Jake Fork	C+	D	D+	A
NH	Courtneyfort	697 Spencer ...	A+	A+	C+	A+
	East Deborah...	271 Ryan Mount	B	C	D+	B-
	Ingramton	430 Calvin U...	C+	D+	C	C-
	North Latoya	603 Clark Mount	D-	A-	B+	B-

We do not have to provide each tuple values for each level. The next example does not include a City-level value for the second tuple:

```
In  [55] neighborhoods.loc[("NE", "Shawnchester"):("NH")]
```

```
Out [55]
```

Category			Culture		Services	
Subcategory			Restaurants	Museums	Police	Schools
State	City	Street				
NE	Shawnchester	802 Cook Cliff	D-	D+	D	A
	South Kennet...	346 Wallace ...	C-	B-	A	A-
	South Nathan	821 Jake Fork	C+	D	D+	A
NH	Courtneyfort	697 Spencer ...	A+	A+	C+	A+
	East Deborah...	271 Ryan Mount	B	C	D+	B-
	Ingramton	430 Calvin U...	C+	D+	C	C-
	North Latoya	603 Clark Mount	D-	A-	B+	B-
	South Tara	559 Michael ...	C-	C-	F	B

Pandas pulls rows starting from ("NE", "Shawnchester") until it reaches the end of all rows with a State value of "NH".

7.4.3 *Extracting one or more rows with iloc*

The iloc accessor extracts rows and columns by index position. The following examples should be a refresher on concepts covered in chapter 4. We can pass an index position to iloc to extract a single row:

```
In  [56] neighborhoods.iloc[25]
```

```
Out [56] Category  Subcategory
         Culture   Restaurants   A+
                   Museums       A
         Services  Police        A+
                   Schools       C+
         Name: (CT, East Jessicaland, 208 Todd Knolls), dtype: object
```

We can pass two arguments to iloc to represent the row and column indices. The next example targets the row with index position 25 and the column with index position 2:

```
In  [57] neighborhoods.iloc[25, 2]
```

```
Out [57] 'A+'
```

We can pull out multiple rows by wrapping their index positions in a list:

```
In  [58] neighborhoods.iloc[[25, 30]]
```

Out [58]

Category			Culture		Services	
Subcategory			Restaurants	Museums	Police	Schools
State	City	Street				
CT	East Jessica...	208 Todd Knolls	A+	A	A+	C+
DC	East Lisaview	910 Sandy Ramp	A-	A+	B	B

There's a big difference between `loc` and `iloc` when it comes to slicing. When we're index slicing with `iloc`, the endpoint is exclusive. In the preceding example, the record with a street of `"910 Sandy Ramp"` has index position 30. When we provide 30 as the `iloc` endpoint in the next example, pandas pulls up to that index but does not include it:

```
In  [59] neighborhoods.iloc[25:30]
```

Out [59]

Category			Culture		Services	
Subcategory			Restaurants	Museums	Police	Schools
State	City	Street				
CT	East Jessica...	208 Todd Knolls	A+	A	A+	C+
	New Adrianhaven	048 Brian Cove	A-	C+	A+	D-
	Port Mike	410 Keith Lodge	D-	A	B+	D
	Sethstad	139 Bailey G...	C	C-	C+	A+
DC	East Jessica	149 Norman C...	A-	C-	C+	A-

Column slicing follows the same principles. The next example pulls the columns from index positions 1 to 3 (exclusive):

```
In  [60] neighborhoods.iloc[25:30, 1:3]
```

Out [60]

Category			Culture	Services
Subcategory			Museums	Police
State	City	Street		
CT	East Jessica...	208 Todd Knolls	A	A+
	New Adrianhaven	048 Brian Cove	C+	A+
	Port Mike	410 Keith Lodge	A	B+
	Sethstad	139 Bailey G...	C-	C+
DC	East Jessica	149 Norman C...	C-	C+

Pandas also permits negative slices. The next example pulls rows starting from the fourth-to-last row and the columns starting from the second-to-last column:

```
In  [61] neighborhoods.iloc[-4:, -2:]
```

Out [61]

Category			Services	
Subcategory			Police	Schools
State	City	Street		
WY	Lake Nicole	933 Jennifer...	A-	C
	Martintown	013 Bell Mills	A-	B-
	Port Jason	624 Faulkner...	C+	C+
	Reneeshire	717 Patel Sq...	D	A

Pandas assigns each `DataFrame` row an index position, not each value in a given index level. Thus, we cannot index across consecutive `MultiIndex` levels with `iloc`. This limitation is an intentional design decision by the pandas development team. As developer Jeff Reback states, `iloc` serves as a "strict positional indexer" that "does not regard the structure [of the `DataFrame`] at all."[2]

7.5   *Cross-sections*

The `xs` method allows us to extract rows by providing a value for *one* `MultiIndex` level. We pass the method a `key` parameter with the value to look for. We pass the `level` parameter either the numeric position or the name of the index level in which to look for the value. For example, let's say we wanted to find all addresses in a city of Lake Nicole, regardless of the state or street. City is the second level in the `Multi-Index`; it has an index position of 1 in the level hierarchy:

```
In  [62] # The two lines below are equivalent
         neighborhoods.xs(key = "Lake Nicole", level = 1)
         neighborhoods.xs(key = "Lake Nicole", level = "City")

Out [62]
```

Category		Culture		Services	
Subcategory		Restaurants	Museums	Police	Schools
State	Street				
OR	650 Angela Track	D	C-	D	F
WY	754 Weaver Turnpike	B	D-	B	D
	933 Jennifer Burg	C	A+	A-	C

There are three addresses in a city of `"Lake Nicole"` across two states. Notice that pandas removes the City level from the new `DataFrame`'s `MultiIndex`. The `City` value is fixed (`"Lake Nicole"`), so there is no need for pandas to include it.

We can apply the same extraction techniques to columns by passing the `axis` parameter an argument of `"columns"`. The next example selects the columns with a key of `"Museums"` in the Subcategory level of the column `MultiIndex`. Only one column fits that description:

```
In  [63] neighborhoods.xs(
             axis = "columns", key = "Museums", level = "Subcategory"
         ).head()

Out [63]
```

---

2 See Jeff Reback, "Inconsistent behavior of loc and iloc for MultiIndex," https://github.com/pandas-dev/pandas/issues/15228.

Category			Culture
State City		Street	
AK	Rowlandchester	386 Rebecca Cove	A-
	Scottstad	082 Leblanc Freeway	C-
		114 Jones Garden	D-
	Stevenshire	238 Andrew Rue	A
AL	Clarkland	430 Douglas Mission	F

Notice that the Subcategory level is not present in the returned `DataFrame`, but the Category level is still present. Pandas includes it because there is still potential for variation (such as multiple values) in the Category level. When we pull out values from an intermediate level, they can belong to multiple top-level labels.

We can also provide the `xs` method with keys across nonconsecutive `MultiIndex` levels. We pass them in a tuple. Suppose that we want the rows with a Street value of `"238 Andrew Rue"` and a State of `"AK"`, irrespective of the City value. That's not a problem with `xs`:

```
In  [64] # The two lines below are equivalent
        neighborhoods.xs(
            key = ("AK", "238 Andrew Rue"), level = ["State", "Street"]
        )

        neighborhoods.xs(
            key = ("AK", "238 Andrew Rue"), level = [0, 2]
        )

Out [64]
```

Category	Culture		Services	
Subcategory	Restaurants	Museums	Police	Schools
City				
Stevenshire	D-	A	A-	A-

The ability to target values in only one level is a powerful feature of `MultiIndexes`.

7.6   *Manipulating the Index*

At the start of the chapter, we contorted our neighborhoods data set into its current shape by altering the parameters to the `read_csv` function. Pandas also allows us to manipulate the index on an existing `DataFrame`. Let's take a look.

7.6.1   *Resetting the index*

The neighborhoods `DataFrame` currently has State as its outermost `MultiIndex` level, followed by City and Street:

```
In  [65] neighborhoods.head()

Out [65]
```

Category			Culture		Services	
Subcategory			Restaurants	Museums	Police	Schools
State City		Street				
AK	Rowlandchester	386 Rebecca Cove	C-	A-	A+	C
	Scottstad	082 Leblanc Fr...	D	C-	D	B+
		114 Jones Garden	D-	D-	D	D

	Stevenshire	238 Andrew Rue		D-	A	A-	A-
AL	Clarkland	430 Douglas Mi...		A	F	C+	B+

The `reorder_levels` method arranges the `MultiIndex` levels in a specified order. We pass its `order` parameter a list of levels in a desired order. The next example swaps the positions of the City and State levels:

```
In  [66] new_order = ["City", "State", "Street"]
         neighborhoods.reorder_levels(order = new_order).head()
```

Out [66]

Category			Culture		Services	
Subcategory			Restaurants	Museums	Police	Schools
City	State	Street				
Rowlandchester	AK	386 Rebecca ...	C-	A-	A+	C
Scottstad	AK	082 Leblanc ...	D	C-	D	B+
		114 Jones Ga...	D-	D-	D	D
Stevenshire	AK	238 Andrew Rue	D-	A	A-	A-
Clarkland	AL	430 Douglas ...	A	F	C+	B+

We can also pass the `order` parameter a list of integers. The numbers must represent the current index positions of the `MultiIndex` levels. If we want State to be the first level in the new `MultiIndex`, for example, we have to start the list with 1—the State level's index position in the current `MultiIndex`. The next code sample returns the same result as the preceding one:

```
In  [67] neighborhoods.reorder_levels(order = [1, 0, 2]).head()
```

Out [67]

Category			Culture		Services	
Subcategory			Restaurants	Museums	Police	Schools
City	State	Street				
Rowlandchester	AK	386 Rebecca ...	C-	A-	A+	C
Scottstad	AK	082 Leblanc ...	D	C-	D	B+
		114 Jones Ga...	D-	D-	D	D
Stevenshire	AK	238 Andrew Rue	D-	A	A-	A-
Clarkland	AL	430 Douglas ...	A	F	C+	B+

What if we want to get rid of the index? Perhaps we want to set a different combination of columns as the index labels. The `reset_index` method returns a new Data-Frame that integrates the former `MultiIndex` levels as columns. Pandas replaces the former `MultiIndex` with its standard numeric one:

```
In  [68] neighborhoods.reset_index().tail()
```

Out [68]

Category	State	City	Street	Culture		Services	
Subcategory				Restaurants	Museums	Police	Schools
246	WY	Lake...	754 ...	B	D-	B	D
247	WY	Lake...	933 ...	C	A+	A-	C
248	WY	Mart...	013 ...	C-	D	A-	B-

| 249 | | WY | Port... | 624 ... | | A- | | F | C+ | C+ |
| 250 | | WY | Rene... | 717 ... | | B | | B+ | D | A |

Notice that the three new columns (State, City, and Street) become values in Category, the outermost level of the columns' `MultiIndex`. To ensure consistency among columns (making each one a tuple of two values), pandas assigns the three new columns a Subcategory value of an empty string.

We can add the three columns to an alternate `MultiIndex` level. Pass the desired level's index position or name to the `reset_index` method's `col_level` parameter. The next example integrates the State, City, and Street columns into the Subcategory level of the columns' `MultiIndex`:

```
In  [69] # The two lines below are equivalent
        neighborhoods.reset_index(col_level = 1).tail()
        neighborhoods.reset_index(col_level = "Subcategory").tail()
```

Out [69]

Category					Culture		Services		
Subcategory	State	City	Street	Restaurants	Museums		Police	Schools	
246	WY	Lake...	754 ...	B	D-		B	D
247	WY	Lake...	933 ...	C	A+		A-	C
248	WY	Mart...	013 ...	C-	D		A-	B-
249	WY	Port...	624 ...	A-	F		C+	C+
250	WY	Rene...	717 ...	B	B+		D	A

Now pandas will default to an empty string for Category, the parent level that holds the Subcategory level under which State, City, and Street fall. We can replace the empty string with a value of our choice by passing an argument to the `col_fill` parameter. In the next example, we group the three new columns under an Address parent level. Now the outer Category level holds the three distinct values Address, Culture, and Services:

```
In  [70] neighborhoods.reset_index(
            col_fill = "Address", col_level = "Subcategory"
        ).tail()
```

Out [70]

Category	Address				Culture		Services		
Subcategory	State	City	Street	Restaurants	Museums		Police	Schools	
246	WY	Lake...	754 ...	B	D-		B	D
247	WY	Lake...	933 ...	C	A+		A-	C
248	WY	Mart...	013 ...	C-	D		A-	B-
249	WY	Port...	624 ...	A-	F		C+	C+
250	WY	Rene...	717 ...	B	B+		D	A

The standard invocation of `reset_index` transforms all index levels into regular columns. We can also move a single index level by passing its name to the `levels` parameter. The next example moves the Street level from the `MultiIndex` to a regular `DataFrame` column:

```
In  [71] neighborhoods.reset_index(level = "Street").tail()
```

Out [71]

| Category | | Street | Culture | | Services | |
| Subcategory | | | Restaurants | Museums | Police | Schools |
State	City					
WY	Lake Nicole	754 Weaver Tur...	B	D-	B	D
	Lake Nicole	933 Jennifer Burg	C	A+	A-	C
	Martintown	013 Bell Mills	C-	D	A-	B-
	Port Jason	624 Faulkner O...	A-	F	C+	C+
	Reneeshire	717 Patel Square	B	B+	D	A

We can move multiple index levels by passing them in a list:

```
In  [72] neighborhoods.reset_index(level = ["Street", "City"]).tail()
```

Out [72]

| Category | | City | Street | Culture | | Services | |
| Subcategory | | | | Restaurants | Museums | Police | Schools |
State							
WY		Lake Nicole	754 Weav...	B	D-	B	D
WY		Lake Nicole	933 Jenn...	C	A+	A-	C
WY		Martintown	013 Bell...	C-	D	A-	B-
WY		Port Jason	624 Faul...	A-	F	C+	C+
WY		Reneeshire	717 Pate...	B	B+	D	A

What about removing a level from the MultiIndex? If we pass the reset_index method's drop parameter a value of True, pandas will delete the specified level instead of adding it to the columns. The next reset_index example removes the Street level:

```
In  [73] neighborhoods.reset_index(level = "Street", drop = True).tail()
```

Out [73]

| Category | | Culture | | Services | |
| Subcategory | | Restaurants | Museums | Police | Schools |
State	City				
WY	Lake Nicole	B	D-	B	D
	Lake Nicole	C	A+	A-	C
	Martintown	C-	D	A-	B-
	Port Jason	A-	F	C+	C+
	Reneeshire	B	B+	D	A

To set ourselves up for section 7.6.2, let's make our index reset permanent by overwriting the neighborhoods variable with the new DataFrame. This operation moves all three index levels to columns in the DataFrame:

```
In  [74] neighborhoods = neighborhoods.reset_index()
```

Now we have seven columns in neighborhoods with a `MultiIndex` on only the column axis.

7.6.2 *Setting the index*

Let's check in on our `DataFrame` to jog our memory:

```
In  [75] neighborhoods.head(3)

Out [75]
```

Category Subcategory	State	City	Street	Culture Restaurants	Museums	Services Police	Schools
0	AK	Rowl...	386 ...	C-	A-	A+	C
1	AK	Scot...	082 ...	D	C-	D	B+
2	AK	Scot...	114 ...	D-	D-	D	D

The `set_index` method sets one or more `DataFrame` columns as the new index. We can pass the column(s) to use to its `keys` parameter:

```
In  [76] neighborhoods.set_index(keys = "City").head()

Out [76]
```

Category Subcategory City	State	Street	Culture Restaurants	Museums	Services Police	Schools
Rowlandchester	AK	386 Rebecca...	C-	A-	A+	C
Scottstad	AK	082 Leblanc...	D	C-	D	B+
Scottstad	AK	114 Jones G...	D-	D-	D	D
Stevenshire	AK	238 Andrew Rue	D-	A	A-	A-
Clarkland	AL	430 Douglas...	A	F	C+	B+

What if we want one of the last four columns to serve as the index?. The next example passes the `keys` parameter a tuple with the values to target at each `MultiIndex` level:

```
In  [77] neighborhoods.set_index(keys = ("Culture", "Museums")).head()

Out [77]
```

Category Subcategory (Cultur...	State	City	Street	Culture Restaurants	Services Police	Schools
A-	AK	Rowlan...	386 Re...	C-	A+	C
C-	AK	Scottstad	082 Le...	D	D	B+
D-	AK	Scottstad	114 Jo...	D-	D	D
A	AK	Steven...	238 An...	D-	A-	A-
F	AL	Clarkland	430 Do...	A	C+	B+

To create a `MultiIndex` on the row axis, we can pass a list with multiple columns to the `keys` parameter:

```
In  [78] neighborhoods.set_index(keys = ["State", "City"]).head()

Out [78]
```

| Category | | Street | Culture | Services | |
| Subcategory | | Restaurants | Museums | Police | Schools |
State City					
AK	Rowlandchester	386 Rebecca...	C-	A-	A+	C
	Scottstad	082 Leblanc...	D	C-	D	B+
	Scottstad	114 Jones G...	D-	D-	D	D
	Stevenshire	238 Andrew Rue	D-	A	A-	A-
AL	Clarkland	430 Douglas...	A	F	C+	B+

As we've seen frequently in pandas, there are many permutations and combinations for shaping a data set for analysis. When defining a `DataFrame`'s indices, ask yourself which values matter most to your current problem. What is the key piece of information? Are several pieces of data intrinsically tied together? Which data points would you like to store as rows versus columns? Do rows or columns comprise a group or category? For many of these problems, a `MultiIndex` can provide an effective solution for storing your data.

7.7   *Coding challenge*

Here's your chance to practice the concepts introduced in this chapter.

7.7.1   *Problems*

The investments.csv data set holds more than 27,000 records of startup investments gathered from the website Crunchbase. Each startup has a Name, a Market, a Status, a State of operation, and a number of Funding Rounds:

```
In  [79] investments = pd.read_csv("investments.csv")
         investments.head()
```

Out [79]

	Name	Market	Status	State	Funding Rounds
0	#waywire	News	Acquired	NY	1
1	&TV Communications	Games	Operating	CA	2
2	-R- Ranch and Mine	Tourism	Operating	TX	2
3	004 Technologies	Software	Operating	IL	1
4	1-4 All	Software	Operating	NC	1

Let's add a `MultiIndex` to this `DataFrame`. We can begin by identifying the number of unique values in each column with the `nunique` method. Columns with a small number of unique items usually represent categorical data and are good candidates for index levels:

```
In  [80] investments.nunique()
```

```
Out [80] Name              27763
         Market              693
         Status                3
         State                61
         Funding Rounds       16
         dtype: int64
```

Let's create a three-level `MultiIndex` with the Status, Funding Rounds, and State columns. We'll order the columns so that the ones with the smallest number of values come first. The fewer unique values in a level, the quicker pandas can extract its rows. We'll also sort the `DataFrame` index to accelerate lookup time:

```
In  [81] investments = investments.set_index(
            keys = ["Status", "Funding Rounds", "State"]
        ).sort_index()
```

Here's what investments currently looks like:

```
In  [82] investments.head()

Out [82]
```

Status	Funding Rounds	State	Name	Market
Acquired	1	AB	Hallpass Media	Games
		AL	EnteGreat	Enterprise Soft...
		AL	Onward Behaviora...	Biotechnology
		AL	Proxsys	Biotechnology
		AZ	Envox Group	Public Relations

Here are the challenges for this section:

1. Extract all rows with a Status of `"Closed"`.
2. Extract all rows with a Status of `"Acquired"` and 10 funding rounds.
3. Extract all rows with a Status of `"Operating"`, six funding rounds, and a State of `"NJ"`.
4. Extract all rows with a Status of `"Closed"` and eight funding rounds. Pull out only the Name column.
5. Extract all rows with a State of `"NJ"`, irrespective of the values in the Status and Funding Rounds levels.
6. Reincorporate the `MultiIndex` levels back into the `DataFrame` as columns.

7.7.2 Solutions

Let's tackle the problems one by one:

1. To extract all rows with a Status of `"Closed"`, we can use the `loc` accessor. We'll pass a tuple with a single value of `"Closed"`. Remember that a one-element tuple requires a comma:

```
In  [83] investments.loc[("Closed",)].head()

Out [83]
```

Funding Rounds	State	Name	Market
1	AB	Cardinal Media Technologies	Social Network Media
	AB	Easy Bill Online	Tracking
	AB	Globel Direct	Public Relations
	AB	Ph03nix New Media	Games
	AL	Naubo	News

2 Next, we need to pull out rows that fit two conditions: a Status value of
"Acquired" and a Funding Rounds value of 10. These are sequential levels in
the MultiIndex. We can pass a tuple with the proper values to the loc accessor:

```
In  [84] investments.loc[("Acquired", 10)]

Out [84]
```

State	Name	Market
NY	Genesis Networks	Web Hosting
TX	ACTIVE Network	Software

3 We can use the same solution that we used for the preceding two problems.
This time around, we need to provide a tuple of three values, one for each MultiIndex level:

```
In  [85] investments.loc[("Operating", 6, "NJ")]

Out [85]
```

Status	Funding Rounds	State	Name	Market
Operating	6	NJ	Agile Therapeutics	Biotechnology
		NJ	Agilence	Retail Technology
		NJ	Edge Therapeutics	Biotechnology
		NJ	Nistica	Web Hosting

4 To extract DataFrame columns, we can pass a second argument to the loc
accessor. For this problem, we'll pass a one-element tuple with the Name column. The first argument still holds the values for the Status and Funding
Rounds levels:

```
In  [86] investments.loc[("Closed", 8), ("Name",)]

Out [86]
```

State	Name
CA	CipherMax
CA	Dilithium Networks
CA	Moblyng
CA	SolFocus
CA	Solyndra
FL	Extreme Enterprises
GA	MedShape
NC	Biolex Therapeutics
WA	Cozi Group

5 The next challenge asks us to extract rows with a value of "NJ" in the State
level. We can use the xs method, passing either the level's index position or the
level's name to the level parameter:

```
In  [87] # The two lines below are equivalent
         investments.xs(key = "NJ", level = 2).head()
         investments.xs(key = "NJ", level = "State").head()
```

Out [87]

Status	Funding Rounds	Name	Market
Acquired	1	AkaRx	Biotechnology
	1	Aptalis Pharma	Biotechnology
	1	Cadent	Software
	1	Cancer Genetics	Health And Wellness
	1	Clacendix	E-Commerce

6 Finally, we want to add the `MultiIndex` levels back to the `DataFrame` as columns. We'll invoke the `reset_index` method to reincorporate the index levels and overwrite the `investments` DataFrame to make the change permanent:

```
In  [88] investments = investments.reset_index()
         investments.head()
```

Out [88]

	Status	Funding Rounds	State	Name	Market
0	Acquired	1	AB	Hallpass Media	Games
1	Acquired	1	AL	EnteGreat	Enterprise Software
2	Acquired	1	AL	Onward Behaviora...	Biotechnology
3	Acquired	1	AL	Proxsys	Biotechnology
4	Acquired	1	AZ	Envox Group	Public Relations

Congratulations on completing the coding challenge!

Summary

- A `MultiIndex` is an index made of multiple levels.
- A `MultiIndex` uses tuples of values to store its labels.
- A `DataFrame` can store a `MultiIndex` on both its row and column axis.
- The `sort_index` method sorts `MultiIndex` levels. Pandas can sort index levels individually or as a group.
- The label-based `loc` and the position-based `iloc` accessors require additional arguments to extract the proper combination of rows and columns.
- Pass tuples to the `loc` and `iloc` accessors to avoid ambiguity.
- The `reset_index` method integrates index levels as `DataFrame` columns.
- Pass the `set_index` method a list of columns to build a `MultiIndex` from existing `DataFrame` columns.

Reshaping and pivoting 8

This chapter covers

- Comparing wide and narrow data
- Generating a pivot table from a `DataFrame`
- Aggregating values by sum, average, count, and more
- Stacking and unstacking `DataFrame` index levels
- Melting a `DataFrame`

A data set can arrive in a format unsuited for the analysis that we'd like to perform on it. Sometimes, issues are confined to a specific column, row, or cell. A column may have the wrong data type, a row may have missing values, or a cell may have incorrect character casing. At other times, a data set may have larger structural problems that extend beyond the data. Perhaps the data set stores its values in a format that makes it easy to extract a single row but difficult to aggregate the data.

Reshaping a data set means manipulating it into a different shape, one that tells a story that could not be gleaned from its original presentation. Reshaping offers a new view or perspective on the data. This skill is critical; one study estimates that 80% of data analysis consists of cleaning up data and contorting it into the proper shape.[1]

In this chapter, we'll explore new pandas techniques for molding data sets into the shapes we desire. First, we'll look at how to summarize a larger data set in a concise pivot table. Then we'll proceed in the opposite direction, learning how to split an aggregated data set. By the end, you'll be a master of contorting data into whatever presentation best fits your analysis.

8.1 Wide vs. narrow data

Before we dive into more methods, let's talk briefly about data set structure. A data set can store its values in wide or narrow format. A *narrow* data set is also called a *long* or a *tall* data set. These names reflect the direction in which the data set expands as we add more values to it. A *wide* data set increases in width; it grows out. A narrow/long/tall data set increases in height; it grows down.

Take a peek at the following table, which measures temperatures in two cities over two days:

	Weekday	Miami	New York
0	Monday	100	65
1	Tuesday	105	70

Consider the *variables*, the measurements that vary. One might think that the only variables in this data set are the weekdays and the temperatures. But an additional variable is hiding in the column names: the city. This data set stores the same variable—temperature—across two columns instead of one. The Miami and New York headers do not describe the data their columns store—that is, `100` is not a type of `Miami` in the same way that `Monday` is a type of `Weekday`. The data set has hidden the varying cities variable by storing it in the column headers. We can categorize this table as being a wide data set. A wide data set expands horizontally.

Suppose that we introduced temperature measurements for two more cities. We would have to add two new columns for the same variable: the temperature. Notice the direction in which the data set expands. The data grows wider, not taller:

	Weekday	Miami	New York	Chicago	San Francisco
0	Monday	100	65	50	60
1	Tuesday	105	70	58	62

Is horizontal expansion a bad thing? Not necessarily. A wide data set is ideal for seeing the aggregate picture—the complete story. If what we care about is the temperatures on Monday and Tuesday, the data set is easy to read and understand. But the wide format has its share of disadvantages too. The data set becomes more difficult to work with as we add more columns. Suppose that we wrote code to calculate the average temperature across all days. Now the temperatures are stored across four columns. If

---

[1] See Hadley Wickham, "Tidy Data," *Journal of Statistical Software*, https://vita.had.co.nz/papers/tidy-data.pdf.

we added another city column, we'd have to alter our calculation logic to include it. The design is less flexible.

A narrow data set grows vertically. A narrow format makes it easier to manipulate existing data and to add new records. Each variable is isolated to a single column. Compare the first table in this section with the following table:

	Weekday	City	Temperature
0	Monday	Miami	100
1	Monday	New York	65
2	Tuesday	Miami	105
3	Tuesday	New York	70

To include temperatures for two more cities, we would add rows instead of columns. The data grows taller, not wider:

	Weekday	City	Temperature
0	Monday	Miami	100
1	Monday	New York	65
2	Monday	Chicago	50
3	Monday	San Francisco	60
4	Tuesday	Miami	105
5	Tuesday	New York	70
6	Tuesday	Chicago	58
7	Tuesday	San Francisco	62

Is it easier to locate the temperatures for cities on Monday? I would argue no because now the data is scattered across four rows. But it is easier to calculate the average temperature because we have isolated the temperature values to a single column. As we add more rows, the average calculation logic remains the same.

The optimal storage format for a data set depends on the insight we're trying to glean from it. Pandas offers tools to transform `DataFrames` from narrow formats to wide formats and vice versa. We'll learn how to apply both transformations throughout the rest of the chapter.

8.2   Creating a pivot table from a DataFrame

Our first data set, sales_by_employee.csv, is a list of business deals at a fictional company. Each row includes the sale's Date, the salesman's Name, the Customer, and the Revenue and Expenses from the deal:

```
In  [1] import pandas as pd

In  [2] pd.read_csv("sales_by_employee.csv").head()

Out [2]
```

	Date	Name	Customer	Revenue	Expenses
0	1/1/20	Oscar	Logistics XYZ	5250	531
1	1/1/20	Oscar	Money Corp.	4406	661
2	1/2/20	Oscar	PaperMaven	8661	1401
3	1/3/20	Oscar	PaperGenius	7075	906
4	1/4/20	Oscar	Paper Pound	2524	1767

For utility's sake, let's convert the strings in the Date column to datetime objects with the `read_csv` function's `parse_dates` parameter. After that change, this import looks good to go. We can assign the `DataFrame` to a `sales` variable:

```
In  [3] sales = pd.read_csv(
           "sales_by_employee.csv", parse_dates = ["Date"]
        )

        sales.tail()

Out [3]
```

	Date	Name	Customer	Revenue	Expenses
21	2020-01-01	Creed	Money Corp.	4430	548
22	2020-01-02	Creed	Average Paper Co.	8026	1906
23	2020-01-02	Creed	Average Paper Co.	5188	1768
24	2020-01-04	Creed	PaperMaven	3144	1314
25	2020-01-05	Creed	Money Corp.	938	1053

With our data set loaded, let's explore how we can aggregate its data with a pivot table.

8.2.1 The pivot_table method

A *pivot table* aggregates a column's values and groups the results by using other columns' values. The word *aggregate* describes a summary computation that involves multiple values. Example aggregations include average, sum, median, and count. A pivot table in pandas is similar to the Pivot Table feature in Microsoft Excel.

As always, an example proves to be most helpful, so let's tackle our first challenge. Multiple salesmen closed deals on the same date. In addition, the same salesmen closed multiple deals on the same date. What if we want to sum the revenue by date and see how much each salesman contributed to the daily totals?

We follow four steps to create a pivot table:

1. Select the column(s) whose values we want to aggregate.
2. Choose the aggregation operation to apply to the column(s).
3. Select the column(s) whose values will group the aggregated data into categories.
4. Determine whether to place the groups on the row axis, the column axis, or both axes.

Let's proceed one step at a time. First, we'll need to invoke the `pivot_table` method on our existing `sales` DataFrame. The method's `index` parameter accepts the column whose values will make up the pivot table's index labels. Pandas will use the unique values from that column to group the results.

The next example uses the Date column's values for the index labels of the pivot table. The Date column contains five unique dates. Pandas applies its default aggregation operation, an average, to all numeric columns in `sales` (Expenses and Revenue):

```
In  [4] sales.pivot_table(index = "Date")

Out [4]
```

	Expenses	Revenue
Date		
2020-01-01	637.500000	4293.500000
2020-01-02	1244.400000	7303.000000
2020-01-03	1313.666667	4865.833333
2020-01-04	1450.600000	3948.000000
2020-01-05	1196.250000	4834.750000

The method returns a regular `DataFrame` object. It may be a bit underwhelming, but this DataFrame is a pivot table! The table shows average expenses and average revenue organized by the five unique dates in the Date column.

We declare the aggregation function with the `aggfunc` parameter; its default argument is `"mean"`. The following code produces the same result as the preceding code:

```
In  [5] sales.pivot_table(index = "Date", aggfunc = "mean")

Out [5]
```

	Expenses	Revenue
Date		
2020-01-01	637.500000	4293.500000
2020-01-02	1244.400000	7303.000000
2020-01-03	1313.666667	4865.833333
2020-01-04	1450.600000	3948.000000
2020-01-05	1196.250000	4834.750000

We'll have to modify some method arguments to reach our original goal: a sum of each date's revenue organized by salesman. First, let's swap the `aggfunc` parameter's argument to `"sum"` to add the values in Expenses and Revenue:

```
In  [6] sales.pivot_table(index = "Date", aggfunc = "sum")

Out [6]
```

	Expenses	Revenue
Date		
2020-01-01	3825	25761
2020-01-02	6222	36515
2020-01-03	7882	29195
2020-01-04	7253	19740
2020-01-05	4785	19339

For now, we care only about summing the values in the Revenue column. The `values` parameter accepts the `DataFrame` column(s) that pandas will aggregate. To aggregate only one column's values, we can pass the parameter a string with the column name:

```
In  [7] sales.pivot_table(
            index = "Date", values = "Revenue", aggfunc = "sum"
        )
```

Out [7]

	Revenue
Date	
2020-01-01	25761
2020-01-02	36515
2020-01-03	29195
2020-01-04	19740
2020-01-05	19339

To aggregate values across multiple columns, we can pass `values` a list of columns.

We have a sum of revenue grouped by date. Our final step is communicating how much each salesman contributed to the daily total. One presentational view that seems to be optimal is placing each salesman's name in a separate column. In other words, we'd like to use the Name column's unique values as the column headers in the pivot table. Let's add a `columns` parameter to the method invocation and pass it an argument of `"Name"`:

```
In  [8] sales.pivot_table(
            index = "Date",
            columns = "Name",
            values = "Revenue",
            aggfunc = "sum"
        )
```

Out [8]

Name	Creed	Dwight	Jim	Michael	Oscar
Date					
2020-01-01	4430.0	2639.0	1864.0	7172.0	9656.0
2020-01-02	13214.0	NaN	8278.0	6362.0	8661.0
2020-01-03	NaN	11912.0	4226.0	5982.0	7075.0
2020-01-04	3144.0	NaN	6155.0	7917.0	2524.0
2020-01-05	938.0	7771.0	NaN	7837.0	2793.0

That's it! We have an aggregated sum of revenue organized by dates on the row axis and salesmen on the column axis. Notice the presence of NaNs in the data set. A NaN denotes that the salesman did not have a row in `sales` with a Revenue value for a given date. Dwight does not have any `sales` row with a Date value of 2020-01-02, for example. The pivot table needs the index label of 2020-01-02 to exist for the four salesmen who have a revenue value for that date. Pandas plugs in the missing holes with NaNs. The presence of NaN values also forces the coercion of integers into floating-point numbers.

We can use the `fill_value` parameter to replace all pivot table NaNs with a fixed value. Let's fill in the data gaps with zeroes:

```
In  [9] sales.pivot_table(
            index = "Date",
            columns = "Name",
            values = "Revenue",
            aggfunc = "sum",
            fill_value = 0
        )
```

Out [9]

Name Date	Creed	Dwight	Jim	Michael	Oscar
2020-01-01	4430	2639	1864	7172	9656
2020-01-02	13214	0	8278	6362	8661
2020-01-03	0	11912	4226	5982	7075
2020-01-04	3144	0	6155	7917	2524
2020-01-05	938	7771	0	7837	2793

We may also want to see the revenue subtotals for each combination of date and salesman. We can pass an argument of True to the margins parameter to add totals for
each row and column:

```
In  [10] sales.pivot_table(
             index = "Date",
             columns = "Name",
             values = "Revenue",
             aggfunc = "sum",
             fill_value = 0,
             margins = True
         )
```

Out [10]

Name Date	Creed	Dwight	Jim	Michael	Oscar	All
2020-01-01 00:00:00	4430	2639	1864	7172	9656	25761
2020-01-02 00:00:00	13214	0	8278	6362	8661	36515
2020-01-03 00:00:00	0	11912	4226	5982	7075	29195
2020-01-04 00:00:00	3144	0	6155	7917	2524	19740
2020-01-05 00:00:00	938	7771	0	7837	2793	19339
All	21726	22322	20523	35270	30709	130550

Notice that the inclusion of "All" in the row labels changes the visual representation
of the dates, which now include the hour, minute, and second. Pandas needs to support both dates and string index labels. A string is the only data type that can represent either a date or a text value. Thus, the library converts the index from a
DatetimeIndex for dates to a plain Index for strings. When converting a datetime
object to its string representation, pandas includes the time; it also assumes the start
of the day for a date without time.

   We can use the margins_name parameter to customize the subtotal labels. The
next example changes the labels from "All" to "Total":

```
In  [11] sales.pivot_table(
             index = "Date",
             columns = "Name",
             values = "Revenue",
             aggfunc = "sum",
             fill_value = 0,
             margins = True,
             margins_name = "Total"
         )
```

Out [11]

Name Date	Creed	Dwight	Jim	Michael	Oscar	Total
2020-01-01 00:00:00	4430	2639	1864	7172	9656	25761
2020-01-02 00:00:00	13214	0	8278	6362	8661	36515
2020-01-03 00:00:00	0	11912	4226	5982	7075	29195
2020-01-04 00:00:00	3144	0	6155	7917	2524	19740
2020-01-05 00:00:00	938	7771	0	7837	2793	19339
Total	21726	22322	20523	35270	30709	130550

Ideally, Excel users will feel right at home with these options.

8.2.2 *Additional options for pivot tables*

A pivot table supports a variety of aggregation operations. Suppose that we're interested in the number of business deals closed per day. We can pass aggfunc an argument of "count" to count the number of sales rows for each combination of date and employee:

```
In  [12] sales.pivot_table(
            index = "Date",
            columns = "Name",
            values = "Revenue",
            aggfunc = "count"
        )
```

Out [12]

Name Date	Creed	Dwight	Jim	Michael	Oscar
2020-01-01	1.0	1.0	1.0	1.0	2.0
2020-01-02	2.0	NaN	1.0	1.0	1.0
2020-01-03	NaN	3.0	1.0	1.0	1.0
2020-01-04	1.0	NaN	2.0	1.0	1.0
2020-01-05	1.0	1.0	NaN	1.0	1.0

Once again, a NaN value indicates that the salesman did not make a sale on a given day. Creed did not close a single sale on 2020-01-03, for example, whereas Dwight closed three. Some additional options for the aggfunc parameter are listed in the following table:

Argument	Description
max	The largest value in the grouping
min	The smallest value in the grouping
std	The standard deviation of the values in the grouping
median	The median (midpoint) of the values in the grouping
size	The number of values in the grouping (equivalent to count)

We can also pass a list of aggregation functions to the `pivot_table` function's `agg-func` parameter. The pivot table will create a `MultiIndex` on the column axis and store the aggregations in its outermost level. The next example aggregates both the sum of revenue by date and the count of revenue by date:

```
In  [13] sales.pivot_table(
             index = "Date",
             columns = "Name",
             values = "Revenue",
             aggfunc = ["sum", "count"],
             fill_value = 0
         )
```

Out [13]

	sum					count				
Name	Creed	Dwight	Jim	Michael	Oscar	Creed	Dwight	Jim	Michael	Oscar
Date										
2020-01-01	4430	2639	1864	7172	9656	1	1	1	1	2
2020-01-02	13214	0	8278	6362	8661	2	0	1	1	1
2020-01-03	0	11912	4226	5982	7075	0	3	1	1	1
2020-01-04	3144	0	6155	7917	2524	1	0	2	1	1
2020-01-05	938	7771	0	7837	2793	1	1	0	1	1

We can apply different aggregations to different columns by passing a dictionary to the `aggfunc` parameter. Use the dictionary's keys to identify `DataFrame` columns and the values to set the aggregation. The next example extracts the minimum revenue and the maximum expense for each combination of date and salesman:

```
In  [14] sales.pivot_table(
             index = "Date",
             columns = "Name",
             values = ["Revenue", "Expenses"],
             fill_value = 0,
             aggfunc = { "Revenue": "min", "Expenses": "max" }
         )
```

Out [14]

	Expenses					Revenue				
Name	Creed	Dwight	Jim	Michael	Oscar	Creed	Dwight	Jim	Michael	Oscar
Date										
20...	548	368	1305	412	531	4430	2639	1864	7172	5250
20...	1768	0	462	685	1401	8026	0	8278	6362	8661
20...	0	758	1923	1772	906	0	4951	4226	5982	7075
20...	1314	0	426	1857	1767	3144	0	3868	7917	2524
20...	1053	1475	0	1633	624	938	7771	0	7837	2793

We can also stack multiple groupings on a single axis by passing the `index` parameter a list of columns. The next example aggregates the sum of expenses by salesman and date on the row axis. Pandas return a `DataFrame` with a two-level `MultiIndex`:

```
In  [15] sales.pivot_table(
             index = ["Name", "Date"], values = "Revenue", aggfunc = "sum"
         ).head(10)
```

```
Out [15]
```

		Revenue
Name	**Date**	
Creed	2020-01-01	4430
	2020-01-02	13214
	2020-01-04	3144
	2020-01-05	938
Dwight	2020-01-01	2639
	2020-01-03	11912
	2020-01-05	7771
Jim	2020-01-01	1864
	2020-01-02	8278
	2020-01-03	4226

Switch the order of strings in the index list to rearrange the levels in the pivot table's
MultiIndex. The next example swaps the positions of Name and Date:

```
In  [16] sales.pivot_table(
             index = ["Date", "Name"], values = "Revenue", aggfunc = "sum"
         ).head(10)
```

```
Out [16]
```

		Revenue
Date	**Name**	
2020-01-01	Creed	4430
	Dwight	2639
	Jim	1864
	Michael	7172
	Oscar	9656
2020-01-02	Creed	13214
	Jim	8278
	Michael	6362
	Oscar	8661
2020-01-03	Dwight	11912

The pivot table first organizes and sorts the Date values, and then organizes and sorts
the Name values within each Date.

8.3 *Stacking and unstacking index levels*

Here's a reminder of what sales looks like currently:

```
In  [17] sales.head()
```

```
Out [17]
```

	Date	Name	Customer	Revenue	Expenses
0	2020-01-01	Oscar	Logistics XYZ	5250	531
1	2020-01-01	Oscar	Money Corp.	4406	661
2	2020-01-02	Oscar	PaperMaven	8661	1401
3	2020-01-03	Oscar	PaperGenius	7075	906
4	2020-01-04	Oscar	Paper Pound	2524	1767

Let's pivot sales to organize revenue by employee name and date. We'll place dates on the column axis and names on the row axis:

```
In  [18] by_name_and_date = sales.pivot_table(
             index = "Name",
             columns = "Date",
             values = "Revenue",
             aggfunc = "sum"
         )

         by_name_and_date.head(2)

Out [18]
```

Date Name	2020-01-01	2020-01-02	2020-01-03	2020-01-04	2020-01-05
Creed	4430.0	13214.0	NaN	3144.0	938.0
Dwight	2639.0	NaN	11912.0	NaN	7771.0

Sometimes, we may want to move an index level from one axis to another. This change offers a different presentation of the data, and we can decide which view we like better.

The `stack` method moves an index level from the column axis to the row axis. The next example moves the Date index level from the column axis to the row axis. Pandas creates a `MultiIndex` to store the two row levels: Name and Date. Because only one column of values remains, pandas returns a `Series`:

```
In  [19] by_name_and_date.stack().head(7)

Out [19]

Name    Date
Creed   2020-01-01      4430.0
        2020-01-02     13214.0
        2020-01-04      3144.0
        2020-01-05       938.0
Dwight  2020-01-01      2639.0
        2020-01-03     11912.0
        2020-01-05      7771.0
dtype: float64
```

Notice that the `DataFrame`'s NaNs are absent from the `Series`. Pandas kept cells with NaNs in the `by_name_and_date` pivot table to maintain the structural integrity of the rows and columns. The shape of this `MultiIndex Series` allows pandas to discard the NaN values.

The complementary `unstack` method moves an index level from the row axis to the column axis. Consider the following pivot table, which groups revenue by customer and salesman. The row axis has a two-level `MultiIndex`, and the column axis has a regular index:

```
In  [20] sales_by_customer = sales.pivot_table(
             index = ["Customer", "Name"],
             values = "Revenue",
```

```
        aggfunc = "sum"
    )

    sales_by_customer.head()
```

Out [20]

		Revenue
Customer	Name	
Average Paper Co.	Creed	13214
	Jim	2287
Best Paper Co.	Dwight	2703
	Michael	15754
Logistics XYZ	Dwight	9209

The unstack method moves the innermost level of the row index to the column index:

In [21] sales_by_customer.unstack()

Out [21]

	Revenue				
Name	Creed	Dwight	Jim	Michael	Oscar
Customer					
Average Paper Co.	13214.0	NaN	2287.0	NaN	NaN
Best Paper Co.	NaN	2703.0	NaN	15754.0	NaN
Logistics XYZ	NaN	9209.0	NaN	7172.0	5250.0
Money Corp.	5368.0	NaN	8278.0	NaN	4406.0
Paper Pound	NaN	7771.0	4226.0	NaN	5317.0
PaperGenius	NaN	2639.0	1864.0	12344.0	7075.0
PaperMaven	3144.0	NaN	3868.0	NaN	8661.0

In the new DataFrame, the column axis now has a two-level MultiIndex, and the row axis has a regular one-level index.

8.4   *Melting a data set*

A pivot table aggregates the values in a data set. In this section, we'll learn how to do the opposite: break an aggregated collection of data into an unaggregated one.

Let's apply our wide-versus-narrow framework to the sales DataFrame. Here's an effective strategy to figure out whether a data set is in narrow format: navigate across one row of values, and ask each cell whether its value is a single measurement of the variable that the column header is describing. Here's the first row of sales:

In [22] sales.head(1)

Out [22]

	Date	Name	Customer	Revenue	Expenses
0	2020-01-01	Oscar	Logistics XYZ	5250	531

In the previous example, "2020-01-01" is a Date, "Oscar" is a Name, "Logistics XYZ" is a Customer, 5250 is a Revenue amount, and 531 is an Expenses amount. The sales DataFrame is an example of a narrow data set. Each row value represents a single observation for a given variable. No variable repeats across multiple columns.

We often have to choose between flexibility and readability when manipulating data in a wide or narrow format. We could represent the last four columns (Name, Customer, Revenue, Expenses) as fields in a single Category column (following example), but there is no real benefit because the four variables are distinct and separate. It is harder to aggregate data when it is stored in a format like this one:

	Date	Category	Value
0	2020-01-01	Name	Oscar
1	2020-01-01	Customer	Logistics XYZ
2	2020-01-01	Revenue	5250
3	2020-01-01	Expenses	531

The next data set, video_game_sales.csv, is a listing of regional sales for more than 16,000 video games. Each row includes the game's name as well as the number of units sold (in millions) in the North America (NA), Europe (EU), Japan (JP), and other (Other) regions:

```
In  [23] video_game_sales = pd.read_csv("video_game_sales.csv")
         video_game_sales.head()

Out [23]
```

	Name	NA	EU	JP	Other
0	Wii Sports	41.49	29.02	3.77	8.46
1	Super Mario Bros.	29.08	3.58	6.81	0.77
2	Mario Kart Wii	15.85	12.88	3.79	3.31
3	Wii Sports Resort	15.75	11.01	3.28	2.96
4	Pokemon Red/Poke...	11.27	8.89	10.22	1.00

Once again, let's traverse a sample row and ask each cell whether it holds the correct piece of information. Here's the first row of video_game_sales:

```
In  [24] video_game_sales.head(1)

Out [24]
```

	Name	NA	EU	JP	Other
0	Wii Sports	41.49	29.02	3.77	8.46

The first cell is fine; `"Wii Sports"` is an example of a Name. The next four cells are problematic. 41.49 is not a type of NA or a measurement of NA. NA (North America) is not a variable whose values vary throughout its column. The NA column's real piece of variable data is the sales numbers. NA represents the region for those sales numbers—a separate and distinct variable.

Thus, video_game_sales stores its data in wide format. Four columns (NA, EU, JP, and Other) store the same data point: the number of units sold. If we added more regional sales columns, the data set would grow horizontally. If we can group multiple column headers in a common category, it is a hint that the data set is storing its data in wide format.

Suppose that we moved the values `"NA"`, `"EU"`, `"JP"`, and `"Other"` to a new Region column. Compare the preceding presentation with the following one:

	Name	Region	Sales
0	Wii Sports	NA	41.49
1	Wii Sports	EU	29.02
2	Wii Sports	JP	3.77
3	Wii Sports	Other	8.46

In a way, we are unpivoting the video_game_sales `DataFrame`. We are converting an aggregate, summary view of the data to one in which each column stores one variable piece of information.

Pandas melts a `DataFrame` with the `melt` method. (*Melting* is the process of converting a wide data set to a narrow one.) The method accepts two primary parameters:

- The `id_vars` parameter sets the identifier column, the column for which the wide data set aggregates data. Name is the identifier column in video_game_sales. The data set aggregates sales per video game.
- The `value_vars` parameter accepts the column(s) whose values pandas will melt and store in a new column.

Let's start simple, melting only the NA column's values. In the next example, pandas loops through each NA column value and assigns it to a separate row in a new `DataFrame`. The library stores the former column name (NA) in a new variable column:

```
In  [25] video_game_sales.melt(id_vars = "Name", value_vars = "NA").head()

Out [25]
```

	Name	variable	value
0	Wii Sports	NA	41.49
1	Super Mario Bros.	NA	29.08
2	Mario Kart Wii	NA	15.85
3	Wii Sports Resort	NA	15.75
4	Pokemon Red/Pokemon Blue	NA	11.27

Next, let's melt all four of the regional sales columns. The next code sample passes the `value_vars` parameter a list of the four regional sales columns from video_game_sales:

```
In  [26] regional_sales_columns = ["NA", "EU", "JP", "Other"]

         video_game_sales.melt(
             id_vars = "Name", value_vars = regional_sales_columns
         )

Out [26]
```

	Name	variable	value
0	Wii Sports	NA	41.49
1	Super Mario Bros.	NA	29.08
2	Mario Kart Wii	NA	15.85
3	Wii Sports Resort	NA	15.75
4	Pokemon Red/Pokemon Blue	NA	11.27
...	...	...	...
66259	Woody Woodpecker in Crazy Castle 5	Other	0.00
66260	Men in Black II: Alien Escape	Other	0.00

```
66261   SCORE International Baja 1000: The Official Game   Other   0.00
66262                                         Know How 2   Other   0.00
66263                                   Spirits & Spells   Other   0.00

66264 rows × 3 columns
```

The melt method returns a DataFrame with 66,264 rows! By comparison, video_game_sales has 16,566 rows. The new data set is four times longer because it has four rows of data for each row in video_games_sales. The data set stores

- 16,566 rows for each video game and its respective NA sales number
- 16,566 rows for each video game and its respective EU sales number
- 16,566 rows for each video game and its respective JP sales number
- 16,566 rows for each video game and its respective Other sales number

The variable column holds the four regional column names from video_game_sales. The value column holds the values from those four regional sales columns. In the previous output, the data tells us that the videogame "Woody Woodpecker in Crazy Castle 5" had a value of 0.00 in the Other column of video_game_sales.

We can customize the melted DataFrame's column names by passing arguments to the var_name and value_name parameters. The next example uses Region for the variable column and Sales for the value column:

```
In  [27] video_game_sales_by_region = video_game_sales.melt(
            id_vars = "Name",
            value_vars = regional_sales_columns,
            var_name = "Region",
            value_name = "Sales"
        )

        video_game_sales_by_region.head()

Out [27]
```

	Name	Region	Sales
0	Wii Sports	NA	41.49
1	Super Mario Bros.	NA	29.08
2	Mario Kart Wii	NA	15.85
3	Wii Sports Resort	NA	15.75
4	Pokemon Red/Pokemon Blue	NA	11.27

Narrow data is easier to aggregate than wide data. Let's say we want to find the sum of each video game's sales across all regions. Given the melted data set, we can use the pivot_table method to accomplish this task with a few lines of code:

```
In  [28] video_game_sales_by_region.pivot_table(
            index = "Name", values = "Sales", aggfunc = "sum"
        ).head()

Out [28]
```

	Sales
Name	
'98 Koshien	0.40
.hack//G.U. Vol.1//Rebirth	0.17
.hack//G.U. Vol.2//Reminisce	0.23
.hack//G.U. Vol.3//Redemption	0.17
.hack//Infection Part 1	1.26

The data set's narrow shape simplified the process of pivoting it.

8.5 *Exploding a list of values*

Sometimes, a data set stores multiple values in the same cell. We may want to break up the data cluster so that each row stores a single value. Consider recipes.csv, a collection of three recipes, each of which has a name and an ingredients list. The ingredients are stored in a single comma-separated string:

```
In  [29] recipes = pd.read_csv("recipes.csv")
         recipes
```

Out [29]

	Recipe	Ingredients
0	Cashew Crusted Chicken	Apricot preserves, Dijon mustard, cu...
1	Tomato Basil Salmon	Salmon filets, basil, tomato, olive ...
2	Parmesan Cheese Chicken	Bread crumbs, Parmesan cheese, Itali...

Do you recall the `str.split` method we introduced in chapter 6? This method uses a delimiter to split a string into substrings. We can split each Ingredients string by the presence of a comma. In the next example, pandas returns a `Series` of lists. Each list stores the ingredients for the row:

```
In  [30] recipes["Ingredients"].str.split(",")
```

Out [30]

```
0    [Apricot preserves,  Dijon mustard,  curry pow...
1    [Salmon filets,  basil,  tomato,  olive oil,  ...
2    [Bread crumbs,  Parmesan cheese,  Italian seas...
Name: Ingredients, dtype: object
```

Let's overwrite the original Ingredients column with the new one:

```
In  [31] recipes["Ingredients"] = recipes["Ingredients"].str.split(",")
         recipes
```

Out [31]

	Recipe	Ingredients
0	Cashew Crusted Chicken	[Apricot preserves, Dijon mustard, ...
1	Tomato Basil Salmon	[Salmon filets, basil, tomato, ol...
2	Parmesan Cheese Chicken	[Bread crumbs, Parmesan cheese, It...

Now, how can we spread out each list's values across multiple rows? The `explode` method creates a separate row for each list element in a `Series`. We invoke the method on a `DataFrame` and pass in the column with lists:

```
In  [32] recipes.explode("Ingredients")

Out [32]
```

	Recipe	Ingredients
0	Cashew Crusted Chicken	Apricot preserves
0	Cashew Crusted Chicken	Dijon mustard
0	Cashew Crusted Chicken	curry powder
0	Cashew Crusted Chicken	chicken breasts
0	Cashew Crusted Chicken	cashews
1	Tomato Basil Salmon	Salmon filets
1	Tomato Basil Salmon	basil
1	Tomato Basil Salmon	tomato
1	Tomato Basil Salmon	olive oil
1	Tomato Basil Salmon	Parmesan cheese
2	Simply Parmesan Cheese	Bread crumbs
2	Simply Parmesan Cheese	Parmesan cheese
2	Simply Parmesan Cheese	Italian seasoning
2	Simply Parmesan Cheese	egg
2	Simply Parmesan Cheese	chicken breasts

Beautiful! We've isolated each ingredient to a separate line. Note that the `explode` method requires a `Series` of lists to work properly.

8.6   Coding challenge

Here's an opportunity to practice the reshaping, pivoting, and melting concepts introduced in this chapter.

8.6.1   Problems

We have two data sets for you to play with. The used_cars.csv file is a listing of used cars for sale on the classifieds website Craigslist. Each row includes the car's manufacturer, year of production, fuel type, transmission type, and price:

```
In  [33] cars = pd.read_csv("used_cars.csv")
         cars.head()

Out [33]
```

	Manufacturer	Year	Fuel	Transmission	Price
0	Acura	2012	Gas	Automatic	10299
1	Jaguar	2011	Gas	Automatic	9500
2	Honda	2004	Gas	Automatic	3995
3	Chevrolet	2016	Gas	Automatic	41988
4	Kia	2015	Gas	Automatic	12995

The minimum_wage.csv data set is a collection of minimum wages across the United States. The data set has a State column and multiple year columns:

```
In  [34] min_wage = pd.read_csv("minimum_wage.csv")
         min_wage.head()

Out [34]
```

	State	2010	2011	2012	2013	2014	2015	2016	2017
0	Alabama	0.00	0.00	0.00	0.00	0.00	0.00	0.00	0.00
1	Alaska	8.90	8.63	8.45	8.33	8.20	9.24	10.17	10.01
2	Arizona	8.33	8.18	8.34	8.38	8.36	8.50	8.40	10.22
3	Arkansas	7.18	6.96	6.82	6.72	6.61	7.92	8.35	8.68
4	California	9.19	8.91	8.72	8.60	9.52	9.51	10.43	10.22

Here are the challenges:

1 Aggregate the sum of car prices in cars. Group the results by fuel type on the row axis.

2 Aggregate the count of cars in cars. Group the results by manufacturer on the index axis and transmission type on the column axis. Show the subtotals for both the rows and columns.

3 Aggregate the average of car prices in cars. Group the results by year and fuel type on the index axis and transmission type on the column axis.

4 Given a DataFrame from the preceding challenge, move the transmission level from the column axis to the row axis.

5 Convert the min_wage from wide format to narrow format. In other words, move the data from the eight year columns (2010–17) to a single column.

8.6.2 Solutions

Let's tackle the problems one by one:

1 The pivot_table method is an optimal solution for adding the values in the Price column and organizing the totals by fuel type. We can use the method's index parameter to set the pivot table's index labels; we'll pass an argument of "Fuel". We'll specify the aggregation operation as "sum" with the aggfunc parameter:

```
In  [35] cars.pivot_table(
             values = "Price", index = "Fuel", aggfunc = "sum"
         )

Out [35]
```

	Price
Fuel	
Diesel	986177143
Electric	18502957
Gas	86203853926
Hybrid	44926064
Other	242096286

2 We can also use the `pivot_table` method to count cars by manufacturer and transmission type. We'll use the `columns` parameter to set the Transmission column's values as the pivot table's column labels. Remember to pass the `margins` parameter an argument of `True` to show subtotals for rows and columns:

```
In  [36] cars.pivot_table(
             values = "Price",
             index = "Manufacturer",
             columns = "Transmission",
             aggfunc = "count",
             margins = True
         ).tail()
```

Out [36]

Transmission Manufacturer	Automatic	Manual	Other	All
Tesla	179.0	NaN	59.0	238
Toyota	31480.0	1367.0	2134.0	34981
Volkswagen	7985.0	1286.0	236.0	9507
Volvo	2665.0	155.0	50.0	2870
All	398428.0	21005.0	21738.0	441171

3 To organize average car prices by year and fuel type on the pivot table's row axis, we can pass a list of strings to the `pivot_table` function's `index` parameter:

```
In  [37] cars.pivot_table(
             values = "Price",
             index = ["Year", "Fuel"],
             columns = ["Transmission"],
             aggfunc = "mean"
         )
```

Out [37]

Transmission Year Fuel		Automatic	Manual	Other
2000	Diesel	11326.176962	14010.164021	11075.000000
	Electric	1500.000000	NaN	NaN
	Gas	4314.675996	6226.140327	3203.538462
	Hybrid	2600.000000	2400.000000	NaN
	Other	16014.918919	11361.952381	12984.642857
...	...	...	...	...
2020	Diesel	63272.595930	1.000000	1234.000000
	Electric	8015.166667	2200.000000	20247.500000
	Gas	34925.857933	36007.270833	20971.045455
	Hybrid	35753.200000	NaN	1234.000000
	Other	22210.306452	NaN	2725.925926

102 rows × 3 columns

Let's assign the previous pivot table to a `report` variable for the next challenge:

```
In  [38] report = cars.pivot_table(
             values = "Price",
             index = ["Year", "Fuel"],
```

```
            columns = ["Transmission"],
            aggfunc = "mean"
        )
```

4 The next exercise is to move the transmission type from the column index to
   the row index. The `stack` method does the trick here. The method returns a
   `MultiIndex Series`. The `Series` has three levels: Year, Fuel, and the newly
   added Transmission:

```
In  [39] report.stack()

Out [39]

Year  Fuel       Transmission
2000  Diesel     Automatic       11326.176962
                 Manual          14010.164021
                 Other           11075.000000
      Electric   Automatic        1500.000000
      Gas        Automatic        4314.675996
                                      ...
2020  Gas        Other           20971.045455
      Hybrid     Automatic       35753.200000
                 Other            1234.000000
      Other      Automatic       22210.306452
                 Other            2725.925926
Length: 274, dtype: float64
```

5 Next, we'd like to convert the `min_wage` data set from wide format to narrow
   format. Eight columns store the same variable: the wages themselves. The solution is the `melt` method. We can declare the State column as the identifier column and the eight year columns as the variable columns:

```
In  [40] year_columns = [
             "2010", "2011", "2012", "2013",
             "2014", "2015", "2016", "2017"
         ]

         min_wage.melt(id_vars = "State", value_vars = year_columns)

Out [40]
```

	State	variable	value
0	Alabama	2010	0.00
1	Alaska	2010	8.90
2	Arizona	2010	8.33
3	Arkansas	2010	7.18
4	California	2010	9.19
...	...	...	...
435	Virginia	2017	7.41
436	Washington	2017	11.24
437	West Virginia	2017	8.94
438	Wisconsin	2017	7.41
439	Wyoming	2017	5.26

440 rows × 3 columns

Here's a bonus tip: we can remove the `value_vars` parameter from the `melt` method invocation and still get the same `DataFrame`. By default, pandas melts data from all columns except the one we pass to the `id_vars` parameter:

```
In  [41] min_wage.melt(id_vars = "State")

Out [41]
```

	State	variable	value
0	Alabama	2010	0.00
1	Alaska	2010	8.90
2	Arizona	2010	8.33
3	Arkansas	2010	7.18
4	California	2010	9.19
...	...	...	...
435	Virginia	2017	7.41
436	Washington	2017	11.24
437	West Virginia	2017	8.94
438	Wisconsin	2017	7.41
439	Wyoming	2017	5.26

440 rows × 3 columns

We can also customize the column names with the `var_name` and `value_name` parameters. The next example uses `"Year"` and `"Wage"` to better explain what each column represents:

```
In  [42] min_wage.melt(
             id_vars = "State", var_name = "Year", value_name = "Wage"
         )

Out [42]
```

	State	Year	Wage
0	Alabama	2010	0.00
1	Alaska	2010	8.90
2	Arizona	2010	8.33
3	Arkansas	2010	7.18
4	California	2010	9.19
...	...	...	...
435	Virginia	2017	7.41
436	Washington	2017	11.24
437	West Virginia	2017	8.94
438	Wisconsin	2017	7.41
439	Wyoming	2017	5.26

440 rows × 3 columns

Congratulations on completing the coding challenge!

Summary

- The `pivot_table` method aggregates a `DataFrame`'s data.
- Pivot table aggregations include sum, count, and average.
- We can customize the pivot table's row labels and column labels.

- We can use one or more columns' values as the index labels of the pivot table.
- The `stack` method moves an index level from the column index to the row index.
- The `unstack` method moves an index level from the row index to the column index.
- The `melt` method "unpivots" an aggregated table by distributing its data across individual rows. The process converts a wide data set to a narrow one.
- The `explode` method creates a separate row entry for each element in a list; it requires a `Series` of lists.

The GroupBy object

The pandas library's `GroupBy` object is a storage container for grouping `Data-Frame` rows into buckets. It provides a set of methods to aggregate and analyze each independent group in the collection. It allows us to extract rows at specific index positions within each group. It also offers a convenient way to iterate over the groups of rows. There's lots of power packed into a `GroupBy` object, so let's see what it's capable of doing.

9.1 Creating a GroupBy object from scratch

Let's create a new Jupyter Notebook and import the pandas library:

```
In  [1] import pandas as pd
```

We'll kick things off with a small example and dive into more of the technical details in section 9.2. Let's begin by creating a `DataFrame` that stores the prices of fruits and vegetables in a supermarket:

```
In  [2] food_data = {
            "Item": ["Banana", "Cucumber", "Orange", "Tomato", "Watermelon"],
            "Type": ["Fruit", "Vegetable", "Fruit", "Vegetable", "Fruit"],
            "Price": [0.99, 1.25, 0.25, 0.33, 3.00]
        }

        supermarket = pd.DataFrame(data = food_data)

        supermarket
```

```
Out [2]
```

	Item	Type	Price
0	Banana	Fruit	0.99
1	Cucumber	Vegetable	1.25
2	Orange	Fruit	0.25
3	Tomato	Vegetable	0.33
4	Watermelon	Fruit	3.00

The Type column identifies the group to which an Item belongs. There are two groups of items in the supermarket data set: fruits and vegetables. We can use terms such as *groups, buckets,* and *clusters* interchangeably to describe the same idea. Multiple rows fall into the same category.

The GroupBy object organizes `DataFrame` rows into buckets based on shared values in a column. Suppose that we are interested in the average price of a fruit and the average price of a vegetable. If we could isolate the `"Fruit"` rows and `"Vegetable"` rows into separate groups, it would be easier to perform the calculations.

Let's begin by invoking the `groupby` method on the supermarket `DataFrame`. We need to pass it the column whose values pandas will use to create the groups. The next example provides the Type column. The method returns an object we haven't seen yet: a `DataFrameGroupBy`. The `DataFrameGroupBy` object is separate and distinct from a `DataFrame`:

```
In  [3] groups = supermarket.groupby("Type")
        groups
```

```
Out [3] <pandas.core.groupby.generic.DataFrameGroupBy object at
        0x114f2db90>
```

The Type column has two unique values, so the `GroupBy` object will store two groups. The `get_group` method accepts a group name and returns a `DataFrame` with the corresponding rows. Let's pull out the `"Fruit"` rows:

```
In  [4] groups.get_group("Fruit")

Out [4]
```

	Item	Type	Price
0	Banana	Fruit	0.99
2	Orange	Fruit	0.25
4	Watermelon	Fruit	3.00

We can also pull out the `"Vegetable"` rows:

```
In  [5] groups.get_group("Vegetable")

Out [5]
```

	Item	Type	Price
1	Cucumber	Vegetable	1.25
3	Tomato	Vegetable	0.33

The `GroupBy` object excels at aggregate operations. Our original goal was to calculate the average price of the fruits and vegetables in supermarket. We can invoke the `mean` method on `groups` to calculate the average price of items within each group. With a few lines of code, we've successfully split, aggregated, and analyzed a data set:

```
In  [6] groups.mean()

Out [6]
```

	Price
Type	
Fruit	1.413333
Vegetable	0.790000

With the foundational knowledge under our belts, let's move on to a more complex data set.

9.2 Creating a GroupBy object from a data set

The Fortune 1000 is a listing of the 1,000 largest companies in the United States by revenue. The list is updated annually by the business magazine *Fortune*. The fortune1000.csv file is a collection of Fortune 1000 companies from 2018. Each row includes a company's name, revenue, profits, employee count, sector, and industry:

```
In  [7] fortune = pd.read_csv("fortune1000.csv")
        fortune

Out [7]
```

	Company	Revenues	Profits	Employees	Sector	Industry
0	Walmart	500343.0	9862.0	2300000	Retailing	General M...
1	Exxon Mobil	244363.0	19710.0	71200	Energy	Petroleum...

2	Berkshire...	242137.0	44940.0	377000	Financials	Insurance...
3	Apple	229234.0	48351.0	123000	Technology	Computers...
4	UnitedHea...	201159.0	10558.0	260000	Health Care	Health Ca...
...	...	...	...	...	...	...
995	SiteOne L...	1862.0	54.6	3664	Wholesalers	Wholesale...
996	Charles R...	1858.0	123.4	11800	Health Care	Health Ca...
997	CoreLogic	1851.0	152.2	5900	Business ...	Financial...
998	Ensign Group	1849.0	40.5	21301	Health Care	Health Ca...
999	HCP	1848.0	414.2	190	Financials	Real estate

1000 rows × 6 columns

A sector can have many companies. Apple and Amazon.com both belong to the "Technology" sector, for example.

An industry is a subcategory within a sector. The "Pipelines" and "Petroleum Refining" industries fall in the "Energy" sector, for example.

The Sector column holds 21 unique sectors. Suppose that we want to find the average revenue across the companies within each sector. Before we use the GroupBy object, let's solve the problem by taking an alternative approach. Chapter 5 showed us how to create a Boolean Series to extract a subset of rows from a DataFrame. The next example pulls out all companies with a Sector value of "Retailing":

```
In [8] in_retailing = fortune["Sector"] == "Retailing"
       retail_companies = fortune[in_retailing]
       retail_companies.head()
```

Out [8]

	Company	Revenues	Profits	Employees	Sector	Industry
0	Walmart	500343.0	9862.0	2300000	Retailing	General Mercha...
7	Amazon.com	177866.0	3033.0	566000	Retailing	Internet Servi...
14	Costco	129025.0	2679.0	182000	Retailing	General Mercha...
22	Home Depot	100904.0	8630.0	413000	Retailing	Specialty Reta...
38	Target	71879.0	2934.0	345000	Retailing	General Mercha...

We can pull out the Revenues column from the subset by using square brackets:

```
In [9] retail_companies["Revenues"].head()
```

```
Out [9] 0     500343.0
        7     177866.0
        14    129025.0
        22    100904.0
        38     71879.0
        Name: Revenues, dtype: float64
```

Finally, we can calculate the Retailing sector's average revenue by invoking the mean method on the Revenues column:

```
In [10] retail_companies["Revenues"].mean()
```

```
Out [10] 21874.714285714286
```

The preceding code is suitable for calculating the average revenue of one sector. We'll need to write a lot of additional code, however, to apply the same logic to the other 20 sectors in fortune. The code is not particularly scalable. Python can automate some of the repetition, but the GroupBy object offers the best solution out of the box. The pandas developers have already solved this problem for us.

Let's invoke the groupby method on the fortune DataFrame. The method accepts the column whose values pandas will use to group the rows. A column is a good candidate for a grouping if it stores categorical data for the rows. Make sure that there are parent categories under which multiple rows fall. The data set has 1,000 unique companies but only 21 unique sectors, for example, so the Sector column is a good fit for aggregate analysis:

```
In  [11] sectors = fortune.groupby("Sector")
```

Let's output the sectors variable to see what kind of object we're working with:

```
In  [12] sectors

Out [12] <pandas.core.groupby.generic.DataFrameGroupBy object at
             0x1235b1d10>
```

A DataFrameGroupBy object is a bundle of DataFrames. Behind the scenes, pandas repeated the extraction process we used for the "Retailing" sector but for all 21 values in the Sector column.

We can count the number of groups in sectors by passing the GroupBy object into Python's built-in len function:

```
In  [13] len(sectors)

Out [13] 21
```

The sectors GroupBy object has 21 DataFrames. The number is equal to the number of unique values in fortune's Sector column, which we can discover by invoking the nunique method:

```
In  [14] fortune["Sector"].nunique()

Out [14] 21
```

What are the 21 sectors, and how many companies from fortune belong to each one? The size method on the GroupBy object returns a Series with an alphabetical list of the groups and their row counts. The following output tells us that 25 fortune companies have a Sector value of "Aerospace & Defense", 14 have a value of "Apparel", and so on:

```
In  [15] sectors.size()

Out [15] Sector
         Aerospace & Defense          25
         Apparel                      14
         Business Services            53
         Chemicals                    33
         Energy                      107
```

```
Engineering & Construction        27
Financials                       155
Food &  Drug Stores               12
Food, Beverages & Tobacco         37
Health Care                       71
Hotels, Restaurants & Leisure     26
Household Products                28
Industrials                       49
Materials                         45
Media                             25
Motor Vehicles & Parts            19
Retailing                         77
Technology                       103
Telecommunications                10
Transportation                    40
Wholesalers                       44
dtype: int64
```

Now that we've bucketed our fortune rows, let's explore what we can do with a GroupBy object.

9.3   *Attributes and methods of a GroupBy object*

One way to visualize our GroupBy object is as a dictionary that maps the 21 sectors to a collection of fortune rows belonging to each one. The groups attribute stores a dictionary with these group-to-row associations; its keys are sector names, and its values are Index objects storing the row index positions from the fortune DataFrame. The dictionary has 21 total key-value pairs, but I've limited the following output to the first two pairs to save space:

```
In  [16] sectors.groups

Out [16]

'Aerospace &  Defense': Int64Index([ 26,  50,  58,  98, 117, 118, 207, 224,
                                     275, 380, 404, 406, 414, 540, 660,
                                     661, 806, 829, 884, 930, 954, 955,
                                     959, 975, 988], dtype='int64'),
 'Apparel': Int64Index([88, 241, 331, 420, 432, 526, 529, 554, 587, 678,
                        766, 774, 835, 861], dtype='int64'),
```

The output tells us that rows with index positions 26, 50, 58, 98, and so on have a value of "Aerospace & Defense" in fortune's Sector column.

Chapter 4 introduced the loc accessor for extracting DataFrame rows and columns by index label. Its first argument is the row index label, and its second argument is the column index label. Let's extract a sample fortune row to confirm that pandas is pulling it into the correct sector group. We'll try 26, the first index position listed in the "Aerospace & Defense" group:

```
In  [17] fortune.loc[26, "Sector"]

Out [17] 'Aerospace &  Defense'
```

What if we want to find the highest-performing company (by revenue) within each sector? The GroupBy object's `first` method extracts the first row listed for each sector in fortune. Because our fortune DataFrame is sorted by revenue, the first company pulled out for each sector will be the highest-performing company within that sector. The return value of `first` is a 21-row DataFrame (one company per sector):

```
In  [18] sectors.first()

Out [18]
```

Sector	Company	Revenues	Profits	Employees	Industry
Aerospace &...	Boeing	93392.0	8197.0	140800	Aerospace ...
Apparel	Nike	34350.0	4240.0	74400	Apparel
Business Se...	ManpowerGroup	21034.0	545.4	29000	Temporary ...
Chemicals	DowDuPont	62683.0	1460.0	98000	Chemicals
Energy	Exxon Mobil	244363.0	19710.0	71200	Petroleum ...
...	...	...	...	...	...
Retailing	Walmart	500343.0	9862.0	2300000	General Me...
Technology	Apple	229234.0	48351.0	123000	Computers,...
Telecommuni...	AT&T	160546.0	29450.0	254000	Telecommun...
Transportation	UPS	65872.0	4910.0	346415	Mail, Pack...
Wholesalers	McKesson	198533.0	5070.0	64500	Wholesaler...

The complementary `last` method extracts the last company from fortune that belongs to each sector. Again, pandas pulls the rows out in the order in which they appear in the DataFrame. Because fortune sorts companies in descending order by revenue, the following results reveal the companies with the lowest revenue per sector:

```
In  [19] sectors.last()

Out [19]
```

Sector	Company	Revenues	Profits	Employees	Industry
Aerospace &...	Aerojet Ro...	1877.0	-9.2	5157	Aerospace ...
Apparel	Wolverine ...	2350.0	0.3	3700	Apparel
Business Se...	CoreLogic	1851.0	152.2	5900	Financial ...
Chemicals	Stepan	1925.0	91.6	2096	Chemicals
Energy	Superior E...	1874.0	-205.9	6400	Oil and Ga...
...	...	...	...	...	...
Retailing	Childrens ...	1870.0	84.7	9800	Specialty ...
Technology	VeriFone S...	1871.0	-173.8	5600	Financial ...
Telecommuni...	Zayo Group...	2200.0	85.7	3794	Telecommun...
Transportation	Echo Globa...	1943.0	12.6	2453	Transporta...
Wholesalers	SiteOne La...	1862.0	54.6	3664	Wholesaler...

The GroupBy object assigns index positions to the rows in each sector group. The first fortune row in the "Aerospace & Defense" sector has an index position of 0 within its group. Likewise, the first fortune row in the "Apparel" sector has an index position of 0 within its group. The index positions are independent between groups.

The nth method extracts the row at a given index position within its group. If we invoke the nth method with an argument of 0, we get the first company within each sector. The next DataFrame is identical to the one returned by the `first` method:

```
In  [20] sectors.nth(0)
```

```
Out [20]
```

	Company	Revenues	Profits	Employees	Industry
Sector					
Aerospace &...	Boeing	93392.0	8197.0	140800	Aerospace ...
Apparel	Nike	34350.0	4240.0	74400	Apparel
Business Se...	ManpowerGroup	21034.0	545.4	29000	Temporary ...
Chemicals	DowDuPont	62683.0	1460.0	98000	Chemicals
Energy	Exxon Mobil	244363.0	19710.0	71200	Petroleum ...
...	...	...	...	...	...
Retailing	Walmart	500343.0	9862.0	2300000	General Me...
Technology	Apple	229234.0	48351.0	123000	Computers,...
Telecommuni...	AT&T	160546.0	29450.0	254000	Telecommun...
Transportation	UPS	65872.0	4910.0	346415	Mail, Pack...
Wholesalers	McKesson	198533.0	5070.0	64500	Wholesaler...

The next example passes an argument of 3 to the `nth` method to pull out the fourth row from each sector in the fortune `DataFrame`. The results include the 21 companies that are ranked fourth-best by revenue in their sector:

```
In  [21] sectors.nth(3)
```

```
Out [21]
```

	Company	Revenues	Profits	Employees	Industry
Sector					
Aerospace &...	General Dy...	30973.0	2912.0	98600	Aerospace ...
Apparel	Ralph Lauren	6653.0	-99.3	18250	Apparel
Business Se...	Aramark	14604.0	373.9	215000	Diversifie...
Chemicals	Monsanto	14640.0	2260.0	21900	Chemicals
Energy	Valero Energy	88407.0	4065.0	10015	Petroleum ...
...	...	...	...	...	...
Retailing	Home Depot	100904.0	8630.0	413000	Specialty ...
Technology	IBM	79139.0	5753.0	397800	Informatio...
Telecommuni...	Charter Co...	41581.0	9895.0	94800	Telecommun...
Transportation	Delta Air ...	41244.0	3577.0	86564	Airlines
Wholesalers	Sysco	55371.0	1142.5	66500	Wholesaler...

Notice that the value for the "Apparel" sector is "Ralph Lauren". We can confirm the output is correct by filtering for the "Apparel" rows in fortune. Notice that "Ralph Lauren" is fourth in line:

```
In  [22] fortune[fortune["Sector"] == "Apparel"].head()
```

```
Out [22]
```

	Company	Revenues	Profits	Employees	Sector	Industry
88	Nike	34350.0	4240.0	74400	Apparel	Apparel
241	VF	12400.0	614.9	69000	Apparel	Apparel
331	PVH	8915.0	537.8	28050	Apparel	Apparel
420	Ralph Lauren	6653.0	-99.3	18250	Apparel	Apparel
432	Hanesbrands	6478.0	61.9	67200	Apparel	Apparel

The `head` method extracts multiple rows from each group. In the next example, `head(2)` extracts the first two rows for each sector within fortune. The result is a Data-Frame with 42 rows (21 unique sectors, with two rows for each sector). Don't confuse this `head` method on a `GroupBy` object with the `head` method on a `DataFrame` object:

```
In  [23] sectors.head(2)
```

Out [23]

	Company	Revenues	Profits	Employees	Sector	Industry
0	Walmart	500343.0	9862.0	2300000	Retailing	General M...
1	Exxon Mobil	244363.0	19710.0	71200	Energy	Petroleum...
2	Berkshire...	242137.0	44940.0	377000	Financials	Insurance...
3	Apple	229234.0	48351.0	123000	Technology	Computers...
4	UnitedHea...	201159.0	10558.0	260000	Health Care	Health Ca...
...	...	...	...	...	...	...
160	Visa	18358.0	6699.0	15000	Business ...	Financial...
162	Kimberly-...	18259.0	2278.0	42000	Household...	Household...
163	AECOM	18203.0	339.4	87000	Engineeri...	Engineeri...
189	Sherwin-W...	14984.0	1772.3	52695	Chemicals	Chemicals
241	VF	12400.0	614.9	69000	Apparel	Apparel

The complementary `tail` method extracts the last rows from each group. `tail(3)` pulls the last three rows for each sector, for example. The result is a 63-row Data-Frame (21 sectors x 3 rows):

```
In  [24] sectors.tail(3)
```

Out [24]

	Company	Revenues	Profits	Employees	Sector	Industry
473	Windstrea...	5853.0	-2116.6	12979	Telecommu...	Telecommu...
520	Telephone...	5044.0	153.0	9900	Telecommu...	Telecommu...
667	Weis Markets	3467.0	98.4	23000	Food & D...	Food and ...
759	Hain Cele...	2853.0	67.4	7825	Food, Bev...	Food Cons...
774	Fossil Group	2788.0	-478.2	12300	Apparel	Apparel
...	...	...	...	...	...	...
995	SiteOne L...	1862.0	54.6	3664	Wholesalers	Wholesale...
996	Charles R...	1858.0	123.4	11800	Health Care	Health Ca...
997	CoreLogic	1851.0	152.2	5900	Business ...	Financial...
998	Ensign Group	1849.0	40.5	21301	Health Care	Health Ca...
999	HCP	1848.0	414.2	190	Financials	Real estate

63 rows × 6 columns

We can use the `get_group` method to extract all rows in a given group. The method returns a `DataFrame` containing the rows. The next example shows all companies in the `"Energy"` sector:

```
In  [25] sectors.get_group("Energy").head()
```

Out [25]

	Company	Revenues	Profits	Employees	Sector	Industry
1	Exxon Mobil	244363.0	19710.0	71200	Energy	Petroleum R...
12	Chevron	134533.0	9195.0	51900	Energy	Petroleum R...

27	Phillips 66	91568.0	5106.0	14600	Energy	Petroleum R...
30	Valero Energy	88407.0	4065.0	10015	Energy	Petroleum R...
40	Marathon Pe...	67610.0	3432.0	43800	Energy	Petroleum R...

Now that we understand a `GroupBy` object's mechanics, let's discuss how we can aggregate the values in every nested group.

9.4 *Aggregate operations*

We can invoke methods on the `GroupBy` object to apply aggregate operations to every nested group. The `sum` method, for example, adds the column values in each group. By default, pandas targets all numeric columns in the original `DataFrame`. In the next example, the `sum` method calculates the sum per sector for the three numeric columns (Revenues, Profits, and Employees) in the fortune `DataFrame`. We invoke the `sum` method on the `GroupBy` object:

```
In [26] sectors.sum().head(10)
```

Out [26]

Sector	Revenues	Profits	Employees
Aerospace & Defense	383835.0	26733.5	1010124
Apparel	101157.3	6350.7	355699
Business Services	316090.0	37179.2	1593999
Chemicals	251151.0	20475.0	474020
Energy	1543507.2	85369.6	981207
Engineering & Construction	172782.0	7121.0	420745
Financials	2442480.0	264253.5	3500119
Food & Drug Stores	405468.0	8440.3	1398074
Food, Beverages & Tobacco	510232.0	54902.5	1079316
Health Care	1507991.4	92791.1	2971189

Let's double-check a sample calculation. Pandas lists the sum of company revenue in `"Aerospace & Defense"` as $383,835. We can use the `get_group` method to retrieve the nested `"Aerospace & Defense"` DataFrame, target its Revenues column, and use the `sum` method to calculate its sum:

```
In [27] sectors.get_group("Aerospace & Defense").head()
```

Out [27]

	Company	Revenues	Profits	Employees	Sector	Industry
26	Boeing	93392.0	8197.0	140800	Aerospace...	Aerospace...
50	United Te...	59837.0	4552.0	204700	Aerospace...	Aerospace...
58	Lockheed ...	51048.0	2002.0	100000	Aerospace...	Aerospace...
98	General D...	30973.0	2912.0	98600	Aerospace...	Aerospace...
117	Northrop ...	25803.0	2015.0	70000	Aerospace...	Aerospace...

```
In [28] sectors.get_group("Aerospace & Defense").loc[:,"Revenues"].head()
```

```
Out [28] 26     93392.0
         50     59837.0
         58     51048.0
```

```
98      30973.0
117     25803.0
Name: Revenues, dtype: float64
```

In [29] sectors.get_group("Aerospace & Defense").loc[:, "Revenues"].sum()

Out [29] 383835.0

The values are equal. Pandas is correct! With a single sum method call, the library applied the calculation logic to each nested DataFrame in the sectors GroupBy object. We've performed an aggregate analysis for all of a column's groups with a minimal amount of code.

The GroupBy object supports many other aggregation methods. The next example invokes the mean method to calculate the average of the Revenues, Profits, and Employees columns per sector. Again, pandas includes only numeric columns in its calculations:

In [30] sectors.mean().head()

Out [30]

Sector	Revenues	Profits	Employees
Aerospace & Defense	15353.400000	1069.340000	40404.960000
Apparel	7225.521429	453.621429	25407.071429
Business Services	5963.962264	701.494340	30075.452830
Chemicals	7610.636364	620.454545	14364.242424
Energy	14425.300935	805.373585	9170.158879

We can target a single fortune column by passing its name inside square brackets after the GroupBy object. Pandas returns a new object, a SeriesGroupBy:

In [31] sectors["Revenues"]

Out [31] <pandas.core.groupby.generic.SeriesGroupBy object at 0x114778210>

Under the hood, the DataFrameGroupBy object stores a collection of Series-GroupBy objects. The SeriesGroupBy objects can perform aggregate operations on individual columns from fortune. Pandas will organize the results by sector. The next example calculates the sum of revenue by sector:

In [32] sectors["Revenues"].sum().head()

Out [32] Sector
         Aerospace & Defense   383835.0
         Apparel   101157.3
         Business Services   316090.0
         Chemicals   251151.0
         Energy   1543507.2
         Name: Revenues, dtype: float64

The next example calculates the average number of employees per sector:

```
In  [33] sectors["Employees"].mean().head()

Out [33] Sector
         Aerospace & Defense     40404.960000
         Apparel                 25407.071429
         Business Services       30075.452830
         Chemicals               14364.242424
         Energy                   9170.158879
         Name: Employees, dtype: float64
```

The max method returns the maximum value from a given column. In the next example, we extract the highest Profits column value for each sector. The best-performing company in the "Aerospace & Defense" sector has profits of $8,197:

```
In  [34] sectors["Profits"].max().head()

Out [34] Sector
         Aerospace & Defense      8197.0
         Apparel                  4240.0
         Business Services        6699.0
         Chemicals                3000.4
         Energy                  19710.0
         Name: Profits, dtype: float64
```

The complementary min method returns the minimum value in a given column. The next example displays the minimum employee count per sector. The smallest number of employees at a company in the "Aerospace & Defense" sector is 5,157:

```
In  [35] sectors["Employees"].min().head()

Out [35] Sector
         Aerospace & Defense     5157
         Apparel                 3700
         Business Services       2338
         Chemicals               1931
         Energy                   593
         Name: Employees, dtype: int64
```

The agg method applies multiple aggregate operations to different columns and accepts a dictionary as its argument. In each key-value pair, the key denotes a DataFrame column, and the value specifies the aggregate operation to apply to the column. The next example extracts the lowest revenue, highest profit, and average number of employees for each sector:

```
In  [36] aggregations = {
             "Revenues": "min",
             "Profits": "max",
             "Employees": "mean"
         }

         sectors.agg(aggregations).head()
```

Out [36]

Sector	Revenues	Profits	Employees
Aerospace & Defense	1877.0	8197.0	40404.960000
Apparel	2350.0	4240.0	25407.071429
Business Services	1851.0	6699.0	30075.452830
Chemicals	1925.0	3000.4	14364.242424
Energy	1874.0	19710.0	9170.158879

Pandas returns a `DataFrame` with the aggregation dictionary's keys as column headers. The sectors remain index labels.

9.5   *Applying a custom operation to all groups*

Suppose that we want to apply a custom operation to each nested group in a `GroupBy` object. In section 9.4, we used the `GroupBy` object's `max` method to find each sector's maximum revenue. Let's say we want to identify the company with the highest revenue in each sector. We solved this problem earlier, but let's now assume that fortune is unordered.

A `DataFrame`'s `nlargest` method extracts the rows with the greatest value in a given column. Here's a quick refresher. The next example returns the five fortune rows with the greatest values in the Profits column:

In [37] fortune.nlargest(n = 5, columns = "Profits")

Out [37]

	Company	Revenues	Profits	Employees	Sector	Industry
3	Apple	229234.0	48351.0	123000	Technology	Computers...
2	Berkshire...	242137.0	44940.0	377000	Financials	Insurance...
15	Verizon	126034.0	30101.0	155400	Telecommu...	Telecommu...
8	AT&T	160546.0	29450.0	254000	Telecommu...	Telecommu...
19	JPMorgan ...	113899.0	24441.0	252539	Financials	Commercia...

If we could invoke the `nlargest` method on each nested `DataFrame` in sectors, we'd get the results we seek. We'd get the company with the highest revenue in each sector.

We can use the `GroupBy` object's `apply` method here. The method expects a function as an argument. It invokes the function once for each group in the `GroupBy` object. Then it collects the return values from the function invocations and returns them in a new `DataFrame`.

First, let's define a `get_largest_row` function that accepts a single argument: a `DataFrame`. The function will return the `DataFrame` row with the greatest value in the Revenues column. The function is dynamic; it can perform the logic on any `DataFrame` as long as it has a Revenues column:

In [38] def get_largest_row(df):
            return df.nlargest(1, "Revenues")

Next, we can invoke the `apply` method and pass in the uninvoked `get_larg-est_row` function. Pandas invokes `get_largest_row` once for each sector and returns a `DataFrame` with the companies with the highest revenue in their sector:

```
In  [39] sectors.apply(get_largest_row).head()
```

```
Out [39]
```

		Company	Revenues	Profits	Employees	Industry
Sector						
Aerospace ...	26	Boeing	93392.0	8197.0	140800	Aerospace...
Apparel	88	Nike	34350.0	4240.0	74400	Apparel
Business S...	142	ManpowerG...	21034.0	545.4	29000	Temporary...
Chemicals	46	DowDuPont	62683.0	1460.0	98000	Chemicals
Energy	1	Exxon Mobil	244363.0	19710.0	71200	Petroleum...

Use the `apply` method when pandas does not support a custom aggregation you'd like to apply to each nested group.

9.6 *Grouping by multiple columns*

We can create a `GroupBy` object with values from multiple `DataFrame` columns. This operation is optimal when a combination of column values serves as the best identifier for a group. The next example passes a list of two strings to the `groupby` method. Pandas groups the rows first by the Sector column's values and then by the Industry column's values. Remember that a company's industry is a subcategory within a larger sector:

```
In  [40] sector_and_industry = fortune.groupby(by = ["Sector", "Industry"])
```

The `GroupBy` object's `size` method now returns a `MultiIndex Series` with a count of rows for each internal group. This `GroupBy` object has a length of 82, which means that fortune has 82 unique combinations of sector and industry:

```
In  [41] sector_and_industry.size()
```

```
Out [41]
```

Sector	Industry	
Aerospace & Defense	Aerospace and Defense	25
Apparel	Apparel	14
Business Services	Advertising, marketing	2
	Diversified Outsourcing Services	14
	Education	2
	..	
Transportation	Trucking, Truck Leasing	11
Wholesalers	Wholesalers: Diversified	24
	Wholesalers: Electronics and Office Equipment	8
	Wholesalers: Food and Grocery	6
	Wholesalers: Health Care	6

Length: 82, dtype: int64

The get_group method requires a tuple of values to extract a nested DataFrame from the GroupBy collection. The next example targets rows with a sector of "Business Services" and industry of "Education":

```
In  [42] sector_and_industry.get_group(("Business Services", "Education"))
```

Out [42]

	Company	Revenues	Profits	Employees	Sector	Industry
567	Laureate ...	4378.0	91.5	54500	Business ...	Education
810	Graham Ho...	2592.0	302.0	16153	Business ...	Education

For all aggregations, pandas returns a MultiIndex DataFrame with the calculations. The next example calculates the sum of the three numeric columns in fortune (Revenues, Profits, and Employees), grouped first by sector and then by the industries within each sector:

```
In  [43] sector_and_industry.sum().head()
```

Out [43]

Sector	Industry	Revenues	Profits	Employees
Aerospace & Defense	Aerospace and Def...	383835.0	26733.5	1010124
Apparel	Apparel	101157.3	6350.7	355699
Business Services	Advertising, mark...	23156.0	1667.4	127500
	Diversified Outso...	74175.0	5043.7	858600
	Education	6970.0	393.5	70653

We can target individual fortune columns for aggregation by using the same syntax as in section 9.5. Enter the column in square brackets after the GroupBy object; then invoke the aggregation method. The next example calculates the average revenue for companies within each sector/industry combo:

```
In  [44] sector_and_industry["Revenues"].mean().head(5)
```

Out [44]

Sector	Industry	
Aerospace & Defense	Aerospace and Defense	15353.400000
Apparel	Apparel	7225.521429
Business Services	Advertising, marketing	11578.000000
	Diversified Outsourcing Services	5298.214286
	Education	3485.000000

Name: Revenues, dtype: float64

In summary, a GroupBy object is an optimal data structure for splitting, organizing, and aggregating a DataFrame's values. If you need to use multiple columns to identify buckets, pass the groupby method a list of columns.

9.7 Coding challenge

This coding challenge's data set, cereals.csv, is a listing of 80 popular breakfast cereals. Each row includes a cereal's name, manufacturer, type, calories, grams of fiber, and grams of sugar. Let's take a look:

```
In  [45] cereals = pd.read_csv("cereals.csv")
         cereals.head()

Out [45]
```

	Name	Manufacturer	Type	Calories	Fiber	Sugars
0	100% Bran	Nabisco	Cold	70	10.0	6
1	100% Natural Bran	Quaker Oats	Cold	120	2.0	8
2	All-Bran	Kellogg's	Cold	70	9.0	5
3	All-Bran with Ex...	Kellogg's	Cold	50	14.0	0
4	Almond Delight	Ralston Purina	Cold	110	1.0	8

Good luck!

9.7.1 Problems

Here are the challenges:

1. Group the cereals, using the Manufacturer column's values.
2. Determine the total number of groups, and the number of cereals per group.
3. Extract the cereals that belong to the manufacturer/group "Nabisco".
4. Calculate the average of values in the Calories, Fiber, and Sugars columns for each manufacturer.
5. Find the maximum value in the Sugars column for each manufacturer.
6. Find the minimum value in the Fiber column for each manufacturer.
7. Extract the cereal with the lowest amount of grams of sugar per manufacturer in a new DataFrame.

9.7.2 Solutions

Let's dive into the solutions:

1. To group the cereals by manufacturer, we can invoke the groupby method on the cereals DataFrame and pass in the Manufacturer column. Pandas will use the column's unique values to organize the groups:

   ```
   In  [46] manufacturers = cereals.groupby("Manufacturer")
   ```

2. To find the total number of groups/manufacturers, we can pass the GroupBy object into Python's built-in len function:

   ```
   In  [47] len(manufacturers)

   Out [47] 7
   ```

If you're curious, the GroupBy object's size method returns a Series with a count of cereals per group:

```
In  [48] manufacturers.size()

Out [48] Manufacturer
         American Home Food Products     1
         General Mills                  22
         Kellogg's                      23
         Nabisco                         6
         Post                            9
         Quaker Oats                     8
         Ralston Purina                  8
         dtype: int64
```

3 To identify cereals belonging to the "Nabisco" group, we can invoke the get_group method on our GroupBy object. Pandas will return the nested DataFrame with "Nabisco" rows:

```
In  [49] manufacturers.get_group("Nabisco")

Out [49]
```

	Name	Manufacturer	Type	Calories	Fiber	Sugars
0	100% Bran	Nabisco	Cold	70	10.0	6
20	Cream of Wheat (Quick)	Nabisco	Hot	100	1.0	0
63	Shredded Wheat	Nabisco	Cold	80	3.0	0
64	Shredded Wheat 'n'Bran	Nabisco	Cold	90	4.0	0
65	Shredded Wheat spoon ...	Nabisco	Cold	90	3.0	0
68	Strawberry Fruit Wheats	Nabisco	Cold	90	3.0	5

4 To calculate the averages of the numeric columns in cereals, we can invoke the mean method on the manufacturers GroupBy object. Pandas will aggregate all numeric columns in cereals by default:

```
In  [50] manufacturers.mean()

Out [50]
```

Manufacturer	Calories	Fiber	Sugars
American Home Food Products	100.000000	0.000000	3.000000
General Mills	111.363636	1.272727	7.954545
Kellogg's	108.695652	2.739130	7.565217
Nabisco	86.666667	4.000000	1.833333
Post	108.888889	2.777778	8.777778
Quaker Oats	95.000000	1.337500	5.250000
Ralston Purina	115.000000	1.875000	6.125000

5 Next, we are tasked with finding the maximum Sugars value per manufacturer. We can use square brackets after a GroupBy object to identify which column's values to aggregate. Then we provide the correct aggregate method, which is max in this case:

```
In  [51] manufacturers["Sugars"].max()

Out [51] Manufacturer
         American Home Food Products    3
         General Mills                 14
         Kellogg's                     15
         Nabisco                        6
         Post                          15
         Quaker Oats                   12
         Ralston Purina                11
         Name: Sugars, dtype: int64
```

6 To find the smallest fiber value per manufacturer, we can swap the column to Fiber and invoke the `min` method:

```
In  [52] manufacturers["Fiber"].min()

Out [52] Manufacturer
         American Home Food Products    0.0
         General Mills                  0.0
         Kellogg's                      0.0
         Nabisco                        1.0
         Post                           0.0
         Quaker Oats                    0.0
         Ralston Purina                 0.0
         Name: Fiber, dtype: float64
```

7 Finally, we need to identify the cereal row for each manufacturer with the lowest value in the Sugars column. We can solve this problem by using the `apply` method and a custom function. The `smallest_sugar_row` function uses the `nsmallest` method to pull the `DataFrame` row with the smallest value in the Sugars column. Then we use `apply` to invoke the custom function on each `GroupBy` group:

```
In  [53] def smallest_sugar_row(df):
             return df.nsmallest(1, "Sugars")

In  [54] manufacturers.apply(smallest_sugar_row)

Out [54]
```

		Name	Manufacturer	Type	Calories	Fiber	Sugars
Manufacturer							
American H...	43	Maypo	American ...	Hot	100	0.0	3
General Mills	11	Cheerios	General M...	Cold	110	2.0	0
Nabisco	20	Cream of ...	Nabisco	Hot	100	1.0	0
Post	33	Grape-Nuts	Post	Cold	110	3.0	3
Quaker Oats	57	Quaker Oa...	Quaker Oats	Hot	100	2.7	-1
Ralston Pu...	61	Rice Chex	Ralston P...	Cold	110	0.0	2

Congratulations on completing the coding challenge!

Summary

- A `GroupBy` object is a container of `DataFrames`.
- Pandas buckets rows into `GroupBy DataFrames` by using values across one or more columns.
- The `first` and `last` methods return the first and last rows from each `GroupBy` group. The row order in the original `DataFrame` determines the row order in each group.
- The `head` and `tail` methods extract multiple rows from each group in the `GroupBy` object based on the row's positions in the original `DataFrame`.
- The `nth` method extracts a row from each `GroupBy` group by its index position.
- Pandas can perform aggregate calculations such as sum, average, max, and min for each group in a `GroupBy` object.
- The `agg` method applies different aggregate operations to different columns. We pass it a dictionary with columns as keys and aggregation as values.
- The `apply` method invokes a function on each `DataFrame` in a `GroupBy` object.

Merging, joining, and concatenating

This chapter covers

- Concatenating `DataFrames` on the vertical and horizontal axes
- Merging `DataFrames` with inner joins, outer joins, and left joins
- Finding unique and shared values between `DataFrames`
- Joining `DataFrames` by index labels

As a business domain grows in complexity, it becomes increasingly difficult to store all data in a single collection. To solve this problem, data administrators split data across multiple tables. Then they associate the tables with one another so it is easy to identify the relationships among them.

You may have previously worked with a database such as PostgreSQL, MySQL, or Oracle. Relational database management systems (RDBMS) follow the paradigm described in the preceding paragraph. A database consists of tables. A table holds records for one domain model. A table consists of rows and columns. A row stores information for one record. A column stores an attribute for that record. Tables connect through column keys. If you haven't worked with databases before, you can consider a table to be effectively equivalent to a pandas `DataFrame`.

Here's a real-world example. Imagine that we're building an e-commerce site and want to create a `users` table to store the website's registered users. Following relational database conventions, we would assign a unique numeric identifier to each record. We'll store the values in an id column. The id column's values are called *primary keys* because they are the primary identifiers for specific rows.

Users				
id	first_name	last_name	email	gender
1	Homer	Simpson	donutfan@simpson.com	Male
2	Bart	Simpson	troublemaker@simpson.com	Male

Let's imagine that our next goal is to keep track of users' orders on our site. We'll create an `orders` table to store order details such as item name and price. But how do we connect each order to the user who placed it? Take a peek at the following table:

Orders				
id	item	price	quantity	user_id
1	Donut Box	4.99	4	1
2	Slingshot	19.99	1	2

To establish a relationship between two tables, database administrators create a column of foreign keys. A *foreign key* is a reference to a record in another table. It is labeled *foreign* because the key exists outside the current table's scope.

Each `orders` table row stores the ID of the *user* who placed the order in the user_id column. Thus, the user_id column stores foreign keys; its values are references to records in another table, the `users` table. Using the established relationship between the two tables, we can determine that order 1 was placed by the user with an id of 1, Homer Simpson.

The advantage of foreign keys is the reduction of data duplication. The `orders` table does not need to copy the user's first name, last name, and email for each order, for example. Rather, it needs only to store a single reference to the correct `users` record. The business entities of users and orders live separately, but we can connect them when necessary.

When it comes time to combine tables, we can always turn to pandas. The library excels at appending, concatenating, joining, merging, and combining `DataFrames` in both vertical and horizontal directions. It can identify unique and shared records between `DataFrames`. It can perform SQL operations such as inner joins, outer joins, left joins, and right joins. In this chapter, we'll explore the differences among these joins and the situations in which each one can prove to be advantageous.

10.1 Introducing the data sets

Let's import the pandas library and assign it an alias of `pd`:

```
In  [1] import pandas as pd
```

This chapter's data sets come from the online social service Meetup, a website where users join groups for common interests such as hiking, literature, and board games. Group organizers schedule remote or in-person events that group members attend. Meetup's domain has several data models, including groups, categories, and cities.

The meetup directory houses all data sets for this chapter. Let's begin our exploration by importing the groups1.csv and groups2.csv files. These files hold a sample of Meetup's registered groups. Each group includes an ID, name, associated category ID, and associated city ID. Here's what groups1 looks like:

```
In  [2] groups1 = pd.read_csv("meetup/groups1.csv")
        groups1.head()
```

```
Out [2]
```

	group_id	name	category_id	city_id
0	6388	Alternative Health NYC	14	10001
1	6510	Alternative Energy Meetup	4	10001
2	8458	NYC Animal Rights	26	10001
3	8940	The New York City Anime Group	29	10001
4	10104	NYC Pit Bull Group	26	10001

Let's also import groups2.csv. Notice that both CSVs have the same four columns. We can imagine that the groups data was somehow split and stored across two files instead of one:

```
In  [3] groups2 = pd.read_csv("meetup/groups2.csv")
        groups2.head()
```

```
Out [3]
```

	group_id	name	category_id	city_id
0	18879327	BachataMania	5	10001
1	18880221	Photoshoot Chicago - Photography and ...	27	60601
2	18880426	Chicago Adult Push / Kick Scooter Gro...	31	60601
3	18880495	Chicago International Soccer Club	32	60601
4	18880695	Impact.tech San Francisco Meetup	2	94101

Each group has a `category_id` foreign key. We can find information on categories in the categories.csv file. Each row in this file stores the category's ID and name:

```
In  [4] categories = pd.read_csv("meetup/categories.csv")

        categories.head()
```

```
Out [4]
```

	category_id	category_name
0	1	Arts & Culture
1	3	Cars & Motorcycles
2	4	Community & Environment
3	5	Dancing
4	6	Education & Learning

Each group also has a `city_id` foreign key. The cities.csv data set stores the city information. A city has a unique ID, name, state, and zip code. Let's take a look:

```
In  [5] pd.read_csv("meetup/cities.csv").head()
```

```
Out [5]
```

	id	city	state	zip
0	7093	West New York	NJ	7093
1	10001	New York	NY	10001
2	13417	New York Mills	NY	13417
3	46312	East Chicago	IN	46312
4	56567	New York Mills	MN	56567

The cities data set has a small issue. Look at the zip value in the first row. 7093 is an invalid zip code; the value in the CSV is in fact 07093. Zip codes can start with a leading zero. Unfortunately, pandas assumes that the zip codes are integers and thus strips the leading zeroes from the values. To solve this problem, we can add the `dtype` parameter to the `read_csv` function. `dtype` accepts a dictionary in which keys denote column names and values denote the data type to assign to that column. Let's make sure that pandas imports the zip column's values as strings:

```
In  [6] cities = pd.read_csv(
            "meetup/cities.csv", dtype = {"zip": "string"}
        )
        cities.head()
```

```
Out [6]
```

	id	city	state	zip
0	7093	West New York	NJ	07093
1	10001	New York	NY	10001
2	13417	New York Mills	NY	13417
3	46312	East Chicago	IN	46312
4	56567	New York Mills	MN	56567

Excellent; we're ready to proceed. To summarize, each group in groups1 and groups2 belongs to a category and a city. The category_id and group_id columns store foreign keys. The category_id column values map to the category_id column in `categories`. The city_id column values map to the id column in cities. With our data tables loaded into Jupyter, we're ready to start joining them.

10.2   Concatenating data sets

The simplest way to combine two data sets is with *concatenation*—appending one DataFrame to the end of another.

The groups1 and groups2 DataFrames both have the same four column names. Let's assume that they are two halves of a greater whole. We'd like to combine their rows into a single DataFrame. Pandas has a convenient concat function at the top level of the library. We can pass its objs parameter a list of DataFrames. Pandas will concatenate the objects in the order in which they appear in the objs list. The next example concatenates the rows in groups2 to the end of groups1:

```
In  [7] pd.concat(objs = [groups1, groups2])

Out [7]
```

	group_id	name	category_id	city_id
0	6388	Alternative Health NYC	14	10001
1	6510	Alternative Energy Meetup	4	10001
2	8458	NYC Animal Rights	26	10001
3	8940	The New York City Anime Group	29	10001
4	10104	NYC Pit Bull Group	26	10001
...	...	...	...	...
8326	26377464	Shinect	34	94101
8327	26377698	The art of getting what you want [...	14	94101
8328	26378067	Streeterville Running Group	9	60601
8329	26378128	Just Dance NYC	23	10001
8330	26378470	FREE Arabic Chicago Evanston North...	31	60601

16330 rows × 4 columns

The concatenated DataFrame has 16,330 rows! As you might have guessed, its length is equal to the sum of the lengths of the groups1 and groups2 DataFrames:

```
In  [8] len(groups1)

Out [8] 7999

In  [9] len(groups2)

Out [9] 8331

In  [10] len(groups1) + len(groups2)

Out [10] 16330
```

Pandas preserves the original index labels from both DataFrames in the concatenation, which is why we see a final index position of 8,330 in the concatenated Data-Frame even though it has more than 16,000 rows. What we are seeing is the 8,330 index from the end of the groups2 DataFrame. Pandas does not care that the same index number appears in both groups1 and groups2. As a result, the concatenated index has duplicate index labels.

We can pass the `concat` function's `ignore_index` parameter an argument of `True` to generate pandas' standard numeric index. The concatenated `DataFrame` will discard the original index labels:

```
In  [11] pd.concat(objs = [groups1, groups2], ignore_index = True)

Out [11]
```

	group_id	name	category_id	city_id
0	6388	Alternative Health NYC	14	10001
1	6510	Alternative Energy Meetup	4	10001
2	8458	NYC Animal Rights	26	10001
3	8940	The New York City Anime Group	29	10001
4	10104	NYC Pit Bull Group	26	10001
...	...	...	...	...
16325	26377464	Shinect	34	94101
16326	26377698	The art of getting what you want ...	14	94101
16327	26378067	Streeterville Running Group	9	60601
16328	26378128	Just Dance NYC	23	10001
16329	26378470	FREE Arabic Chicago Evanston Nort...	31	60601

16330 rows × 4 columns

What if we wanted the best of both worlds: to create a nonduplicate index but also preserve which `DataFrame` each row of data came from? One solution is to add a `keys` parameter and pass it a list of strings. Pandas will associate each string in the `keys` list with the `DataFrame` at the same index position in the `objs` list. The `keys` and `objs` lists must be of equal length.

The next example assigns the `groups1` `DataFrame` a key of `"G1"` and the `groups2` `DataFrame` a key of `"G2"`. The `concat` function returns a `MultiIndex` `DataFrame`. The `MultiIndex`'s first level stores the keys, and its second level stores the index labels from the respective `DataFrame`:

```
In  [12] pd.concat(objs = [groups1, groups2], keys = ["G1", "G2"])

Out [12]
```

		group_id	name	category_id	city_id
G1	0	6388	Alternative Health NYC	14	10001
	1	6510	Alternative Energy Meetup	4	10001
	2	8458	NYC Animal Rights	26	10001
	3	8940	The New York City Anime Group	29	10001
	4	10104	NYC Pit Bull Group	26	10001
...	...	...	...	...	...
G2	8326	26377464	Shinect	34	94101
	8327	26377698	The art of getting what you wan...	14	94101
	8328	26378067	Streeterville Running Group	9	60601
	8329	26378128	Just Dance NYC	23	10001
	8330	26378470	FREE Arabic Chicago Evanston No...	31	60601

16330 rows × 4 columns

We can extract the original `DataFrames` by accessing the `G1` or `G2` keys on the first level of the `MultiIndex`. (See chapter 7 for a refresher on using the `loc` accessor on `MultiIndex` `DataFrames`.) Before we proceed, let's assign the concatenated `DataFrame` to a `groups` variable:

```
In [13] groups = pd.concat(objs = [groups1, groups2], ignore_index = True)
```

We'll come back to `groups` in section 10.4.

10.3 *Missing values in concatenated DataFrames*

When concatenating two `DataFrames`, pandas places `NaNs` at intersections of row labels and column labels that the data sets do not share. Consider the following two `DataFrames`, both of which have a Football column. The sports_champions_A `DataFrame` has an exclusive Baseball column, and the sports_champions_B `DataFrame` has an exclusive Hockey column:

```
In [14] sports_champions_A = pd.DataFrame(
            data = [
                ["New England Patriots", "Houston Astros"],
                ["Philadelphia Eagles", "Boston Red Sox"]
            ],
            columns = ["Football", "Baseball"],
            index = [2017, 2018]
        )

        sports_champions_A

Out [14]
```

	Football	Baseball
2017	New England Patriots	Houston Astros
2018	Philadelphia Eagles	Boston Red Sox

```
In [15] sports_champions_B = pd.DataFrame(
            data = [
                ["New England Patriots", "St. Louis Blues"],
                ["Kansas City Chiefs", "Tampa Bay Lightning"]
            ],
            columns = ["Football", "Hockey"],
            index = [2019, 2020]
        )

        sports_champions_B

Out [15]
```

	Football	Hockey
2019	New England Patriots	St. Louis Blues
2020	Kansas City Chiefs	Tampa Bay Lightning

If we concatenate the `DataFrames`, we will create missing values in the Baseball and Hockey columns. The sports_champions_A `DataFrame` has no values to place in the Hockey column, and the sports_champions_B `DataFrame` has no values to place in the Baseball column:

```
In  [16] pd.concat(objs = [sports_champions_A, sports_champions_B])

Out [16]
```

	Football	Baseball	Hockey
2017	New England Patriots	Houston Astros	NaN
2018	Philadelphia Eagles	Boston Red Sox	NaN
2019	New England Patriots	NaN	St. Louis Blues
2020	Kansas City Chiefs	NaN	Tampa Bay Lightning

By default, pandas concatenates rows on the horizontal axis. Sometimes, we want to append the rows on the vertical axis instead. Consider the sports_champions_C `DataFrame`, which has the same two index labels as sports_champions_A (2017 and 2018) but two different columns, Hockey and Basketball:

```
In  [17] sports_champions_C = pd.DataFrame(
            data = [
                ["Pittsburgh Penguins", "Golden State Warriors"],
                ["Washington Capitals", "Golden State Warriors"]
            ],
            columns = ["Hockey", "Basketball"],
            index = [2017, 2018]
        )

        sports_champions_C

Out [17]
```

	Hockey	Basketball
2017	Pittsburgh Penguins	Golden State Warriors
2018	Washington Capitals	Golden State Warriors

When we concatenate sports_champions_A and sports_champions_C, pandas appends the rows of the second `DataFrame` to the end of the first. The process creates duplicate 2017 and 2018 index labels:

```
In  [18] pd.concat(objs = [sports_champions_A, sports_champions_C])

Out [18]
```

	Football	Baseball	Hockey	Basketball
2017	New England P...	Houston Astros	NaN	NaN
2018	Philadelphia ...	Boston Red Sox	NaN	NaN
2017	NaN	NaN	Pittsburgh Pe...	Golden State ...
2018	NaN	NaN	Washington Ca...	Golden State ...

This result is not what we want. Rather, we'd like to align the duplicate index labels (2017 and 2018) so that the columns have no missing values.

The concat function includes an axis parameter. We can pass that parameter an argument of either 1 or "columns" to concatenate the DataFrames across the column axis:

```
In  [19] # The two lines below are equivalent
        pd.concat(
            objs = [sports_champions_A, sports_champions_C],
            axis = 1
        )
        pd.concat(
            objs = [sports_champions_A, sports_champions_C],
            axis = "columns"
        )
```

```
Out [19]
```

	Football	Baseball	Hockey	Basketball
2017	New England P...	Houston Astros	Pittsburgh Pe...	Golden State ...
2018	Philadelphia ...	Boston Red Sox	Washington Ca...	Golden State ...

Much better!

In summary, the concat function combines two DataFrames by appending one to the end of the other on either the horizontal axis or the vertical axis. I like to describe the process as "gluing" two data sets together.

10.4 Left joins

Compared with a concatenation, a *join* uses a logical criterion to determine which rows or columns to merge between two data sets. A join can target only rows with shared values between both data sets, for example. The following sections cover three types of joins: left, inner, and outer. Let's walk through them one by one.

A *left join* uses keys from one data set to pull in values from another. It is equivalent to a VLOOKUP operation in Excel. A left join is optimal when one data set is the focal point of the analysis. We pull in the second data set to provide supplemental information related to the primary data set. Consider the diagram in figure 10.1. Think of each circle as being a DataFrame. The DataFrame on the left is the focus of the analysis.

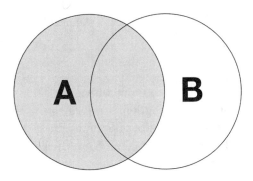

Figure 10.1 Left join diagram

Here's a quick reminder of what our groups data set looks like:

```
In [20] groups.head(3)

Out [20]
```

	group_id	name	category_id	city_id
0	6388	Alternative Health NYC	14	10001
1	6510	Alternative Energy Meetup	4	10001
2	8458	NYC Animal Rights	26	10001

The foreign keys in the category_id column reference the IDs in the categories data set:

```
In [21] categories.head(3)

Out [21]
```

	category_id	category_name
0	1	Arts & Culture
1	3	Cars & Motorcycles
2	4	Community & Environment

Let's execute a left join on groups to add category information for each group. We'll use the merge method to merge one DataFrame into another. The method's first parameter, right, accepts a DataFrame. The terminology comes from the previous diagram. The right DataFrame is the circle on the right, the "second" data set. We can pass a string denoting the type of join to the method's how parameter; we'll pass in "left". We also must tell pandas which columns to use to match values between the two DataFrames. Let's add an on parameter with a value of "category_id". We can use the on parameter only when the column name is equal between DataFrames. In our case, both the groups and categories DataFrames have a category_id column:

```
In [22] groups.merge(categories, how = "left", on = "category_id").head()

Out [22]
```

	group_id	name	category_id	city_id	category_name
0	6388	Alternative Heal...	14	10001	Health & Wellbeing
1	6510	Alternative Ener...	4	10001	Community & Envi...
2	8458	NYC Animal Rights	26	10001	NaN
3	8940	The New York Cit...	29	10001	Sci-Fi & Fantasy
4	10104	NYC Pit Bull Group	26	10001	NaN

There it is! Pandas pulls in the categories table's columns whenever it finds a match for the category_id value in groups. The one exception is the category_id column, which is listed only once. Note that when the library does not find a category_id in categories, it displays NaN values in the category_name column from categories. We can see an example on rows 2 and 4 of the previous output.

10.5   *Inner joins*

An *inner join* targets values that exist across two DataFrames. Consider figure 10.2; an inner join targets the colored overlap in the middle of the circles.

In an inner join, pandas excludes values that exist only in the first Data-Frame and only in the second Data-Frame.

Here's a reminder of what the groups and categories data sets look like:

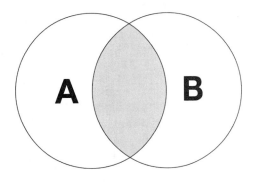

Figure 10.2   Inner join diagram

```
In  [23] groups.head(3)
```

```
Out [23]
```

	group_id	name	category_id	city_id
0	6388	Alternative Health NYC	14	10001
1	6510	Alternative Energy Meetup	4	10001
2	8458	NYC Animal Rights	26	10001

```
In  [24] categories.head(3)
```

```
Out [24]
```

	category_id	category_name
0	1	Arts & Culture
1	3	Cars & Motorcycles
2	4	Community & Environment

Let's identify the categories that exist in both data sets. From a technical perspective, we once again want to target the rows from the two DataFrames with equal values in the category_id columns. In this situation, it doesn't matter whether we invoke the merge method on group or categories. An inner join identifies common elements in both data sets; the results will be the same regardless. For the next example, let's call the merge method on groups:

```
In  [25] groups.merge(categories, how = "inner", on = "category_id")
```

```
Out [25]
```

	group_id	name	category_id	city_id	category_name
0	6388	Alternative He...	14	10001	Health & Wellb...
1	54126	Energy Healers...	14	10001	Health & Wellb...
2	67776	Flourishing Li...	14	10001	Health & Wellb...
3	111855	Hypnosis & NLP...	14	10001	Health & Wellb...
4	129277	The Live Food ...	14	60601	Health & Wellb...
...	...	...	...	...	...

8032	25536270	New York Cucko...	17	10001	Lifestyle
8033	25795045	Pagans Paradis...	17	10001	Lifestyle
8034	25856573	Fuck Yeah Femm...	17	94101	Lifestyle
8035	26158102	Chicago Crossd...	17	60601	Lifestyle
8036	26219043	Corporate Goes...	17	10001	Lifestyle

8037 rows × 5 columns

The merged `DataFrame` includes all columns from both the groups and categories `DataFrames`. The values in the category_id column appear in both groups and categories. The category_id column is listed only once. We don't need a duplicate column because the values in category_id are the same for groups and categories in an inner join.

Let's add some context to what pandas did. The first four rows in the merged `DataFrame` have a category_id of 14. We can filter for that ID in the groups and categories `DataFrames`:

```
In  [26] groups[groups["category_id"] == 14]
```

Out [26]

	group_id	name	category_id	city_id
0	6388	Alternative Health NYC	14	10001
52	54126	Energy Healers NYC	14	10001
78	67776	Flourishing Life Meetup	14	10001
121	111855	Hypnosis & NLP NYC - Update Your ...	14	10001
136	129277	The Live Food Chicago Community	14	60601
...	...	...	...	...
16174	26291539	The Transformation Project: Colla...	14	94101
16201	26299876	Cognitive Empathy, How To Transla...	14	10001
16248	26322976	Contemplative Practices Group	14	94101
16314	26366221	The art of getting what you want:...	14	94101
16326	26377698	The art of getting what you want ...	14	94101

870 rows × 4 columns

```
In  [27] categories[categories["category_id"] == 14]
```

Out [27]

	category_id	category_name
8	14	Health & Wellbeing

The merged `DataFrame` creates one row for each group_id match across the two `DataFrames`. There are 870 rows in groups and one row in categories with a group_id of 14. Pandas pairs each of the 870 rows in groups with the single row in categories and creates a total of 870 rows in the merged `DataFrame`. Because an inner join creates a new row for each value match, the merged `DataFrame` can be significantly larger than the original ones. If there were three categories with an ID of 14, for example, pandas would create 2610 rows (870 x 3).

10.6 *Outer joins*

An *outer join* combines all records across two data sets. Exclusivity does not matter with an outer join. Figure 10.3 shows the results of an outer join; pandas includes all values irrespective of whether they belong in one data set or both data sets.

Here's a reminder of what the groups and cities `DataFrames` look like:

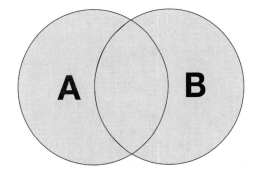

Figure 10.3 Outer join diagram

```
In  [28] groups.head(3)
```

```
Out [28]
```

	group_id	name	category_id	city_id
0	6388	Alternative Health NYC	14	10001
1	6510	Alternative Energy Meetup	4	10001
2	8458	NYC Animal Rights	26	10001

```
In  [29] cities.head(3)
```

```
Out [29]
```

	id	city	state	zip
0	7093	West New York	NJ	07093
1	10001	New York	NY	10001
2	13417	New York Mills	NY	13417

Let's merge groups and cities with an outer join. We'll pull in all cities: the ones exclusive to groups, the ones exclusive to cities, and the ones common to both.

So far, we've used only shared column names to merge data sets. When column names differ between data sets, we must pass different parameters to the `merge` method. Instead of the `on` parameter, we can use the `merge` method's `left_on` and `right_on` parameters. We pass `left_on` the column name in the left `DataFrame` and `right_on` the column name in the right `DataFrame`. Here, we perform an outer join to merge city information from cities into the groups `DataFrame`:

```
In  [30] groups.merge(
            cities, how = "outer", left_on = "city_id", right_on = "id"
         )
```

```
Out [30]
```

	group_id	name	category_id	city_id	city	state	zip
0	6388.0	Altern...	14.0	10001.0	New York	NY	10001
1	6510.0	Altern...	4.0	10001.0	New York	NY	10001
2	8458.0	NYC An...	26.0	10001.0	New York	NY	10001
3	8940.0	The Ne...	29.0	10001.0	New York	NY	10001
4	10104.0	NYC Pi...	26.0	10001.0	New York	NY	10001
...	...	...	...	...	...	...	...

```
16329    243034...   Midwes...      34.0    60064.0   North ...   IL   60064
16330       NaN        NaN           NaN       NaN     New Yo...   NY   13417
16331       NaN        NaN           NaN       NaN     East C...   IN   46312
16332       NaN        NaN           NaN       NaN     New Yo...   MN   56567
16333       NaN        NaN           NaN       NaN     Chicag...   CA   95712
```

16334 rows × 8 columns

The final `DataFrame` has all city IDs from both data sets. If pandas finds a values match between the city_id and id columns, it merges the columns from the two `Data-Frames` in a single row. We can see some examples in the first five rows. The city_id column stores the common id.

If one `DataFrame` has a value that the other does not, pandas places a NaN value in the city_id column. We can see some examples at the end of the data set. This placement will happen irrespective of whether groups or cities has the exclusive value.

We can pass `True` to the `merge` method's `indicator` parameter to identify which `DataFrame` a value belongs to. The merged `DataFrame` will include a _merge column that stores the values "both", "left_only", and "right_only":

```
In  [31] groups.merge(
            cities,
            how = "outer",
            left_on = "city_id",
            right_on = "id",
            indicator = True
        )
```

Out [31]

	group_id	name	category_id	city_id	city	state	zip	_merge
0	6388.0	Alt...	14.0	100...	New...	NY	10001	both
1	6510.0	Alt...	4.0	100...	New...	NY	10001	both
2	8458.0	NYC...	26.0	100...	New...	NY	10001	both
3	8940.0	The...	29.0	100...	New...	NY	10001	both
4	101...	NYC...	26.0	100...	New...	NY	10001	both
...	...	...	...	...	...	...	...	...
16329	243...	Mid...	34.0	600...	Nor...	IL	60064	both
16330	NaN	NaN	NaN	NaN	New...	NY	13417	rig...
16331	NaN	NaN	NaN	NaN	Eas...	IN	46312	rig...
16332	NaN	NaN	NaN	NaN	New...	MN	56567	rig...
16333	NaN	NaN	NaN	NaN	Chi...	CA	95712	rig...

16334 rows × 9 columns

We can use the _merge column to filter rows that belong to either of the `DataFrames`. The next example extracts rows with a value of "right_only" in the _merge column or, equivalently, the city IDs that are present only in cities, the right `DataFrame`:

```
In  [32] outer_join = groups.merge(
            cities,
            how = "outer",
            left_on = "city_id",
            right_on = "id",
            indicator = True
        )
```

```
        in_right_only = outer_join["_merge"] == "right_only"

        outer_join[in_right_only].head()
```

Out [32]

	group_id	name	category_id	city_id	city	state	zip	_merge
16330	NaN	NaN	NaN	NaN	New Y...	NY	13417	right...
16331	NaN	NaN	NaN	NaN	East ...	IN	46312	right...
16332	NaN	NaN	NaN	NaN	New Y...	MN	56567	right...
16333	NaN	NaN	NaN	NaN	Chica...	CA	95712	right...

With a few lines of code, we can easily filter out exclusive values in each data set.

10.7 Merging on index labels

Imagine that a `DataFrame` we'd like to join stores its primary keys in its index. Let's simulate this scenario. We can invoke the `set_index` method on cities to set its id column as its `DataFrame` index:

```
In  [33] cities.head(3)
```

Out [33]

	id	city	state	zip
0	7093	West New York	NJ	07093
1	10001	New York	NY	10001
2	13417	New York Mills	NY	13417

```
In  [34] cities = cities.set_index("id")

In  [35] cities.head(3)
```

Out [35]

id	city	state	zip
7093	West New York	NJ	07093
10001	New York	NY	10001
13417	New York Mills	NY	13417

Let's use a left join to merge cities into groups again. Here's a quick reminder of what groups looks like:

```
In  [36] groups.head(3)
```

Out [36]

	group_id	name	category_id	city_id
0	6388	Alternative Health NYC	14	10001
1	6510	Alternative Energy Meetup	4	10001
2	8458	NYC Animal Rights	26	10001

Now we want to compare the values in the city_id column in groups with the index labels of cities. When we invoke the `merge` method, we'll pass the how parameter an argument of `"left"` for a left join. We'll use the `left_on` parameter to tell pandas to look for matches in the city_id column in groups, the left `DataFrame`. To look for matches in the index of the right `DataFrame`, we can provide a different parameter, `right_index`, and set it to `True`. The argument tells pandas to look for city_id matches in the right `DataFrame`'s index:

```
In  [37] groups.merge(
            cities,
            how = "left",
            left_on = "city_id",
            right_index = True
        )
```

Out [37]

	group_id	name	category_id	city_id	city	state	zip
0	6388	Alterna...	14	10001	New York	NY	10001
1	6510	Alterna...	4	10001	New York	NY	10001
2	8458	NYC Ani...	26	10001	New York	NY	10001
3	8940	The New...	29	10001	New York	NY	10001
4	10104	NYC Pit...	26	10001	New York	NY	10001
...	...	...	...	...	...	...	...
16325	26377464	Shinect	34	94101	San Fra...	CA	94101
16326	26377698	The art...	14	94101	San Fra...	CA	94101
16327	26378067	Streete...	9	60601	Chicago	IL	60290
16328	26378128	Just Da...	23	10001	New York	NY	10001
16329	26378470	FREE Ar...	31	60601	Chicago	IL	60290

16330 rows × 7 columns

The method also supports a complementary `left_index` parameter. Pass that parameter an argument of `True` to tell pandas to look for matches in the left `DataFrame`'s index. The left `DataFrame` is the one that we invoke the `merge` method on.

10.8 *Coding challenge*

We've reached the end of our exploration; thanks for joining us (pun intended)! Let's practice the concepts introduced in this chapter.

This coding challenge's tables summarize sales in a fictional restaurant. The week_1_sales.csv and week_2_sales.csv files hold listings of weekly transactions. Each restaurant order includes the ID of a customer who placed an order and the ID of the food item they purchased. Here's a preview of the first five rows of week_1_sales:

```
In  [38] pd.read_csv("restaurant/week_1_sales.csv").head()
```

Out [38]

	Customer ID	Food ID
0	537	9
1	97	4
2	658	1
3	202	2
4	155	9

The week_2_sales data set has an identical shape. Let's import the two CSVs and assign them to week1 and week2 variables:

```
In [39] week1 = pd.read_csv("restaurant/week_1_sales.csv")
        week2 = pd.read_csv("restaurant/week_2_sales.csv")
```

The Customer ID columns hold foreign keys that reference values in the ID column in customers.csv. Each record in customers.csv includes a customer's first name, last name, gender, company, and occupation. Let's import that data set with the read_csv function and set its ID column as the DataFrame index with the index_col parameter:

```
In [40] pd.read_csv("restaurant/customers.csv", index_col = "ID").head()

Out [40]
```

ID	First Name	Last Name	Gender	Company	Occupation
1	Joseph	Perkins	Male	Dynazzy	Community Outreach Specialist
2	Jennifer	Alvarez	Female	DabZ	Senior Quality Engineer
3	Roger	Black	Male	Tagfeed	Account Executive
4	Steven	Evans	Male	Fatz	Registered Nurse
5	Judy	Morrison	Female	Demivee	Legal Assistant

```
In [41] customers = pd.read_csv(
            "restaurant/customers.csv", index_col = "ID"
        )
```

There's another column of foreign keys in the weeks1 and weeks2 DataFrames. The Food ID foreign key connects to the ID column in foods.csv. A food item includes an ID, a name, and a price. When we import this data set, let's set its Food ID column as the DataFrame index:

```
In [42] pd.read_csv("restaurant/foods.csv", index_col = "Food ID")

Out [42]
```

Food ID	Food Item	Price
1	Sushi	3.99
2	Burrito	9.99
3	Taco	2.99
4	Quesadilla	4.25
5	Pizza	2.49
6	Pasta	13.99
7	Steak	24.99
8	Salad	11.25
9	Donut	0.99
10	Drink	1.75

```
In [43] foods = pd.read_csv("restaurant/foods.csv", index_col = "Food ID")
```

With the data sets imported, we're ready to tackle the exercises.

10.8.1 Problems

Here are the challenges:

1 Concatenate the two weeks of sales data into one DataFrame. Assign the week1 DataFrame a key of "Week 1" and the week2 DataFrame a key of "Week 2".
2 Find the customers who ate at the restaurant both weeks.
3 Find the customers who ate at the restaurant both weeks and ordered the same item each week.

HINT   You can join data sets on multiple columns by passing the on parameter a list of columns.

4 Identify which customers came in only on Week 1 and only on Week 2.
5 Each row in the week1 DataFrame identifies a customer who purchased a food item. For each row, pull in the customer's information from the customers DataFrame.

10.8.2 Solutions

Let's explore the solutions:

1 Our first challenge is to combine the two weeks of restaurant sales data into a single DataFrame. The concat function at the top level of pandas offers a perfect solution. We can pass the two DataFrames in a list to the function's objs parameter. To assign a MultiIndex level to each DataFrame in the result, we'll also provide the keys parameter a list with the level labels:

```
In  [44] pd.concat(objs = [week1, week2], keys = ["Week 1", "Week 2"])

Out [44]
```

		Customer ID	Food ID
Week 1	0	537	9
	1	97	4
	2	658	1
	3	202	2
	4	155	9
	...	...	...
Week 2	245	783	10
	246	556	10
	247	547	9
	248	252	9
	249	249	6

```
500 rows × 2 columns
```

2 Next, we want to identify customers who visited the restaurant both weeks. From a technical perspective, we need to find the Customer IDs present in both the week1 and week2 DataFrames. An inner join is what we're looking for here. Let's invoke the merge method on week1 and pass in week2 as the right DataFrame. We'll declare the join type as "inner" and tell pandas to look for shared values in the Customer ID columns:

```
In  [45] week1.merge(
             right = week2, how = "inner", on = "Customer ID"
         ).head()
```

Out [45]

	Customer ID	Food ID_x	Food ID_y
0	537	9	5
1	155	9	3
2	155	1	3
3	503	5	8
4	503	5	9

Remember that the inner join shows all matches of customer IDs across the week1 and week2 DataFramess. Thus, there are duplicates in the result (customers 155 and 503). If we wanted to remove duplicates, we could invoke the drop_duplicates method introduced in chapter 5:

```
In  [46] week1.merge(
             right = week2, how = "inner", on = "Customer ID"
         ).drop_duplicates(subset = ["Customer ID"]).head()
```

Out [46]

	Customer ID	Food ID_x	Food ID_y
0	537	9	5
1	155	9	3
3	503	5	8
5	550	6	7
6	101	7	4

3 The third challenge asks to find the customers who visited the restaurant both weeks and ordered the same item. Once again, an inner join is the right option for finding values present in both the left and right DataFrames. This time around, however, we have to pass the on parameter a list with two columns. The values in both the Customer ID and Food ID columns must match between week1 and week2:

```
In  [47] week1.merge(
             right = week2,
             how = "inner",
             on = ["Customer ID", "Food ID"]
         )
```

Out [47]

	Customer ID	Food ID
0	304	3
1	540	3
2	937	10
3	233	3
4	21	4
5	21	4
6	922	1
7	578	5
8	578	5s

4 One solution to identify the customers who came in only one week is to use an outer join. We can match records across the two DataFrames by using values in the Customer ID column. Let's pass the indicator parameter a value of True to add a _merge column. Pandas will indicate whether the Customer ID exists in only the left table ("left_only"), only the right table ("right_only"), or both tables ("both"):

```
In  [48] week1.merge(
              right = week2,
              how = "outer",
              on = "Customer ID",
              indicator = True
          ).head()
```

Out [48]

	Customer ID	Food ID_x	Food ID_y	_merge
0	537	9.0	5.0	both
1	97	4.0	NaN	left_only
2	658	1.0	NaN	left_only
3	202	2.0	NaN	left_only
4	155	9.0	3.0	both

5 The final challenge asks to pull customer information into the week1 table. A left join is an optimal solution. Invoke the merge method on the week1 Data-Frame, passing in the customers DataFrame as the right data set. Pass the how parameter an argument of "left".

The tricky part of this challenge is that the week1 DataFrame stores the customer IDs in its Customer ID column, whereas the customers DataFrame stores them in its index labels. To solve the problem, we can pass the left_on parameter the column name from the week1 DataFrame and the right_index parameter a value of True:

```
In  [49] week1.merge(
              right = customers,
              how = "left",
              left_on = "Customer ID",
              right_index = True
          ).head()
```

Out [49]

	Customer ID	Food ID	First Name	Last Name	Gender	Company	Occupation
0	537	9	Cheryl	Carroll	Female	Zoombeat	Regist...
1	97	4	Amanda	Watkins	Female	Ozu	Accoun...
2	658	1	Patrick	Webb	Male	Browsebug	Commun...
3	202	2	Louis	Campbell	Male	Rhynoodle	Accoun...
4	155	9	Carolyn	Diaz	Female	Gigazoom	Databa...

Congratulations on completing the coding challenge!

Summary

- A *primary key* is a unique identifier for a record in a data set.
- A *foreign key* is a reference to a record in another data set.
- The `concat` function concatenates `DataFrame`s on either the horizontal or vertical axis.
- The `merge` method joins two `DataFrame`s based on some logical criterion.
- An *inner join* identifies common values between two `DataFrame`s. For any matches, pandas pulls all columns from the right `DataFrame` into the left `DataFrame`.
- An *outer join* merges two `DataFrame`s. Pandas includes values whether they are exclusive to one data set or shared.
- A *left join* pulls in columns from the right `DataFrame` when their values exist in the left `DataFrame`. The operation is equivalent to a `VLOOKUP` in Excel.
- A left join is ideal when the second `DataFrame` contains supplemental information that we'd like to attach to the primary `DataFrame`.

Working with dates and times

11

This chapter covers

- Converting `Series` of strings to datetimes
- Retrieving date and time information from datetime objects
- Rounding dates to week, month, and quarter ends
- Adding and subtracting datetimes to and from each other

A *datetime* is a data type for storing date and time. It can model a specific date (such as October 4, 2021), a particular time (such as 11:50 a.m.), or both (such as October 4, 2021 at 11:50 a.m.). Datetimes are valuable because they allow us to track trends over time. A financial analyst may use datetimes to determine the weekdays when a stock performs best. A restaurant owner may use them to discover the peak hours that customers are patronizing the business. An operations manager may use them to identify the parts of a process that are creating bottlenecks in production. The *when* in a data set can often lead to the *why*.

In this chapter, we'll review Python's built-in datetime objects and see how pandas improves them with its `Timestamp` and `Timedelta` objects. We'll also learn how to use the library to convert strings to dates, add and subtract offsets of time, calculate durations, and more. There's no time to waste (pun intended), so let's dive in.

11.1 Introducing the Timestamp object

A *module* is a file with Python code. Python's standard library is a collection of more than 250 modules baked into the language that provide battle-tested solutions to common problems such as database connections, mathematics, and testing. The standard library exists so developers can write software that uses core language features rather than install additional dependencies. It's often said that Python comes with "batteries included"; like a toy, the language is ready to be used out of the box.

11.1.1 How Python works with datetimes

To reduce memory consumption, Python does not autoload its standard library modules by default. Instead, we must explicitly import any desired modules into our project. As with an external package (such as pandas), we can import a module with the import keyword and assign it an alias with the as keyword. The standard library's datetime module is our target; it stores classes for working with dates and times. dt is a popular alias for the datetime module. Let's spin up a fresh Jupyter Notebook and import datetime along with the pandas library:

```
In  [1] import datetime as dt
        import pandas as pd
```

Let's review four classes in the module: date, time, datetime, and timedelta. (See appendix B for more details on classes and objects.)

A date models a single day in history. The object does not store any time. The date class constructor accepts sequential year, month, and day parameters. All parameters expect integers. The next example instantiates a date object for my birthday, April 12, 1991:

```
In  [2] # The two lines below are equivalent
        birthday = dt.date(1991, 4, 12)
        birthday = dt.date(year = 1991, month = 4, day = 12)
        birthday

Out [2] datetime.date(1991, 4, 12)
```

The date object saves the constructor's arguments as object attributes. We can access their values with the year, month, and day attributes:

```
In  [3] birthday.year

Out [3] 1991

In  [4] birthday.month

Out [4] 4
```

```
In  [5] birthday.day
```

```
Out [5] 12
```

A date object is *immutable*—we cannot change its internal state after we create it. Python will raise an AttributeError exception if we attempt to overwrite any date attributes:

```
In  [6] birthday.month = 10
```

```
---------------------------------------------------------------------------
AttributeError                             Traceback (most recent call last)
<ipython-input-15-2690a31d7b19> in <module>
----> 1 birthday.month = 10

AttributeError: attribute 'month' of 'datetime.date' objects is not writable
```

The complementary time class models a specific time of day. The date is irrelevant. The time constructor's first three parameters accept integer arguments for hour, minute, and second. Like a date object, a time object is immutable. The next example instantiates a time object modeling 6:43:25 a.m.:

```
In  [7] # The two lines below are equivalent
        alarm_clock = dt.time(6, 43, 25)
        alarm_clock = dt.time(hour = 6, minute = 43, second = 25)
        alarm_clock
```

```
Out [7] datetime.time(6, 43, 25)
```

The default argument for all three parameters is 0. If we instantiate a time object without arguments, it will represent midnight (12:00:00 a.m.). Midnight is 0 hours, 0 minutes, and 0 seconds into the day:

```
In  [8] dt.time()
```

```
Out [8] datetime.time(0, 0)
```

The next example passes in 9 for the hour parameter, 42 for the second parameter, and no value for the minute parameter. The time object substitutes 0 for the minutes value. The resulting time is 9:00:42 a.m.:

```
In  [9] dt.time(hour = 9, second = 42)
```

```
Out [9] datetime.time(9, 0, 42)
```

The time constructor uses a 24-hour clock; we can pass it an hour value greater than or equal to 12 to represent a time in the afternoon or evening,. The next example models 19:43:22 or, equivalently, 7:43:22 p.m.:

```
In  [10] dt.time(hour = 19, minute = 43, second = 22)
```

```
Out [10] datetime.time(19, 43, 22)
```

The `time` object saves our constructor arguments as object attributes. We can access their values with the `hour`, `minute`, and `second` attributes:

```
In  [11] alarm_clock.hour
```

```
Out [11] 6
```

```
In  [12] alarm_clock.minute
```

```
Out [12] 43
```

```
In  [13] alarm_clock.second
```

```
Out [13] 25
```

Next in line is the `datetime` object, which holds both a date and a time. Its first six parameters are the `year`, `month`, `day`, `hour`, `minute`, and `second`:

```
In  [14] # The two lines below are equivalent
         moon_landing = dt.datetime(1969, 7, 20, 22, 56, 20)
         moon_landing = dt.datetime(
             year = 1969,
             month = 7,
             day = 20,
             hour = 22,
             minute = 56,
             second = 20
         )
         moon_landing
```

```
Out [14] datetime.datetime(1969, 7, 20, 22, 56, 20)
```

The `year`, `month`, and `day` parameters are required. The time-related attributes are optional and default to 0. The next example models midnight on January 1, 2020 (12:00:00 a.m.). We explicitly pass in the `year`, `month`, and `day` parameters; the `hour`, `minute`, and `second` parameters implicitly fall back to 0:

```
In  [15] dt.datetime(2020, 1, 1)
```

```
Out [15] datetime.datetime(2020, 1, 1, 0, 0)
```

Our final noteworthy object from the `datetime` module is `timedelta`, which models a duration—a length of time. Its constructor's parameters include `weeks`, `days`, and `hours`. All the parameters are optional and default to 0. The constructor adds the time lengths to calculate the total duration. In the next example, we add 8 weeks and 6 days for a total of 62 days (8 weeks * 7 days + 6 days). Python also adds 3 hours, 58 minutes, and 12 seconds for a grand total of 14,292 seconds (238 minutes * 60 seconds + 12 seconds):

```
In  [16] dt.timedelta(
             weeks = 8,
             days = 6,
             hours = 3,
```

```
        minutes = 58,
        seconds = 12
    )
```

Out [16] datetime.timedelta(days=62, seconds=14292)

Now that we've familiarized ourselves with how Python models dates, times, and durations, let's explore how pandas builds on these concepts.

11.1.2 *How pandas works with datetimes*

Python's datetime module has had its share of criticism. Some common complaints include

- A large number of modules to keep track of. We introduced only datetime in this chapter, but additional modules are available for calendars, time conversions, utility functions, and more.
- A large number of classes to remember.
- Complex, difficult object APIs for time-zone logic.

Pandas introduces the Timestamp object as a replacement for Python's datetime object. We can view the Timestamp and datetime objects as being siblings; they are often interchangeable in the pandas ecosystem, such as when being passed as method arguments. Much as the Series expands on a Python list, the Timestamp adds features to the more primitive datetime object. We'll see some of these bells and whistles as we progress through the chapter.

The Timestamp constructor is available at the top level of pandas; it accepts the same parameters as a datetime constructor. The three date-related parameters (year, month, and day) are required. Time-related parameters are optional and default to 0. Here, we again model April 12, 1991, a glorious day:

```
In  [17] # The two lines below are equivalent
         pd.Timestamp(1991, 4, 12)
         pd.Timestamp(year = 1991, month = 4, day = 12)
```

Out [17] Timestamp('1991-04-12 00:00:00')

Pandas considers a Timestamp to be equal to a date/datetime if the two objects store the same information. We can use the == symbols to compare object equality:

```
In  [18] (pd.Timestamp(year = 1991, month = 4, day = 12)
          == dt.date(year = 1991, month = 4, day = 12))
```

Out [18] True

```
In  [19] (pd.Timestamp(year = 1991, month = 4, day = 12, minute = 2)
          == dt.datetime(year = 1991, month = 4, day = 12, minute = 2))
```

Out [19] True

The two objects will be unequal if there is any difference in date or time. The next example instantiates a Timestamp with a minute value of 2 and a datetime with a minute value of 1. The equality comparison yields False:

```
In  [20] (pd.Timestamp(year = 1991, month = 4, day = 12, minute = 2)
            == dt.datetime(year = 1991, month = 4, day = 12, minute = 1))

Out [20] False
```

The `Timestamp` constructor is remarkably flexible and accepts a variety of inputs. The next example passes the constructor a string instead of a sequence of integers. The text stores a date in the common YYYY-MM-DD format (four-digit year, two-digit month, two-digit day). Pandas correctly deciphers the month, day, and year from the input:

```
In  [21] pd.Timestamp("2015-03-31")

Out [21] Timestamp('2015-03-31 00:00:00')
```

Pandas recognizes many standard datetime string formats. The next example replaces the dashes in the date string with slashes:

```
In  [22] pd.Timestamp("2015/03/31")

Out [22] Timestamp('2015-03-31 00:00:00')
```

The next example passes a string in MM/DD/YYYY format, which is no problem for pandas:

```
In  [23] pd.Timestamp("03/31/2015")

Out [23] Timestamp('2015-03-31 00:00:00')
```

We can also include the time in a variety of written formats:

```
In  [24] pd.Timestamp("2021-03-08 08:35:15")

Out [24] Timestamp('2021-03-08 08:35:15')

In  [25] pd.Timestamp("2021-03-08 6:13:29 PM")

Out [25] Timestamp('2021-03-08 18:13:29')
```

Finally, the `Timestamp` constructor accepts Python's native `date`, `time`, and `datetime` objects. The next example parses data from a `datetime` object:

```
In  [26] pd.Timestamp(dt.datetime(2000, 2, 3, 21, 35, 22))

Out [26] Timestamp('2000-02-03 21:35:22')
```

The `Timestamp` object implements all `datetime` attributes, such as `hour`, `minute`, and `second`. The next example saves the previous `Timestamp` to a variable and then outputs several attributes:

```
In  [27] my_time = pd.Timestamp(dt.datetime(2000, 2, 3, 21, 35, 22))
         print(my_time.year)
         print(my_time.month)
         print(my_time.day)
         print(my_time.hour)
         print(my_time.minute)
         print(my_time.second)
```

```
Out [27] 2000
         2
         3
         21
         35
         22
```

Pandas does its best to ensure that its datetime objects work similarly to Python's built-in ones. We can consider the objects to be effectively swappable in pandas operations.

11.2   *Storing multiple timestamps in a DatetimeIndex*

An *index* is the collection of identifier labels attached to a pandas data structure. The most common index we've encountered so far is the `RangeIndex`, a sequence of ascending or descending numeric values. We can access the index of a `Series` or a `DataFrame` via the `index` attribute:

```
In  [28] pd.Series([1, 2, 3]).index

Out [28] RangeIndex(start=0, stop=3, step=1)
```

Pandas uses an `Index` object to store a collection of string labels. In the next example, notice that the index object pandas attaches to a `Series` changes based on its contents:

```
In  [29] pd.Series([1, 2, 3], index = ["A", "B", "C"]).index

Out [29] Index(['A', 'B', 'C'], dtype='object')
```

The `DatetimeIndex` is an index for storing `Timestamp` objects. If we pass a list of `Timestamps` to the `Series` constructor's `index` parameter, pandas will attach a `DatetimeIndex` to the `Series`:

```
In  [30] timestamps = [
             pd.Timestamp("2020-01-01"),
             pd.Timestamp("2020-02-01"),
             pd.Timestamp("2020-03-01"),
         ]

         pd.Series([1, 2, 3], index = timestamps).index

Out [30] DatetimeIndex(['2020-01-01', '2020-02-01', '2020-03-01'],
         dtype='datetime64[ns]', freq=None)
```

Pandas will also use a `DatetimeIndex` if we pass a list of Python `datetime` objects:

```
In  [31] datetimes = [
             dt.datetime(2020, 1, 1),
             dt.datetime(2020, 2, 1),
             dt.datetime(2020, 3, 1),
         ]

         pd.Series([1, 2, 3], index = datetimes).index

Out [31] DatetimeIndex(['2020-01-01', '2020-02-01', '2020-03-01'],
         dtype='datetime64[ns]', freq=None)
```

We can also create a `DatetimeIndex` from scratch. Its constructor is available at the top level of pandas. The constructor's `data` parameter accepts any iterable collection of dates. We can pass the dates as strings, datetimes, `Timestamps`, or even a mix of data types. Pandas will convert all values to equivalent `Timestamps` and store them within the index:

```
In  [32] string_dates = ["2018/01/02", "2016/04/12", "2009/09/07"]
         pd.DatetimeIndex(data = string_dates)

Out [32] DatetimeIndex(['2018-01-02', '2016-04-12', '2009-09-07'],
         dtype='datetime64[ns]', freq=None)

In  [33] mixed_dates = [
             dt.date(2018, 1, 2),
             "2016/04/12",
             pd.Timestamp(2009, 9, 7)
         ]

         dt_index = pd.DatetimeIndex(mixed_dates)
         dt_index

Out [33] DatetimeIndex(['2018-01-02', '2016-04-12', '2009-09-07'],
         dtype='datetime64[ns]', freq=None)
```

Now that we have a `DatetimeIndex` assigned to a `dt_index` variable, let's attach it to a pandas data structure. The next example connects the index to a sample `Series`:

```
In  [34] s = pd.Series(data = [100, 200, 300], index = dt_index)
         s

Out [34] 2018-01-02    100
         2016-04-12    200
         2009-09-07    300
         dtype: int64
```

Date- and time-related operations become possible in pandas only when we store our values as `Timestamps` rather than strings. Pandas can't deduce a day of the week from a string like `"2018-01-02"` because it views it as being a collection of digits and dashes, not an actual date. That's why it's imperative to convert all relevant string columns to datetimes when importing a data set for the first time.

We can use the `sort_index` method to sort a `DatetimeIndex` in ascending or descending order. The next example sorts the index dates in ascending order (earliest to latest):

```
In  [35] s.sort_index()

Out [35] 2009-09-07    300
         2016-04-12    200
         2018-01-02    100
         dtype: int64
```

Pandas accounts for both date and time when sorting or comparing datetimes. If two `Timestamps` use the same date, pandas will compare their hours, minutes, seconds, and so on.

A variety of sorting and comparison operations are available for `Timestamps` out of the box. The less-than symbol (`<`) , for example, checks whether one `Timestamp` occurs earlier than another:

```
In  [36] morning = pd.Timestamp("2020-01-01 11:23:22 AM")
         evening = pd.Timestamp("2020-01-01 11:23:22 PM")

         morning < evening
```

```
Out [36] True
```

In section 11.7, we'll learn how to apply these types of comparisons to all values in a `Series`.

11.3   *Converting column or index values to datetimes*

Our first data set for this chapter, disney.csv, holds nearly 60 years' worth of stock prices for the Walt Disney Company, one of the world's most recognized entertainment brands. Each row includes a date, the stock's highest and lowest value throughout that day, and its opening and closing price:

```
In  [37] disney = pd.read_csv("disney.csv")
         disney.head()
```

```
Out [37]
```

	Date	High	Low	Open	Close
0	1962-01-02	0.096026	0.092908	0.092908	0.092908
1	1962-01-03	0.094467	0.092908	0.092908	0.094155
2	1962-01-04	0.094467	0.093532	0.094155	0.094155
3	1962-01-05	0.094779	0.093844	0.094155	0.094467
4	1962-01-08	0.095714	0.092285	0.094467	0.094155

The `read_csv` function defaults to importing all values in non-numeric columns as strings. We can access the `dtypes` attribute on the `DataFrame` to see the columns' data types. Notice that the Date column has a data type of `"object"`, the pandas designation for a string:

```
In  [38] disney.dtypes
```

```
Out [38] Date      object
         High      float64
         Low       float64
         Open      float64
         Close     float64
         dtype: object
```

We must explicitly tell pandas which columns' values to convert to datetimes. One option we've seen before is the `read_csv` function's `parse_dates` parameter, introduced in chapter 3. We can pass the parameter a list of columns whose values pandas should convert to datetimes:

```
In  [39] disney = pd.read_csv("disney.csv", parse_dates = ["Date"])
```

An alternative solution is the `to_datetime` conversion function at the top level of pandas. The function accepts an iterable object (such as a Python list, tuple, `Series`, or index), converts its values to datetimes, and returns the new values in a `DatetimeIndex`. Here's a small example:

```
In  [40] string_dates = ["2015-01-01", "2016-02-02", "2017-03-03"]
         dt_index = pd.to_datetime(string_dates)
         dt_index

Out [40] DatetimeIndex(['2015-01-01', '2016-02-02', '2017-03-03'],
         dtype='datetime64[ns]', freq=None)
```

Let's pass the Date `Series` from the disney `DataFrame` to the `to_datetime` function:

```
In  [41] pd.to_datetime(disney["Date"]).head()

Out [41] 0    1962-01-02
         1    1962-01-03
         2    1962-01-04
         3    1962-01-05
         4    1962-01-08
         Name: Date, dtype: datetime64[ns]
```

We've got a `Series` of datetimes, so let's overwrite the original `DataFrame`. The next code sample replaces the original Date column with the new datetime `Series`. Remember that Python evaluates the right side of an equal sign first:

```
In  [42] disney["Date"] = pd.to_datetime(disney["Date"])
```

Let's check on the Date column again via the `dtypes` attribute:

```
In  [43] disney.dtypes

Out [43] Date      datetime64[ns]
         High             float64
         Low              float64
         Open             float64
         Close            float64
         dtype: object
```

Excellent; we have a datetime column! With our Date values stored correctly, we can explore the powerful datetime functionalities that pandas provides out of the box.

11.4 Using the DatetimeProperties object

A datetime `Series` holds a special `dt` attribute that exposes a `DatetimeProperties` object:

```
In  [44] disney["Date"].dt

Out [44] <pandas.core.indexes.accessors.DatetimeProperties object at
         0x116247950>
```

We can access attributes and invoke methods on the `DatetimeProperties` object to extract information from the columns' datetime values. The `dt` attribute is to date-times what the `str` attribute is to strings. (See chapter 6 for a review of `str`.) Both attributes specialize in manipulations of a specific type of data.

Let's begin our exploration of the `DatetimeProperties` object with the day attribute, which pulls out the day from each date. Pandas returns the values in a new `Series`:

```
In  [45] disney["Date"].head(3)

Out [45] 0    1962-01-02
         1    1962-01-03
         2    1962-01-04
         Name: Date, dtype: datetime64[ns]

In  [46] disney["Date"].dt.day.head(3)

Out [46] 0    2
         1    3
         2    4
         Name: Date, dtype: int64
```

The `month` attribute returns a `Series` with the month numbers. January has a `month` value of 1, February has a `month` value of 2, and so on. It's important to note that this is different from how we typically count in Python/pandas, where we assign the first item a value of 0:

```
In  [47] disney["Date"].dt.month.head(3)

Out [47] 0    1
         1    1
         2    1
         Name: Date, dtype: int64
```

The `year` attribute returns a new `Series` with the years:

```
In  [48] disney["Date"].dt.year.head(3)

Out [48] 0    1962
         1    1962
         2    1962
         Name: Date, dtype: int64
```

The previous attributes are pretty simple. We can ask pandas to extract more-interesting pieces of information. One example is the `dayofweek` attribute, which returns a `Series` of numbers for each date's day of the week. 0 denotes Monday, 1 denotes Tuesday, and so on up to 6 for Sunday. In the following output, the value of 1 at index position 0 indicates that January 2, 1962, fell on a Tuesday:

```
In  [49] disney["Date"].dt.dayofweek.head()

Out [49] 0    1
         1    2
         2    3
         3    4
```

```
4    0
Name: Date, dtype: int64
```

What if we wanted the weekday's name instead of its number? The day_name method does the trick. Be careful with the syntax. We invoke the method on the dt object, not on the Series itself:

```
In  [50] disney["Date"].dt.day_name().head()

Out [50] 0       Tuesday
         1     Wednesday
         2      Thursday
         3        Friday
         4        Monday
         Name: Date, dtype: object
```

We can pair these dt attributes and methods with other pandas features for advanced analyses. Here's an example. Let's calculate the average performance of Disney's stock by weekday. We'll begin by attaching the Series returned from the dt.day_name method to the disney DataFrame:

```
In  [51] disney["Day of Week"] = disney["Date"].dt.day_name()
```

We can group the rows based on the values in the new Day of Week column (a technique introduced in chapter 7):

```
In  [52] group = disney.groupby("Day of Week")
```

We can invoke the GroupBy object's mean method to calculate the average of values for each grouping:

```
In  [53] group.mean()

Out [53]
```

Day of Week	High	Low	Open	Close
Friday	23.767304	23.318898	23.552872	23.554498
Monday	23.377271	22.930606	23.161392	23.162543
Thursday	23.770234	23.288687	23.534561	23.540359
Tuesday	23.791234	23.335267	23.571755	23.562907
Wednesday	23.842743	23.355419	23.605618	23.609873

In three lines of code, we've calculated the average stock performance by day of week.

Let's come back to dt object methods. The complementary month_name method returns a Series with the dates' month names:

```
In  [54] disney["Date"].dt.month_name().head()

Out [54] 0       January
         1       January
         2       January
         3       January
         4       January
         Name: Date, dtype: object
```

Some attributes on the `dt` object return Booleans. Suppose that we want to explore Disney's stock performance at the start of each quarter in its history. The four quarters of a business year start on January 1, April 1, July 1, and October 1. The `is_quarter_start` attribute returns a Boolean `Series` in which `True` denotes that the row's date fell on a quarter start day:

```
In  [55] disney["Date"].dt.is_quarter_start.tail()

Out [55] 14722    False
         14723    False
         14724    False
         14725     True
         14726    False
         Name: Date, dtype: bool
```

We can use the Boolean `Series` to extract the disney rows that fell at the beginning of a quarter. The next example uses the familiar square-bracket syntax to pull out the rows:

```
In  [56] disney[disney["Date"].dt.is_quarter_start].head()

Out [56]
```

	Date	High	Low	Open	Close	Day of Week
189	1962-10-01	0.064849	0.062355	0.063913	0.062355	Monday
314	1963-04-01	0.087989	0.086704	0.087025	0.086704	Monday
377	1963-07-01	0.096338	0.095053	0.096338	0.095696	Monday
441	1963-10-01	0.110467	0.107898	0.107898	0.110467	Tuesday
565	1964-04-01	0.116248	0.112394	0.112394	0.116248	Wednesday

We can use the `is_quarter_end` attribute to pull out dates that fell at the end of a quarter:

```
In  [57] disney[disney["Date"].dt.is_quarter_end].head()

Out [57]
```

	Date	High	Low	Open	Close	Day of Week
251	1962-12-31	0.074501	0.071290	0.074501	0.072253	Monday
440	1963-09-30	0.109825	0.105972	0.108541	0.107577	Monday
502	1963-12-31	0.101476	0.096980	0.097622	0.101476	Tuesday
564	1964-03-31	0.115605	0.112394	0.114963	0.112394	Tuesday
628	1964-06-30	0.101476	0.100191	0.101476	0.100834	Tuesday

The complementary `is_month_start` and `is_month_end` attributes confirm that a date fell at the beginning or end of a month:

```
In  [58] disney[disney["Date"].dt.is_month_start].head()

Out [58]
```

	Date	High	Low	Open	Close	Day of Week
22	1962-02-01	0.096338	0.093532	0.093532	0.094779	Thursday
41	1962-03-01	0.095714	0.093532	0.093532	0.095714	Thursday
83	1962-05-01	0.087296	0.085426	0.085738	0.086673	Tuesday
105	1962-06-01	0.079814	0.077943	0.079814	0.079814	Friday
147	1962-08-01	0.068590	0.068278	0.068590	0.068590	Wednesday

```
In  [59] disney[disney["Date"].dt.is_month_end].head()
```

```
Out [59]
```

	Date	High	Low	Open	Close	Day of Week
21	1962-01-31	0.093844	0.092908	0.093532	0.093532	Wednesday
40	1962-02-28	0.094779	0.093220	0.094155	0.093220	Wednesday
82	1962-04-30	0.087608	0.085738	0.087608	0.085738	Monday
104	1962-05-31	0.082308	0.079814	0.079814	0.079814	Thursday
146	1962-07-31	0.069214	0.068278	0.068278	0.068590	Tuesday

The `is_year_start` attribute returns `True` if a date falls at the start of a year. The next example returns an empty `DataFrame`; the stock market is closed on New Year's Day, so no dates in the data set fit the criteria:

```
In  [60] disney[disney["Date"].dt.is_year_start].head()
```

```
Out [60]
```

Date	High	Low	Open	Close	Day of Week

The complementary `is_year_end` attribute returns `True` if a date falls at the end of a year:

```
In  [61] disney[disney["Date"].dt.is_year_end].head()
```

```
Out [61]
```

	Date	High	Low	Open	Close	Day of Week
251	1962-12-31	0.074501	0.071290	0.074501	0.072253	Monday
502	1963-12-31	0.101476	0.096980	0.097622	0.101476	Tuesday
755	1964-12-31	0.117853	0.116890	0.116890	0.116890	Thursday
1007	1965-12-31	0.154141	0.150929	0.153498	0.152214	Friday
1736	1968-12-31	0.439301	0.431594	0.434163	0.436732	Tuesday

Regardless of the attribute, the filtering process remains the same: create a Boolean `Series` and then pass it inside square brackets after the `DataFrame`.

11.5 Adding and subtracting durations of time

We can add or subtract consistent durations of time with the `DateOffset` object. Its constructor is available at the top level of pandas. The constructor accepts parameters for `years`, `months`, `days`, and more. The next example models a time of three years, four months, and three days:

```
In  [62] pd.DateOffset(years = 3, months = 4, days = 5)
```

```
Out [62] <DateOffset: days=5, months=4, years=3>
```

Here's a reminder of the first five rows of the disney `DataFrame`:

```
In  [63] disney["Date"].head()
```

```
Out [63] 0    1962-01-02
         1    1962-01-03
         2    1962-01-04
```

```
3    1962-01-05
4    1962-01-08
Name: Date, dtype: datetime64[ns]
```

For the sake of example, let's imagine that our recordkeeping system malfunctioned, and the dates in the Date column are off by five days. We can add a consistent amount of time to each date in a datetime `Series` with a plus sign (+) and a `DateOffset` object. The plus sign means "move forward" or "into the future." The next example adds five days to each date in the Date column:

```
In  [64] (disney["Date"] + pd.DateOffset(days = 5)).head()

Out [64] 0    1962-01-07
         1    1962-01-08
         2    1962-01-09
         3    1962-01-10
         4    1962-01-13
         Name: Date, dtype: datetime64[ns]
```

When paired with a `DateOffset`, the minus sign (-) subtracts a duration from each date in a datetime `Series`. The minus sign means "move backward" or "into the past." The next example moves each date back three days:

```
In  [65] (disney["Date"] - pd.DateOffset(days = 3)).head()

Out [65] 0    1961-12-30
         1    1961-12-31
         2    1962-01-01
         3    1962-01-02
         4    1962-01-05
         Name: Date, dtype: datetime64[ns]
```

Although the previous output does not show it, the `Timestamp` objects *do* store a time internally. When we converted the Date column's values to datetimes, pandas assumed a time of midnight for each date. The next example adds an `hours` parameter to the `DateOffset` constructor to add a consistent time to each datetime in Date. The resulting `Series` displays the date and time:

```
In  [66] (disney["Date"] + pd.DateOffset(days = 10, hours = 6)).head()

Out [66] 0    1962-01-12 06:00:00
         1    1962-01-13 06:00:00
         2    1962-01-14 06:00:00
         3    1962-01-15 06:00:00
         4    1962-01-18 06:00:00
         Name: Date, dtype: datetime64[ns]
```

Pandas applies the same logic when subtracting a duration. The next example subtracts one year, three months, ten days, six hours, and three minutes from each date:

```
In  [67] (
             disney["Date"]
             - pd.DateOffset(
                 years = 1, months = 3, days = 10, hours = 6, minutes = 3
```

```
                )
            ).head()

Out [67] 0    1960-09-21 17:57:00
         1    1960-09-22 17:57:00
         2    1960-09-23 17:57:00
         3    1960-09-24 17:57:00
         4    1960-09-27 17:57:00
         Name: Date, dtype: datetime64[ns]
```

The `DateOffset` constructor supports additional keyword parameters for seconds, microseconds, and nanoseconds. See the pandas documentation for more info.

11.6   *Date offsets*

The `DateOffset` object is optimal for adding or subtracting a consistent amount of time to or from each date. Real-world analyses often demand a more dynamic calculation. Let's say we want to round each date to the end of its current month. Each date is a different number of days from the end of its month, so a consistent `DateOffset` addition won't suffice.

Pandas ships with prebuilt offset objects for dynamic time-based calculations. These objects are defined in `offsets.py`, a module within the library. In our code, we have to prefix these offsets with their complete path: `pd.offsets`.

One sample offset is `MonthEnd`, which rounds each date to the next month-end. Here's a refresher on the last five rows in the Date column:

```
In  [68] disney["Date"].tail()

Out [68] 14722    2020-06-26
         14723    2020-06-29
         14724    2020-06-30
         14725    2020-07-01
         14726    2020-07-02
         Name: Date, dtype: datetime64[ns]
```

We can apply the addition and subtraction syntax from section 11.5 to pandas' offset objects. The next example returns a new `Series` that rounds each datetime to the month-end. The plus sign moves forward in time, so we move to the next month-end:

```
In  [69] (disney["Date"] + pd.offsets.MonthEnd()).tail()

Out [69] 14722    2020-06-30
         14723    2020-06-30
         14724    2020-07-31
         14725    2020-07-31
         14726    2020-07-31
         Name: Date, dtype: datetime64[ns]
```

There has to be some movement in the intended direction. Pandas cannot round a date to the same date. Thus, if a date falls at the end of a month, the library rounds it to the end of the following month. Pandas rounds 2020-06-30 at index position 14724 to 2020-07-31, the next available month-end.

The minus sign moves each date backward in time. The next example uses the MonthEnd offset to round the dates to the previous month-end. Pandas rounds the first three dates (2020-06-26, 2020-06-29, and 2020-06-30) to 2020-05-31, the last day in May. It rounds the final two dates (2020-07-01 and 2020-07-02) to 2020-06-30, the last day in June:

```
In   [70] (disney["Date"] - pd.offsets.MonthEnd()).tail()

Out  [70] 14722    2020-05-31
          14723    2020-05-31
          14724    2020-05-31
          14725    2020-06-30
          14726    2020-06-30
          Name: Date, dtype: datetime64[ns]
```

The complementary MonthBegin offset rounds to the first date of a month. The next example uses a + sign to round each date to the next month's beginning. Pandas rounds the first three dates (2020-06-26, 2020-06-29, and 2020-06-30) to 2020-07-01, the beginning of July. Pandas rounds the two remaining July dates (2020-07-01 and 2020-07-02) to 2020-08-01, the first day of August:

```
In   [71] (disney["Date"] + pd.offsets.MonthBegin()).tail()

Out  [71] 14722    2020-07-01
          14723    2020-07-01
          14724    2020-07-01
          14725    2020-08-01
          14726    2020-08-01
          Name: Date, dtype: datetime64[ns]
```

We can pair the MonthBegin offset with the minus sign to round dates backward to the beginning of a month. In the next example, pandas rounds the first three dates (2020-06-26, 2020-06-29, and 2020-06-30) to the start of June, 2020-06-01. It rounds the last date, 2020-07-02, to the beginning of July, 2020-07-01. The curious case is 2020-07-01 at index position 14725. As we mentioned earlier, pandas cannot round a date to the same date. There has to be some movement backward, so pandas rounds to the previous month's start, 2020-06-01:

```
In   [72] (disney["Date"] - pd.offsets.MonthBegin()).tail()

Out  [72] 14722    2020-06-01
          14723    2020-06-01
          14724    2020-06-01
          14725    2020-06-01
          14726    2020-07-01
          Name: Date, dtype: datetime64[ns]
```

A special group of offsets is available for business time calculations; their names begin with a capital "B". The Business Month End (BMonthEnd) offset, for example, rounds to the month's last business day. The five business days are Monday, Tuesday, Wednesday, Thursday, and Friday.

Consider the following `Series` of three datetimes. The three dates fall on Thursday, Friday, and Saturday, respectively:

```
In  [73] may_dates = ["2020-05-28", "2020-05-29", "2020-05-30"]
         end_of_may = pd.Series(pd.to_datetime(may_dates))
         end_of_may

Out [73] 0    2020-05-28
         1    2020-05-29
         2    2020-05-30
         dtype: datetime64[ns]
```

Let's compare the `MonthEnd` and `BMonthEnd` offsets. When we pair the `MonthEnd` offset with a plus sign, pandas rounds all three dates to the last day of May, 2020-05-31. Whether that date falls on a business day or the weekend is irrelevant:

```
In  [74] end_of_may + pd.offsets.MonthEnd()

Out [74] 0    2020-05-31
         1    2020-05-31
         2    2020-05-31
         dtype: datetime64[ns]
```

The `BMonthEnd` offset returns a different set of results. The last business day of May 2020 is Friday, May 29. Pandas rounds the first date in the `Series`, 2020-05-28, to the 29th. The next date, 2020-05-29, falls *on* the month's last business date. Pandas cannot round a date to the same date, so it rounds 2020-05-29 to June's last business day, 2020-06-30, a Tuesday. The last date in the `Series`, 2020-05-30, is a Saturday. No business days are left in May, so pandas similarly rounds the date to June's last business day, 2020-06-30:

```
In  [75] end_of_may + pd.offsets.BMonthEnd()

Out [75] 0    2020-05-29
         1    2020-06-30
         2    2020-06-30
         dtype: datetime64[ns]
```

The `pd.offsets` module includes additional offsets for rounding to the starts and ends of quarters, business quarters, years, business years, and more. Feel free to explore them in your free time.

11.7   *The Timedelta object*

You may recall Python's native `timedelta` object from earlier in the chapter. A `timedelta` models duration—the distance between two times. A duration such as one hour represents a length of time; it does not have a specific date or time attached. Pandas models a duration with its own `Timedelta` object.

> **NOTE**   It's easy to confuse the two objects. `timedelta` is built into Python, whereas `Timedelta` is built into pandas. The two are interchangeable when used with pandas operations.

The Timedelta constructor is available at the top level of pandas. It accepts keyword parameters for units of time such as days, hours, minutes, and seconds. The next example instantiates a Timedelta modeling eight days, seven hours, six minutes, and five seconds:

```
In  [76] duration = pd.Timedelta(
            days = 8,
            hours = 7,
            minutes = 6,
            seconds = 5
         )

         duration

Out [76] Timedelta('8 days 07:06:05')
```

The to_timedelta function at the top level of pandas converts its argument to a Timedelta object. We can pass in a string, as in the next example:

```
In  [77] duration = pd.to_timedelta("3 hours, 5 minutes, 12 seconds")

Out [77] Timedelta('0 days 03:05:12')
```

We can also pass an integer to the to_timedelta function along with a unit parameter. The unit parameter declares the unit of time that the number represents. Accepted arguments include "hour", "day", and "minute". The next example's Timedelta models a five-hour duration:

```
In  [78] pd.to_timedelta(5, unit = "hour")

Out [78] Timedelta('0 days 05:00:00')
```

We can pass an iterable object such as a list to the to_timedelta function to convert its values to Timedeltas. Pandas will store the Timedeltas in a TimedeltaIndex, a pandas index for storing durations:

```
In  [79] pd.to_timedelta([5, 10, 15], unit = "day")

Out [79] TimedeltaIndex(['5 days', '10 days', '15 days'],
             dtype='timedelta64[ns]', freq=None)
```

Usually, Timedelta objects are derived rather than created from scratch. The subtraction of one Timestamp from another, for example, returns a Timedelta automatically:

```
In  [80] pd.Timestamp("1999-02-05") - pd.Timestamp("1998-05-24")

Out [80] Timedelta('257 days 00:00:00')
```

Now that we've gotten acquainted with Timedeltas, let's import our second data set for the chapter: deliveries.csv. The CSV tracks product shipments for a fictional company. Each row includes an order date and a delivery date:

```
In  [81] deliveries = pd.read_csv("deliveries.csv")
         deliveries.head()

Out [81]
```

	order_date	delivery_date
0	5/24/98	2/5/99
1	4/22/92	3/6/98
2	2/10/91	8/26/92
3	7/21/92	11/20/97
4	9/2/93	6/10/98

Let's practice converting the values in the two columns to datetimes. Yes, we can use the parse_dates parameter, but let's try another approach. One option is invoking the to_datetime function twice, once for the order_date column and once for the delivery_date column, and overwriting the existing DataFrame columns:

```
In  [82] deliveries["order_date"] = pd.to_datetime(
             deliveries["order_date"]
         )

         deliveries["delivery_date"] = pd.to_datetime(
             deliveries["delivery_date"]
         )
```

A more scalable solution is to iterate over the column names with a for loop. We can reference a deliveries column dynamically, use to_datetime to create a Datetime-Index of Timestamps from it, and then overwrite the original column:

```
In  [83] for column in ["order_date", "delivery_date"]:
             deliveries[column] = pd.to_datetime(deliveries[column])
```

Let's take a look at deliveries. The new column format confirms that we've converted the strings to datetimes:

```
In  [84] deliveries.head()

Out [84]
```

	order_date	delivery_date
0	1998-05-24	1999-02-05
1	1992-04-22	1998-03-06
2	1991-02-10	1992-08-26
3	1992-07-21	1997-11-20
4	1993-09-02	1998-06-10

Let's calculate the duration of each shipment. With pandas, this calculation is as simple as subtracting the order_date column from the delivery_date column:

```
In  [85] (deliveries["delivery_date"] - deliveries["order_date"]).head()

Out [85] 0      257 days
         1     2144 days
         2      563 days
```

```
3    1948 days
4    1742 days
dtype: timedelta64[ns]
```

Pandas returns a `Series` of `timedeltas`. Let's attach the new `Series` to the end of the deliveries `DataFrame`:

```
In  [86] deliveries["duration"] = (
             deliveries["delivery_date"] - deliveries["order_date"]
         )
         deliveries.head()

Out [86]
```

	order_date	delivery_date	duration
0	1998-05-24	1999-02-05	257 days
1	1992-04-22	1998-03-06	2144 days
2	1991-02-10	1992-08-26	563 days
3	1992-07-21	1997-11-20	1948 days
4	1993-09-02	1998-06-10	1742 days

Now we have two `Timestamp` columns and one `Timedelta` column:

```
In  [87] deliveries.dtypes

Out [87] order_date        datetime64[ns]
         delivery_date     datetime64[ns]
         duration          timedelta64[ns]
         dtype: object
```

We can add or subtract `Timedeltas` from `Timestamp` objects. The next example subtracts each row's duration from the delivery_date column. Predictably, the values in the new `Series` are identical to the values in the order_date column:

```
In  [88] (deliveries["delivery_date"] - deliveries["duration"]).head()

Out [88] 0    1998-05-24
         1    1992-04-22
         2    1991-02-10
         3    1992-07-21
         4    1993-09-02
         dtype: datetime64[ns]
```

A plus symbol adds a `Timedelta` to a `Timestamp`. Let's say we wanted to find the date of delivery if each package took twice as long to arrive. We can add the `Timedelta` values in the duration column to the `Timestamp` values in the delivery_date column:

```
In  [89] (deliveries["delivery_date"] + deliveries["duration"]).head()

Out [89] 0    1999-10-20
         1    2004-01-18
         2    1994-03-12
         3    2003-03-22
         4    2003-03-18
         dtype: datetime64[ns]
```

The `sort_values` method works with `Timedelta Series`. The next example sorts the duration column in ascending order, from the shortest delivery to the longest one:

```
In  [90] deliveries.sort_values("duration")

Out [90]
```

	order_date	delivery_date	duration
454	1990-05-24	1990-06-01	8 days
294	1994-08-11	1994-08-20	9 days
10	1998-05-10	1998-05-19	9 days
499	1993-06-03	1993-06-13	10 days
143	1997-09-20	1997-10-06	16 days
...	...	...	...
152	1990-09-18	1999-12-19	3379 days
62	1990-04-02	1999-08-16	3423 days
458	1990-02-13	1999-11-15	3562 days
145	1990-03-07	1999-12-25	3580 days
448	1990-01-20	1999-11-12	3583 days

```
501 rows × 3 columns
```

Mathematical methods are also available on `Timedelta Series`. The next few examples highlight three methods we've used throughout the book: `max` for the largest value, `min` for the smallest value, and `mean` for the average:

```
In  [91] deliveries["duration"].max()

Out [91] Timedelta('3583 days 00:00:00')

In  [92] deliveries["duration"].min()

Out [92] Timedelta('8 days 00:00:00')

In  [93] deliveries["duration"].mean()

Out [93] Timedelta('1217 days 22:53:53.532934')
```

Here's the next challenge. Let's filter the `DataFrame` for packages that took more than a year to deliver. We can use the greater-than symbol (>) to compare each duration column value to a fixed duration. We can specify the length of time as a `Timedelta` or as a string. The next example uses `"365 days"`:

```
In  [94] # The two lines below are equivalent
         (deliveries["duration"] > pd.Timedelta(days = 365)).head()
         (deliveries["duration"] > "365 days").head()

Out [94] 0      False
         1      True
         2      True
         3      True
         4      True
         Name: Delivery Time, dtype: bool
```

Let's use the Boolean `Series` to filter for the `deliveries` rows with a delivery time greater than 365 days:

```
In [95] deliveries[deliveries["duration"] > "365 days"].head()

Out [95]
```

	order_date	delivery_date	duration
1	1992-04-22	1998-03-06	2144 days
2	1991-02-10	1992-08-26	563 days
3	1992-07-21	1997-11-20	1948 days
4	1993-09-02	1998-06-10	1742 days
6	1990-01-25	1994-10-02	1711 days

We can get as granular as needed with the comparison duration. The next example includes the days, hours, and minutes in the string, separating the units of time with commas:

```
In [96] long_time = (
            deliveries["duration"] > "2000 days, 8 hours, 4 minutes"
        )

        deliveries[long_time].head()

Out [96]
```

	order_date	delivery_date	duration
1	1992-04-22	1998-03-06	2144 days
7	1992-02-23	1998-12-30	2502 days
11	1992-10-17	1998-10-06	2180 days
12	1992-05-30	1999-08-15	2633 days
15	1990-01-20	1998-07-24	3107 days

As a reminder, Pandas can sort `Timedelta` columns. To discover the longest or shortest durations, we can invoke the `sort_values` method on the duration `Series`.

11.8 Coding challenge

Here's your chance to practice the concepts introduced in this chapter.

11.8.1 Problems

Citi Bike NYC is New York City's official bike-sharing program. Residents and tourists can pick up and drop off bicycles at hundreds of locations around the city. Ride data is publicly available and released monthly by the city at https://www.citibikenyc.com/system-data. citibike.csv is a collection of ~1.9 million rides that cyclists took in June 2020. For simplicity's sake, the data set has been modified from its original version and includes only two columns: each ride's start time and end time. Let's import the data set and assign it to a `citi_bike` variable:

```
In [97] citi_bike = pd.read_csv("citibike.csv")
        citi_bike.head()

Out [97]
```

	start_time	stop_time
0	2020-06-01 00:00:03.3720	2020-06-01 00:17:46.2080
1	2020-06-01 00:00:03.5530	2020-06-01 01:03:33.9360
2	2020-06-01 00:00:09.6140	2020-06-01 00:17:06.8330
3	2020-06-01 00:00:12.1780	2020-06-01 00:03:58.8640
4	2020-06-01 00:00:21.2550	2020-06-01 00:24:18.9650

The datetime entries in the start_time and stop_time columns include the year, month, day, hour, minute, second, and microsecond. (A *microsecond* is a unit of time equal to one millionth of a second.)

We can use the info method to print a summary that includes the DataFrame's length, the columns' data types, and the memory use. Notice that pandas has imported the two columns' values as strings:

```
In  [98] citi_bike.info()

Out [98]

<class 'pandas.core.frame.DataFrame'>
RangeIndex: 1882273 entries, 0 to 1882272
Data columns (total 2 columns):
 #   Column      Dtype
---  ------      -----
 0   start_time  object
 1   stop_time   object
dtypes: object(2)
memory usage: 28.7+ MB
```

Here are the challenges for this section:

1. Convert the start_time and stop_time columns to store datetime (Timestamp) values instead of strings.
2. Count the rides that occurred on each day of the week (Monday, Tuesday, and so on). Which weekday is the most popular for a bike ride? Use the start_time column as your starting point.
3. Count the rides per week for each week within the month. To do so, round each date in the start_time column to its previous or current Monday. Assume that each week starts on a Monday and ends on a Sunday. Thus, the first week of June would be Monday, June 1 through Sunday, June 7.
4. Calculate the duration of each ride, and save the results to a new duration column.
5. Find the average duration of a bike ride.
6. Extract the five longest bike rides by duration from the data set.

11.8.2 Solutions

Let's tackle the problems one by one:

1. The to_datetime conversion function at the top level of pandas works well to convert the start_time and end_time columns' values to Timestamps. The next

code sample iterates over a list of the column names with a `for` loop, passes each column into the `to_datetime` function, and overwrites the existing string column with the new datetime `Series`:

```
In  [99] for column in ["start_time", "stop_time"]:
             citi_bike[column] = pd.to_datetime(citi_bike[column])
```

Let's invoke the `info` method again to confirm that the two columns store date-time values:

```
In  [100] citi_bike.info()
```

```
Out [100]
```

```
<class 'pandas.core.frame.DataFrame'>
RangeIndex: 1882273 entries, 0 to 1882272
Data columns (total 2 columns):
 #   Column       Dtype
---  ------       -----
 0   start_time   datetime64[ns]
 1   stop_time    datetime64[ns]
dtypes: datetime64[ns](2)
memory usage: 28.7 MB
```

2 We'll have to take two steps to count the number of bike rides per weekday. First, we extract the weekday from each datetime in the start_time column; then we count the weekdays' occurrences. The `dt.day_name` method returns a `Series` with the weekday names for each date:

```
In  [101] citi_bike["start_time"].dt.day_name().head()
```

```
Out [101] 0     Monday
          1     Monday
          2     Monday
          3     Monday
          4     Monday
          Name: start_time, dtype: object
```

Then we can invoke the trusty `value_counts` method on the returned `Series` to count the weekdays. In June 2020, Tuesday was the most popular day for a bike ride:

```
In  [102] citi_bike["start_time"].dt.day_name().value_counts()
```

```
Out [102] Tuesday      305833
          Sunday       301482
          Monday       292690
          Saturday     285966
          Friday       258479
          Wednesday    222647
          Thursday     215176
          Name: start_time, dtype: int64
```

3 The next challenge requires us to group each date into its corresponding week bucket. We can do so by rounding the date to its previous or current Monday. Here's a clever solution: we can use the `dayofweek` attribute to return a `Series` of numbers. 0 denotes Monday, 1 denotes Tuesday, 6 denotes Sunday, and so on:

```
In  [103] citi_bike["start_time"].dt.dayofweek.head()

Out [103] 0    0
          1    0
          2    0
          3    0
          4    0
             Name: start_time, dtype: int64
```

The weekday number also represents the distance in days from the closest Monday. Monday, June 1, for example, has a `dayofweek` value of 0. The date is 0 days away from the closest Monday. Similarly, Tuesday, June 2, has a `dayofweek` value of 1. The date is one day away from the closest Monday (June 1). Let's save this `Series` to a `days_away_from_monday` variable:

```
In  [104] days_away_from_monday = citi_bike["start_time"].dt.dayofweek
```

If we subtract a date's `dayofweek` value from the date itself, we'll effectively round each date to its previous Monday. We can pass the `dayofweek` `Series` into the `to_timedelta` function to convert it to a `Series` of durations. We'll pass a unit parameter set to `"day"` to tell pandas to treat the numeric values as the number of days:

```
In  [105] citi_bike["start_time"] - pd.to_timedelta(
              days_away_from_monday, unit = "day"
          )

Out [105] 0           2020-06-01 00:00:03.372
          1           2020-06-01 00:00:03.553
          2           2020-06-01 00:00:09.614
          3           2020-06-01 00:00:12.178
          4           2020-06-01 00:00:21.255
                             . . .
          1882268     2020-06-29 23:59:41.116
          1882269     2020-06-29 23:59:46.426
          1882270     2020-06-29 23:59:47.477
          1882271     2020-06-29 23:59:53.395
          1882272     2020-06-29 23:59:53.901
          Name: start_time, Length: 1882273, dtype: datetime64[ns]
```

Let's save the new `Series` to a `dates_rounded_to_monday` variable:

```
In  [106] dates_rounded_to_monday = citi_bike[
              "start_time"
          ] - pd.to_timedelta(days_away_from_monday, unit = "day")
```

We're halfway there. We've rounded the dates to the correct Mondays, but the `value_counts` method won't work yet. The differences in times between the dates will lead pandas to deem them unequal:

```
In  [107] dates_rounded_to_monday.value_counts().head()

Out [107] 2020-06-22 20:13:36.208    3
          2020-06-08 17:17:26.335    3
          2020-06-08 16:50:44.596    3
          2020-06-15 19:24:26.737    3
          2020-06-08 19:49:21.686    3
          Name: start_time, dtype: int64
```

Let's use the `dt.date` attribute to return a `Series` with the dates from each datetime:

```
In  [108] dates_rounded_to_monday.dt.date.head()

Out [108] 0     2020-06-01
          1     2020-06-01
          2     2020-06-01
          3     2020-06-01
          4     2020-06-01
          Name: start_time, dtype: object
```

Now that we've isolated the dates, we can invoke the `value_counts` method to count each value's occurrences. The week of Monday, June 15 to Sunday, June 21 saw the highest number of bike rides throughout the month:

```
In  [109] dates_rounded_to_monday.dt.date.value_counts()

Out [109] 2020-06-15    481211
          2020-06-08    471384
          2020-06-22    465412
          2020-06-01    337590
          2020-06-29    126676
          Name: start_time, dtype: int64
```

4   To calculate each ride's duration, we can subtract the start_time column from the stop_time column. Pandas will return a `Series` of `Timedeltas`. We'll need to save this `Series` for the next example, so let's attach it to the `DataFrame` as a new column called duration:

```
In  [110] citi_bike["duration"] = (
              citi_bike["stop_time"] - citi_bike["start_time"]
          )

          citi_bike.head()

Out [110]
```

	start_time	stop_time	duration
0	2020-06-01 00:00:03.372	2020-06-01 00:17:46.208	0 days 00:17:42.836000
1	2020-06-01 00:00:03.553	2020-06-01 01:03:33.936	0 days 01:03:30.383000
2	2020-06-01 00:00:09.614	2020-06-01 00:17:06.833	0 days 00:16:57.219000

```
3 2020-06-01 00:00:12.178 2020-06-01 00:03:58.864 0 days 00:03:46.686000
4 2020-06-01 00:00:21.255 2020-06-01 00:24:18.965 0 days 00:23:57.710000
```

Note that the previous subtraction would raise an error if the columns were storing strings; that's why it's imperative to convert them to datetimes first.

5 Next up, we have to find the average duration of all bike rides. This process is a simple one: we can invoke the mean method on the new duration column for the calculation. The average ride was 27 minutes and 19 seconds:

```
In  [111] citi_bike["duration"].mean()

Out [111] Timedelta('0 days 00:27:19.590506853')
```

6 The final question asks to identify the five longest bike rides in the data set. One solution is to sort the duration column values in descending order with the sort_values method and then use the head method to view the first five rows. These sessions likely belonged to people who forgot to check their bikes in after finishing their ride:

```
In  [112] citi_bike["duration"].sort_values(ascending = False).head()

Out [112] 50593    32 days 15:01:54.940000
          98339    31 days 01:47:20.632000
          52306    30 days 19:32:20.696000
          15171    30 days 04:26:48.424000
          149761   28 days 09:24:50.696000
          Name: duration, dtype: timedelta64[ns]
```

Another option is the nlargest method. We can invoke this method on either the duration Series or the DataFrame as a whole. Let's go with the latter approach:

```
In  [113] citi_bike.nlargest(n = 5, columns = "duration")

Out [113]
```

	start_time	stop_time	duration
50593	2020-06-01 21:30:17...	2020-07-04 12:32:12...	32 days 15:01:54.94...
98339	2020-06-02 19:41:39...	2020-07-03 21:29:00...	31 days 01:47:20.63...
52306	2020-06-01 22:17:10...	2020-07-02 17:49:31...	30 days 19:32:20.69...
15171	2020-06-01 13:01:41...	2020-07-01 17:28:30...	30 days 04:26:48.42...
149761	2020-06-04 14:36:53...	2020-07-03 00:01:44...	28 days 09:24:50.69...

There you have it: the five longest bike rides in the data set. Congratulations on completing the coding challenge!

Summary

- The pandas Timestamp object is a flexible, powerful replacement for Python's native datetime object.
- The dt accessor on a datetime Series reveals a DatetimeProperties object with attributes and methods for extracting the day, month, weekday name, and more.

- The `Timedelta` object models a duration.
- Pandas creates a `Timedelta` object when we subtract two `Timestamp` objects from each other.
- The offsets in the `pd.offsets` package dynamically round dates to the closest week, month, quarter, and more. We can round forward with the plus sign and backward with the minus sign.
- A `DatetimeIndex` is a container for `Timestamp` values. We can add it as an index or column to a pandas data structure.
- The `TimedeltaIndex` is a container for `Timedelta` objects.
- The top-level `to_datetime` function converts an iterable of values to a `DatetimeIndex` of `Timestamps`.

High *12* appears as a large decorative chapter number

Imports and exports

This chapter covers

- Importing JSON data
- Flattening a nested collection of records
- Downloading a CSV from an online website
- Reading from and writing to Excel workbooks

Data sets come in a variety of file formats: comma-separated values (CSV), tab-separated values (TSV), Excel workbooks (XLSX), and more. Some data formats do not store data in tabular format; instead, they nest collections of related data inside a key-value store. Consider the following two examples. Figure 12.1 stores data in a table, and figure 12.2 stores the same data in a Python dictionary.

Year	Award	Winner
2000	Best Actor	Russell Crowe
2000	Best Actress	Julia Roberts
2001	Best Actor	Denzel Washington
2001	Best Actress	Halle Berry

Figure 12.1   A table of Oscar winners

Python's dictionary is an example of a key-value data structure:

```
{
    2000: [
        {
            "Award": "Best Actor",
            "Winner": "Russell Crowe"
        },
        {
            "Award": "Best Actress",
            "Winner": "Julia Roberts"
        }
    ],
    2001: [
        {
            "Award": "Best Actor",
            "Winner": "Denzel Washington"
        },
        {
            "Award": "Best Actress",
            "Winner": "Halle Berry"
        }
    ]
}
```

Figure 12.2   A Python dictionary (key-value store) with the same data

Pandas ships with utility functions to manipulate key-value data into tabular data and vice versa. When we have the data in a `DataFrame`, we can apply all our favorite techniques to it. But contorting the data into the right shape often proves to be the most challenging part of an analysis. In this chapter, we'll learn how to resolve common problems in data imports. We'll also explore the other side of the equation: exporting `DataFrames` to various file types and data structures.

12.1   Reading from and writing to JSON files

Let's kick things off by talking about JSON, perhaps the most popular key-value storage format available today. *JavaScript Object Notation* (JSON) is a format for storing and transferring text data. Although the JavaScript programming language inspires its syntax, JSON itself is language-independent. Most languages today, including Python, can generate and parse JSON.

A JSON response consists of key-value pairs, in which a key serves as a unique identifier for a value. The colon symbol (:) connects a key to a value:

```
"name":"Harry Potter"
```

Keys must be strings. Values can be of any data type, including strings, numbers, and Booleans. JSON is similar to Python's dictionary object.

JSON is a popular response format for many modern application programming interfaces (APIs), such as website servers. A raw JSON response from an API looks like a plain string. Here's what a response might look like:

```
{"name":"Harry Potter","age":17,"wizard":true}
```

Software programs called *linters* format JSON responses by placing each key-value pair on a separate line. One popular example is JSONLint (https://jsonlint.com). Running the previous JSON through JSONLint produces the following output:

```
{
    "name": "Harry Potter",
    "age": 17,
    "wizard": true,
}
```

There is no technical difference between the two preceding code samples, but the latter is more readable.

The JSON response holds three key-value pairs:

- The `"name"` key has a string value of `"Harry Potter"`.
- The `"age"` key has an integer value of 17.
- The `"wizard"` key has a Boolean value of `true`. In JSON, Booleans are spelled in lowercase. The concept is identical to a Python Boolean.

A key can also point to an *array*, an ordered collection of elements equivalent to a Python list. The `"friends"` key in the next JSON example maps to an array of two strings:

```
{
    "name": "Harry Potter",
    age": 17,
    "wizard": true,
    "friends": ["Ron Weasley", "Hermione Granger"],
}
```

JSON can store additional key-value pairs within nested objects, such as `"address"` in the following example. In Pythonic terms, we can think of `"address"` as a dictionary nested within another dictionary:

```
{
    "name": "Harry Potter",
    "age": 17,
    "wizard": true,
    "friends": ["Ron Weasley", "Hermione Granger"],
    "address": {
        "street": "4 Privet Drive",
        "town": "Little Whinging"
    }
}
```

Nested stores of key-value pairs help simplify the data by grouping related fields.

12.1.1   *Loading a JSON file into a DataFrame*

Let's create a new Jupyter Notebook and import the pandas library. Make sure to create the Notebook in the same directory as this chapter's data files:

```
In  [1] import pandas as pd
```

JSON can be stored in a plain-text file with a .json extension. This chapter's prizes.json file is a saved JSON response from the Nobel Prize API. The API stores Nobel Prize laureates dating back to 1901. You can view the raw JSON response in your web browser by navigating to http://api.nobelprize.org/v1/prize.json. Here's a preview of the JSON shape:

```
{
  "prizes": [
    {
      "year": "2019",
      "category": "chemistry",
      "laureates": [
        {
          "id": "976",
          "firstname": "John",
          "surname": "Goodenough",
          "motivation": "\"for the development of lithium-ion batteries\"",
          "share": "3"
        },
        {
          "id": "977",
          "firstname": "M. Stanley",
          "surname": "Whittingham",
          "motivation": "\"for the development of lithium-ion batteries\"",
          "share": "3"
        },
        {
          "id": "978",
          "firstname": "Akira",
          "surname": "Yoshino",
          "motivation": "\"for the development of lithium-ion batteries\"",
          "share": "3"
        }
      ]
    },
```

The JSON consists of a top-level `prizes` key that maps to an array of dictionaries, one for each combination of year and category (`"chemistry"`, `"physics"`, `"literature"`, and so on). The `"year"` and `"category"` keys are present for all winners, whereas the `"laureates"` and `"overallMotivation"` keys are present for only some. Here's a sample dictionary with an `"overallMotivation"` key:

```
{
    year: "1972",
    category: "peace",
    overallMotivation: "No Nobel Prize was awarded this year. The prize
    money for 1972 was allocated to the Main Fund."
}
```

The `"laureates"` key connects to an array of dictionaries, each with its own `"id"`, `"firstname"`, `"surname"`, `"motivation"`, and `"share"` keys. The `"laureates"` key stores an array to accommodate years in which multiple people were awarded a Nobel Prize in the same category. The `"laureates"` key uses a list even if a year had only one winner. Here is an example:

```
{
    year: "2019",
    category: "literature",
    laureates: [
        {
            id: "980",
            firstname: "Peter",
            surname: "Handke",
            motivation: "for an influential work that with linguistic
            ingenuity has explored the periphery and the specificity of
            human experience",
            share: "1"
        }
    ]
},
```

Import functions in pandas have a consistent naming scheme; each one consists of a read prefix followed by a file type. We've used the `read_csv` function many times throughout the book, for example. To import a JSON file, we'll use the complementary `read_json` function. Its first argument is the file path. The next example passes the nobel.json file. Pandas returns a one-column `DataFrame` with a prizes column:

```
In  [2] nobel = pd.read_json("nobel.json")
        nobel.head()

Out [2]
```

	prizes
0	{'year': '2019', 'category': 'chemistry', 'laureates': [{'id': '97...
1	{'year': '2019', 'category': 'economics', 'laureates': [{'id': '98...
2	{'year': '2019', 'category': 'literature', 'laureates': [{'id': '9...
3	{'year': '2019', 'category': 'peace', 'laureates': [{'id': '981', ...
4	{'year': '2019', 'category': 'physics', 'overallMotivation': '"for...

We've successfully imported the file into pandas, but unfortunately, not in a format that's ideal for analysis. Pandas set the JSON's top-level `prizes` key as the column name and created a Python dictionary for each key-value pair it parsed from the JSON. Here's a sample row value:

```
In  [3] nobel.loc[2, "prizes"]

Out [3] {'year': '2019',
         'category': 'literature',
         'laureates': [{'id': '980',
           'firstname': 'Peter',
           'surname': 'Handke',
```

```
    'motivation': '"for an influential work that with linguistic
        ingenuity has explored the periphery and the specificity of
        human experience"',
    'share': '1'}]}
```

The next example passes the row value into Python's built-in `type` function. We indeed have a `Series` of dictionaries:

```
In  [4] type(nobel.loc[2, "prizes"])

Out [4] dict
```

Our goal is to convert the data to tabular format. To do so, we'll need to extract the JSON's top-level key-value pairs (year, category) to separate `DataFrame` columns. We'll also need to iterate over each dictionary in the `"laureates"` list and extract its nested information. Our goal is a separate row for each Nobel laureate, connected to their year and category. The `DataFrame` we're aiming for looks like this:

	id	firstname	surname	motivation	share	year	category
0	976	John	Goodenough	"for the develop...	3	2019	chemistry
1	977	M. Stanley	Whittingham	"for the develop...	3	2019	chemistry
2	978	Akira	Yoshino	"for the develop...	3	2019	chemistry

The process of moving nested records of data into a single, one-dimensional list is called *flattening* or *normalizing*. The pandas library includes a built-in `json_normalize` function to take care of the heavy lifting. Let's try it on a small example: a sample dictionary from the `nobel` `DataFrame`. We'll use the `loc` accessor to access the first row's dictionary and assign it to a `chemistry_2019` variable:

```
In  [5] chemistry_2019 = nobel.loc[0, "prizes"]
        chemistry_2019

Out [5] {'year': '2019',
         'category': 'chemistry',
         'laureates': [{'id': '976',
          'firstname': 'John',
          'surname': 'Goodenough',
          'motivation': '"for the development of lithium-ion batteries"',
          'share': '3'},
         {'id': '977',
          'firstname': 'M. Stanley',
          'surname': 'Whittingham',
          'motivation': '"for the development of lithium-ion batteries"',
          'share': '3'},
         {'id': '978',
          'firstname': 'Akira',
          'surname': 'Yoshino',
          'motivation': '"for the development of lithium-ion batteries"',
          'share': '3'}]}
```

Let's pass the `chemistry_2019` dictionary to the `json_normalize` function's `data` parameter. The good news is that pandas extracts the three top-level dictionary keys (`"year"`, `"category"`, and `"laureates"`) to separate columns in a new

DataFrame. Unfortunately, the library still keeps the nested dictionaries from the
`"laureates"` list. Ultimately, we'd like to store the data in separate columns.

```
In  [6] pd.json_normalize(data = chemistry_2019)

Out [6]
```

year	category	laureates
0 2019	chemistry	[{'id': '976', 'firstname': 'John', 'surname':...

We can use the `json_normalize` function's `record_path` parameter to normalize
the nested `"laureates"` records. We pass the parameter a string denoting which key
in the dictionary holds the nested records. Let's pass it `"laureates"`:

```
In  [7] pd.json_normalize(data = chemistry_2019, record_path = "laureates")

Out [7]
```

	id	firstname	surname	motivation	share
0	976	John	Goodenough	"for the development of li...	3
1	977	M. Stanley	Whittingham	"for the development of li...	3
2	978	Akira	Yoshino	"for the development of li...	3

One step forward, one step back. Pandas expanded the nested `"laureates"` dictionaries into new columns, but now we've lost the original year and category columns.
To preserve these top-level key-value pairs, we can pass a list with their names to a
parameter called `meta`:

```
In  [8] pd.json_normalize(
            data = chemistry_2019,
            record_path = "laureates",
            meta = ["year", "category"],
        )

Out [8]
```

	id	firstname	surname	motivation	share	year	category
0	976	John	Goodenough	"for the develop...	3	2019	chemistry
1	977	M. Stanley	Whittingham	"for the develop...	3	2019	chemistry
2	978	Akira	Yoshino	"for the develop...	3	2019	chemistry

That's exactly the `DataFrame` we want. Our normalization strategy has worked successfully on a single dictionary from the prizes column. Luckily, the `json_normalize`
function is smart enough to accept a `Series` of dictionaries and repeat the extraction
logic for each entry. Let's see what happens when we pass it the `prizes` Series:

```
In  [9] pd.json_normalize(
            data = nobel["prizes"],
            record_path = "laureates",
            meta = ["year", "category"]
        )

-----------------------------------------------------------------
KeyError                                    Traceback (most recent call last)
<ipython-input-49-e09a24c19e5b> in <module>
      2     data = nobel["prizes"],
```

```
     3      record_path = "laureates",
----> 4      meta = ["year", "category"]
     5  )
```

```
KeyError: 'laureates'
```

Unfortunately, Pandas raises a `KeyError` exception. Some dictionaries in the prizes `Series` do not have a `"laureates"` key. The `json_normalize` function is unable to extract nested laureates information from a nonexistent list. One way we can solve this problem is to identify the dictionaries that lack a `"laureates"` key and manually assign them the key. In those situations, we can provide the `"laureates"` key a value of an empty list.

Let's take a second to review the `setdefault` method on a Python dictionary. Consider this dictionary:

```
In  [10] cheese_consumption = {
             "France": 57.9,
             "Germany": 53.2,
             "Luxembourg": 53.2
         }
```

The `setdefault` method assigns a key-value pair to a dictionary, but only if the dictionary does not have the key. If the key exists, the method returns its existing value. The method's first argument is the key, and its second argument is the value.

The following example attempts to add the key `"France"` to the `cheese_consumption` dictionary with a value of `100`. The key exists, so nothing changes. Python keeps the original value of `57.9`:

```
In  [11] cheese_consumption.setdefault("France", 100)
```

```
Out [11] 57.9
```

```
In  [12] cheese_consumption["France"]
```

```
Out [12] 57.9
```

By comparison, the next example invokes `setdefault` with an argument of `"Italy"`. The key `"Italy"` does not exist in the dictionary, so Python adds it and assigns it a value of `48`:

```
In  [13] cheese_consumption.setdefault("Italy", 48)
```

```
Out [13] 48
```

```
In  [14] cheese_consumption
```

```
Out [14] {'France': 57.9, 'Germany': 53.2, 'Luxembourg': 53.2, 'Italy': 48}
```

Let's apply this technique to each nested dictionary within prizes. If a dictionary does not have a `laureates` key, we'll use the `setdefault` method to add the key with a value of an empty list. As a reminder, we can use the `apply` method to iterate individually over each `Series` element. This method, introduced in chapter 3, accepts a function as an argument and passes each `Series` row to the function in sequence. The next example defines an `add_laureates_key` function to update a single dictionary and then passes the function to the `apply` method as an argument:

```
In  [15] def add_laureates_key(entry):
             entry.setdefault("laureates", [])

         nobel["prizes"].apply(add_laureates_key)

Out [15] 0        [{'id': '976', 'firstname': 'John', 'surname':...
         1        [{'id': '982', 'firstname': 'Abhijit', 'surnam...
         2        [{'id': '980', 'firstname': 'Peter', 'surname'...
         3        [{'id': '981', 'firstname': 'Abiy', 'surname':...
         4        [{'id': '973', 'firstname': 'James', 'surname'...
                                      ...
         641      [{'id': '160', 'firstname': 'Jacobus H.', 'sur...
         642      [{'id': '569', 'firstname': 'Sully', 'surname'...
         643      [{'id': '462', 'firstname': 'Henry', 'surname'...
         644      [{'id': '1', 'firstname': 'Wilhelm Conrad', 's...
         645      [{'id': '293', 'firstname': 'Emil', 'surname':...
         Name: prizes, Length: 646, dtype: object
```

The `setdefault` method mutates the dictionaries within prizes, so there is no need to overwrite the original `Series`.

Now that all nested dictionaries have a `laureates` key, we can reinvoke the `json_normalize` function. Once again, we'll pass a list to the `meta` parameter with the two top-level dictionary keys we'd like to keep. We'll also use `record_path` to specify the top-level attribute with a nested list of records:

```
In  [16] winners = pd.json_normalize(
             data = nobel["prizes"],
             record_path = "laureates",
             meta = ["year", "category"]
         )

         winners

Out [16]
```

	id	firstname	surname	motivation	share	year	category
0	976	John	Goodenough	"for the de...	3	2019	chemistry
1	977	M. Stanley	Whittingham	"for the de...	3	2019	chemistry
2	978	Akira	Yoshino	"for the de...	3	2019	chemistry
3	982	Abhijit	Banerjee	"for their ...	3	2019	economics
4	983	Esther	Duflo	"for their ...	3	2019	economics
...	...	...	...	...	...	...	...
945	569	Sully	Prudhomme	"in special...	1	1901	literature
946	462	Henry	Dunant	"for his hu...	2	1901	peace
947	463	Frédéric	Passy	"for his li...	2	1901	peace
948	1	Wilhelm Con...	Röntgen	"in recogni...	1	1901	physics
949	293	Emil	von Behring	"for his wo...	1	1901	medicine

950 rows × 7 columns

Success! We've normalized the JSON data, converted it to tabular format, and stored it in a two-dimensional `DataFrame`.

12.1.2 *Exporting a DataFrame to a JSON file*

Now let's attempt the process in reverse: converting a `DataFrame` to a JSON representation and writing it to a JSON file. The `to_json` method creates a JSON string from a pandas data structure; its `orient` parameter customizes the format in which pandas returns the data. The next example uses an argument of `"records"` to return a JSON array of key-value objects. Pandas stores the column names as dictionary keys that point to the row's respective values. Here's an example with the first two rows of `winners`, the `DataFrame` we created in section 12.1.1:

```
In  [17] winners.head(2)
```

```
Out [17]
```

	id	firstname	surname	motivation	share	year	category
0	976	John	Goodenough	"for the develop...	3	2019	chemistry
1	977	M. Stanley	Whittingham	"for the develop...	3	2019	chemistry

```
In  [18] winners.head(2).to_json(orient = "records")
```

```
Out [18]
```

```
'[{"id":"976","firstname":"John","surname":"Goodenough","motivation":"\\
"for the development of lithium-ion
batteries\\"","share":"3","year":"2019","category":"chemistry"},{"id":"9
77","firstname":"M.
Stanley","surname":"Whittingham","motivation":"\\"for the development of
lithium-ion
batteries\\"","share":"3","year":"2019","category":"chemistry"}]'
```

By comparison, we can pass an argument of `"split"` to return a dictionary with separate `columns`, `index`, and `data` keys. This option prevents the duplication of column names for each row entry:

```
In  [19] winners.head(2).to_json(orient = "split")
```

```
Out [19]
```

```
'{"columns":["id","firstname","surname","motivation","share","year","category
    "],"index":[0,1],"data":[["976","John","Goodenough","\\"for the
    development of lithium-ion
    batteries\\"","3","2019","chemistry"],["977","M.
    Stanley","Whittingham","\\"for the development of lithium-ion
    batteries\\"","3","2019","chemistry"]]}'
```

Additional arguments available for the `orient` parameter include `"index"`, `"columns"`, `"values"`, and `"table"`.

When the JSON format fits your expectations, pass the JSON file name as the first argument to the `to_json` method. Pandas will write the string to a JSON file in the same directory as the Jupyter Notebook:

```
In  [20] winners.to_json("winners.json", orient = "records")
```

> **WARNING** Be mindful when executing the same cell twice. If a win-
> ners.json file exists in the directory, pandas will overwrite it when we exe-
> cute the previous cell. The library will not warn us that it is replacing the file.
> For this reason, I strongly recommend giving output files a different name
> from input files.

12.2 Reading from and writing to CSV files

Our next data set is a collection of baby names in New York City. Each row includes the
name, birth year, gender, ethnicity, count, and popularity rank. The CSV file is hosted
on New York City's government website and is available at http://mng.bz/MgzQ.

We can access the website in our web browser and download the CSV file to our
computer for local storage. As an alternative, we can pass the URL as the first argument to the read_csv function. Pandas will automatically fetch the data set and
import it into a DataFrame. Hardcoded URLs are helpful when we have real-time
data that changes frequently because they save us the manual work of downloading
the data set each time we rerun our analysis:

```
In  [21] url = "https://data.cityofnewyork.us/api/views/25th-nujf/rows.csv"
         baby_names = pd.read_csv(url)
         baby_names.head()

Out [21]
```

	Year of Birth	Gender	Ethnicity	Child's First Name	Count	Rank
0	2011	FEMALE	HISPANIC	GERALDINE	13	75
1	2011	FEMALE	HISPANIC	GIA	21	67
2	2011	FEMALE	HISPANIC	GIANNA	49	42
3	2011	FEMALE	HISPANIC	GISELLE	38	51
4	2011	FEMALE	HISPANIC	GRACE	36	53

Note that pandas will raise an HTTPError exception if the link is invalid.

Let's try writing the baby_names DataFrame to a plain CSV file with the to_csv
method. Without an argument, the method outputs the CSV string directly in our
Jupyter Notebook. Following CSV conventions, pandas separates rows with line breaks
and row values with commas. As a reminder, a \n character marks a line break in
Python. Here's a small preview of the method's output for the first ten rows of
baby_names:

```
In  [22] baby_names.head(10).to_csv()

Out [22]
```

```
",Year of Birth,Gender,Ethnicity,Child's First
    Name,Count,Rank\n0,2011,FEMALE,HISPANIC,GERALDINE,13,75\n1,2011,FEMALE,H
    ISPANIC,GIA,21,67\n2,2011,FEMALE,HISPANIC,GIANNA,49,42\n3,2011,FEMALE,HI
    SPANIC,GISELLE,38,51\n4,2011,FEMALE,HISPANIC,GRACE,36,53\n5,2011,FEMALE,
    HISPANIC,GUADALUPE,26,62\n6,2011,FEMALE,HISPANIC,HAILEY,126,8\n7,2011,FE
    MALE,HISPANIC,HALEY,14,74\n8,2011,FEMALE,HISPANIC,HANNAH,17,71\n9,2011,F
    EMALE,HISPANIC,HAYLEE,17,71\n"
```

By default, pandas includes the DataFrame index in the CSV string. Notice the comma at the beginning of the string and the numeric values (0, 1, 2, and so on) after each \n symbol. Figure 12.3 highlights the commas in the output from the to_csv method.

```
",Year of Birth,Gender,Ethnicity,Child's First
Name,Count,Rank\n0,2011,FEMALE,HISPANIC,GERALDINE,13,75\n1,2011,FEMALE,HISP
ANIC,GIA,21,67\n2,2011,FEMALE,HISPANIC,GIANNA,49,42\n3,2011,FEMALE,HISPANIC
,GISELLE,38,51\n4,2011,FEMALE,HISPANIC,GRACE,36,53\n5,2011,FEMALE,HISPANIC,
GUADALUPE,26,62\n6,2011,FEMALE,HISPANIC,HAILEY,126,8\n7,2011,FEMALE,HISPANI
C,HALEY,14,74\n8,2011,FEMALE,HISPANIC,HANNAH,17,71\n9,2011,FEMALE,HISPANIC,
HAYLEE,17,71\n"
```

Figure 12.3   The CSV output with arrows highlighting the index labels

We can exclude the index by passing the index parameter an argument of False:

```
In  [23] baby_names.head(10).to_csv(index = False)

Out [23]

"Year of Birth,Gender,Ethnicity,Child's First
    Name,Count,Rank\n2011,FEMALE,HISPANIC,GERALDINE,13,75\n2011,FEMALE,HISPA
    NIC,GIA,21,67\n2011,FEMALE,HISPANIC,GIANNA,49,42\n2011,FEMALE,HISPANIC,G
    ISELLE,38,51\n2011,FEMALE,HISPANIC,GRACE,36,53\n2011,FEMALE,HISPANIC,GUA
    DALUPE,26,62\n2011,FEMALE,HISPANIC,HAILEY,126,8\n2011,FEMALE,HISPANIC,HA
    LEY,14,74\n2011,FEMALE,HISPANIC,HANNAH,17,71\n2011,FEMALE,HISPANIC,HAYLE
    E,17,71\n"
```

To write the string to a CSV file, we can pass the desired filename as the first argument to the to_csv method. Make sure to include the .csv extension in the string. If we do not provide a specific path, pandas will write the file to the same directory as the Jupyter Notebook:

```
In  [24] baby_names.to_csv("NYC_Baby_Names.csv", index = False)
```

The method produces no output below the Notebook cell. If we flip back to the Jupyter Notebook navigation interface, however, we see that pandas has created the CSV file. Figure 12.4 shows the saved NYC_Baby_Names.csv file.

Chapter 12 - Imports and Exports.ipynb

Multiple Worksheets.xlsx

nobel.json

NYC_Baby_Names.csv

Figure 12.4   The NYC_Baby_Names.csv file saved to the same directory as the Jupyter Notebook

By default, pandas writes all `DataFrame` columns to the CSV file. We can choose which columns to export by passing a list of names to the `columns` parameter. The next example creates a CSV with only the Gender, Child's First Name, and Count columns:

```
In  [25] baby_names.to_csv(
             "NYC_Baby_Names.csv",
             index = False,
             columns = ["Gender", "Child's First Name", "Count"]
          )
```

Please note that if a NYC_Baby_Names.csv file exists in the directory, pandas will overwrite the existing file.

12.3 Reading from and writing to Excel workbooks

Excel is the most popular spreadsheet application in use today. Pandas makes it easy to read from and write to Excel workbooks and even specific worksheets. But first, we'll need to do a little housekeeping to integrate the two pieces of software.

12.3.1 Installing the xlrd and openpyxl libraries in an Anaconda environment

Pandas needs the `xlrd` and `openpyxl` libraries to interact with Excel. These packages are the glue that connects Python to Excel.

Here's a refresher on installing a package in an Anaconda environment. For a more in-depth overview, see appendix A. If you've already installed these libraries in your Anaconda environment, feel free to skip to section 12.3.2.

1 Launch the Terminal (macOS) or Anaconda Prompt (Windows) application.

2 Use the `conda info --envs` command to see your available Anaconda environments:

```
$ conda info --envs

# conda environments:
#
base                     *  /opt/anaconda3
pandas_in_action            /opt/anaconda3/envs/pandas_in_action
```

3 Activate the Anaconda environment in which you'd like to install the libraries. Appendix A shows how to create a `pandas_in_action` environment for this book. If you chose a different environment name, replace `pandas_in_action` with it in the following command:

```
$ conda activate pandas_in_action
```

4 Install the `xlrd` and `openpyxl` libraries with the `conda install` command:

```
(pandas_in_action) $ conda install xlrd openpyxl
```

5 When Anaconda lists the required package dependencies, enter `"Y"` and press Enter to start the installation.

6 When the installation completes, execute `jupyter notebook` to start the Jupyter server again, and navigate back to the Jupyter Notebook for the chapter.

Don't forget to execute the cell with the `import pandas as pd` command at the top.

12.3.2 *Importing Excel workbooks*

The `read_excel` function at the top level of pandas imports an Excel workbook into a `DataFrame`. Its first parameter, `io`, accepts a string with the workbook's path. Make sure to include the .xlsx extension in the filename. By default, pandas will import only the first worksheet in the workbook.

The Single Worksheet.xlsx Excel workbook is a good place to start because it contains a single Data worksheet:

```
In  [26] pd.read_excel("Single Worksheet.xlsx")

Out [26]
```

	First Name	Last Name	City	Gender
0	Brandon	James	Miami	M
1	Sean	Hawkins	Denver	M
2	Judy	Day	Los Angeles	F
3	Ashley	Ruiz	San Francisco	F
4	Stephanie	Gomez	Portland	F

The `read_excel` function supports many of the same parameters as `read_csv`, including `index_col` to set the index columns, `usecols` to select the columns, and `squeeze` to coerce a one-column `DataFrame` into a `Series` object. The next example sets the City column as the index and keeps only three of the data set's four columns. Note that if we pass a column to the `index_col` parameter, we must also include the column in the `usecols` list:

```
In  [27] pd.read_excel(
            io = "Single Worksheet.xlsx",
            usecols = ["City", "First Name", "Last Name"],
            index_col = "City"
        )

Out [27]
```

City	First Name	Last Name
Miami	Brandon	James
Denver	Sean	Hawkins
Los Angeles	Judy	Day
San Francisco	Ashley	Ruiz
Portland	Stephanie	Gomez

The complexity increases slightly when a workbook contains multiple worksheets. The Multiple Worksheets.xlsx workbook holds three worksheets: Data 1, Data 2, and Data 3. By default, pandas imports only the first worksheet in the workbook:

```
In  [28] pd.read_excel("Multiple Worksheets.xlsx")

Out [28]
```

	First Name	Last Name	City	Gender
0	Brandon	James	Miami	M
1	Sean	Hawkins	Denver	M
2	Judy	Day	Los Angeles	F
3	Ashley	Ruiz	San Francisco	F
4	Stephanie	Gomez	Portland	F

During import, pandas assigns each worksheet an index position starting at 0. We can import a specific worksheet by passing the worksheet's index position or its name to the sheet_name parameter. The parameter's default argument is 0 (the first worksheet). Therefore, the following two statements return the same DataFrame:

```
In  [29] # The two lines below are equivalent
         pd.read_excel("Multiple Worksheets.xlsx", sheet_name = 0)
         pd.read_excel("Multiple Worksheets.xlsx", sheet_name = "Data 1")

Out [29]
```

	First Name	Last Name	City	Gender
0	Brandon	James	Miami	M
1	Sean	Hawkins	Denver	M
2	Judy	Day	Los Angeles	F
3	Ashley	Ruiz	San Francisco	F
4	Stephanie	Gomez	Portland	F

To import all worksheets, we can pass an argument of None to the sheet_name parameter. Pandas will store each worksheet in a separate DataFrame. The read_excel function returns a dictionary with the worksheets' names as keys and the respective DataFrames as values:

```
In  [30] workbook = pd.read_excel(
             "Multiple Worksheets.xlsx", sheet_name = None
         )

         workbook

Out [30] {'Data 1':   First Name Last Name           City Gender
         0     Brandon     James          Miami  M
         1        Sean   Hawkins         Denver  M
         2        Judy       Day    Los Angeles  F
         3      Ashley      Ruiz  San Francisco  F
         4   Stephanie     Gomez       Portland  F,
         'Data 2':   First Name Last Name           City Gender
         0      Parker     Power        Raleigh  F
         1     Preston  Prescott   Philadelphia  F
         2     Ronaldo   Donaldo         Bangor  M
         3       Megan   Stiller  San Francisco  M
         4      Bustin    Jieber         Austin  F,
         'Data 3':   First Name Last Name  City Gender
         0      Robert    Miller  Seattle  M
         1        Tara    Garcia  Phoenix  F
         2     Raphael Rodriguez  Orlando  M}
```

```
In  [31] type(workbook)
```

```
Out [31] dict
```

To access a `DataFrame`/worksheet, we access a key in the dictionary. Here, we access the `DataFrame` for the Data 2 worksheet:

```
In  [32] workbook["Data 2"]
```

```
Out [32]
```

	First Name	Last Name	City	Gender
0	Parker	Power	Raleigh	F
1	Preston	Prescott	Philadelphia	F
2	Ronaldo	Donaldo	Bangor	M
3	Megan	Stiller	San Francisco	M
4	Bustin	Jieber	Austin	F

To specify a subset of worksheets to import, we can pass the `sheet_name` parameter a list of index positions or worksheet names. Pandas still returns a dictionary. The dictionary's keys will match the strings in the `sheet_name` list. The next example imports only the Data 1 and Data 3 worksheets:

```
In  [33] pd.read_excel(
             "Multiple Worksheets.xlsx",
             sheet_name = ["Data 1", "Data 3"]
         )
```

```
Out [33] {'Data 1':    First Name Last Name           City Gender
          0   Brandon      James         Miami       M
          1      Sean    Hawkins        Denver       M
          2      Judy        Day   Los Angeles       F
          3    Ashley       Ruiz San Francisco       F
          4 Stephanie      Gomez      Portland       F,
          'Data 3':    First Name  Last Name   City Gender
          0    Robert     Miller  Seattle       M
          1      Tara     Garcia  Phoenix       F
          2   Raphael  Rodriguez  Orlando      M}
```

The next example targets index positions 1 and 2 or, equivalently, the second and third worksheets:

```
In  [34] pd.read_excel("Multiple Worksheets.xlsx", sheet_name = [1, 2])
```

```
Out [34] {1:    First Name Last Name           City Gender
          0   Parker      Power       Raleigh       F
          1  Preston   Prescott  Philadelphia       F
          2  Ronaldo    Donaldo        Bangor       M
          3    Megan    Stiller San Francisco       M
          4   Bustin     Jieber        Austin       F,
          2:   First Name  Last Name    City Gender
          0    Robert     Miller  Seattle       M
          1      Tara     Garcia  Phoenix       F
          2   Raphael  Rodriguez  Orlando      M}
```

After we've imported the `DataFrame`, we're free to invoke whatever methods we like on it. The original source of the data has no impact on our available operations.

12.3.3 Exporting Excel workbooks

Let's return to the baby_names `DataFrame` that we downloaded from the city of New York. Here's a reminder of what it looks like:

```
In  [35] baby_names.head()

Out [35]
```

	Year of Birth	Gender	Ethnicity	Child's First Name	Count	Rank
0	2011	FEMALE	HISPANIC	GERALDINE	13	75
1	2011	FEMALE	HISPANIC	GIA	21	67
2	2011	FEMALE	HISPANIC	GIANNA	49	42
3	2011	FEMALE	HISPANIC	GISELLE	38	51
4	2011	FEMALE	HISPANIC	GRACE	36	53

Let's say we want to split the data set into two `DataFrames`, one for each gender. Then we'd like to write each `DataFrame` to a separate worksheet in a new Excel workbook. We can begin by filtering the baby_names `DataFrame`, using the values in the Gender column. Chapter 5 introduced the following syntax:

```
In  [36] girls = baby_names[baby_names["Gender"] == "FEMALE"]
         boys = baby_names[baby_names["Gender"] == "MALE"]
```

Writing to an Excel workbook requires a few more steps than writing to a CSV. First up, we need to create an `ExcelWriter` object. This object serves as the foundation of the workbook. We'll attach individual worksheets to it in a moment.

The `ExcelWriter` constructor is available as a top-level attribute of the pandas library. Its first parameter, `path`, accepts the new workbook's filename as a string. If we do not provide a path to a directory, pandas will create the Excel file in the same directory as the Jupyter Notebook. Make sure to save the `ExcelWriter` object to a variable. The following example uses `excel_file`:

```
In  [37] excel_file = pd.ExcelWriter("Baby_Names.xlsx")
         excel_file

Out [37] <pandas.io.excel._openpyxl._OpenpyxlWriter at 0x118a7bf90>
```

Next, we need to connect our girls and boys `DataFrames` to individual worksheets in the workbook. Let's start with the former.

A `DataFrame` includes a `to_excel` method for writing to an Excel workbook. The method's first parameter, `excel_writer`, accepts an `ExcelWriter` object, like the one we created in the preceding example. The method's `sheet_name` parameter accepts the worksheet name as a string. Finally, we can pass the `index` parameter a value of `False` to exclude the `DataFrame` index:

```
In  [38] girls.to_excel(
             excel_writer = excel_file, sheet_name = "Girls", index = False
         )
```

Note that we have not created the Excel workbook yet. Rather, we've wired up the `Excel-Writer` object to include the girls `DataFrame` when we do create the workbook.

Next, let's connect our boys `DataFrame` to the Excel workbook. We'll invoke the `to_excel` method on boys, passing the `excel_writer` parameter the same `Excel-Writer` object. Now pandas knows that it should write both data sets to the same workbook. Let's also alter the string argument to the `sheet_name` parameter. To export only a subset of columns, let's pass a custom list to the `columns` parameter. The next example instructs pandas to include only the Child's First Name, Count, and Rank columns when writing the boys `DataFrame` to the "Boys" worksheet in the workbook:

```
In  [39] boys.to_excel(
             excel_file,
             sheet_name = "Boys",
             index = False,
             columns = ["Child's First Name", "Count", "Rank"]
         )
```

Now that we've configured the Excel workbook's plumbing, we're clear to write it to disk. Invoke the `save` method on the `excel_file` ExcelWriter object to complete the process:

```
In  [40] excel_file.save()
```

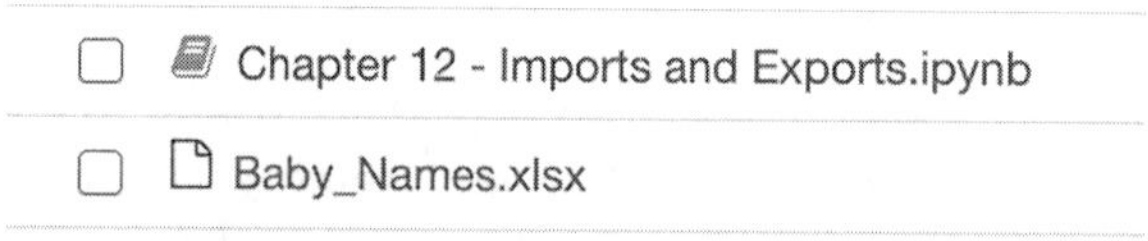

☐ 📄 Chapter 12 - Imports and Exports.ipynb

☐ 📄 Baby_Names.xlsx

Figure 12.5   The XLSX Excel file saved to the same directory as the Jupyter Notebook

Check out the Jupyter Notebook interface to see the result. Figure 12.5 shows the new Baby_Names.xlsx file in the same folder.

And there you have it. Now you know how to export JSON, CSV, and XLSX files from pandas. The library offers additional functions for exporting its data structures to other file formats.

12.4   Coding challenge

Let's practice the concepts introduced in this chapter. The tv_shows.json file is an aggregate collection of TV show episodes pulled from the Episodate.com API (see https://www.episodate.com/api). The JSON includes data for three TV shows: *The X-Files*, *Lost*, and *Buffy the Vampire Slayer*.

```
In  [41] tv_shows_json = pd.read_json("tv_shows.json")
         tv_shows_json
```

```
Out [41]
```

	shows
0	{'show': 'The X-Files', 'runtime': 60, 'network': 'FOX',...
1	{'show': 'Lost', 'runtime': 60, 'network': 'ABC', 'episo...
2	{'show': 'Buffy the Vampire Slayer', 'runtime': 60, 'net...

The JSON consists of a top-level `"shows"` key that connects to a list of three dictionaries, one for each of the three shows:

```
{
    "shows": [{}, {}, {}]
}
```

Each nested show dictionary includes `"show"`, `"runtime"`, `"network"`, and `"episodes"` keys. Here's a truncated preview of the first row's dictionary:

```
In   [42] tv_shows_json.loc[0, "shows"]

Out [42] {'show': 'The X-Files',
          'runtime': 60,
          'network': 'FOX',
          'episodes': [{'season': 1,
           'episode': 1,
           'name': 'Pilot',
           'air_date': '1993-09-11 01:00:00'},
          {'season': 1,
           'episode': 2,
           'name': 'Deep Throat',
           'air_date': '1993-09-18 01:00:00'},
```

The `"episodes"` key maps to a list of dictionaries. Each dictionary holds data for one show episode. In the previous example, we see the data for the first two episodes of season 1 of *The X-Files*.

12.4.1 Problems

Your challenges are

1 Normalize the nested episode data for each dictionary in the shows column. The goal is a `DataFrame` with a separate row for each episode. Each row should include the episode's relevant metadata (season, episode, name, and air_date) as well as the show's top-level information (show, runtime, and network).

2 Filter the normalized data set into three separate `DataFrames`, one for each of the shows (`"The X-Files"`, `"Lost"`, and `"Buffy the Vampire Slayer"`).

3 Write the three `DataFrames` to an episodes.xlsx Excel workbook, and save each TV show's episode data to a separate worksheet. (The worksheet names are up to you.)

12.4.2 Solutions

Let's tackle the problems:

1 We can use the `json_normalize` function to extract each TV show's nested batch of episodes. The episodes are available under the `"episodes"` key, which we can pass to the method's `record_path` parameter. To preserve the top-level show data, we can pass the `meta` parameter a list of the top-level keys to keep:

```
In  [43] tv_shows = pd.json_normalize(
             data = tv_shows_json["shows"],
             record_path = "episodes",
             meta = ["show", "runtime", "network"]
         )

         tv_shows
```

Out [43]

	season	episode	name	air_date	show	runtime	network
0	1	1	Pilot	1993-09-1...	The X-Files	60	FOX
1	1	2	Deep Throat	1993-09-1...	The X-Files	60	FOX
2	1	3	Squeeze	1993-09-2...	The X-Files	60	FOX
3	1	4	Conduit	1993-10-0...	The X-Files	60	FOX
4	1	5	The Jerse...	1993-10-0...	The X-Files	60	FOX
...	...	...	...	...	...	...	...
477	7	18	Dirty Girls	2003-04-1...	Buffy the...	60	UPN
478	7	19	Empty Places	2003-04-3...	Buffy the...	60	UPN
479	7	20	Touched	2003-05-0...	Buffy the...	60	UPN
480	7	21	End of Days	2003-05-1...	Buffy the...	60	UPN
481	7	22	Chosen	2003-05-2...	Buffy the...	60	UPN

482 rows × 7 columns

2 Our next challenge is to split the data set into three DataFrames, one for each TV show. We can filter the rows in tv_shows based on the values in the show column:

```
In  [44] xfiles = tv_shows[tv_shows["show"] == "The X-Files"]
         lost = tv_shows[tv_shows["show"] == "Lost"]
         buffy = tv_shows[tv_shows["show"] == "Buffy the Vampire Slayer"]
```

3 Finally, let's write the three DataFrames to an Excel workbook. We'll begin by instantiating an ExcelWriter object and saving it to a variable. We can pass in the workbook name as the first argument. I've chosen to call it episodes.xlsx:

```
In  [45] episodes = pd.ExcelWriter("episodes.xlsx")
         episodes
```

Out [45] <pandas.io.excel._openpyxl._OpenpyxlWriter at 0x11e5cd3d0>

Next, we must invoke the to_excel method on the three DataFrames to connect them to individual worksheets in the workbook. We'll pass the same episodes ExcelWriter object to the excel_writer parameter in each invocation. We'll make sure to provide a unique name for each worksheet via the sheet_name parameter. Finally, we'll pass the index parameter a value of False to exclude the DataFrame index:

```
In  [46] xfiles.to_excel(
             excel_writer = episodes, sheet_name = "X-Files", index = False
         )
```

```
In  [47] lost.to_excel(
             excel_writer = episodes, sheet_name = "Lost", index = False
         )

In  [48] buffy.to_excel(
             excel_writer = episodes,
             sheet_name = "Buffy the Vampire Slayer",
             index = False
         )
```

With the worksheets wired up, we can invoke the save method on the episodes ExcelWriter object to create the episodes.xlsx workbook:

```
In  [49] episodes.save()
```

Congratulations on completing the coding challenge!

Summary

- The read_json function parses a JSON file into a DataFrame.
- The json_normalize function converts nested JSON data to a tabular DataFrame.
- We can pass URLs to import functions such as read_csv, read_json, and read_excel. Pandas will download the data set from the provided link.
- The read_excel function imports an Excel workbook. The method's sheet_name parameter sets the worksheets to import. When we import multiple worksheets, pandas stores the resulting DataFrames in a dictionary.
- To write one or more DataFrames to an Excel workbook, instantiate an ExcelWriter object, attach the DataFrames to it via the to_excel method, and then invoke the save method on the ExcelWriter object.

Configuring pandas

13

This chapter covers

- Configuring pandas display settings for both the Notebook and single cells
- Limiting the number of printed `DataFrame` rows and columns
- Altering the precision of decimal-point numbers
- Truncating a cell's text content
- Rounding numeric values when they fall below a floor

As we've worked through the book's data sets, we've seen how pandas improves our user experience by making sensible decisions on data presentation. When we output a 1,000-row `DataFrame`, for example, the library assumes that we'd prefer to see 30 rows from the beginning and end rather than the whole data set, which can clutter the screen. Sometimes, we may want to break from pandas' assumptions and alter its settings to fit our custom display needs. Luckily, the library exposes many of its internal settings for us to alter. In this chapter, we'll learn how to configure options such as row and column limits, floating-point precision, and value rounding. Let's get our hands dirty and see how we can switch things up.

310

13.1 Getting and setting pandas options

We'll begin by importing the pandas library and assigning it an alias of `pd`:

```
In  [1] import pandas as pd
```

This chapter's data set, happiness.csv, is a ranking of the world's nations by happiness. The polling firm Gallup gathers the data with support from the United Nations. Each row includes a nation's aggregate happiness score alongside individual scores for gross domestic product (GDP) per capita, social support, life expectancy, and generosity. The data set holds 6 columns and 156 rows:

```
In  [2] happiness = pd.read_csv("happiness.csv")
        happiness.head()
```

```
Out [2]
```

	Country	Score	GDP per cap…	Social sup…	Life expect…	Generosity
0	Finland	7.769	1.340	1.587	0.986	0.153
1	Denmark	7.600	1.383	1.573	0.996	0.252
2	Norway	7.554	1.488	1.582	1.028	0.271
3	Iceland	7.494	1.380	1.624	1.026	0.354
4	Netherlands	7.488	1.396	1.522	0.999	0.322

Pandas stores its settings in a single `options` object at the top level of the library. Each option belongs to a parent category. Let's start with the `display` category, which holds settings for the printed representation of pandas' data structures.

The top-level `describe_option` function returns the documentation for a given setting. We can pass it a string with the setting's name. Let's look into the `max_rows` option, which is nested within the `display` parent category. The `max_rows` setting configures the maximum number of rows that pandas prints before it truncates a DataFrame:

```
In  [3] pd.describe_option("display.max_rows")
```

```
Out [3]
```

```
display.max_rows : int
    If max_rows is exceeded, switch to truncate view. Depending on
    `large_repr`, objects are either centrally truncated or printed
    as a summary view. 'None' value means unlimited.

    In case python/IPython is running in a terminal and
    `large_repr` equals 'truncate' this can be set to 0 and pandas
    will auto-detect the height of the terminal and print a
    truncated object which fits the screen height. The IPython
    notebook, IPython qtconsole, or IDLE do not run in a terminal
    and hence it is not possible to do correct auto-detection.
    [default: 60] [currently: 60]
```

Notice that the end of the documentation includes the setting's default value and its current value.

Pandas will print all library options that match the string argument. The library uses regular expressions to compare `describe_option`'s argument with its available settings. As a reminder, a *regular expression* is a search pattern for text; see appendix E for a detailed overview. The next example passes an argument of `"max_col"`. Pandas prints documentation for the two settings that match the term:

```
In  [4] pd.describe_option("max_col")

Out [4]

display.max_columns : int
    If max_cols is exceeded, switch to truncate view. Depending on
    `large_repr`, objects are either centrally truncated or printed as
    a summary view. 'None' value means unlimited.

    In case python/IPython is running in a terminal and `large_repr`
    equals 'truncate' this can be set to 0 and pandas will auto-detect
    the width of the terminal and print a truncated object which fits
    the screen width. The IPython notebook, IPython qtconsole, or IDLE
    do not run in a terminal and hence it is not possible to do
    correct auto-detection.
    [default: 20] [currently: 5]
display.max_colwidth : int or None
    The maximum width in characters of a column in the repr of
    a pandas data structure. When the column overflows, a "..."
    placeholder is embedded in the output. A 'None' value means unlimited.
    [default: 50] [currently: 9]
```

Although regular expressions are appealing, I recommend writing out the full name of the setting, including its parent category. Explicit code tends to lead to fewer errors.

There are two ways to get a setting's current value. The first way is the `get_option` function at the top level of pandas; like `describe_option`, it accepts a string argument with the setting's name. The second approach is to access the parent category and the specific setting as attributes on the top-level `pd.options` object.

The following example shows the syntax for both strategies. Both lines of code return 60 for the `max_rows` setting, which means that pandas will truncate any Data-Frame output greater than 60 rows in length:

```
In  [5] # The two lines below are equivalent
        pd.get_option("display.max_rows")
        pd.options.display.max_rows

Out [5] 60
```

Similarly, there are two ways to *set* a new value for a configuration setting. The `set_option` function at the top level of pandas accepts the setting as its first argument and its new value as the second argument. Alternatively, we can access the option via attributes on the `pd.options` object and assign the new value with an equal sign:

```
In  [6] # The two lines below are equivalent
        pd.set_option("display.max_rows", 6)
        pd.options.display.max_rows = 6
```

We've instructed pandas to truncate the `DataFrame` output if it is longer than six rows:

```
In [7] pd.options.display.max_rows

Out [7] 6
```

Let's see the change in action. The next example asks pandas to print the first six rows of happiness. The threshold of six maximum rows is not crossed, so pandas outputs the `DataFrame` without truncation:

```
In [8] happiness.head(6)

Out [8]
```

	Country	Score	GDP per cap...	Social sup...	Life expect...	Generosity
0	Finland	7.769	1.340	1.587	0.986	0.153
1	Denmark	7.600	1.383	1.573	0.996	0.252
2	Norway	7.554	1.488	1.582	1.028	0.271
3	Iceland	7.494	1.380	1.624	1.026	0.354
4	Netherlands	7.488	1.396	1.522	0.999	0.322
5	Switzerland	7.480	1.452	1.526	1.052	0.263

Now let's cross the threshold and ask pandas to print the first seven rows of happiness. The library always aims to print an equal number of rows before and after the truncation. In the next example, it prints three rows from the beginning of the output and three rows from the end of the output, truncating the middle row (index 3):

```
In [9] happiness.head(7)

Out [9]
```

	Country	Score	GDP per cap...	Social sup...	Life expect...	Generosity
0	Finland	7.769	1.340	1.587	0.986	0.153
1	Denmark	7.600	1.383	1.573	0.996	0.252
2	Norway	7.554	1.488	1.582	1.028	0.271
...	...	...	...	...	...	...
4	Netherlands	7.488	1.396	1.522	0.999	0.322
5	Switzerland	7.480	1.452	1.526	1.052	0.263
6	Sweden	7.343	1.387	1.487	1.009	0.267

7 rows × 6 columns

The `max_rows` setting declares the number of printed rows. The complementary `display.max_columns` option sets the maximum number of printed columns. The default value is 20:

```
In [10] # The two lines below are equivalent
        pd.get_option("display.max_columns")
        pd.options.display.max_columns

Out [10] 20
```

Again, to assign a new value, we can use the `set_option` function or access the nested `max_columns` attribute directly:

```
In  [11] # The two lines below are equivalent
         pd.set_option("display.max_columns", 2)
         pd.options.display.max_columns = 2
```

If we set an even number of max columns, pandas will exclude the truncation column from its max column count. The happiness `DataFrame` has six columns, but the following output displays only two of them. Pandas includes the first and last columns, Country and Generosity, and places a truncation column between the two:

```
In  [12] happiness.head(7)

Out [12]
```

	Country	...	Generosity
0	Finland		0.153
1	Denmark	...	0.252
2	Norway	...	0.271
...	...	...	...
4	Netherlands	...	0.322
5	Switzerland	...	0.263
6	Sweden	...	0.267

```
7 rows × 6 columns
```

If we set an odd number of max columns, pandas will include the truncation column in its column count. An odd number ensures that pandas can pack an equal number of columns on both sides of the truncation. The next example sets the `max_columns` value to 5. The happiness output displays the two leftmost columns (Country and Score), the truncation column, and the two rightmost columns (Life expectancy and Generosity). Pandas prints four of the original six columns:

```
In  [13] # The two lines below are equivalent
         pd.set_option("display.max_columns", 5)
         pd.options.display.max_columns = 5

In  [14] happiness.head(7)

Out [14]
```

	Country	Score	...	Life expectancy	Generosity
0	Finland	7.769	...	0.986	0.153
1	Denmark	7.600	...	0.996	0.252
2	Norway	7.554	...	1.028	0.271
...	...	...	...	...	...
4	Netherlands	7.488	...	0.999	0.322
5	Switzerland	7.480	...	1.052	0.263
6	Sweden	7.343	...	1.009	0.267

```
5 rows × 6 columns
```

To return a setting to its original value, pass its name to the reset_option function at the top level of pandas. The next example resets the max_rows setting:

```
In  [15] pd.reset_option("display.max_rows")
```

We can confirm the change by invoking the get_option function again:

```
In  [16] pd.get_option("display.max_rows")

Out [16] 60
```

Pandas has reset the max_rows setting to its default value of 60.

13.2 *Precision*

Now that we're comfortable with pandas' API for changing settings, let's walk through a few popular configuration options.

The display.precision option sets the number of digits after a floating-point number. The default value is 6:

```
In  [17] pd.describe_option("display.precision")

Out [17]

        display.precision : int
            Floating point output precision (number of significant
            digits). This is only a suggestion
            [default: 6] [currently: 6]
```

The next example sets the precision to 2. The setting affects values in all four of the floating-point columns in happiness:

```
In  [18] # The two lines below are equivalent
         pd.set_option("display.precision", 2)
         pd.options.display.precision = 2

In  [19] happiness.head()

Out [19]
```

	Country	Score	...	Life expectancy	Generosity
0	Finland	7.77	...	1.34	0.15
1	Denmark	7.60	...	1.38	0.25
2	Norway	7.55	...	1.49	0.27
3	Iceland	7.49	...	1.38	0.35
4	Netherlands	7.49	...	1.40	0.32

```
5 rows × 6 columns
```

The precision setting alters only the presentation of floating-point numbers. Pandas preserves the original values within the DataFrame, which we can prove by using the loc accessor to extract a sample value from a floating-point column like Score:

```
In  [20] happiness.loc[0, "Score"]

Out [20] 7.769
```

The Score column's original value, 7.769, is still present. Pandas changes the presentation of the value to 7.77 when it prints the DataFrame.

13.3 *Maximum column width*

The display.max_colwidth setting sets the maximum number of characters pandas prints before truncating a cell's text:

```
In  [21] pd.describe_option("display.max_colwidth")

Out [21]

         display.max_colwidth : int or None
             The maximum width in characters of a column in the repr of
             a pandas data structure. When the column overflows, a "..."
             placeholder is embedded in the output. A 'None' value means
             unlimited.
             [default: 50] [currently: 50]
```

The next example asks pandas to truncate text if its length is greater than nine characters:

```
In  [22] # The two lines below are equivalent
         pd.set_option("display.max_colwidth", 9)
         pd.options.display.max_colwidth = 9
```

Let's see what happens when we output happiness:

```
In  [23] happiness.tail()

Out [23]
```

	Country	Score	...	Life expectancy	Generosity
151	Rwanda	3.33	...	0.61	0.22
152	Tanzania	3.23	...	0.50	0.28
153	Afgha...	3.20	...	0.36	0.16
154	Central Afr...	3.08	...	0.10	0.23
155	South...	2.85	...	0.29	0.20

5 rows × 6 columns

Pandas shortens the last three Country values (Afghanistan, Central African Republic, and South Sudan). The first two values in the output (Rwanda at six characters and Tanzania at eight characters) remain unaffected.

13.4 *Chop threshold*

In some analyses, we may consider values to be insignificant if they are reasonably close to 0. Your business domain, for example, may consider the value 0.10 to be "as good as 0" or "effectively 0". The display.chop_threshold option sets the floor that a floating-point value must cross to be printed. Pandas will display any value below the threshold as 0:

```
In  [24] pd.describe_option("display.chop_threshold")

Out [24]

        display.chop_threshold : float or None
            if set to a float value, all float values smaller then the
            given threshold will be displayed as exactly 0 by repr and
            friends.
        [default: None] [currently: None]
```

This example sets 0.25 as the chop threshold:

```
In  [25] pd.set_option("display.chop_threshold", 0.25)
```

In the next output, notice that pandas prints the values in the Life expectancy and Generosity columns for index 154 (0.105 and 0.235, respectively) as 0.00 in the output:

```
In  [26] happiness.tail()

Out [26]
```

	Country	Score	...	Life expectancy	Generosity
151	Rwanda	3.33	...	0.61	0.00
152	Tanzania	3.23	...	0.50	0.28
153	Afghanistan	3.20	...	0.36	0.00
154	Central Afr...	3.08	...	0.00	0.00
155	South Sudan	2.85	...	0.29	0.00

```
5 rows × 6 columns
```

Much like the `precision` setting, `chop_threshold` does not change the underlying values in the `DataFrame`—only their printed representation.

13.5   *Option context*

The settings we've altered so far have been global. When we change them, we alter the output of all Jupyter Notebook cells executed afterward. A global setting persists until we assign a new value to it. If we set `display.max_columns` to 6, for example, Jupyter will output `DataFrame`s with a maximum of six columns for all future cell executions.

Sometimes, we want to customize presentation options for a single cell. We can accomplish this task with pandas' top-level `option_context` function. We pair the function with Python's built-in `with` keyword to create a context block. Think of a *context block* as being a temporary execution environment. The `option_context` function sets temporary values for pandas options while the code inside the block executes; global pandas settings are not affected.

We pass settings to the `option_context` function as sequential arguments. The next example prints the happiness `DataFrame` with

- `display.max_columns` set to 5
- `display.max_rows` set to 10
- `display.precision` set to 3

Jupyter does not recognize the with block's contents as the final statement of a Notebook cell. Thus, we need to use a Notebook function called display to output the DataFrame manually:

```
In [27] with pd.option_context(
            "display.max_columns", 5,
            "display.max_rows", 10,
            "display.precision", 3
        ):
            display(happiness)
```

```
Out [27]
```

	Country	Score	...	Life expectancy	Generosity
0	Finland	7.769	...	0.986	0.153
1	Denmark	7.600	...	0.996	0.252
2	Norway	7.554	...	1.028	0.271
3	Iceland	7.494	...	1.026	0.354
4	Netherlands	7.488	...	0.999	0.322
...	...	...	...	...	...
151	Rwanda	3.334	...	0.614	0.217
152	Tanzania	3.231	...	0.499	0.276
153	Afghanistan	3.203	...	0.361	0.158
154	Central Afr...	3.083	...	0.105	0.235
155	South Sudan	2.853	...	0.295	0.202

156 rows × 6 columns

Because we used the with keyword, we did not alter global Notebook settings for these three options; they retain their original values.

The option_context function is helpful for assigning different options to different cell executions. If you'd like a uniform presentation for all output, I recommend setting the options once in a cell at the top of your Jupyter Notebook.

Summary

- The describe_option function returns documentation for a pandas setting.
- The set_option function sets a new value for a setting.
- We can also change a setting by accessing and overwriting attributes on the pd.options object.
- The reset_option function changes a pandas setting back to its default value.
- The display.max_rows and display.max_columns options set the maximum rows/columns that pandas shows in the output.
- The display.precision setting alters the number of digits after a decimal point.
- The display.max_colwidth option sets the numeric threshold at which pandas truncates printed characters.
- The display.chop_threshold option sets a numeric floor. If values do not cross the threshold, pandas will print them as zeroes.
- Pair the option_context function and the with keyword to create a temporary execution context for a block completely.

Visualization 14

This chapter covers

- Installing the Matplotlib library for data visualization
- Rendering graphs and charts with pandas and Matplotlib
- Applying color templates to visualizations

Text-based `DataFrame` summaries are helpful, but many times, a story can best be told by a visualization. A line chart can quickly communicate a trend over time; a bar graph can distinctly identify unique categories and their counts; a pie chart can represent proportions in an easily digestible manner, and so on. Fortunately, pandas seamlessly integrates with many popular Python data visualization libraries, including Matplotlib, seaborn, and ggplot. In this chapter, we'll learn how to use Matplotlib to render dynamic charts from our `Series` and `DataFrames`. I hope that these visualizations help you add that little spark to your data presentations.

14.1   *Installing matplotlib*

By default, pandas relies on the open source Matplotlib package to render charts and graphs. Let's install it in our Anaconda environment.

Begin by launching the Terminal (macOS) or Anaconda Prompt (Windows) application for your operating system. The default Anaconda environment, base, should be listed in parentheses to the left. base is the currently active environment.

When we installed Anaconda (see appendix A), we created an environment called pandas_in_action. Let's execute the conda activate command to activate it. If you chose a different environment name, replace pandas_in_action with that name, as follows:

```
(base) ~$ conda activate pandas_in_action
```

The parentheses should change to reflect the active environment. Execute the command conda install matplotlib to install the Matplotlib library within the pandas_in_action environment:

```
(pandas_in_action) ~$ conda install matplotlib
```

When the prompt asks you to confirm, enter 'Y' for yes and press Enter. When installation completes, execute jupyter notebook and create a new Notebook.

14.2   *Line charts*

As always, let's begin by importing the pandas library. We'll also import the pyplot package from within the Matplotlib library. In this context, a *package* means a nested folder within the top library. We can access the pyplot package using dot syntax, the same way we access any library attribute. A common community alias for pyplot is plt.

By default, Jupyter Notebook renders each Matplotlib visualization in a separate browser window, like a pop-up window on a website. The windows can be a bit jarring, especially when there are multiple charts on the screen. We can add an extra line—%matplotlib inline—to force Jupyter to render visualizations directly below the code in a cell. %matplotlib inline is an example of a magic function, a syntactical shortcut for setting a configuration option in the Notebook:

```
In  [1] import pandas as pd
        import matplotlib.pyplot as plt
        %matplotlib inline
```

Now on to the data! This chapter's data set, space_missions.csv, includes more than 100 space flights throughout 2019 and 2020. Each record consists of a mission's date, sponsoring company, location, cost, and status ("Success" or "Failure"):

```
In  [2] pd.read_csv("space_missions.csv").head()
```

```
Out [2]
```

	Date	Company Name	Location	Cost	Status
0	2/5/19	Arianespace	France	200.00	Success
1	2/22/19	SpaceX	USA	50.00	Success
2	3/2/19	SpaceX	USA	50.00	Success
3	3/9/19	CASC	China	29.15	Success
4	3/22/19	Arianespace	France	37.00	Success

Let's adjust two settings before we assign the imported `DataFrame` to a `space` variable. First, we'll use the `parse_dates` parameter to import the values in the Date column as datetimes. Next, we'll set the Date column as the index of the `DataFrame`:

```
In  [3] space = pd.read_csv(
            "space_missions.csv",
            parse_dates = ["Date"],
            index_col = "Date"
        )

        space.head()
```

```
Out [3]
```

Date	Company Name	Location	Cost	Status
2019-02-05	Arianespace	France	200.00	Success
2019-02-22	SpaceX	USA	50.00	Success
2019-03-02	SpaceX	USA	50.00	Success
2019-03-09	CASC	China	29.15	Success
2019-03-22	Arianespace	France	37.00	Success

Suppose that we want to plot the flight costs over the two years in this data set. A *time-series* graph is an optimal chart for observing a trend over time. We can plot time on the x-axis and values on the y-axis. First, let's extract the Cost column from the space `DataFrame`. The result is a `Series` with numeric values and a datetime index:

```
In  [4] space["Cost"].head()

Out [4] Date
        2019-02-05    200.00
        2019-02-22     50.00
        2019-03-02     50.00
        2019-03-09     29.15
        2019-03-22     37.00
        Name: Cost, dtype: float64
```

To render a visualization, invoke the `plot` method on a pandas data structure. By default, Matplotlib draws a line graph. Jupyter also prints the location of the graph object in the computer's memory. The location will be different with each cell execution, so feel free to ignore it:

```
In  [5] space["Cost"].plot()

Out [5] <matplotlib.axes._subplots.AxesSubplot at 0x11e1c4650>
```

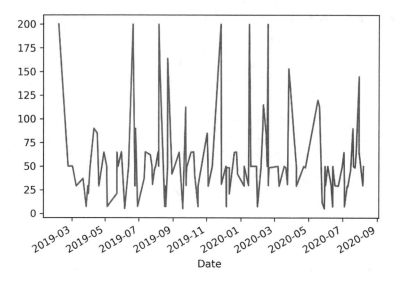

Pretty fancy! We have rendered a line chart with Matplotlib using values from pandas. By default, the library plots the index labels (in this case, the datetimes) on the x-axis and the `Series`' values on the y-axis. Matplotlib also calculates reasonable intervals for the range of values on both axes.

We can also invoke the `plot` method on the space `DataFrame` itself. In this scenario, pandas produces the same output, but only because the data set has only one numeric column:

```
In  [6] space.plot()

Out [6] <matplotlib.axes._subplots.AxesSubplot at 0x11ea18790>
```

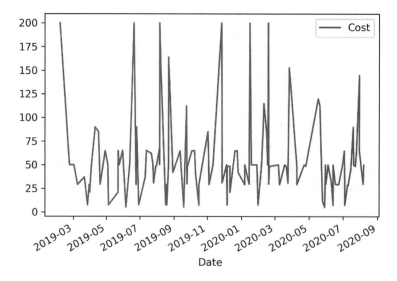

If a `DataFrame` holds multiple numeric columns, Matpotlib will draw a separate line for each one. Be careful: if there is a large gap in the magnitude of values between columns (if one numeric column has values in the millions and another has values in the hundreds, for example), the larger values can easily dwarf the smaller ones. Consider this `DataFrame`:

```
In  [7] data = [
            [2000, 3000000],
            [5000, 5000000]
        ]

        df = pd.DataFrame(data = data, columns = ["Small", "Large"])
        df

Out [7]
```

	Small	Large
0	2000	3000000
1	5000	5000000

When we plot the df `DataFrame`, Matplotlib adjusts the graph scale to accommodate the Large column's values. The trend in the Small column's values becomes impossible to see:

```
In  [8] df.plot()

Out [8] <matplotlib.axes._subplots.AxesSubplot at 0x7fc48279b6d0>
```

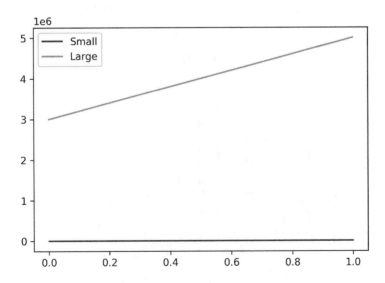

Let's come back to space. The `plot` method accepts a `y` parameter to identify the `DataFrame` column whose values Matplotlib should plot. The next example passes the Cost column and is another way to render the same time-series graph:

```
In   [9] space.plot(y = "Cost")
```

```
Out [9] <matplotlib.axes._subplots.AxesSubplot at 0x11eb0b990>
```

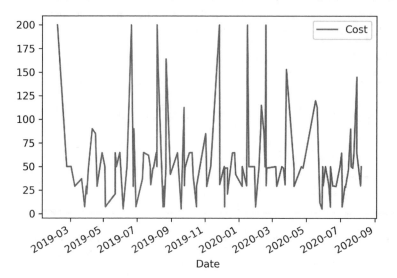

We can use the `colormap` parameter to alter the aesthetics of the visualization. Think of this process as setting the color theme of the graph. The parameter accepts a string with a predefined color palette from the Matplotlib library. The following example uses a `"gray"` theme that renders the line chart in black and white:

```
In   [10] space.plot(y = "Cost", colormap = "gray")
```

```
Out [10] <matplotlib.axes._subplots.AxesSubplot at 0x11ebef350>
```

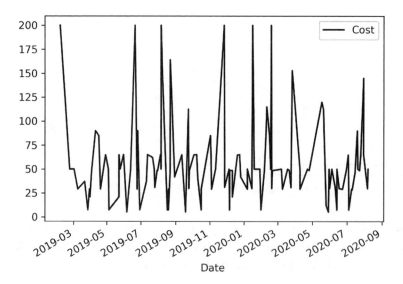

To see a list of valid inputs for the `colormaps` parameter, invoke the `colormaps` method on the `pyplot` library (aliased to `plt` in our Notebook). Note that we can apply some of these themes only if certain criteria are met, such as a minimum number of graph lines:

```
In  [11] print(plt.colormaps())

Out [11] ['Accent', 'Accent_r', 'Blues', 'Blues_r', 'BrBG', 'BrBG_r',
         'BuGn', 'BuGn_r', 'BuPu', 'BuPu_r', 'CMRmap', 'CMRmap_r',
         'Dark2', 'Dark2_r', 'GnBu', 'GnBu_r', 'Greens', 'Greens_r',
         'Greys', 'Greys_r', 'OrRd', 'OrRd_r', 'Oranges', 'Oranges_r',
         'PRGn', 'PRGn_r', 'Paired', 'Paired_r', 'Pastel1', 'Pastel1_r',
         'Pastel2', 'Pastel2_r', 'PiYG', 'PiYG_r', 'PuBu', 'PuBuGn',
         'PuBuGn_r', 'PuBu_r', 'PuOr', 'PuOr_r', 'PuRd', 'PuRd_r',
         'Purples', 'Purples_r', 'RdBu', 'RdBu_r', 'RdGy', 'RdGy_r',
         'RdPu', 'RdPu_r', 'RdYlBu', 'RdYlBu_r', 'RdYlGn', 'RdYlGn_r',
         'Reds', 'Reds_r', 'Set1', 'Set1_r', 'Set2', 'Set2_r', 'Set3',
         'Set3_r', 'Spectral', 'Spectral_r', 'Wistia', 'Wistia_r', 'YlGn',
         'YlGnBu', 'YlGnBu_r', 'YlGn_r', 'YlOrBr', 'YlOrBr_r', 'YlOrRd',
         'YlOrRd_r', 'afmhot', 'afmhot_r', 'autumn', 'autumn_r', 'binary',
         'binary_r', 'bone', 'bone_r', 'brg', 'brg_r', 'bwr', 'bwr_r',
         'cividis', 'cividis_r', 'cool', 'cool_r', 'coolwarm',
         'coolwarm_r', 'copper', 'copper_r', 'cubehelix', 'cubehelix_r',
         'flag', 'flag_r', 'gist_earth', 'gist_earth_r', 'gist_gray',
         'gist_gray_r', 'gist_heat', 'gist_heat_r', 'gist_ncar',
         'gist_ncar_r', 'gist_rainbow', 'gist_rainbow_r', 'gist_stern',
         'gist_stern_r', 'gist_yarg', 'gist_yarg_r', 'gnuplot',
         'gnuplot2', 'gnuplot2_r', 'gnuplot_r', 'gray', 'gray_r', 'hot',
         'hot_r', 'hsv', 'hsv_r', 'inferno', 'inferno_r', 'jet', 'jet_r',
         'magma', 'magma_r', 'nipy_spectral', 'nipy_spectral_r', 'ocean',
         'ocean_r', 'pink', 'pink_r', 'plasma', 'plasma_r', 'prism',
         'prism_r', 'rainbow', 'rainbow_r', 'seismic', 'seismic_r',
         'spring', 'spring_r', 'summer', 'summer_r', 'tab10', 'tab10_r',
         'tab20', 'tab20_r', 'tab20b', 'tab20b_r', 'tab20c', 'tab20c_r',
         'terrain', 'terrain_r', 'twilight', 'twilight_r',
         'twilight_shifted', 'twilight_shifted_r', 'viridis', 'viridis_r',
         'winter', 'winter_r']
```

Matplotlib has more than 150 available color maps to choose among. The library also offers ways to customize the graphs manually.

14.3 *Bar graphs*

The `plot` method's `kind` parameter alters the type of chart that Matplotlib renders. A bar graph is an excellent choice to display the counts of unique values in a data set, so let's use it to visualize how many space flights each company sponsored.

First, we'll target the Company Name column and invoke the `value_counts` method to return a `Series` of mission counts by company:

```
In  [12] space["Company Name"].value_counts()

Out [12] CASC            35
         SpaceX          25
         Roscosmos       12
```

```
        Arianespace      10
        Rocket Lab        9
        VKS RF            6
        ULA               6
        Northrop          5
        ISRO              5
        MHI               3
        Virgin Orbit      1
        JAXA              1
        ILS               1
        ExPace            1
        Name: Company Name, dtype: int64
```

Next, let's invoke the `plot` method on the `Series`, passing an argument of `"bar"` to the `kind` parameter. Matplotlib once again plots the index labels on the x-axis and the values on the y-axis. It looks as though CASC has the most entries in the data set, followed by SpaceX:

```
In   [13]  space["Company Name"].value_counts().plot(kind = "bar")
```

```
Out  [13]  <matplotlib.axes._subplots.AxesSubplot at 0x11ecd6310>
```

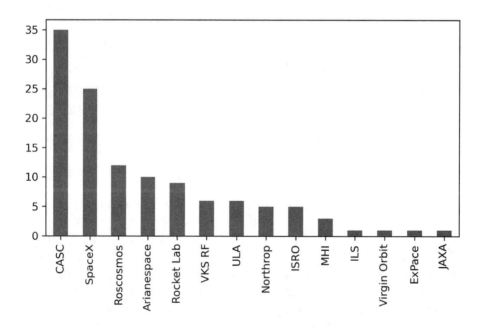

The graph is a good start, but we have to twist our heads to read the labels. Ouch. Let's change the `kind` argument to `"barh"` to render a horizontal bar graph instead:

```
In   [14]  space["Company Name"].value_counts().plot(kind = "barh")
```

```
Out  [14]  <matplotlib.axes._subplots.AxesSubplot at 0x11edf0190>
```

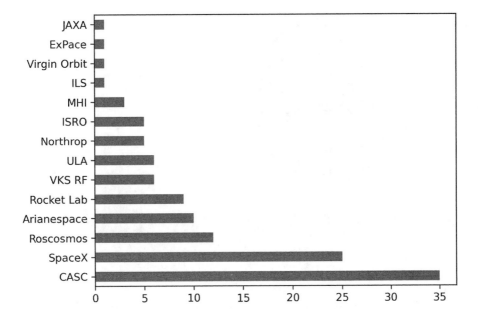

That's a lot better! Now we can easily identify which companies had the greatest number of space flights in the data set.

14.4 Pie charts

A *pie chart* is a visualization in which colored slices add up to form a whole circular pie (much like slices of a pizza). Each piece visually represents the proportion it contributes to the total amount.

Let's use a pie chart to compare the ratio of successful missions to failed missions. The Status column has only two unique values: `"Success"` and `"Failure"`. First, we'll use the `value_counts` method to count the number of occurrences of each:

```
In  [15] space["Status"].value_counts()

Out [15] Success    114
         Failure      6
         Name: Status, dtype: int64
```

Let's invoke the `plot` method again. This time around, we'll pass the `kind` parameter an argument of `"pie"`:

```
In  [16] space["Status"].value_counts().plot(kind = "pie")

Out [16] <matplotlib.axes._subplots.AxesSubplot at 0x11ef9ea90>
```

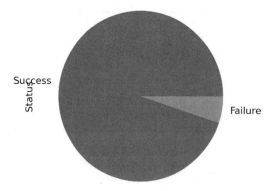

Good news! It looks as though the majority of space flights were successful.

To add a legend to a visualization like this one, we can pass the `legend` parameter an argument of `True`:

```
In  [17] space["Status"].value_counts().plot(kind = "pie", legend = True)

Out [17] <matplotlib.axes._subplots.AxesSubplot at 0x11eac1a10>
```

Matplotlib supports a wide variety of additional charts and graphs, including histograms, scatterplots, and boxplots. We can include additional parameters to customize the aesthetics, labels, legends, and interactivity of these visualizations. We've only scratched the surface of what this powerful library can render.

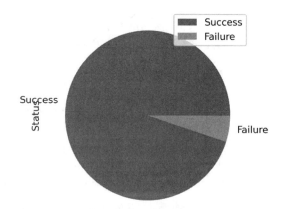

Summary

- Pandas seamlessly integrates with the Matplotlib library for data visualization. It also plays well with additional plotting libraries within Python's data science ecosystem.
- The `plot` method on a `Series` or `DataFrame` renders a visualization with data from the pandas data structure.
- The default Matplotlib chart is a line graph.
- The `kind` parameter to the `plot` method alters the type of the rendered visualization. Options include line graphs, bar graphs, and pie charts.
- The `colormap` parameter changes the color scheme of the rendered graphic. Matplotlib has dozens of predefined templates, and users can also create their own by adjusting method parameters.

appendix A
Installation and setup

Welcome to the supplementary material! This appendix walks you through installing the Python programming language and the pandas library for the macOS and Windows operating systems. A *library* (also called a *package*) is a toolbox of features that expands a core programming language's functionalities—an expansion pack or add-on that offers solutions to common challenges that developers face when working with the language. The Python ecosystem includes thousands of packages for domains such as statistics, HTTP requests, and database management.

A *dependency* is a piece of software that we need to install to run another piece of software. Pandas is not a stand-alone package; it has a set of dependencies including the libraries NumPy and pytz. These libraries may require their own dependencies. We don't have to understand what all these other packages do, but we need to install them for pandas to function.

A.1 *The Anaconda distribution*

Open source libraries are often developed by independent teams of contributors on different timelines. Unfortunately, the isolated development cycles can introduce compatibility issues between library versions. Installing the latest version of a library without upgrading its dependencies may render it dysfunctional, for example.

To simplify the installation and management of pandas and its dependencies, we'll rely on a Python distribution called Anaconda. A *distribution* is a collection of software that bundles multiple applications and their dependencies in one straightforward installer. With a user base of more than 20 million, Anaconda is the most popular distribution for getting up and running with data science in Python.

Anaconda installs Python and a powerful environment management system called `conda`. An *environment* is an independent sandbox for code execution—a playground of sorts where we can install Python and a selection of packages. To experiment with a different version of Python, a different version of pandas, a different combination of packages, or anything in between, we create a new `conda`

Environment 1		Environment 2		Environment 3
Python 2.7		Python 3.9		Python 3.8
pandas 0.20.3		pandas 1.2.0		django 3.0.7
numpy 1.9.1		numpy 1.16.6		flask 1.1.12

Figure A.1   Three Anaconda environments with different Python versions and different packages

environment. Figure A.1 depicts three hypothetical `conda` environments, each with a different version of Python.

The advantage of environments is isolation. Changes in one environment do not affect any other environment, as `conda` stores them in different folders. Thus, we can easily work on multiple projects, each of which requires a different configuration. When you're installing packages to an environment, `conda` also installs the appropriate dependencies and ensures compatibility between different library versions. In short, `conda` is an effective way to enable multiple installations and configurations of Python tools on your computer.

That's a big-picture introduction! Now let's get down to business and install Anaconda. Head to www.anaconda.com/products/individual, and find the section of the page with installer downloads for your operating system. You'll likely see multiple versions of the Anaconda installer:

- If you're given a choice between a Graphical Installer and a Command Line Installer, choose the Graphical Installer.
- If you're given a choice of Python versions, target the most up-to-date one. As with most software, a larger version number denotes a more recent release. Python 3 is newer than Python 2, and Python 3.9 is newer than Python 3.8. When you're learning a new technology, it's best to get started with the latest release. Don't worry; `conda` permits you to create environments with earlier versions of Python if you need them.
- If you're a Windows user, you may be given a choice between a 64-bit and a 32-bit installer. We'll discuss which one to select in section A.3.

At this point, the setup process diverges for the macOS and Windows operating systems. Find the appropriate subsection in this appendix, and continue from there.

A.2   The macOS setup process

Let's walk through installing Anaconda on a macOS computer.

A.2.1   Installing Anaconda in macOS

Your Anaconda download will consist of a single .pkg installer file. The filename will likely include the Anaconda version number and the operating system (such as

Anaconda3-2021.05-MacOSX-x86_64). Locate the installer in your file system, and double-click it to start the installation.

Click the Continue button on the first screen. On the README screen, the installer provides a quick overview of Anaconda that is worth perusing (see figure A.2).

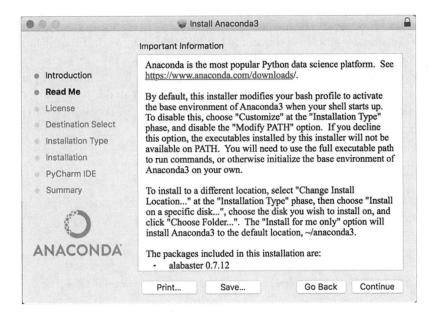

Figure A.2 Anaconda installation screen on a macOS computer

The installation creates a starter `conda` environment called `base` with a collection of more than 250 preselected data analysis packages. You will be able to create additional environments later. The installer also informs you that it will activate this `base` environment whenever you start your shell; we'll discuss how this process works in section A.2.2. For now, trust that this part of the installation process is required, and proceed onward.

Continue through any remaining screens. Accept the license agreement and the space requirements. You'll be given the option to customize your installation directory; whether you do is entirely up to you. Note that the distribution is self-contained; Anaconda installs itself within one directory on your computer. Thus, if you'd ever like to uninstall Anaconda, you can delete that directory.

Installation may take up to a few minutes. When it completes, click Next until you exit the installer.

A.2.2 *Launching Terminal*

Anaconda ships with a graphical program called Navigator that makes it easy to create and manage `conda` environments. Before we launch it, though, we'll use the more traditional Terminal application to issue commands to the `conda` environment manager.

Terminal is an application for issuing commands to the macOS operating system. Before modern graphical user interfaces (GUIs) existed, users relied exclusively on text-based applications to interact with the computer. In Terminal, you enter text and then press the Enter key to execute it. I'd like us to master Terminal before Anaconda Navigator because it's important to understand the complexity that a piece of software abstracts from us before we rely on its shortcuts.

Open a Finder window, and navigate to the Applications directory, where you'll find the Terminal application within the Utilities folder. Launch the application. I also recommend dragging the Terminal app's icon to the Dock for easy access.

Terminal should list the active `conda` environment inside a pair of parentheses before its flashing prompt. As a reminder, Anaconda created a `base` starter environment during installation. Figure A.3 shows a sample Terminal window with the `base` environment activated.

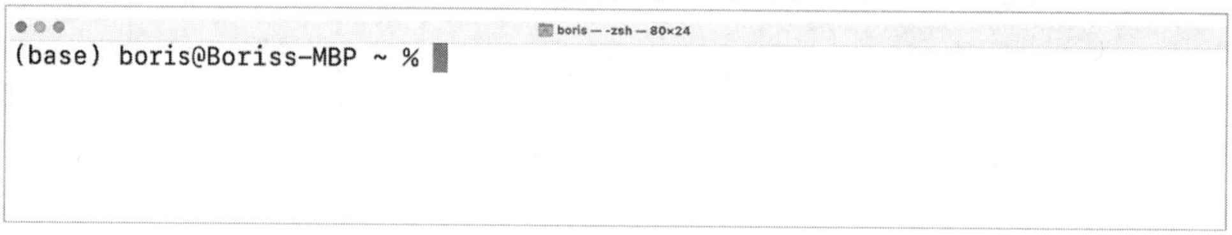

Figure A.3   Terminal on a macOS machine. The active `conda` environment is `base`.

Anaconda will activate the `conda` environment manager and this `base` environment whenever we start Terminal.

A.2.3   *Common Terminal commands*

We need to memorize only a few commands to work effectively with Terminal. In Terminal, we can navigate through our computer's directories the same way that we do in the Finder. The `pwd` (print working directory) command outputs the folder we are in:

```
(base) ~$ pwd
/Users/boris
```

The `ls` (list) command lists the files and folders inside the current directory:

```
(base) ~$ ls
Applications Documents   Google Drive Movies     Pictures    anaconda3
Desktop      Downloads   Library      Music      Public
```

Some commands accept flags. A *flag* is a configuration option we add after a command to modify how it executes. Its syntax consists of a sequence of dashes and text characters. Here's one example. The `ls` command by itself shows only public files and folders. We can add the `--all` flag to the command to display the hidden files as well. Some flags support multiple syntax options. `ls -a` , for example, is a shortcut for `ls --all`. Try both commands for yourself.

The `cd` (change directory) command navigates into a specified directory. Enter the directory name immediately after the command, making sure to include a space. In the next example, we navigate into the Desktop directory:

```
(base) ~$ cd Desktop
```

We can output our current location with the `pwd` command:

```
(base) ~/Desktop$ pwd
/Users/boris/Desktop
```

A pair of dots after `cd` navigates upward in the folder hierarchy:

```
(base) ~/Desktop$ cd ..

(base) ~$ pwd
/Users/boris
```

Terminal has a powerful autocomplete feature. Inside your user directory, enter `cd Des` and press the Tab key to autocomplete it to `cd Desktop`. Terminal looks at the list of available files and folders, and determines that only `Desktop` matches the `Des` pattern we typed. If there are multiple matches, Terminal will complete a portion of the name. If a directory contains two folders, `Anaconda` and `Analytics`, and you enter the letter `A`, Terminal will autocomplete `Ana`, the common letters in the two options. You'll have to type an additional letter and press the Tab key again for Terminal to autocomplete the remainder of the name.

At this point, we've acquired all the knowledge we need to start working with the `conda` environment manager. Skip to section A.4, where we'll meet up with our Windows friends and set up our first `conda` environment!

A.3 The Windows setup process

Let's walk through installing Anaconda on a Windows computer.

A.3.1 Installing Anaconda in Windows

The Anaconda installer for Windows is available in both 32-bit and 64-bit versions. These options describe the type of processor installed with your computer. If you are unsure which option to download, open the Start menu, and choose the System Information app. On the app's main screen, you will see a table consisting of Item and Value columns. Look for the `System Type` item; its value will include `x64` if your computer runs a 64-bit version of Windows or `x86` if your computer runs a 32-bit version of Windows. Figure A.4 shows the System Information app on a Windows computer with the System Type row highlighted.

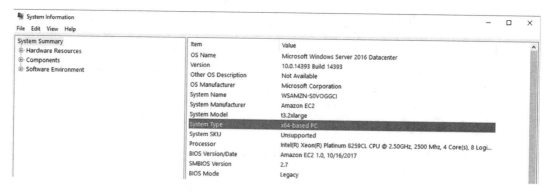

Figure A.4   The System Information app on a 64-bit Windows computer

Your Anaconda download will consist of a single .exe installer file. The filename will include the Anaconda version number and the operating system (such as Anaconda3-2021.05-Windows-x86_64). Locate the file on your file system and double-click it to launch the installer.

Proceed through the first few installation screens. You will be prompted to accept the license agreement, choose whether to install Anaconda for one or all users, and select the installation directory. Selecting the default options is fine.

When you reach the Advanced Installation Options screen, it might be a good idea to deselect the Register Anaconda As My Default Python check box if you already have Python installed on your computer. Deselecting the item prevents the installation from setting Anaconda as the default Python version on your computer. If you're installing Python for the first time, keeping the option selected should be fine.

The installation creates a starter `conda` environment called `base` with a collection of more than 250 preselected data analysis packages. You will be able to create additional environments later.

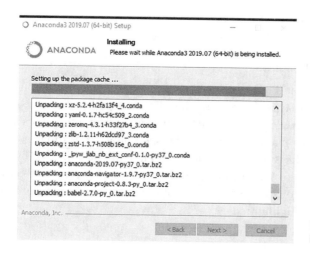

Installation can take up to a few minutes. Figure A.5 shows a sample of the installation process. When installation is complete, exit the installer.

Figure A.5   In-progress Anaconda installation on a Windows computer

If you ever want to uninstall Anaconda, launch the Start menu, and choose Add or Remove Programs. Locate the Anaconda program, click the Uninstall button, and follow the steps in the prompt to remove the distribution from your computer. Note that this process will remove all `conda` environments as well as their installed packages and Python versions.

A.3.2 Launching Anaconda Prompt

Anaconda ships with a graphical program called Navigator that makes it easy to create and manage `conda` environments. Before we launch it, though, we'll use a more traditional command-line application to issue commands to the `conda` environment manager. It's important to understand the problems that Navigator solves for us before we rely on its shortcuts.

Anaconda Prompt is an application for issuing text commands to the Windows operating system. We enter a command and then press the Enter key to execute it. Before modern GUIs existed, users relied exclusively on command-based applications like this one to interact with the computer. Open the Start menu, find Anaconda Prompt, and launch the application.

Anaconda Prompt should always list the active `conda` environment in a pair of parentheses before its flashing prompt. Right now, you should see `base`, the starter environment that Anaconda created during installation. Figure A.6 displays Anaconda Prompt with an active `base` environment.

Figure A.6 Anaconda Prompt on a Windows machine. The active `conda` environment is `base`.

Anaconda Prompt will activate the `base` environment when it launches. In section A.3.4, we'll walk through how to create and activate new environments with `conda`.

A.3.3 Common Anaconda Prompt commands

We need to memorize only a few commands to work effectively with Anaconda Prompt. We can navigate through our computer's directories the same way that we do in Windows Explorer. The `dir` (directory) command lists all files and folders in the current directory:

```
(base) C:\Users\Boris>dir
     Volume in drive C is OS
     Volume Serial Number is 6AAC-5705

 Directory of C:\Users\Boris
```

```
08/15/2019 03:16 PM <DIR> .
   08/15/2019 03:16 PM <DIR> ..
   09/20/2017 02:45 PM <DIR> Contacts
   08/18/2019 11:21 AM <DIR> Desktop
   08/13/2019 03:50 PM <DIR> Documents
   08/15/2019 02:51 PM <DIR> Downloads
   09/20/2017 02:45 PM <DIR> Favorites
   05/07/2015 09:56 PM <DIR> Intel
   06/25/2018 03:35 PM <DIR> Links
   09/20/2017 02:45 PM <DIR> Music
   09/20/2017 02:45 PM <DIR> Pictures
   09/20/2017 02:45 PM <DIR> Saved Games
   09/20/2017 02:45 PM <DIR> Searches
   09/20/2017 02:45 PM <DIR> Videos
                  1 File(s) 91 bytes
                 26 Dir(s) 577,728,139,264 bytes free
```

The `cd` (change directory) command navigates into a specified directory. Enter the directory name immediately after the command, making sure to include a space. In the next example, we navigate into the Desktop directory:

```
(base) C:\Users\Boris>cd Desktop

(base) C:\Users\Boris\Desktop>
```

A pair of dots after `cd` navigates upward in the folder hierarchy:

```
(base) C:\Users\Boris\Desktop>cd ..

(base) C:\Users\Boris>
```

Anaconda Prompt has a powerful autocomplete feature. Inside your user directory, enter `cd Des` and press the Tab key to autocomplete it to `cd Desktop`. Anaconda Prompt looks at the list of available files and folders, and determines that only `Desktop` matches the `Des` pattern we typed. If there are multiple matches, Anaconda Prompt will complete a portion of the name. If a directory contains two folders, `Anaconda` and `Analytics`, and you enter the letter `A`, Anaconda Prompt will autocomplete `Ana`, the common letters in the two options. You'll have to type an additional letter and press the Tab key again for Prompt to autocomplete the remainder of the name.

At this point, we have all the knowledge we need to start working with the `conda` environment manager. Let's create our first `conda` environment!

A.4 *Creating a new Anaconda environment*

Congratulations—you've successfully installed the Anaconda distribution on your macOS or Windows machine. Now let's create a sample `conda` environment that we'll use as we work through the book. Please note that the code samples in this section are from a macOS computer. Although outputs may vary slightly between the two operating systems, the Anaconda commands remain the same.

Open Terminal (macOS) or Anaconda Prompt (Windows). Anaconda's default `base` environment should be active. Look for the presence of parentheses with the word `base` to the left of the prompt.

First, let's confirm that we successfully installed the conda environment manager by issuing a sample command. Here's an easy one: ask conda for its version number. Note that your version may differ from the one in the following output, but as long as the command returns any number at all, conda is successfully installed:

```
(base) ~$ conda --version
conda 4.10.1
```

The conda info command returns a list of technical details about conda. The output includes the currently active environment and its location on your hard drive. Here is an abbreviated version of the output:

```
(base) ~$ conda info

    active environment : base
   active env location : /opt/anaconda3
           shell level : 1
      user config file : /Users/boris/.condarc
 populated config files : /Users/boris/.condarc
         conda version : 4.10.1
   conda-build version : 3.18.9
        python version : 3.7.4.final.0
```

We can use flags to customize and configure conda commands. A *flag* is a configuration option we add after a command to modify how it executes. Its syntax consists of a sequence of dashes and text characters. The --envs flag to the info command lists all environments and their locations on the computer. An asterisk (*) marks the active environment:

```
(base) ~$ conda info --envs
# conda environments:
#
base                     *  /Users/boris/anaconda3
```

Every conda command supports the --help flag, which outputs documentation for the command. Let's add the flag to the conda info command:

```
(base) ~$ conda info --help
usage: conda info [-h] [--json] [-v] [-q] [-a] [--base] [-e] [-s]
                  [--unsafe-channels]

Display information about current conda install.

Options:

optional arguments:
  -h, --help          Show this help message and exit.
  -a, --all           Show all information.
  --base              Display base environment path.
  -e, --envs          List all known conda environments.
  -s, --system        List environment variables.
  --unsafe-channels   Display list of channels with tokens exposed.
```

```
Output, Prompt, and Flow Control Options:
   --json                  Report all output as json. Suitable for using conda
                           programmatically.
   -v, --verbose           Use once for info, twice for debug, three times for
                           trace.
   -q, --quiet             Do not display progress bar.
```

Let's create a new playground to play in. The conda create command generates a new conda environment. We have to use the --name flag to provide a name for the environment. I've chosen a fitting title of pandas_in_action; you're welcome to choose whatever environment name you like. When conda prompts for confirmation, enter y (for yes) and press Enter to confirm:

```
(base) ~$ conda create --name pandas_in_action
Collecting package metadata (current_repodata.json): done
Solving environment: done

## Package Plan ##

  environment location: /opt/anaconda3/envs/pandas_in_action


Proceed ([y]/n)? y

Preparing transaction: done
Verifying transaction: done
Executing transaction: done
#
# To activate this environment, use
#
#     $ conda activate pandas_in_action
#
# To deactivate an active environment, use
#
#     $ conda deactivate
```

By default, conda installs the latest version of Python in the new environment. To customize the language version, add the keyword python at the end of the command, enter an equal sign, and declare the desired version. The next example shows how to create an environment called sample with Python 3.7:

```
(base) ~$ conda create --name sample python=3.7
```

Use the conda env remove command to delete an environment. Provide the --name flag with the environment you'd like to remove. The next code sample deletes the sample environment we created:

```
(base) ~$ conda env remove --name sample
```

Now that the pandas_in_action environment exists, we can activate it. The conda activate command sets the active environment in Terminal or Anaconda Prompt. The text in parentheses before the prompt will change to reflect the new active environment:

```
(base) ~$ conda activate pandas_in_action

(pandas_in_action) ~$
```

All conda commands execute in the context of the active environment. If we ask conda to install a Python package, for example, conda will now install it within pandas_in_action. We want to install the following packages:

- The core pandas library
- The jupyter development environment where we'll be writing our code
- The bottleneck and numexpr libraries for speed accelerations

The conda install command downloads and install packages in the active conda environment. Add the four packages immediately after the command, separated by spaces:

```
(pandas_in_action) ~$ conda install pandas jupyter bottleneck numexpr
```

As mentioned earlier, these four libraries have dependencies. The conda environment manager will output a list of all packages that it needs to install. Following is a shortened version of the output. It's OK if you see a different list of libraries or version numbers; conda takes care of compatibility.

```
Collecting package metadata (repodata.json): done
Solving environment: done

## Package Plan ##

  environment location: /opt/anaconda3/envs/pandas_in_action

  added / updated specs:
    - bottleneck
    - jupyter
    - numexpr
    - pandas


The following packages will be downloaded:

    package                    |              build
    ---------------------------|-----------------
    appnope-0.1.2              |py38hecd8cb5_1001          10 KB
    argon2-cffi-20.1.0         |   py38haf1e3a3_1          44 KB
    async_generator-1.10       |             py_0          24 KB
    certifi-2020.12.5          |   py38hecd8cb5_0         141 KB
    cffi-1.14.4                |   py38h2125817_0         217 KB
    ipython-7.19.0             |   py38h01d92e1_0         982 KB
    jedi-0.18.0                |   py38hecd8cb5_0         906 KB
    #... more libraries
```

Type y for yes and press Enter to install all packages and their dependencies.

If you ever forget the packages installed in an environment, use the `conda list` command to see a complete list. The output includes each library's version:

```
(pandas_in_action) ~$ conda list

# packages in environment at /Users/boris/anaconda3/envs/pandas_in_action:
#
# Name                    Version                   Build  Channel
jupyter                   1.0.0                     py39hecd8cb5_7
pandas                    1.2.4                     py39h23ab428_0
```

If you ever want to remove a package from an environment, use the `conda unin-stall` command. Here's what that command would look like with pandas:

```
(pandas_in_action) ~$ conda uninstall pandas
```

We're ready to explore our development environment. We can launch the Jupyter Notebook application with the command `jupyter notebook`:

```
(pandas_in_action) ~$ jupyter notebook
```

Jupyter Notebook starts a local server on your computer to run the core Jupyter application. We need a server running continually so that it can observe the Python code we write and execute it immediately.

The Jupyter Notebook application should open in your system's default web browser. You can also access the application by navigating to localhost:8888/ in the address bar; localhost refers to your computer, and 8888 is the port on which the app is running. Much as a dock includes multiple ports to welcome multiple ships, your computer (localhost) has multiple ports to allow multiple programs to run on your computer's local server. Figure A.7 shows the main interface of the Jupyter Notebook interface, listing the files and folders in the current directory.

The Jupyter Notebook interface is similar to the Finder (macOS) or Windows Explorer (Windows). Folders and files are organized in alphabetical order. You can click through folders to navigate into the next directory and use the breadcrumbs on

Figure A.7   Jupyter Notebook's main interface

top to navigate upward. Poke around for a few seconds. When you get the hang of navigation, close the browser.

Note that closing the browser does not shut down the running Jupyter server. We need to press the keyboard shortcut Ctrl-C twice in Terminal or Anaconda Prompt to terminate the Jupyter server.

Note that every time you launch Terminal (macOS) or Anaconda Prompt (Windows), you'll have to activate the `pandas_in_action` environment again. Although Anaconda's `base` environment includes pandas, I recommend creating a new environment for every Python book or tutorial you work through. Multiple environments ensure separation between Python dependencies across different projects. One tutorial may use pandas 1.1.3, for example, and another may use pandas 1.2.0. There are fewer chances for technical errors when you install, upgrade, and work with dependencies in isolation.

Here's a reminder of what to do each time you launch Terminal or Anaconda Prompt:

```
(base) ~$ conda activate pandas_in_action

(pandas_in_action) ~$ jupyter notebook
```

The first command activates the `conda` environment, and the second command launches Jupyter Notebook.

A.5 *Anaconda Navigator*

Anaconda Navigator is a graphical program for managing `conda` environments. Although its feature set is not as comprehensive as that of the `conda` command-line tool, Anaconda Navigator offers a visual, beginner-friendly way to create and manage environments with `conda`. You can find Anaconda Navigator inside the Applications folder in the Finder (macOS) or on the Start menu (Windows). Figure A.8 shows the home screen of the Anaconda Navigator app.

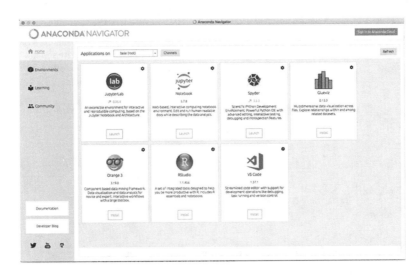

Figure A.8 Anaconda Navigator home screen

Click the Environments tab on the left menu to display a list of all environments. Select a conda environment to see its installed packages, including their descriptions and version numbers.

On the bottom pane, click the Create button to launch a new environment-creation prompt. Give the environment a name, and select a version of Python to install. The resulting dialog box displays the location where conda will create the environment (figure A.9).

Create new environment   X

Name: pandas_playbox

Location: /Users/boris/anaconda3/envs/pandas_playbox

Packages: ☑ Python   3.7   ⌄

            ☐ R   r   ⌄

                                    Cancel   Create

Figure A.9   Creating a new Anaconda environment

To install a package, select an environment in the left list. Above the list of packages, click the drop-down menu and choose All to see all packages (figure A.10).

In the search box on the right, search for a sample library, such as pandas. Locate it in the search results, and select the corresponding check box (figure A.11).

Finally, click the green Apply button in the bottom-right corner to install the library.

Figure A.10 Anaconda package search

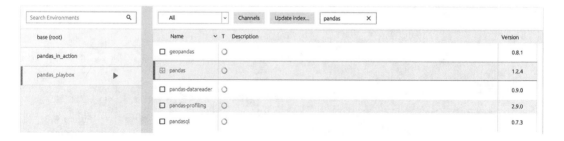

Figure A.11   Searching for and selecting the pandas package in Anaconda Navigator

Let's delete the `pandas_playbox` environment we created. We don't need it because we already created a `pandas_in_action` environment in Terminal or Anaconda Prompt. Make sure to select `pandas_playbox` in the left-side environment list. Then click the Remove button on the bottom panel and again in the confirmation dialog box (figure A.12).

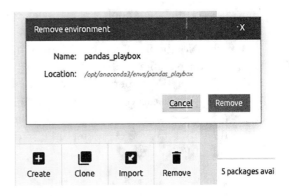

To launch Jupyter Notebook from Anaconda Navigator, click the Home tab of the left navigation menu. On this screen, you'll see tiles for the applications installed in the current environment. The top of the screen has a drop-down menu from which you can choose the active `conda` environment. Make sure to select the `pandas_in_action` environment we created for this book. Then you can launch Jupyter Notebook by clicking its application tile. This action is equivalent to executing `jupyter notebook` from Terminal or Anaconda Prompt.

Figure A.12   Deleting the environment we created in Anaconda Navigator

A.6   *The basics of Jupyter Notebook*

Jupyter Notebook is an interactive development environment for Python, consisting of one or more cells, each of which holds Python code or Markdown. *Markdown* is a text formatting standard that we can use to add headers, text paragraphs, bulleted lists, embedded images, and more to the Notebook. We use Python to write our logic and Markdown to organize our thoughts. As you proceed through the book, feel free to use Markdown to take notes on the material. The complete documentation for Markdown is available at https://daringfireball.net/projects/markdown/syntax.

On the Jupyter launch screen, click the New button on the right menu, and choose Python 3 to create a new Notebook (figure A.13).

Figure A.13   Creating a Jupyter Notebook

To give the Notebook a name, click the Untitled text at the top and enter a name in the dialog box. Jupyter Notebook saves its files with the .ipynb extension, short for IPython Notebooks, the predecessor of Jupyter Notebooks. You can navigate back to your Jupyter Notebook tab to see the new .ipynb file in the directory.

A Notebook operates in two modes: Command and Edit. Clicking a cell or pressing Enter while the cell is focused triggers Edit mode. Jupyter highlights the cell with a green border. In Edit mode, Jupyter interprets your keyboard presses literally. We use this mode to type characters in a selected cell. Figure A.14 displays a sample Jupyter cell in Edit mode.

Figure A.14   Empty Jupyter Notebook cell in Edit mode

Below the Notebook's navigation menu, you'll find a toolbar for common shortcuts. A drop-down menu at the right end of the toolbar displays the focused cell's type. Click the drop-down menu to reveal a list of available cell options, and choose Code or Markdown to change a cell to that type (figure A.15).

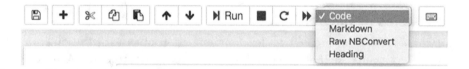

Figure A.15   Changing the type of a Jupyter Notebook cell

One of the best features of Jupyter Notebooks is its trial-and-error approach to development. We enter Python code in a `Code` cell and then execute it. Jupyter outputs the result below the cell. We check whether the result matches what we expect and continue the process. This approach encourages active experimentation; we're always a keyboard press away from seeing the difference that a line of code makes.

Let's execute some basic Python code. Enter the following mathematical expression inside the Notebook's first cell and then click the Run button on the toolbar to execute it:

```
In  [1]: 1 + 1

Out [1]: 2
```

The box to the left of the code (displaying the number 1 in the preceding example) marks the cell's execution order relative to the launch or restart of the Jupyter Notebook. You can execute the cells in any order, and you can execute the same cell multiple times.

As you read through the book, I encourage you to experiment by executing differ-ent snippets of code in your Jupyter cells. Thus, it is OK if your execution numbers do not match those in the text.

If a cell contains multiple lines of code, Jupyter will output the evaluation of the last expression. Note that Python still runs all the code in the cell; we see only the last expression.

```
In  [2]: 1 + 1
         3 + 2

Out [2]: 5
```

The *interpreter* is the software that parses your Python source code and executes it. Jupyter Notebook relies on IPython (Inter-active Python), an enhanced interpreter with extra features for developer productiv-ity. As one example, you can use the Tab key to reveal available methods and attributes on any Python object. The next example shows the available methods on a Python string. Type any string and a dot; then press Tab to see the dialog box. Figure A.16 shows an example with a string. If you're unfamiliar with Python's core data structures, see appendix B for a comprehensive introduction to the language.

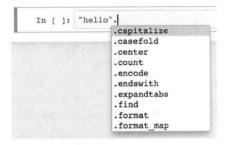

Figure A.16   Jupyter Notebook's autocomplete features

You can enter any amount of Python in a Code cell, but it's best to keep a cell's size reasonably small to improve readability and comprehension. If your logic is complex, split the operations across several cells.

You can use either of two keyboard shortcuts to execute a cell in Jupyter Notebook. Press Shift-Enter to execute a cell and move focus to the next cell, and press Ctrl-Enter to execute a cell and maintain focus on the original cell. Practice reexecuting the first two cells to see this difference in action.

Press the Esc key to activate Command mode, a management mode for the Note-book. The available operations in this mode are more global; they affect the Note-book as a whole rather than one specific cell. In this mode, keyboard characters serve as shortcuts. Here are some helpful keyboard shortcuts to use when the Notebook is in Command mode:

Keyboard shortcut	Description
Up- and down-arrow keys	Navigate through Notebook cells.
a	Create a new cell above the selected cell.
b	Create a new cell below the selected cell.

Keyboard shortcut	Description
c	Copy the contents of a cell.
x	Cut the contents of a cell.
v	Paste a copied or cut cell into the cell below the selected one.
d+d	Delete a cell.
z	Reverse a deletion.
y	Change the cell type to `Code`.
m	Change the cell type to `Markdown`.
h	Show the help menu, which has a complete list of keyboard shortcuts.
Command-S (macOS) or Ctrl-S (Windows)	Save the Notebook. Note that Jupyter Notebook also has autosave functionality.

To clear everything from the Notebook's memory, choose Kernel from the top-level menu and then choose Restart. Additional options are available to clear cell outputs and rerun all cells in the Notebook.

Let's say that we've had enough fun with our Notebook for the day and decide it's time to exit. A Notebook continues running in the background even when we close its browser tab. To close it, navigate to the Running tab on the top menu of the Jupyter launch screen, and click the Shutdown button next to the Notebook (figure A.17).

Figure A.17   Shutting down a Jupyter Notebook

After we shut down all Notebooks, we have to terminate the Jupyter Notebook application. Close the browser tab with the Jupyter application. In Terminal or Anaconda Prompt, press Ctrl+C twice to terminate the local Jupyter server.

At this point, you're all set to start writing Python and pandas code in Jupyter. Good luck!

appendix B
Python crash course

The pandas library is built on top of Python, a popular programming language first released in 1991 by Dutch developer Guido van Rossum. A *library* (also called a *package*) is a toolbox of features that expands the core functionalities of a programming language. Libraries accelerate developer productivity by providing solutions to everyday problems such as database connections, code quality, and testing. Most Python projects use libraries. After all, why solve a problem from scratch if somebody has already solved it? More than 300,000 libraries are available to download from the Python Package Index (PyPi), a centralized online repository of Python packages. Pandas is one of those 300,000 libraries; it implements complex data structures that excel at storing and manipulating multidimensional data. Before we explore what pandas adds to Python, it's important to see what's available in the base language.

Python is an object-oriented programming (OOP) language. The OOP paradigm views a software program as being a collection of objects that talk to one another. An *object* is a digital data structure that stores information and provides ways for it to be accessed and manipulated. Each object has a responsibility or purpose for existing. We can think of each object as being an actor in a play and the software program as being a performance.

A helpful way to think of objects is as digital building blocks. Consider a spreadsheet software like Excel. As users, we can discern the differences among a workbook, a worksheet, and a cell. A workbook holds worksheets, a worksheet holds cells, and cells hold values. We view these three entities as three distinct containers of business logic, each with a designated responsibility, and we interact with them in different ways. When building object-oriented computer programs, developers think in the same manner, identifying and building the "blocks" that need to exist for a program to run.

You'll often hear the expression "Everything is an object" in the Python community. The statement means that the language implements all its data types, even simple ones such as numbers and text, as objects. Libraries like pandas add a new collection of objects—an additional set of building blocks—to the language.

As a data analyst turned software engineer, I've witnessed the Python proficiency requirements for many roles in the industry. I can state from experience that you do not need to be an advanced programmer to be productive with pandas. Basic understanding of Python's core mechanics, however, will significantly accelerate the speed at which you can pick up the library. This appendix highlights the key language essentials you need to know to be successful.

B.1   Simple data types

Data comes in a variety of types. A whole number like 5 is of a different type than a decimal number like 8.46. Both 5 and 8.46 are different from a text value like `"Bob"`.

Let's begin with an exploration of the core data types built into Python. Make sure that you've installed the Anaconda distribution and set up a `conda` environment that includes the Jupyter Notebook coding environment. If you need help, see the installation instructions in appendix A. Activate the `conda` environment you created for this book, execute the command `jupyter notebook`, and create a new Notebook.

A quick note before we start: in Python, the hashtag symbol (`#`) creates a comment. A *comment* is a line of text that Python ignores when it processes the code. Developers use comments to provide inline documentation for their code. Here's an example:

```
# Adds two numbers together
1 + 1
```

We can also add a comment after a piece of code. Python ignores everything after the hashtag symbol. The rest of the line executes normally:

```
1 + 1 # Adds two numbers together
```

Although the previous example evaluates to 2, the next example produces no output. The comment effectively disables the line, so Python ignores the addition:

```
# 1 + 1
```

I've used comments in code cells throughout the book to provide supplemental commentary on the operations at hand. You do not need to copy the comments into your Jupyter Notebook.

B.1.1   Numbers

An *integer* is a whole number; it has no fractional or decimal component. An example is 20:

```
In  [1] 20

Out [1] 20
```

An integer can be any positive number, negative number, or zero. Negative numbers are prefixed by a minus sign (–):

```
In  [2] -13
Out [2] -13
```

A *floating-point number* (colloquially called a *float*) is a number with a fractional or decimal component. We use a dot to declare a decimal point. 7.349 is an example of a float:

```
In  [3] 7.349
Out [3] 7.349
```

Integers and floating-point numbers represent different data types in Python or, equivalently, different objects. Look for the presence of a decimal point to distinguish between the two. The value 5.0 is a floating-point object, for example, whereas 5 is an integer object.

B.1.2 Strings

A *string* is a collection of zero or more text characters. We declare a string by wrapping a piece of text in a pair of single, double, or triple quotes. There are differences among the three options, but they are insignificant for beginners. We'll be sticking with double quotes throughout the book. Jupyter Notebook's output for the three syntax options is identical:

```
In  [4] 'Good morning'
Out [4] 'Good morning'
In  [5] "Good afternoon"
Out [5] 'Good afternoon'
In  [6] """Good night"""
Out [6] 'Good night'
```

Strings are not limited to alphabetic characters; they can include digits, spaces, and symbols. Consider the next example, which includes seven alphabetic characters, a dollar sign, two digits, a space, and an exclamation point:

```
In  [7] "$15 dollars!"
Out [7] '$15 dollars!'
```

Use the presence of quotes to identify a string visually. Many beginners are confused by a value like "5", which is a string that holds a single numeric character. "5" is not an integer.

An *empty string* has no characters. We create it with a pair of quotes with nothing between them:

```
In  [8] ""
Out [8] ''
```

The length of a string refers to the count of its characters. The string `"Monkey business"`, for example, has a length of 15 characters; there are six characters in `Monkey`, eight characters in `business`, and one space between the two words.

Python assigns a number to every string character based on its order in line. The number is called the *index*, and it starts counting from 0. In the string `"car"`,

- `"c"` is at index position 0.
- `"a"` is at index position 1.
- `"r"` is at index position 2.

A string's final index position is always one less than its length. The string `"car"` has a length of 3, so its final index position is 2. Zero-based indexes tend to confuse new developers; it's a difficult mental shift to make because we have been taught since grade school to start counting from 1.

We can extract any character from a string by its index position. After the string, enter a pair of square brackets with the index value. The next example pulls out the `"h"` character in `"Python"`. The `"h"` character is the fourth character in sequence, so it has an index of 3:

```
In  [9] "Python"[3]

Out [9] 'h'
```

To pull from the end of the string, provide a negative value within the square brackets. A value of `-1` extracts the last character, `-2` extracts the second-to-last character, and so on. The next example targets the fourth-to-last character in Python, the `"t"`:

```
In  [10] "Python"[-4]

Out [10] 't'
```

In the preceding example, `"Python"[2]` would yield the same `"t"` output.

We can use a special syntax to extract multiple characters from a string. The process is called *slicing*. Place two numbers inside the square brackets, separated by a colon. The left-side value sets the starting index. The right-side value sets the final index. The starting index is inclusive; Python includes the character at that index. The ending index is exclusive; Python excludes the character at that index. Tricky, I know.

The next example pulls all characters from index position 2 (inclusive) up to index position 5 (exclusive). The slice includes the characters `"t"` at index 2, `"h"` at index 3, and `"o"` at index 4:

```
In  [11] "Python"[2:5]

Out [11] 'tho'
```

If 0 is the starting index, we can remove it from the square brackets and get the same result. Choose whatever syntax option fits you better:

```
In  [12] # The two lines below are equivalent
         "Python"[0:4]
         "Python"[:4]

Out [12] 'Pyth'
```

Here's another shortcut: to extract characters from an index to the string's end, remove the ending index. The following example shows two options for pulling out the characters from "h" (index 3) to the end of the "Python" string:

```
In  [13] # The two lines below are equivalent
         "Python"[3:6]
         "Python"[3:]

Out [13] 'hon'
```

We can also remove both numbers. A single colon tells Python "Go from the beginning to the end." The result is a copy of the string:

```
In  [14] "Python"[:]

Out [14] 'Python'
```

We can mix and match positive and negative index positions in a string slice. Let's pull from index 1 ("y") up to the last character in the string ("n"):

```
In  [15] "Python"[1:-1]

Out [15] 'ytho'
```

We can also pass an optional third number to set the *step interval*—the gap to jump between every two index positions. The next example pulls out the characters from index positions 0 (inclusive) up to 6 (exclusive) in intervals of 2. This slice includes the characters "P", "t", and "o", which are at index positions 0, 2, and 4:

```
In  [16] "Python"[0:6:2]

Out [16] 'Pto'
```

Here's a cool trick: we can pass in -1 as the third number to proceed backward from the end of the list to the beginning. The result is a reversed string:

```
In  [17] "Python"[::-1]

Out [17] 'nohtyP'
```

Slicing comes in handy for extracting snippets of text from larger strings—a topic we cover extensively in chapter 6.

B.1.3 Booleans

The *Boolean* data type represents the logical idea of truth. It can be only one of two values: True or False. The Boolean is named after English mathematician and philosopher George Boole. It usually models an either-or relationship: yes or no, on or off, valid or invalid, active or inactive, and so on.

```
In  [18] True

Out [18] True

In  [19] False

Out [19] False
```

We often arrive at a Boolean data type through a calculation or comparison, which we'll see in section B.2.2.

B.1.4   *The None object*

The None object represents nothingness or the absence of a value. Like a Boolean, it's a tricky type to wrap our heads around because it's more abstract than a concrete value such as an integer.

Suppose that we decide to measure our town's daily temperature for a week but forget to take a reading on Friday. The temperatures for six of the seven days would be integers. How could we log the temperature for the missing day? We might enter something like "missing" or "unknown" or "null". The None object models the same idea in Python. The language needs something to communicate the absence of a value. It requires an object that stands in and announces that a value is missing, does not exist, or is not needed. Jupyter Notebook outputs nothing when we execute a cell with None:

```
In  [20] None
```

As with a Boolean, we'll usually arrive at a None value rather than create it manually. We'll explore the object in greater detail as we work through the book.

B.2   *Operators*

An *operator* is a symbol that performs an operation. One classic example from elementary school is the addition operator: the plus sign (+). The values that an operator works on are called *operands*. In the expression 3 + 5,

- + is the operator.
- 3 and 5 are the operands.

In this section, we'll explore the various mathematical and logical operators built into Python.

B.2.1   *Mathematical operators*

Let's write out the mathematical expression from the introduction. Jupyter will output the calculation directly below the cell:

```
In  [21] 3 + 5

Out [21] 8
```

It is conventional to add a space on both sides of an operator to make the code easier to read. The next two examples illustrate subtraction (-) and multiplication (*):

```
In  [22] 3 - 5

Out [22] -2

In  [23] 3 * 5

Out [23] 15
```

** is the exponentiation operator. The next example raises 3 to the power of 5 (3 multiplied by itself 5 times):

```
In  [24] 3 ** 5
Out [24] 243
```

The / symbol performs division. The next example divides 3 by 5:

```
In  [25] 3 / 5
Out [25] 0.6
```

In mathematical terminology, the *quotient* is the result of dividing one number by another. Division with the / operator always returns a floating-point quotient, even if the divisor fits evenly into the dividend:

```
In  [26] 18 / 6
Out [26] 3.0
```

Floor division is an alternative type of division that removes the decimal remainder from a quotient. It requires two forward slashes (//) and returns an integer quotient. The next example demonstrates the differences between the two operators:

```
In  [27] 8 / 3
Out [27] 2.6666666666666665
In  [28] 8 // 3
Out [28] 2
```

The *modulo* operator (%) returns the remainder of a division. 2 is the remainder when 5 is divided by 3:

```
In  [29] 5 % 3
Out [29] 2
```

We can also use the addition and multiplication operators with strings. The plus sign joins two strings. The technical word for this process is *concatenation*.

```
In  [30] "race" + "car"
Out [30] 'racecar'
```

The multiplication sign repeats a string a given number of times:

```
In  [31] "Mahi" * 2
Out [31] 'MahiMahi'
```

An object's type determines the operations and operators that it supports. We can divide integers, for example, but we cannot divide strings. The primary skill in OOP is identifying the object you're working with and the actions it can perform.

We can concatenate a string to another string, and we can add a number to another number. But what happens when we try to add a string and a number?

```
In  [32] 3 + "5"
```

```
--------------------------------------------------------------------------
TypeError                                 Traceback (most recent call last)
<ipython-input-9-d4e36ca990f8> in <module>
----> 1 3 + "5"

TypeError: unsupported operand type(s) for +: 'int' and 'str'
```

Uh-oh. This example is our first exposure to a Python error—one of several dozen built into the language. The technical name for an error is an *exception*. Like everything else in Python, an exception is an object. Whenever we make a syntactical or logical mistake, Jupyter Notebook displays an analysis that includes the name of the error and the line number that triggered it. The technical term *raise* is often used to indicate that Python encountered an exception. We could say, "I tried to add a number and a string, and Python raised an exception."

Python raises a `TypeError` exception when we use a wrong data type in an operation. In the preceding example, Python observed a number and a plus sign, and assumed that another number would follow. Instead, it received a string, which it cannot add to an integer. We'll see how we can convert an integer to a string (and vice versa) in section B.4.1.

B.2.2   *Equality and inequality operators*

Python considers two objects to be equal if they hold the same value. We can compare the equality of two objects by placing them on opposite sides of the equality operator (`==`). The operator returns `True` if the two objects are equal. As a reminder, `True` is a Boolean value.

```
In  [33] 10 == 10
```

```
Out [33] True
```

Be careful: the equality operator has two equal signs. Python reserves a single equal sign for a completely different operation that we'll cover in section B.3.

The equality operator returns `False` if the two objects are unequal. `True` and `False` are the only valid values for Booleans:

```
In  [34] 10 == 20
```

```
Out [34] False
```

Here are some examples of the equality operator with strings:

```
In  [35] "Hello" == "Hello"
```

```
Out [35] True
```

```
In  [36] "Hello" == "Goodbye"
```

```
Out [36] False
```

Case sensitivity matters when comparing two strings. In the next example, one string starts with a capital "H", and the other starts with a lowercase "h", so Python considers the two strings to be unequal:

```
In  [37] "Hello" == "hello"

Out [37] False
```

The inequality operator (!=) is the inverse of the equality operator; it returns True if two objects are unequal. It is True, for example, that 10 is not equal to 20:

```
In  [38] 10 != 20

Out [38] True
```

Similarly, the string "Hello" is not equal to the string "Goodbye":

```
In  [39] "Hello" != "Goodbye"

Out [39] True
```

The inequality operator returns False if the two objects are equal:

```
In  [40] 10 != 10

Out [40] False

In  [41] "Hello" != "Hello"

Out [41] False
```

Python supports mathematical comparisons between numbers. The < operator checks whether the operand on the left side is smaller than the operand on the right side. The next example checks whether -5 is less than 3:

```
In  [42] -5 < 3

Out [42] True
```

The > operator checks whether the operand on the left side is greater than the operand on the right side. The next example evaluates whether 5 is greater than 7; the result is False.

```
In  [43] 5 > 7

Out [43] False
```

The <= operand checks whether the left-side operand is less than or equal to the right-side operand. Here, we check whether 11 is less than or equal to 11:

```
In  [44] 11 <= 11

Out [44] True
```

The complementary >= operand checks whether the left-side operand is greater than or equal to the right-side operand. The next example checks whether 4 is greater than or equal to 5:

```
In  [45] 4 >= 5

Out [45] False
```

Pandas enables us to apply comparisons like these to whole columns of data, a topic we cover in chapter 5.

B.3   *Variables*

A *variable* is a name we assign to an object; we can compare it with the address of a house, because it is a label, a reference, and an identifier. Variable names should be clear and descriptive, describing the data that the object is storing and the purpose it serves in our application. `revenues_for_quarter4` is a better variable name than `r` or `r4`, for example.

We assign a variable to an object with the assignment operator, a single equal sign (=). The next example assigns four variables (name, age, high_school_gpa, and is_handsome) to four different data types (string, integer, floating-point, and Boolean):

```
In  [46] name = "Boris"
         age = 28
         high_school_gpa = 3.7
         is_handsome = True
```

The execution of a cell with a variable assignment does not yield any output in Jupyter Notebook, but afterward we are able to use the variable in any cell in the Notebook. The variable is a substitute for the value it holds:

```
In  [47] name

Out [47] 'Boris'
```

A variable name must start with a letter or an underscore. After the first letter, it can hold only letters, numbers, or underscores.

As their name suggests, variables can hold values that vary over a program's execution. Let's reassign the age variable to a new value of 35. After we execute the cell, the age variable's reference to its former value, 28, will be lost:

```
In  [48] age = 35
         age

Out [48] 35
```

We can use the same variable on both sides of the assignment operator. Python always evaluates the right side of the equal sign first. In the next example, Python adds the value of age at the start of the cell's execution, 35, to 10. The resulting sum, 45, is saved to the age variable:

```
In  [49] age = age + 10
         age

Out [49] 45
```

Python is a *dynamically typed* language, which means that variables do not know anything about data types. A variable is a placeholder name for any object in the program. Only the object knows its data type. Therefore, we can reassign variables from an object of one type to another. The next example reassigns the `high_school_gpa` variable from its original floating-point value of `3.7` to a string of `"A+"`:

```
In [50] high_school_gpa = "A+"
```

Python raises a `NameError` exception when a variable does not exist in the program:

```
In  [51] last_name

---------------------------------------------------------------------
NameError                                 Traceback (most recent call last)
<ipython-input-5-e1aeda7b4fde> in <module>
----> 1 last_name

NameError: name 'last_name' is not defined
```

You'll typically encounter a `NameError` exception when you mistype a variable name. This exception is nothing to fear; correct the spelling, and execute the cell again.

B.4   *Functions*

A *function* is a procedure consisting of one or more steps. Think of a function as being a cooking recipe in a programming language—a series of instructions that yields a consistent result. Functions enable reusability in software. Because a function captures a piece of business logic from start to finish, we can reuse it when we have to perform the same operation multiple times.

We declare a function and then execute it. In the declaration, we write the steps that the function should take. In the execution, we run the function. Sticking to our cooking analogy, declaring a function is equivalent to writing down a recipe, and executing a function is equivalent to cooking the recipe. The technical term for executing a function is *calling* it or *invoking* it.

B.4.1   *Arguments and return values*

Python ships with more than 65 built-in functions. We can also declare our own custom functions. Let's dive into an example. The built-in `len` function returns the length of a given object. The concept of length varies from data type to data type; for a string, it's a count of its characters.

We invoke a function by entering its name and a pair of opening and closing parentheses. Much as a cooking recipe can accept ingredients, a function invocation can accept inputs called *arguments*. We pass arguments sequentially inside the parentheses, separated by commas.

The `len` function expects one argument: the object whose length it should calculate. The next example passes a string argument of `"Python is fun"` to the function:

```
In  [52] len("Python is fun")

Out [52] 13
```

A cooking recipe produces a final output of a meal. Similarly, a Python function produces a final output called a *return value*. In the preceding example, `len` was the invoked function, `"Python is fun"` was its single argument, and 13 was the return value.

That's all there is to it! A function is a procedure that is invoked with zero or more arguments and produces a return value.

Here are three more popular built-in functions in Python:

- `int`, which converts its argument to an integer
- `float`, which converts its argument to a floating-point number
- `str`, which converts its argument to a string

The next three examples showcase these functions in action. The first example invokes the `int` function with a string argument of `"20"` and produces a return value of 20. Can you identify the arguments and return values for the remaining two functions?

```
In  [53] int("20")

Out [53] 20

In  [54] float("14.3")

Out [54] 14.3

In  [55] str(5)

Out [55] '5'
```

Here's another common error: Python raises a `ValueError` exception when a function receives an argument with the right data type but an inappropriate value. In the next example, the `int` function receives a string (an appropriate type), but the string is one from which it is impossible to extract an integer:

```
In  [56] int("xyz")

---------------------------------------------------------------------------
ValueError                                Traceback (most recent call last)
<ipython-input-6-ed77017b9e49> in <module>
----> 1 int("xyz")

ValueError: invalid literal for int() with base 10: 'xyz'
```

Another popular built-in function is `print`, which outputs text to the screen. It accepts any number of arguments. The function often proves to be helpful when we want to observe a variable's value throughout a program's execution. The next example invokes the `print` function four times with the `value` variable, whose value changes several times:

```
In  [57] value = 10
         print(value)

         value = value - 3
         print(value)
```

```
        value = value * 4
        print(value)

        value = value / 2
        print(value)
Out [57] 10
        7
        28
        14.0
```

If a function accepts multiple arguments, we must separate every two subsequent ones with a comma. Developers often add a space after the comma for readability.

When we pass the `print` function multiple arguments, it outputs all of them in sequence. In the next example, notice that Python separates the three printed elements with a space:

```
In  [58] print("Cherry", "Strawberry", "Key Lime")

Out [58] Cherry Strawberry Key Lime
```

A *parameter* is a name given to an expected function argument. Each argument in an invocation corresponds to a parameter. In previous examples, we passed in arguments to the `print` function sequentially without specifying their parameter.

We have to write parameter names out explicitly for certain arguments. The `print` function's sep (separator) parameter, for example, customizes the string that Python inserts between every two printed values. We have to explicitly write out the sep parameter if we'd like to pass it a custom argument. We assign an argument to a function's keyword parameter with an equal sign. The next example outputs the same three strings but instructs the `print` function to separate them with exclamation points:

```
In  [59] print("Cherry", "Strawberry", "Key Lime", sep = "!")

Out [59] Cherry!Strawberry!Key Lime
```

Let's come back to the example before the last one. Why were the three values printed with a space in between every two subsequent values?

A *default argument* is a fallback value that Python passes to a parameter if the function invocation does not explicitly provide one. The sep parameter to the `print` function has a default argument of " ". If we invoke the `print` function without an argument for the sep parameter, Python will automatically pass in a string with one space. The following two lines of code produce the same output:

```
In  [60] # The two lines below are equivalent
        print("Cherry", "Strawberry", "Key Lime")
        print("Cherry", "Strawberry", "Key Lime", sep=" ")

Out [60] Cherry Strawberry Key Lime
        Cherry Strawberry Key Lime
```

We call parameters like `sep` *keyword arguments.* We have to write their specific parameter name when passing arguments to them. Python requires us to pass keyword arguments after sequential arguments. Here's another example of a `print` function invocation that passes a different string argument to the `sep` parameter:

```
In  [61] print("Cherry", "Strawberry", "Key Lime", sep="*!*")

Out [61] Cherry*!*Strawberry*!*Key Lime
```

The `print` function's end parameter customizes the string Python adds to the end of all output. The parameter's default argument is `"\n"`, a special character that Python recognizes as a line break. In the next example, we explicitly pass the same `"\n"` argument to the end parameter:

```
In  [62] print("Cherry", "Strawberry", "Key Lime", end="\n")
         print("Peach Cobbler")

Out [62] Cherry Strawberry Key Lime
         Peach Cobbler
```

We can pass multiple keyword arguments to a function invocation. The technical rules still apply: separate every two arguments with a comma. The next example invokes the `print` function twice. The first invocation separates its three arguments with a `"!"` and ends the output with a `"***"`. Because the first invocation does not force a line break, the second invocation's output continues where the first one concludes:

```
In  [63] print("Cherry", "Strawberry", "Key Lime", sep="!", end="***")
         print("Peach Cobbler")

Out [63] Cherry!Strawberry!Key Lime***Peach Cobbler
```

Take a second to reflect on the code formatting in the preceding example. Long lines of code can be difficult to read, especially when we clump multiple parameters together. The Python community favors several formatting solutions. One option is placing all arguments on a separate line:

```
In  [64] print(
             "Cherry", "Strawberry", "Key Lime", sep="!", end="***"
         )

Out [64] Cherry!Strawberry!Key Lime***
```

Another option is adding a line break between arguments:

```
In  [65] print(
             "Cherry",
             "Strawberry",
             "Key Lime",
             sep="!",
             end="***",
         )

Out [65] Cherry!Strawberry!Key Lime***
```

All three of these code samples are technically valid. There are multiple ways to format Python code. I use several formatting options throughout the book. My ultimate goal is readability. You do not have to follow the formatting conventions I use. I will do my best to communicate which differences are technical and which ones are aesthetic.

B.4.2 *Custom functions*

We can declare custom functions in our programs. The goal of a function is to capture a distinct piece of business logic in a single, reusable procedure. A common mantra in software engineering circles is *DRY*, an acronym for *don't repeat yourself.* This acronym is a warning that duplication of the same logic or behavior can lead to an unstable program. The more places you repeat code, the more places you have to edit if requirements change. A function solves the DRY problem.

Let's explore an example. Suppose that we are meteorologists working with weather data. Our work requires us to convert temperatures in our program from Fahrenheit to Celsius. There is a simple, consistent formula to the conversion. Writing a function to convert *one* temperature from °F to °C is a good idea because we can isolate the conversion logic and reuse it as needed.

We begin a function definition with the `def` keyword. We follow `def` with the function's name, a pair of opening and closing parentheses, and a colon. Function names and variable names with multiple words follow a `snake_case` naming convention. The convention separates every two words with an underscore, which causes the name to resemble a snake. Let's call our function `convert_to_fahrenheit`:

```
def convert_to_fahrenheit():
```

To review, a *parameter* is a name for an expected function argument. We want the `convert_to_fahrenheit` function to accept a single parameter: a Celsius temperature. Let's call the parameter `celsius_temp`:

```
def convert_to_fahrenheit(celsius_temp):
```

If we define a parameter when we declare a function, we must pass an argument for that parameter when invoking it. Thus, we must always provide a value for `celsius_temp` whenever we run `convert_to_fahrenheit`.

Our next step is defining what the function does. We declare a function's steps in its body, an indented section of code below its name. Python uses indentation to establish relationships between constructs in the program. A function's body is an example of a *block*, a section of code nested within another section of code. According to PEP-8,[1] the Python community's style guide, we should indent each line in a block with four spaces:

```
def convert_to_fahrenheit(celsius_temp):
    # This indented line belongs to the function
    # So does this indented line

# This line is not indented, so it does not belong to convert_to_fahrenheit
```

---

[1] See "PEP 8—Style Guide for Python Code," https://www.python.org/dev/peps/pep-0008.

We can use a function's parameters in its body. In our example, we can use the `celsius_temp` parameter anywhere in the body of the `convert_to_fahrenheit` function.

We can declare variables in a function body. These variables are called *local variables* because they are bound to the scope of the function execution. Python throws local variables out of memory as soon as the function is done running.

Let's write out the logic for the conversion! The formula to convert a Celsius temperature to Fahrenheit is to multiply it by 9/5 and add 32:

```
def convert_to_fahrenheit(celsius_temp):
    first_step = celsius_temp * (9 / 5)
    fahrenheit_temperature = first_step + 32
```

At this juncture, our function correctly calculates the Fahrenheit temperature, but it does not send the evaluation back to the main program. We need to use the `return` keyword to mark the Fahrenheit temperature as the final output of the function. We are returning it to the outside world:

```
In  [66] def convert_to_fahrenheit(celsius_temp):
            first_step = celsius_temp * (9 / 5)
            fahrenheit_temperature = first_step + 32
            return fahrenheit_temperature
```

Our function is complete, so let's test it! We invoke custom functions with a pair of parentheses, the same syntax we use for Python's built-in functions. The next example invokes the `convert_to_fahrenheit` function with a sample argument of 10. Python runs through the function body with the `celsius_temp` parameter set to 10. The function returns a value of `50.0`:

```
In  [67] convert_to_fahrenheit(10)

Out [67] 50.0
```

We can provide keyword arguments instead of positional ones. The next example writes the `celsius_temp` parameter name out explicitly. The following code is equivalent to the preceding code:

```
In  [68] convert_to_fahrenheit(celsius_temp = 10)

Out [68] 50.0
```

Although they are not required, keyword arguments help add clarity to our program. The preceding example better communicates what the `convert_to_fahrenheit` function's input represents.

B.5 Modules

A *module* is a single Python file. The Python *standard library* is a collection of more than 250 modules built into the language to accelerate productivity. The modules assist with technical operations such as mathematics, audio analysis, and URL requests. To reduce a program's memory consumption, Python does not load these modules by default. We have to import the specific modules we want manually when our program requires them.

The syntax to import built-in modules and external packages is identical: enter the `import` keyword, followed by the module or package's name. Let's import Python's `datetime` module, which helps us work with dates and times:

```
In [69] import datetime
```

An *alias* is an alternative name for an import—a shortcut that we can assign to a module so we don't have to write out its complete name when we reference it. The alias is technically up to us, but certain nicknames have established themselves as favorites among Python developers. A popular alias for the `datetime` module, for example, is `dt`. We assign aliases with the `as` keyword:

```
In [70] import datetime as dt
```

Now we can reference the module with `dt` instead of `datetime`.

B.6   *Classes and objects*

All the data types that we've explored so far—integers, floats, Booleans, strings, exceptions, functions, and even modules—are objects. An *object* is a digital data structure, a container for storing, accessing, and manipulating a type of data.

A *class* is a blueprint for creating objects. Think of it as being a schematic or template from which Python builds the objects.

We call an object constructed from a class an *instance* of the class. The act of creating an object from a class is called *instantiation*.

Python's built-in `type` function returns the class of the object we pass in as an argument. The next example invokes the `type` function twice with two different strings: `"peanut butter"` and `"jelly"`. Although their content is unequal, the strings are made from the same blueprint, the same class, the `str` class. They are both strings:

```
In  [71] type("peanut butter")

Out [71] str

In  [72] type("jelly")

Out [72] str
```

These examples are fairly simple. The `type` function is helpful when we are unsure what kind of object we're working with. If we invoke a custom function and are unsure what type of object it returns, we can pass its return value to `type` to find out.

A *literal* is a shorthand syntax that creates an object from a class. One example we've encountered so far is double quotes, which create strings (`"hello"`). For more-complex objects, we need to use a different creation process.

The `datetime` module we imported in section B.5 has a `date` class that models a date in time. Suppose that we're trying to represent Leonardo da Vinci's birthday, April 15, 1452, as a `date` object.

To create an instance from a class, write the class name followed by a pair of parentheses. `date()`, for example, creates a `date` object from the `date` class. The syntax is identical to invoking a function. When instantiating an object, we can sometimes pass arguments to the constructor, the function that creates the objects. The first three arguments to the `date` constructor represent the year, month, and day the `date` object will hold. The three arguments are required:

```
In  [73] da_vinci_birthday = dt.date(1452, 4, 15)
         da_vinci_birthday

Out [73] datetime.date(1452, 4, 15)
```

Now we have a `da_vinci_birthday` variable that holds a `date` object representing April 15, 1452.

B.7 *Attributes and methods*

An *attribute* is a piece of internal data belonging to an object, a characteristic or detail that exposes information about the object. We access an object's attributes with dot syntax. Three sample attributes on a `date` object are day, month, and year:

```
In  [74] da_vinci_birthday.day

Out [74] 15

In  [75] da_vinci_birthday.month

Out [75] 4

In  [76] da_vinci_birthday.year

Out [76] 1452
```

A *method* is an action or command that we can issue to the object. Think of a method as being a function that belongs to an object. *Attributes* make up the object's *state*, and methods represent the object's behavior. Like a function, a method can accept arguments and produce a return value.

We invoke a method with a pair of parentheses after its name. Be sure to add a dot between the object and the method name. One sample method a `date` object has is weekday. The `weekday` method returns the date's day of the week as an integer. 0 denotes Sunday, and 6 denotes Saturday:

```
In  [77] da_vinci_birthday.weekday()

Out [77] 3
```

Leonardo was born on a Wednesday!

The easiness and reusability of methods such as weekday is why date objects exist. Imagine how difficult it would be to model date logic with a text string. Imagine if every developer built their own custom solution. Ouch. Python's developers anticipated that users would need to work with dates, so they built a reusable date class to model that real-world construct.

The key takeaway is that the Python standard library offers developers many utility classes and functions to solve common problems. As programs grow in complexity, however, it becomes difficult to model real-world ideas with only Python's core objects. To solve this problem, developers add custom objects to the language. These objects model business logic pertinent to a specific domain. Developers bundle these objects into libraries. That's all pandas is: a bundle of additional classes to solve specific problems in the domain of data analysis.

B.8   *String methods*

A string object has its own set of methods. Here are a few examples.

The upper method returns a new string with all characters in uppercase:

```
In  [78] "Hello".upper()

Out [78] "HELLO"
```

We can invoke methods on variables. Recall that a *variable* is a placeholder name for an object. Python will substitute the variable for the object that it references. The next example invokes the upper method on the string that the greeting variable references. The output is the same as that of the preceding code example:

```
In  [79] greeting = "Hello"
         greeting.upper()

Out [79] "HELLO"
```

There are two categories of objects: mutable and immutable. A *mutable* object is capable of change. An *immutable* object is incapable of change. Strings, numbers, and Booleans are examples of immutable objects; we cannot modify them after we create them. The string "Hello" will always be the string "Hello". The number 5 will always be the number 5.

In the preceding example, the upper method call did not modify the original "Hello" string assigned to the greeting variable. Rather, the method invocation returned a new string with all capital letters. We can output the greeting variable to confirm that the characters have their original casing:

```
In  [80] greeting

Out [80] 'Hello'
```

A string is immutable, so its methods will not modify the original object. We'll explore some mutable objects starting in section B.9.

The complementary `lower` method returns a new string with all characters in lowercase:

```
In  [81] "1611 BROADWAY".lower()

Out [81] '1611 broadway'
```

There's even a `swapcase` method that returns a new string with each character case inverted. Uppercase letters become lowercase, and lowercase letters become uppercase:

```
In  [82] "uPsIdE dOwN".swapcase()

Out [82] 'UpSiDe DoWn'
```

A method can accept arguments. Let's take a peek at the `replace` method, which swaps all occurrences of a substring with a specified character sequence. The functionality is similar to the Find and Replace feature in a word processing program. The `replace` method accepts two arguments:

- The substring to look for
- The value to replace it with

The next example replaces all occurrences of `"S"` with `"$"`:

```
In  [83] "Sally Sells Seashells by the Seashore".replace("S", "$")

Out [83] '$ally $ells $eashells by the $eashore'
```

In this example,

- `"Sally Sells Seashells by the Seashore"` is the original string *object*.
- `replace` is the *method* invoked on the string.
- `"S"` is the *first argument* passed to the `replace` method invocation.
- `"$"` is the *second argument* passed to the `replace` method invocation.
- `"$ally $ells $eashells by the $eashore"` is the *return value* of the `replace` method.

A method's return value can be of a different data type than the original object. The `isspace` method, for example, is invoked on a string but returns a Boolean. The method returns `True` if the string consists of only spaces; otherwise, it returns `False`.

```
In  [84] "  ".isspace()

Out [84] True

In  [85] "3 Amigos".isspace()

Out [85] False
```

Strings have a family of methods for removing whitespace. The `rstrip` (right strip) method removes whitespace from the end of a string:

```
In  [86] data = "   10/31/2019   "
         data.rstrip()

Out [86] '   10/31/2019'
```

The `lstrip` (left strip) method removes whitespace from the beginning of a string:

```
In  [87] data.lstrip()

Out [87] '10/31/2019   '
```

The `strip` method removes whitespace from both ends of the string:

```
In  [88] data.strip()

Out [88] '10/31/2019'
```

The `capitalize` method capitalizes the first character of a string. This method often proves to be helpful for working with lowercase names, places, or organizations:

```
In  [89] "robert".capitalize()

Out [89] 'Robert'
```

The `title` method capitalizes the first letter of every word in a string, using a space to identify where each word begins and ends:

```
In  [90] "once upon a time".title()

Out [90] 'Once Upon A Time'
```

We can invoke multiple methods in sequence on a single line. This technique is called *method chaining*. In the next example, the `lower` method returns a new string object upon which we invoke the `title` method. The return value from `title` is yet another new string object:

```
In  [91] "BENJAMIN FRANKLIN".lower().title()

Out [91] 'Benjamin Franklin'
```

The `in` keyword checks whether a substring exists in another string. Enter the string to search for before the keyword and the string to search within after the keyword. The operation returns a Boolean:

```
In  [92] "tuna" in "fortunate"

Out [92] True

In  [93] "salmon" in "fortunate"

Out [93] False
```

The `startswith` method checks whether a substring exists at the beginning of a string:

```
In  [94] "factory".startswith("fact")

Out [94] True
```

The `endswith` method checks whether a substring exists at the end of a string:

```
In  [95] "garage".endswith("rage")

Out [95] True
```

The count method counts the occurrences of a substring within a string. The next example counts the number of "e" characters in "celebrate":

```
In  [96] "celebrate".count("e")

Out [96] 3
```

The find and index methods locate the index position of a character or substring. The methods return the first index position at which the argument occurs. Recall that index positions start counting at 0. The next example searches for the index of the first "e" in "celebrate". Python locates it at index 1:

```
In  [97] "celebrate".find("e")

Out [97] 1

In  [98] "celebrate".index("e")

Out [98] 1
```

What's the difference between the find and index methods? If the string does not contain the argument, find will return -1, and index will raise a ValueError exception:

```
In  [99] "celebrate".find("z")

Out [99] -1

In  [100] "celebrate".index("z")

---------------------------------------------------------------------
ValueError                             Traceback (most recent call last)
<ipython-input-5-bf78a69262aa> in <module>
----> 1 "celebrate".index("z")

ValueError: substring not found
```

Each method exists for a specific situation; neither option is better than the other. If your program depends on a substring existing within a larger string, for example, you may use the index method and react to the error. By comparison, if the absence of a substring does not prohibit your program from executing, you can use the find method to avoid crashing.

B.9   Lists

A *list* is a container for storing objects in order. The purpose of lists is twofold: to provide a "box" to store values and to keep them in sequence. We refer to the items within a list as *elements*. In other programming languages, this data structure is often called an *array*.

We declare a list with a pair of opening and closing square brackets. We write our elements inside the square brackets, separating every two with a comma. The next example creates a list of five strings:

```
In  [101] backstreet_boys = ["Nick", "AJ", "Brian", "Howie", "Kevin"]
```

The length of a list is equal to its number of elements. Remember the trusty `len` function? It can help us figure how many members are in the greatest boy band of all time:

```
In  [102] len(backstreet_boys)

Out [102] 5
```

An *empty list* is a list without elements. It has a length of 0:

```
In  [103] []

Out [103] []
```

A list can store elements of any data type: strings, numbers, floats, Booleans, and more. A *homogeneous* list is one in which all elements have the same type. The following three lists are homogeneous. The first holds integers, the second holds floating-points, and the third holds Booleans:

```
In  [104] prime_numbers = [2, 3, 5, 7, 11]

In  [105] stock_prices_for_last_four_days = [99.93, 105.23, 102.18, 94.45]

In  [106] settings = [True, False, False, True, True, False]
```

Lists can also store elements of different data types. A *heterogeneous* list is one in which elements have different data types. The following list has a string, an integer, a Boolean, and a floating-point number:

```
In [107] motley_crew = ["rhinoceros", 42, False, 100.05]
```

Much as it does for each character in a string, Python assigns each list element an index position. The index represents an element's place in line and starts counting from 0. In the following three-item `favorite_foods` list,

- `"Sushi"` occupies index position 0.
- `"Steak"` occupies index position 1.
- `"Barbeque"` occupies index position 2.

```
In [108] favorite_foods = ["Sushi", "Steak", "Barbeque"]
```

Two quick notes on list formatting. First, Python permits us to insert a comma after a list's last element. The comma does not affect the list whatsoever; it is an alternative syntax:

```
In [109] favorite_foods = ["Sushi", "Steak", "Barbeque",]
```

Second, some Python style guides recommend breaking up long lists so that each element occupies a single line. This format also does not affect the list in any technical way. The syntax looks like this:

```
In [110] favorite_foods = [
             "Sushi",
             "Steak",
             "Barbeque",
         ]
```

Throughout the examples in this book, I've used whatever formatting style I believe best enhances readability. You are welcome to use whichever format feels best to you.

We can access a list element by its index position. Pass the index between a pair of square brackets after the list (or the variable that references it):

```
In  [111] favorite_foods[1]

Out [111] 'Steak'
```

In section B.1.2, we introduced a slicing syntax to extract characters from a string. We can use the same syntax to extract elements from a list. The next example pulls out the elements from index positions 1 to 3. Remember that in a list slice, the starting index is inclusive, and the ending index is exclusive:

```
In  [112] favorite_foods[1:3]

Out [112] ['Steak', 'Barbeque']
```

We can remove the number before the colon to pull from the beginning of the list. The next example extracts elements from the start of the list to index 2 (exclusive):

```
In  [113] favorite_foods[:2]

Out [113] ['Sushi', 'Steak']
```

We can remove the number after the colon to pull to the end of the list. The next example extracts elements from index 2 to the end of the list:

```
In  [114] favorite_foods[2:]

Out [114] ['Barbeque']
```

Leave out both numbers to create a copy of the list:

```
In  [115] favorite_foods[:]

Out [115] ['Sushi', 'Steak', 'Barbeque']
```

Finally, we can provide an optional third number in the square brackets to extract elements in intervals. The next example pulls elements from index position 0 (inclusive) to index position 3 (exclusive) in increments of 2:

```
In  [116] favorite_foods[0:3:2]

Out [116] ['Sushi', 'Barbeque']
```

All slicing options return a new list.

Let's walk through some list methods. The append method adds a new element to the end of a list:

```
In  [117] favorite_foods.append("Burrito")
          favorite_foods

Out [117] ['Sushi', 'Steak', 'Barbeque', 'Burrito']
```

Do you recall our discussion on mutability versus immutability? A list is an example of a mutable object, an object that is *capable* of change. We can add, remove, or replace elements within a list after we create it. In the preceding example, the append method mutated the list referenced by the `favorite_foods` variable. We did not create a new list.

By comparison, a string is an example of an immutable object. When we invoke a method like upper, Python returns a new string; the original string remains unaffected. Immutable objects cannot change.

Lists include a variety of mutational methods. The extend method adds multiple elements to the end of a list. It accepts one argument, a list with the values to add:

```
In  [118] favorite_foods.extend(["Tacos", "Pizza", "Cheeseburger"])
          favorite_foods

Out [118] ['Sushi', 'Steak', 'Barbeque', 'Burrito', 'Tacos', 'Pizza',
          'Cheeseburger']
```

The insert method adds an element to the list at a specific index position. Its first argument is the index where we want to inject the element, and its second argument is the new element. Python pushes values at and after the specified index position to the next slot. The next example inserts the string "Pasta" at index position 2. The list shifts the value "Barbeque" and all subsequent elements up one index position:

```
In  [119] favorite_foods.insert(2, "Pasta")
          favorite_foods

Out [119] ['Sushi',
           'Steak',
           'Pasta',
           'Barbeque',
           'Burrito',
           'Tacos',
           'Pizza',
           'Cheeseburger']
```

The in keyword can check whether a list includes an element. "Pizza" exists in our `favorite_foods` list, and "Caviar" does not:

```
In  [120] "Pizza" in favorite_foods

Out [120] True

In  [121] "Caviar" in favorite_foods

Out [121] False
```

The not in operator confirms the absence of an element from a list. It returns the inverse Boolean of the in operator:

```
In  [122] "Pizza" not in favorite_foods

Out [122] False
```

```
In  [123] "Caviar" not in favorite_foods

Out [123] True
```

The `count` method counts the number of times an element appears in the list:

```
In  [124] favorite_foods.append("Pasta")
          favorite_foods

Out [124] ['Sushi',
           'Steak',
           'Pasta',
           'Barbeque',
           'Burrito',
           'Tacos',
           'Pizza',
           'Cheeseburger',
           'Pasta']

In  [125] favorite_foods.count("Pasta")

Out [125] 2
```

The `remove` method deletes the first occurrence of an element from the list. Note that Python does not remove subsequent occurrences of the element:

```
In  [126] favorite_foods.remove("Pasta")
          favorite_foods

Out [126] ['Sushi',
           'Steak',
           'Barbeque',
           'Burrito',
           'Tacos',
           'Pizza',
           'Cheeseburger',
           'Pasta']
```

Let's get rid of the other `"Pasta"` string at the end of the list. The `pop` method removes and returns the last element from the list:

```
In  [127] favorite_foods.pop()

Out [127] 'Pasta'

In  [128] favorite_foods

Out [128] ['Sushi', 'Steak', 'Barbeque', 'Burrito', 'Tacos', 'Pizza',
           'Cheeseburger']
```

The `pop` method also accepts an integer argument with the index position of the value Python should delete. The next example removes the `"Barbeque"` value at index position 2. The `"Burrito"` string slides into index position 2, and the elements after it also shift down by one index:

```
In  [129] favorite_foods.pop(2)

Out [129] 'Barbeque'
```

```
In  [130] favorite_foods

Out [130] ['Sushi', 'Steak', 'Burrito', 'Tacos', 'Pizza', 'Cheeseburger']
```

A list can hold any object, including other lists. The next example declares a list with three nested lists. Each nested list contains three integers:

```
In  [131] spreadsheet = [
              [1, 2, 3],
              [4, 5, 6],
              [7, 8, 9]
          ]
```

Let's take a second to reflect on the preceding visual. Can you see any parallels with a spreadsheet? A nested list is one way we can represent a multidimensional, tabular collection of data. We can view the outermost list as being a worksheet and each internal list as being a row of data.

B.9.1 *List iteration*

A list is an example of a collection object. It is capable of storing multiple values—a *collection* of values. To *iterate* means to move over a collection object's elements one at a time.

The most common way to iterate over a list's items is with a `for` loop. Its syntax looks like this:

```
for variable_name in some_list:
    # Do something
```

A `for` loop consists of several components:

- The `for` keyword.
- A variable name that will store each list element one at a time as the iteration runs.
- The `in` keyword.
- The list to iterate over.
- A block of code that Python will run during each iteration. We can use the variable name in this block of code.

As a reminder, a *block* is a section of indented code. Python uses indentation to associate constructs in our program. The block below a function name defines what the function does. Similarly, the block below a `for` loop defines what happens during each iteration.

The next example iterates over a list of four strings, printing the length of each one:

```
In  [132] for season in ["Winter", "Spring", "Summer", "Fall"]:
              print(len(season))

Out [132] 6
          6
          6
          4
```

The preceding iteration consists of four loops. The `season` variable holds the values `"Winter"`, `"Spring"`, `"Summer"`, and `"Fall"` in sequence. During each iteration, we pass the current string to the `len` function. The `len` function returns a number, which we print out.

Suppose that we want to add the lengths of the strings together. We have to combine a `for` loop with some other Python concepts. In the next example, we first initialize a `letter_count` variable to hold a cumulative sum. Inside the `for` loop block, we calculate the length of the current string with the `len` function and then overwrite the running total. Finally, we output the value of `letter_count` after the loop completes:

```
In  [133] letter_count = 0

          for season in ["Winter", "Spring", "Summer", "Fall"]:
              letter_count = letter_count + len(season)

          letter_count

Out [133] 22
```

The `for` loop is the most conventional option for iterating over a list. Python also supports another syntax, which we discuss in section B.9.2.

B.9.2   List comprehension

List comprehension is a shorthand syntax to create a list from a collection object. Suppose that we have a list of six numbers:

```
In  [134] numbers = [4, 8, 15, 16, 23, 42]
```

Let's say that we want to create a new list with the squares of those numbers. In other words, we want to apply a consistent operation to each element in the original list. One solution is to iterate over each integer in `numbers`, take its square, and add the result to a new list. As a reminder, the `append` method adds an element to the end of a list:

```
In  [135] squares = []

          for number in numbers:
              squares.append(number ** 2)

          squares

Out [135] [16, 64, 225, 256, 529, 1764]
```

List comprehension can produce the same list of squares in a single line of code. Its syntax requires a pair of opening and closing square brackets. Inside the brackets, we first describe what we'd like to do with each element we iterate over and then the collection from which the iterable items will come.

The next example still iterates over the `numbers` list and assigns each list element to a `number` variable. We declare what we'd like to do with each `number` before the for keyword. We move the number `** 2` calculation to the beginning and the `for in` logic to the end:

```
In  [136] squares = [number ** 2 for number in numbers]
          squares
```

```
Out [136] [16, 64, 225, 256, 529, 1764]
```

List comprehension is considered to be the more Pythonic way to create a new list from an existing data structure. The *Pythonic way* describes the collection of recommended practices adopted by Python developers over time.

B.9.3 *Converting a string to a list and vice versa*

We're familiar with lists and strings now, so let's see how we can use them together. Suppose that we have a string in our program that holds an address:

```
In  [137] empire_state_bldg = "20 West 34th Street, New York, NY, 10001"
```

What if we want to break the address into smaller components: street, city, state, and zip code? Notice that the string uses a comma to separate the four pieces.

A string's `split` method breaks a string apart by using a *delimiter*, a sequence of one or more characters marking a boundary. The next example asks the `split` method to split `empire_state_building` on every occurrence of a comma. The method returns a list consisting of the smaller strings:

```
In  [138] empire_state_bldg.split(",")
```

```
Out [138] ['20 West 34th Street', ' New York', ' NY', ' 10001']
```

This code is a step in the right direction. But notice that the last three elements in the list have a leading space. Although we could iterate over the list's elements and call the `strip` on each one to remove its whitespace, a more optimal solution is to add the space to the `split` method's delimiter argument:

```
In  [139] empire_state_bldg.split(", ")
```

```
Out [139] ['20 West 34th Street', 'New York', 'NY', '10001']
```

We've successfully broken the string into a list of strings.

The process also works in reverse. Suppose that we stored our address in a list and want to concatenate the list's elements into a single string:

```
In  [140] chrysler_bldg = ["405 Lexington Ave", "New York", "NY", "10174"]
```

First, we must declare the string that we'd like Python to inject between every two list elements. Then we can invoke the `join` method on the string and pass in a list as the argument. Python will join the list's elements, separating each two with the delimiter. The next example uses a delimiter of a comma and a space:

```
In  [141] ", ".join(chrysler_bldg)
```

```
Out [141] '405 Lexington Ave, New York, NY, 10174'
```

The split and join methods are helpful for working with text data, which often needs to be separated and remerged.

B.10 *Tuples*

A *tuple* is a similar data structure to a Python list. A tuple also stores elements in order, but unlike a list, it is immutable. We cannot add, remove, or replace elements within the tuple after we create it.

The only technical requirement for defining a tuple is to declare multiple elements and separate every subsequent two with a comma. The following example declares a three-element tuple:

```
In  [142] "Rock", "Pop", "Country"

Out [142] ('Rock', 'Pop', 'Country')
```

Usually, however, we declare a tuple with a pair of parentheses. The syntax makes it easier to identify the object visually:

```
In  [143] music_genres = ("Rock", "Pop", "Country")
          music_genres

Out [143] ('Rock', 'Pop', 'Country')
```

The len function returns the length of a tuple:

```
In  [144] len(music_genres)

Out [144] 3
```

To declare a tuple with one element, we must include a comma after the element. Python needs the comma to identify the tuple. Compare the differences in the next two outputs. The first example does not use a comma; Python reads the value as a string.

```
In  [145] one_hit_wonders = ("Never Gonna Give You Up")
          one_hit_wonders

Out [145] 'Never Gonna Give You Up'
```

By comparison, the syntax here returns a tuple. Yes, one symbol can make a world of difference in Python:

```
In  [146] one_hit_wonders = ("Never Gonna Give You Up",)
          one_hit_wonders

Out [146] ('Never Gonna Give You Up',)
```

Use the tuple function to create an *empty tuple*, which is one without elements:

```
In  [147] empty_tuple = tuple()
          empty_tuple

Out [147] ()

In  [148] len(empty_tuple)

Out [148] 0
```

As with a list, you can access tuple elements by index position. As with a list, you can iterate over tuple elements with a `for` loop. The only thing you can't do is modify the tuple. Because of its immutability, a tuple doesn't include mutational methods such as append, pop, and `insert`.

If you have a collection of elements in order, and you know that it will not change, you can prefer a tuple over a list to store it.

B.11 Dictionaries

Lists and tuples are optimal data structures for storing objects in order. We need another data structure to solve a different kind of problem: establishing associations between objects.

Consider a restaurant menu. Each menu item is a unique identifier that we use to look up a corresponding price. The menu item and its cost are associated. The order of items is not what's important; it's the *connection* between two pieces of data.

A *dictionary* is a mutable, unordered collection of key-value pairs. A pair consists of a key and a value. Each key serves as an identifier for a value. Keys must be unique. Values can contain duplicates.

We declare a dictionary with a pair of curly braces (`{}`). The following example creates an empty dictionary:

```
In  [149] {}

Out [149] {}
```

Let's model a sample restaurant menu in Python. Inside the curly braces, we assign a key to its value with a colon (`:`). The following example declares a dictionary with one key-value pair. The string key `"Cheeseburger"` is assigned the floating-point value 7.99:

```
In  [150] { "Cheeseburger": 7.99 }

Out [150] {'Cheeseburger': 7.99}
```

When declaring a dictionary with multiple key-value pairs, separate every two pairs with a comma. Let's expand our menu dictionary to hold three key-value pairs. Notice that the values for the `"French Fries"` and `"Soda"` keys are identical:

```
In  [151] menu = {"Cheeseburger": 7.99, "French Fries": 2.99, "Soda": 2.99}
          menu

Out [151] {'Cheeseburger': 7.99, 'French Fries': 2.99, 'Soda': 2.99}
```

We can count the number of key-value pairs in a dictionary by passing it to Python's built-in `len` function:

```
In  [152] len(menu)

Out [152] 3
```

We use keys to retrieve values from dictionaries. Place a pair of square brackets with the key immediately after the dictionary. The syntax is identical to accessing a list element by index position. The following example extracts the value for the "French Fries" key:

```
In  [153] menu["French Fries"]

Out [153] 2.99
```

In a list, the index position is always a number. In a dictionary, a key can be any immutable data type: integers, floats, strings, Booleans, and more.

Python raises a KeyError exception if the key does not exist in the dictionary. KeyError is another example of a native Python error:

```
In  [154] menu["Steak"]

---------------------------------------------------------------------
KeyError                                  Traceback (most recent call last)
<ipython-input-19-0ad3e3ec4cd7> in <module>
----> 1 menu["Steak"]

KeyError: 'Steak'
```

As always, case sensitivity matters. If a single character is mismatched, Python will not be able to find a key. The key "soda" does not exist in our dictionary. Only "Soda" does:

```
In  [155] menu["soda"]

---------------------------------------------------------------------
KeyError                                  Traceback (most recent call last)
<ipython-input-20-47940ceca824> in <module>
----> 1 menu["soda"]

KeyError: 'soda'
```

The get method also extracts a dictionary value by using a key:

```
In  [156] menu.get("French Fries")

Out [156] 2.99
```

The get method's advantage is that it returns None if the key does not exist rather than raise an error. Remember that None is an object that Python uses to represent the idea of absence or nullness. The None value produces no visual output in Jupyter Notebook. But we can wrap the invocation in a print function to force Python to print None's string representation:

```
In  [157] print(menu.get("Steak"))

Out [157] None
```

The second argument to the get method is a custom value to return if the key does not exist in the dictionary. In the next example, the string "Steak" does not exist as a key in the menu dictionary, so Python returns 99.99 instead:

```
In  [158] menu.get("Steak", 99.99)

Out [158] 99.99
```

A dictionary is a mutable data structure. We can add key-value pairs to or remove key-value pairs from the dictionary after we create it. To add a new key-value pair, provide the key in square brackets, and assign a value to it with the assignment operator (=):

```
In  [159] menu["Taco"] = 0.99
          menu

Out [159] {'Cheeseburger': 7.99, 'French Fries': 2.99, 'Soda': 1.99,
           'Taco': 0.99}
```

If the key already exists in the dictionary, Python will overwrite its original value. The next example changes the value of the "Cheeseburger" key from 7.99 to 9.99:

```
In  [160] print(menu["Cheeseburger"])
          menu["Cheeseburger"] = 9.99
          print(menu["Cheeseburger"])

Out [160] 7.99
          9.99
```

The pop method removes a key-value pair from a dictionary; it accepts a key as an argument and returns its value. Python will raise a KeyError exception if the key does not exist in the dictionary:

```
In  [161] menu.pop("French Fries")

Out [161] 2.99

In  [162] menu

Out [162] {'Cheeseburger': 9.99, 'Soda': 1.99, 'Taco': 0.99}
```

The in keyword checks whether an element exists in the dictionary's keys:

```
In  [163] "Soda" in menu

Out [163] True

In  [164] "Spaghetti" in menu

Out [164] False
```

To check for inclusion among the dictionary's values, invoke the values method on the dictionary. The method returns a listlike object that contains the dictionary's values. We can use the in operator in combination with the values method's return value:

```
In  [165] 1.99 in menu.values()

Out [165] True

In  [166] 499.99 in menu.values()

Out [166] False
```

The `values` method returns a different type of object from the lists, tuples, and dictionaries we've already seen. We don't necessarily need to know what the object is, however. All we care about is how we can work with it. The `in` operator checks for the inclusion of a value in an object, and the object returned by the `values` method knows how to handle it.

B.11.1 Dictionary Iteration

We should always assume that a dictionary's key-value pairs are unordered. If you need a data structure that maintains order, use a list or a tuple. If you need to create associations between objects, use a dictionary.

Even if we cannot guarantee a deterministic iteration order, we can still loop over a dictionary one key-value pair at a time with a `for` loop. The dictionary's `items` method yields a two-item tuple on each iteration. The tuple holds a key and its respective value. We can declare multiple variables after the `for` keyword to store each key and value. In the next example, the `state` variable holds each dictionary key, and the `capital` variable holds each value:

```
In  [167] capitals = {
            "New York": "Albany",
            "Florida": "Tallahassee",
            "California": "Sacramento"
          }

          for state, capital in capitals.items():
              print("The capital of " + state + " is " + capital + ".")

          The capital of New York is Albany.
          The capital of Florida is Tallahassee.
          The capital of California is Sacramento.
```

In the first iteration, Python yields a tuple of (`"New York"`, `"Albany"`). In the second iteration, it yields a tuple of (`"Florida"`, `"Tallahassee"`), and so on.

B.12 Sets

List and dictionary objects help solve the problems of order and association. A set assists with another common need: uniqueness. A *set* is an unordered, mutable collection of unique elements. It prohibits duplicates.

We declare a set with a pair of curly braces. We populate the braces with elements, separating every two with a comma. The next example declares a set of six numbers:

```
In [168] favorite_numbers = { 4, 8, 15, 16, 23, 42 }
```

Readers with a sharp eye may notice that the curly-brace syntax for declaring a set is identical to the syntax for declaring a dictionary. Python can distinguish between the two types of objects based on the presence or absence of key-value pairs.

Because Python interprets an empty pair of curly braces as an empty dictionary, the only way to create an empty set is with the built-in `set` function:

```
In  [169] set()

Out [169] set()
```

Here are some helpful set methods. The `add` method adds a new element to the set:

```
In  [170] favorite_numbers.add(100)
          favorite_numbers

Out [170] {4, 8, 15, 16, 23, 42, 100}
```

Python will add an element to a set only if the set does not already have it. The next example attempts to add 15 to `favorite_numbers`. Python sees that 15 already exists within the set, so the object remains unchanged:

```
In  [171] favorite_numbers.add(15)
          favorite_numbers

Out [171] {4, 8, 15, 16, 23, 42, 100}
```

A set has no concept of order. Python will raise a `TypeError` exception if we attempt to access a set element by index position:

```
In  [172] favorite_numbers[2]

-------------------------------------------------------------------------
TypeError                                 Traceback (most recent call last)
<ipython-input-17-e392cd51c821> in <module>
----> 1 favorite_numbers[2]

TypeError: 'set' object is not subscriptable
```

Python raises a `TypeError` exception when we attempt to apply an operation to an invalid object. Set elements are unordered, so elements do not have index positions.

In addition to preventing duplicates, sets are ideal for identifying similarities and differences between two collections of data. Let's define two sets of strings:

```
In  [173] candy_bars = { "Milky Way", "Snickers", "100 Grand" }
          sweet_things = { "Sour Patch Kids", "Reeses Pieces", "Snickers" }
```

The `intersection` method returns a new set with elements found in both of the original sets. The `&` symbol performs the same logic. In the next example, `"Snickers"` is the only string in common between `candy_bars` and `sweet_things`:

```
In  [174] candy_bars.intersection(sweet_things)

Out [174] {'Snickers'}

In  [175] candy_bars & sweet_things

Out [175] {'Snickers'}
```

The union method returns a set that combines all elements of the two sets. The |
symbol performs the same logic. Keep in mind that duplicate values such as "Snick-
ers" will appear only once:

```
In  [176] candy_bars.union(sweet_things)

Out [176] {'100 Grand', 'Milky Way', 'Reeses Pieces', 'Snickers', 'Sour
          Patch Kids'}

In  [177] candy_bars | sweet_things

Out [177] {'100 Grand', 'Milky Way', 'Reeses Pieces', 'Snickers', 'Sour
          Patch Kids'}
```

The difference method returns a set of elements that are present in the set the
method is called on but not present in the set passed in as an argument. We can use
the - symbol as a shortcut. In the next example, "100 Grand" and "Milky Way" are
present in candy_bars but not in sweet_things:

```
In  [178] candy_bars.difference(sweet_things)

Out [178] {'100 Grand', 'Milky Way'}

In  [179] candy_bars - sweet_things

Out [179] {'100 Grand', 'Milky Way'}
```

The symmetric_difference method returns a set with elements found in either of
the sets but not both. The ^ syntax accomplishes the same result:

```
In  [180] candy_bars.symmetric_difference(sweet_things)

Out [180] {'100 Grand', 'Milky Way', 'Reeses Pieces', 'Sour Patch Kids'}

In  [181] candy_bars ^ sweet_things

Out [181] {'100 Grand', 'Milky Way', 'Reeses Pieces', 'Sour Patch Kids'}
```

And that's all there is to cover! We've learned quite a bit of Python: data types, functions, iterations, and more. It's OK if you don't remember all the details. Rather, come
back to this appendix whenever you need a refresher on the core mechanics of
Python. We'll be using and reviewing a lot of these ideas as we work with the pandas
library.

appendix C
NumPy crash course

The open source NumPy (Numerical Python) library is a dependency of pandas that exposes a powerful `ndarray` object for storing homogeneous, *n*-dimensional arrays. That's quite a mouthful, so let's break it down. An *array* is an ordered collection of values akin to a Python list. *Homogeneous* means that the values within the array are of the same data type. *N-dimensional* means that the array can hold any number of dimensions. (We'll talk about dimensions in section C.1.) NumPy was developed by data scientist Travis Oliphant, who founded Anaconda, the company that builds the Python distribution we used to set up our development environment.

We can use NumPy to generate randomized data sets of any size and shape; in fact, the official pandas documentation does so extensively. Basic knowledge of the library will help enhance our understanding of the underlying mechanics of pandas.

C.1   Dimensions

Dimensions refers to the number of reference points needed to extract a single value from a data structure. Consider a collection of temperatures across several cities on a given day:

	Temperature
New York	38
Chicago	36
San Francisco	51
Miami	73

If I asked you to find a specific temperature in this data set, you'd need only one point of reference: the city's name (such as "San Francisco") or its order (such as "the third city in the list"). Thus, the table depicts a one-dimensional data set.

Compare that table with a data set of temperatures for multiple cities over multiple days:

	Monday	Tuesday	Wednesday	Thursday	Friday
New York	38	41	35	32	35
Chicago	36	39	31	27	25
San Francisco	51	52	50	49	53
Miami	73	74	72	71	74

How many points of reference do you need now to extract a specific value from this data set? The answer is 2. We need a city and a day of the week (such as "San Francisco on Thursday") or a row number and a column number (such as "row 3 and column 4"). Neither the city nor the weekday is a sufficient identifier by itself, because each one associates with multiple values in the data set. The combination of a city and a weekday (or, equivalently, a row and a column) filters the results down to one value; thus, this data set is two-dimensional.

A data set's number of rows and columns does not affect its number of dimensions. A table with 1 million rows and 1 million columns would still be two-dimensional. We would still need a combination of a row position and a column position to pull out a value.

Every additional point of reference adds another dimension. We might collect temperatures over two weeks:

Week 1

	Monday	Tuesday	Wednesday	Thursday	Friday
New York	38	41	35	32	35
Chicago	36	39	31	27	25
San Francisco	51	52	50	49	53
Miami	73	74	72	71	74

Week 2

	Monday	Tuesday	Wednesday	Thursday	Friday
New York	40	42	38	36	28
Chicago	32	28	25	31	25
San Francisco	49	55	54	51	48
Miami	75	78	73	76	71

The city and weekday are no longer sufficient to extract a single value. We now need three points of reference (Week, City, and Day), so we can classify this data set as being three-dimensional.

C.2 *The ndarray object*

Let's begin by creating a new Jupyter Notebook and importing the NumPy library, which is typically assigned the alias np:

```
In [1] import numpy as np
```

NumPy excels at generating both random and nonrandom data. Let's begin with a simple challenge: creating a sequential range of numbers.

C.2.1 *Generating a numeric range with the arange method*

The arange function returns a one-dimensional ndarray object with a range of sequential numeric values. When we invoke arange with one argument, NumPy will set 0 as the lower bound, the value at which the range begins. The first argument will set the upper bound, the number at which the range terminates. The upper bound is exclusive; NumPy will go up to that value but not include it. An argument of 3, for example, will produce an ndarray holding the values 0, 1, and 2:

```
In  [2] np.arange(3)

Out [2] array([0, 1, 2])
```

We can also pass arange two arguments, which will declare the lower and upper bounds of the range. The lower bound is inclusive; the range will include its value. The endpoint remains exclusive. In the next example, notice that NumPy includes 2 but not 6:

```
In  [3] np.arange(2, 6)

Out [3] array([2, 3, 4, 5])
```

The first two arguments to arange correspond to start and stop keyword parameters. We can write the keyword arguments out explicitly. The preceding and following code samples produce the same array:

```
In  [4] np.arange(start = 2, stop = 6)

Out [4] array([2, 3, 4, 5])
```

The arange function's optional third parameter, step, sets the interval between every two values. It helps to think about this concept mathematically. Start at the lower bound, and add the interval value until you reach the upper bound. The next example creates a range from 0 to 111 (exclusive) in gaps of 10:

```
In  [5] np.arange(start = 0, stop = 111, step = 10)

Out [5] array([  0,  10,  20,  30,  40,  50,  60,  70,  80,  90, 100, 110])
```

Let's save that last `ndarray` to a tens variable:

```
In  [6] tens = np.arange(start = 0, stop = 111, step = 10)
```

Now the tens variable points to an `ndarray` object that holds 12 numbers.

C.2.2   *Attributes on a ndarray object*

The NumPy library's `ndarray` object has its own set of attributes and methods. As a reminder, an *attribute* is a piece of data that belongs to an object. A *method* is a command we can send to an object.

The `shape` attribute returns a tuple with the array's dimensions. The length of the shape tuple is equal to the `ndarray`'s number of dimensions. The following output communicates that `tens` is a one-dimensional array with 12 values:

```
In  [7] tens.shape

Out [7] (12,)
```

We can also ask for the `ndarray`'s number of dimensions with the `ndim` attribute:

```
In  [8] tens.ndim

Out [8] 1
```

The `size` attribute returns the number of elements in the array:

```
In  [9] tens.size

Out [9] 12
```

Next up, let's see how we can manipulate the shape of the 12 elements in the array.

C.2.3   *The reshape method*

Currently, our 12-element `tens` `ndarray` is one-dimensional. We can access any element with one reference point, its position in the array:

```
In  [10] tens

Out [10] array([  0,  10,  20,  30,  40,  50,  60,  70,  80,  90, 100,
         110])
```

We may want to manipulate an existing one-dimensional array into a multidimensional one with a different shape. Let's say that our 12 values represent a collection of 3 daily measurements captured across 4 days. It's easier to think about the data in a 4 x 3 shape than in a 12 x 1 shape.

The `reshape` method uses its arguments to return a new `ndarray` object with a specified shape. The next example contorts `tens` into a new two-dimensional array with 4 rows and 3 columns:

```
In  [11] tens.reshape(4, 3)
```

```
Out [11] array([[  0,  10,  20],
                [ 30,  40,  50],
                [ 60,  70,  80],
                [ 90, 100, 110]])
```

The number of arguments passed to reshape will equal the number of dimensions in the new ndarray:

```
In  [12] tens.reshape(4, 3).ndim
```

```
Out [12] 2
```

We must ensure that the product of the arguments equals the number of elements within the original array. The values 4 and 3 are valid arguments because their product is 12, and tens has 12 values. Another valid example is a two-dimensional array with 2 rows and 6 columns:

```
In  [13] tens.reshape(2, 6)
```

```
Out [13] array([[  5,  15,  25,  35,  45,  55],
                [ 65,  75,  85,  95, 105, 115]])
```

NumPy raises a ValueError exception if it cannot contort the original array into the requested shape. In the next example, the library is unable to fit the 12 values in tens into a 2 x 5 array:

```
In  [14] tens.reshape(2, 5)
```

```
Out [14]
```

```
---------------------------------------------------------------------
ValueError                              Traceback (most recent call last)
<ipython-input-68-5b9588276555> in <module>
----> 1 tens.reshape(2, 5)

ValueError: cannot reshape array of size 12 into shape (2,5)
```

Can an ndarray store more than two dimensions of data? Absolutely. Let's provide a third argument to reshape to see it in action. The next example shapes the one-dimensional tens array into a three-dimensional array with a 2 x 3 x 2 shape:

```
In  [15] tens.reshape(2, 3, 2)
```

```
Out [15] array([[[  5,  15],
                 [ 25,  35],
                 [ 45,  55]],

                [[ 65,  75],
                 [ 85,  95],
                 [105, 115]]])
```

Let's access the `ndim` attribute on the new array. The data structure does indeed have three dimensions:

```
In  [16] tens.reshape(2, 3, 2).ndim

Out [16] 3
```

We can also pass an argument of -1 to `reshape` to denote an unknown dimension. NumPy will infer the correct number of values to populate within that dimension. The next example passes arguments of 2 and -1. NumPy calculates that the new two-dimensional array should have a 2 x 6 shape:

```
In  [17] tens.reshape(2, -1)

Out [17] array([[  0,  10,  20,  30,  40,  50],
                [ 60,  70,  80,  90, 100, 110]])
```

In the next example, the library calculates that the returned `ndarray` should have a 2 x 3 x 2 shape:

```
In  [18] tens.reshape(2, -1, 2)

Out [18] array([[[  0,  10],
                 [ 20,  30],
                 [ 40,  50]],

                [[ 60,  70],
                 [ 80,  90],
                 [100, 110]]])
```

We can pass only one unknown dimension into a `reshape` method invocation.

The `reshape` method returns a new `ndarray` object. The original array is not mutated. Thus, our `tens` array still has its original 1 x 12 shape.

C.2.4   *The randint function*

The `randint` function generates one or more random numbers between a range. When passed a single argument, it returns a random integer from 0 up to the value. The next example returns a random value between 0 and 5 (exclusive):

```
In  [19] np.random.randint(5)

Out [19] 3
```

We can pass `randint` two arguments to declare an inclusive lower bound and an exclusive upper bound. NumPy will select a number from within the range:

```
In  [20] np.random.randint(1, 10)

Out [20] 9
```

What if we want to generate an array of random integers? We can pass a third argument to `randint` to specify the desired array shape. We can pass either a single integer or a one-element list to create a one-dimensional array:

```
In  [21] np.random.randint(1, 10, 3)

Out [21] array([4, 6, 3])

In  [22] np.random.randint(1, 10, [3])

Out [22] array([9, 1, 6])
```

To create a multidimensional ndarray, we pass a list specifying the number of values in each dimension. The following example populates a two-dimensional 3 x 5 array of values between 1 and 10 (exclusive):

```
In  [23] np.random.randint(1, 10, [3, 5])

Out [23] array([[2, 9, 8, 8, 7],
                [9, 8, 7, 3, 2],
                [4, 4, 5, 3, 9]])
```

You can provide any number of values inside the list to create ndarrays with more dimensions. A list with three values, for example, will create a three-dimensional array.

C.2.5   *The randn function*

The randn function returns an ndarray with random values from the standard normal distribution. Each sequential argument to the function sets the number of values to store in a dimension. If we pass one argument, the ndarray will have one dimension. The next example creates a 1 x 3 (1 row by 3 column) array:

```
In  [24] np.random.randn(3)

Out [24] array([-1.04474993,  0.46965268, -0.74204863])
```

If we pass two arguments to the randn function, the ndarray will have two dimensions, and so on. The next example creates a 2 x 4 two-dimensional array:

```
In  [25] np.random.randn(2, 4)

Out [25] array([[-0.35139565,  1.15677736,  1.90854535,  0.66070779],
                [-0.02940895, -0.86612595,  1.41188378, -1.20965709]])
```

The next example creates a 3-dimensional array with a 2 x 4 x 3 shape. We can think of this shape as being two data sets, each with four rows and three columns:

```
In  [26] np.random.randn(2, 4, 3)

Out [26] array([[[ 0.38281118,  0.54459183,  1.49719148],
                 [-0.03987083,  0.42543538,  0.11534431],
                 [-1.38462105,  1.54316814,  1.26342648],
                 [ 0.6256691 ,  0.51487132,  0.40268548]],

                [[-0.24774185, -0.64730832,  1.65089833],
                 [ 0.30635744,  0.21157744, -0.5644958 ],
                 [ 0.35393732,  1.80357335,  0.63604068],
                 [-1.5123853 ,  1.20420021,  0.22183476]]])
```

The rand family of functions is a phenomenal way to generate fake numeric data. We can also create fake data of different types and categories such as names, addresses, or credit cards. For more on that topic, see appendix D.

C.3   *The nan object*

The NumPy library uses a special nan object to represent a missing or invalid value. The acronym nan is short for *not a number*, a generic catch-all term for missing data. We'll be seeing nan frequently throughout the book as we import data sets with missing values into pandas. For now, we can access the nan object directly as a top-level attribute on the np package:

```
In   [27] np.nan
```

```
Out [27] nan
```

A nan object is not equal to any value:

```
In   [28] np.nan == 5
```

```
Out [28] False
```

A nan value is also unequal to another nan. From NumPy's perspective, nan values are missing or absent. We cannot say with certainty that they are the same, so we assume that they are different.

```
In   [29] np.nan == np.nan
```

```
Out [29] False
```

And that's it! Those are the most important details about the NumPy library, which pandas uses underneath its hood.

In your spare time, take a peek at the pandas documentation (https://pandas .pydata.org/docs/user_guide/10min.html). You'll likely see many examples that use NumPy to generate random data.

appendix D
Generating fake
data with Faker

Faker is a Python library for generating fake data. It specializes in creating lists of names, phone numbers, street addresses, emails, and the like. In combination with NumPy, which can generate random numeric data, it can quickly create data sets of any size, shape, and type. If you're looking to practice pandas concepts but can't find the perfect data set to apply them to, Faker offers a fantastic solution. In this appendix, we'll walk through everything you need to know to get started with the library.

D.1 Installing Faker

First, let's install the Faker library in our `conda` environment. In Terminal (macOS) or Anaconda Prompt (Windows), activate the `conda` environment you've set up for this book. When I created an environment for appendix A, I called mine `pandas_in_action`:

```
conda activate pandas_in_action
```

If you've forgotten your available Anaconda environments, you can execute `conda info --envs` to see a list of them. When the environment is active, install the Faker library with the `conda install` command:

```
conda install faker
```

When prompted to confirm, enter `"Y"` for Yes and press Enter. Anaconda will download and install the library. When the process completes, launch Jupyter Notebook and create a new Notebook.

D.2   *Getting started with Faker*

Let's explore some core features of Faker and then pair it with NumPy to generate a 1,000-row `DataFrame`. First, we'll import the pandas and NumPy libraries and assign them to their respective aliases (pd and np). Let's also import the `faker` library:

```
In  [1] import pandas as pd
        import numpy as np
        import faker
```

The `faker` package exports a `Faker` class (notice the capital `F`). As a reminder, a *class* is a blueprint for an object—a template for a data structure. `Series` and `DataFrame` are two sample classes from the pandas library, and `Faker` is a sample class from the Faker library.

Let's create an instance of the `Faker` class with a pair of parentheses and assign the resulting `Faker` object to a `fake` variable:

```
In  [2] fake = faker.Faker()
```

A `Faker` object includes many instance methods, each of which returns a random value from a given category. The `name` instance method, for example, returns a string with a person's full name:

```
In  [3] fake.name()
```

```
Out [3] 'David Lee'
```

Due to Faker's inherent randomness, the return values will likely vary when you execute the code on your computer. That's totally fine.

We can invoke the complementary `name_male` and `name_female` methods to return full names by gender:

```
In  [4] fake.name_male()
```

```
Out [4] 'James Arnold'
```

```
In  [5] fake.name_female()
```

```
Out [5] 'Brianna Hall'
```

Use the `first_name` and `last_name` methods to return only a first name or last name:

```
In  [6] fake.first_name()
```

```
Out [6] 'Kevin'
```

```
In  [7] fake.last_name()
```

```
Out [7] 'Soto'
```

There are also gender-specific `first_name_male` and `first_name_female` methods:

```
In  [8] fake.first_name_male()
```

```
Out [8] 'Brian'
```

```
In   [9]  fake.first_name_female()
```

```
Out  [9]  'Susan'
```

As you can see, Faker's syntax is simple but powerful. Here's another example. Suppose that we want to generate some random locations for a data set. The `address` method returns a string with a complete address, including a street, city, state, and postal code:

```
In   [10]  fake.address()
```

```
Out  [10]  '6162 Chase Corner\nEast Ronald, SC 68701'
```

Note that the address is completely fake; it is not an actual location on a map. Faker simply follows conventions on what an address usually looks like.

Notice that Faker separates the street and the remainder of the address with a line break (\n). You can wrap the return value in a `print` function call to break the address across multiple lines:

```
In   [11]  print(fake.address())
```

```
Out  [11]  602 Jason Ways Apt. 358
           Hoganville, NV 37296
```

We can generate the individual components of an address with methods such as `street_address`, `city`, `state`, and `postcode`:

```
In   [12]  fake.street_address()
```

```
Out  [12]  '58229 Heather Walk'
```

```
In   [13]  fake.city()
```

```
Out  [13]  'North Kristinside'
```

```
In   [14]  fake.state()
```

```
Out  [14]  'Oklahoma'
```

```
In   [15]  fake.postcode()
```

```
Out  [15]  '94631'
```

We can generate business-related data with another batch of methods. The following methods return a random company, catchphrase, job title, and URL:

```
In   [16]  fake.company()
```

```
Out  [16]  'Parker, Harris and Sutton'
```

```
In   [17]  fake.catch_phrase()
```

```
Out  [17]  'Switchable systematic task-force'
```

```
In   [18]  fake.job()
```

```
Out  [18]  'Copywriter, advertising'
```

```
In   [19] fake.url()

Out  [19] 'https://www.gutierrez.com/'
```

Faker also supports email addresses, phone numbers, and credit card numbers:

```
In   [20] fake.email()

Out  [20] 'sharon13@taylor.com'

In   [21] fake.phone_number()

Out  [21] '680.402.4787'

In   [22] fake.credit_card_number()

Out  [22] '4687538791240162'
```

The Faker website (https://faker.readthedocs.io/en/master) offers complete documentation for the Faker object's instance methods. The library groups methods into parent categories such as address, automotive, and bank. Figure D.1 shows a sample page from the Faker documentation.

Figure D.1   A sample documentation page on Faker's official website

Take some time to explore Faker's available categories. A little variety can help make the next fake data set you generate a lot more intriguing.

D.3   *Populating a DataFrame with fake values*

Now that we're comfortable using Faker to generate one fake value, let's use it to populate a whole data set. Our goal is to create a 1,000-row `DataFrame` with four columns: Name, Company, Email, and Salary.

Here's how we'll tackle the problem: we'll use a `for` loop to iterate 1,000 times, and in each iteration, we'll ask Faker to generate a fake name, company, and email address. We'll also ask NumPy to generate a random number to represent the salary.

We can use Python's `range` function for the iteration. The function accepts an integer argument. It returns an iterable sequence of ascending numbers, starting at 0 and proceeding up to (but not including) the argument. In the next example, we use a `for` loop to iterate over a range of values from 0 (inclusive) to 5 (exclusive):

```
In  [23] for i in range(5):
            print(i)

Out [23] 0
         1
         2
         3
         4
```

To generate our data set, we'll use `range(1000)` to iterate 1,000 times.

The `DataFrame`'s class constructor accepts various inputs for its `data` parameter, including a list of dictionaries. Pandas maps each dictionary key to a `DataFrame` column and each value to the row's value for that column. Here's a preview of what we want our input to look like:

```
[
    {
        'Name': 'Ashley Anderson',
        'Company': 'Johnson Group',
        'Email': 'jessicabrooks@whitaker-crawford.biz',
        'Salary': 62883
    },
    {
        'Name': 'Katie Lee',
        'Company': 'Ward-Aguirre',
        'Email': 'kennethbowman@fletcher.com',
        'Salary': 102971
    }
    # … and 998 more dictionaries
]
```

You'll notice some logical inconsistencies in the Faker-generated data. The first person's name is Ashley Anderson, for example, but the email is jessicabrooks@whitaker-crawford.biz. This inconsistency is due to the randomness of Faker. For the following examples, we're not going to worry about these imperfections. If we want our data set to be more "accurate," however, we can combine Faker with regular Python code to generate whatever values we desire. We can ask Faker for a first name (`"Morgan"`) and last name (`"Robinson"`), for example, and then concatenate the two strings to form a more realistic email address (`"MorganRobinson@gmail.com"`):

```
In   [24] first_name = fake.first_name_female()
          last_name = fake.last_name()
          email = first_name + last_name + "@gmail.com"
          email

Out  [24] 'MorganRobinson@gmail.com'
```

Back to business. Let's use list comprehension with the `range` function to create a list of 1,000 dictionaries. Within each dictionary, we'll declare the same four keys: `"Name"`, `"Company"`, `"Email"`, and `"Salary`. For the first three values, we'll invoke the name, company, and email instance methods on our `Faker` object. Remember that Python will invoke these methods on *each* iteration, so the values will differ each time. For the `"Salary"` value, we'll use NumPy's `randint` function to return a random integer between 50,000 and 200,000. For a more in-depth tutorial on NumPy functions, see appendix C.

```
In   [25] data = [
              { "Name": fake.name(),
                "Company": fake.company(),
                "Email": fake.email(),
                "Salary": np.random.randint(50000, 200000)
              }
              for i in range(1000)
          ]
```

Our `data` variable holds a list of 1,000 dictionaries. The last step is passing the list of dictionaries to the `DataFrame` constructor at the top level of pandas:

```
In   [26] df = pd.DataFrame(data = data)
          df

Out  [26]
```

	Name	Company	Email	Salary
0	Deborah Lowe	Williams Group	ballbenjamin@gra...	147540
1	Jennifer Black	Johnson Inc	bryannash@carlso...	135992
2	Amy Reese	Mitchell, Hughes...	ajames@hotmail.com	101703
3	Danielle Moore	Porter-Stevens	logan76@ward.com	133189
4	Jennifer Wu	Goodwin Group	vray@boyd-lee.biz	57486
...	...	...	...	...
995	Joseph Stewart	Rangel, Garcia a...	sbrown@yahoo.com	123897
996	Deborah Curtis	Rodriguez, River...	smithedward@yaho...	51908
997	Melissa Simmons	Stevenson Ltd	frederick96@hous...	108791
998	Tracie Martinez	Morales-Moreno	caseycurry@lopez...	181615
999	Phillip Andrade	Anderson and Sons	anthony23@glover...	198586

1000 rows × 4 columns

And there you have it—a `DataFrame` with 1,000 rows of random data to practice with. Feel free to explore the Faker and NumPy documentation to see what other types of random data you can generate.

appendix E
Regular expressions

A *regular expression* (often abbreviated *RegEx*) is a search pattern for text. It defines a logical sequence of characters that the computer should look for in a string.

Here's a simple example. You've likely used the Find feature in your web browser at some point. In most web browsers, you can access this feature by pressing Ctrl-F in Windows or Command-F in macOS. The browser reveals a dialog box in which we type a sequence of characters. Then the browser searches for those characters on the web page. Figure E.1 shows an example of the browser searching for and finding romance in the page's content.

The History and
Romance of
Crime

FROM THE EARLIEST TIMES
TO THE PRESENT DAY

Figure E.1 Searching for the text romance by using the Find feature in Google Chrome

Chrome's Find feature is a simple example of RegEx in action. The tool does have its limitations. We can search for characters only in the exact order in which they

397

appear, for example. We can search for the character sequence `"cat"`, but we cannot declare a condition such as either the letter `"c"` or `"a"` or `"t"`. Regular expressions make this kind of dynamic search possible.

A regular expression describes how to look for content in a piece of text. We can search for characters such as letters, digits, or spaces, but we can also use special symbols to declare conditions. Here are a few examples of what we can search for:

- Any two digits in a row
- A sequence of three or more alphabetic characters followed by a space
- The character `s`, but only at the beginning of a word

In this appendix, we'll explore how regular expressions work in Python and then apply our knowledge to a data set in pandas. Entire textbooks and college courses are dedicated to RegEx, so our hope here is to scratch the surface of this complex field of study. RegEx is easy to get started with and difficult to master.

E.1   *Introduction to Python's re module*

Let's begin by creating a new Jupyter Notebook. We'll import pandas and a special module called `re`. The `re` (regular expressions) module is part of Python's standard library and is built into the language:

```
In  [1] import re
        import pandas as pd
```

The `re` module has a `search` function that looks for a substring in a string. The function accepts two arguments: a search sequence and a string in which to look for it. The next example looks for the string `"flower"` within the string `"field of flowers"`:

```
In  [2] re.search("flower", "field of flowers")

Out [2] <re.Match object; span=(9, 15), match='flower'>
```

The `search` function returns a `Match` object if Python finds the character sequence in the target string. The `Match` object stores information on what content matched the search pattern and where it exists in the target string. The preceding output communicates that `"flower"` was found in a span of characters from index positions 9 to 15. The first index is inclusive, and the second index is exclusive. If we count character index positions in `"field of flowers"`, we see that index 9 is the lowercase `"f"` in `"flowers"`, and index 15 is the `"s"` in `"flowers"`.

The `search` function returns `None` if the search pattern does not exist in the target string. By default, Jupyter Notebook will not output anything for a `None` value. But we can wrap the `search` invocation in a `print` function to force Jupyter to print the value:

```
In  [3] print(re.search("flower", "Barney the Dinosaur"))

Out [3] None
```

The `search` function returns only the first match in the target string. We can use the `findall` function to find all matches. This function accepts the same two arguments—

a search sequence and a target string—and returns a list of strings that match the search sequence. In the next example, Python finds the search pattern `"flower"` twice within `"Picking flowers in the flower field"`:

```
In  [4] re.findall("flower", "Picking flowers in the flower field")

Out [4] ['flower', 'flower']
```

Note that the search is case-sensitive.

E.2 *Metacharacters*

Now let's declare a more complex search pattern using regular expressions. We'll start by assigning a long string to a `sentence` variable. The next code sample breaks the string across multiple lines for readability, but you are welcome to type it in a single line in Jupyter Notebook:

```
In  [5] sentence = "I went to the store and bought " \
                   "5 apples, 4 oranges, and 15 plums."

        sentence

Out [5] 'I went to the store and bought 5 apples, 4 oranges, and 15 plums.'
```

Inside a regular expression, we can declare *metacharacters*—special symbols that define search patterns. The \d metacharacter, for example, instructs Python to match any digit. Let's say we want to identify all digits in our `sentence` string. The next example invokes the `findall` function with the regular expression `"\d"` as the search pattern:

```
In  [6] re.findall("\d", sentence)

Out [6] ['5', '4', '1', '5']
```

The function's return value is a list of the four digits in `sentence` in the order in which they appear:

- the `"5"` in `"5 apples"`
- the `"4"` in `"4 oranges"`
- the `"1"` in `"15 plums"`
- the `"5"` in `"15 plums"`

We've learned our first metacharacter! With a simple \d symbol, we've created a search pattern that matches any digit in a target string.

Two points are worth mentioning before we move forward:

- When a list contains many elements, Jupyter Notebook likes to print each element on a separate line. This stylistic approach makes the output easier to read but also causes it to take up significant space. To force Jupyter to print the list normally—add line breaks only after a certain threshold of characters has been output—we'll wrap our `findall` function calls inside Python's built-in `print` function from this point on.

- We'll pass our RegEx arguments to the `findall` function as raw strings. Python interprets each character in a raw string literally. This parsing option prevents conflicts between regular expressions and escape sequences. Consider the character sequence \b. It has a symbolic meaning in a plain Python string and a different meaning in a regular expression. When we use a raw string, we instruct Python to treat \b as a literal backslash character followed by a literal b character. This syntax guarantees that Python will parse the regular expression's metacharacters correctly.

We declare a raw string with an `"r"` character before the double quotes. Let's rewrite the preceding example with a `print` function call and a raw string:

```
In   [7] print(re.findall(r"\d", sentence))

Out  [7] ['5', '4', '1', '5']
```

To declare the inverse of an operation, we swap the letter casing of the metacharacter. If \d means "match any digit," for example, \D means "match any nondigit." Nondigit characters consist of letters, spaces, commas, and symbols. In the next example, we use \D to identify all nondigit characters in `sentence`:

```
In   [8] print(re.findall(r"\D", sentence))

Out  [8] ['I', ' ', 'w', 'e', 'n', 't', ' ', 't', 'o', ' ', 't', 'h', 'e', '
         ', 's', 't', 'o', 'r', 'e', ' ', 'a', 'n', 'd', ' ', 'b', 'o',
         'u', 'g', 'h', 't', ' ', ' ', 'a', 'p', 'p', 'l', 'e', 's', ',', '
         ', ' ', 'o', 'r', 'a', 'n', 'g', 'e', 's', ',', ' ', 'a', 'n',
         'd', ' ', ' ', 'p', 'l', 'u', 'm', 's', '.']
```

Now that you understand the basics of regular expressions, the next step is learning more metacharacters and building complex search queries. Here's another example. The \w metacharacter matches any word character, a category that includes letters, digits, and underscores:

```
In   [9] print(re.findall(r"\w", sentence))

Out  [9] ['I', 'w', 'e', 'n', 't', 't', 'o', 't', 'h', 'e', 's', 't', 'o',
         'r', 'e', 'a', 'n', 'd', 'b', 'o', 'u', 'g', 'h', 't', '5', 'a',
         'p', 'p', 'l', 'e', 's', '4', 'o', 'r', 'a', 'n', 'g', 'e', 's',
         'a', 'n', 'd', '1', '5', 'p', 'l', 'u', 'm', 's']
```

The inverse \W metacharacter matches any nonword character. Nonword characters include spaces, commas, and periods:

```
In   [10] print(re.findall(r"\W", sentence))

Out  [10] [' ', ' ', ' ', ' ', ' ', ' ', ' ', ' ', ',', ' ', ' ', ',', ' ',
          ' ', ' ', '.']
```

The \s metacharacter searches for any whitespace character:

```
In   [11] print(re.findall(r"\s", sentence))

Out  [11] [' ', ' ', ' ', ' ', ' ', ' ', ' ', ' ', ' ', ' ', ' ', ' ']
```

The inverse \S metacharacter searches for any nonwhitespace character:

```
In  [12] print(re.findall(r"\S", sentence))

Out [12] ['I', 'w', 'e', 'n', 't', 't', 'o', 't', 'h', 'e', 's', 't', 'o',
         'r', 'e', 'a', 'n', 'd', 'b', 'o', 'u', 'g', 'h', 't', '5', 'a',
         'p', 'p', 'l', 'e', 's', ',', '4', 'o', 'r', 'a', 'n', 'g', 'e',
         's', ',', 'a', 'n', 'd', '1', '5', 'p', 'l', 'u', 'm', 's', '.']
```

To search for a specific character, declare it literally in the search pattern. The next example searches for all occurrences of the letter "t". This syntax is the same one we used in this appendix's first examples:

```
In  [13] print(re.findall(r"t", sentence))

Out [13] ['t', 't', 't', 't', 't']
```

To search for a sequence of characters, write them in order in the search pattern. The next example searches for the letters "to" in the sentence string. Python finds it twice (the "to" word and the "to" in "store"):

```
In  [14] print(re.findall(r"to", sentence))

Out [14] ['to', 'to']
```

The \b metacharacter declares a word boundary. A *word boundary* mandates where a character must exist relative to a space. The next example searches for "\bt". The logic translates to "any t character after a word boundary" or, equivalently, "any t character after a space." The pattern matches the "t" characters in "to" and "the":

```
In  [15] print(re.findall(r"\bt", sentence))

Out [15] ['t', 't']
```

Let's flip the symbols around. If we use "t\b", we search for "any t character before a word boundary" or, equivalently, "any t character before a space." The "t" characters that Python matches are different. These are the "t" characters at the end of "went" and "bought":

```
In  [16] print(re.findall(r"t\b", sentence))

Out [16] ['t', 't']
```

The inverse \B metacharacter declares a nonword boundary. "\Bt", for example, means "any t character that does not come after a word boundary" or, equivalently, "any t character that does not come after a space":

```
In  [17] print(re.findall(r"\Bt", sentence))

Out [17] ['t', 't', 't']
```

The preceding example matched the "t" characters in "went", "store", and "bought". Python ignored the "t" characters in "to" and "the" because they appear after a word boundary.

E.3   *Advanced search patterns*

In review, a *metacharacter* is a symbol that designates a search sequence in a regular expression. Section E.2 explored the \d, \w, \s, and \b metacharacters for digits, word characters, spaces, and word boundaries. Let's learn some new metacharacters and then combine them into a complex search query.

The dot (.) metacharacter matches any character whatsoever:

```
In  [18] soda = "coca cola."
         soda

Out [18] 'coca cola.'

In  [19] print(re.findall(r".", soda))

Out [19] ['c', 'o', 'c', 'a', ' ', 'c', 'o', 'l', 'a', '.']
```

At first glance, this metacharacter may not seem to be particularly helpful, but it works wonders when paired with other symbols. The regular expression "c.", for example, searches for the character "c" followed by any character. There are three such matches in our string:

```
In  [20] print(re.findall(r"c.", soda))

Out [20] ['co', 'ca', 'co']
```

What if we want to search for a literal dot in a string? In that case, we have to escape it with a backslash in the regular expression. The "\." in the next example locates the period at the end of the soda string:

```
In  [21] print(re.findall(r"\.", soda))

Out [21] ['.']
```

Earlier, we saw that we could combine characters to search for them in sequence in the target string. Here, we search for the exact sequence of "co":

```
In  [22] print(re.findall(r"co", soda))

Out [22] ['co', 'co']
```

What if we want to search for either the character "c" or the character "o"? To do so, we can wrap the characters in a pair of square brackets. The matches will include any occurrence of either "c" or "o" in the target string:

```
In  [23] print(re.findall(r"[co]", soda))

Out [23] ['c', 'o', 'c', 'c', 'o']
```

The order of characters in the square brackets does not affect the result:

```
In  [24] print(re.findall(r"[oc]", soda))

Out [24] ['c', 'o', 'c', 'c', 'o']
```

Suppose that we want to target any characters between `"c"` and `"l"`. One option would be to write out the complete sequence of alphabetic characters within the square brackets:

```
In  [25] print(re.findall(r"[cdefghijkl]", soda))
```

```
Out [25] ['c', 'c', 'c', 'l']
```

A better solution is to use the dash symbol (-) to declare a range of characters. The following code sample yields the same list as the preceding code:

```
In  [26] print(re.findall(r"[c-l]", soda))
```

```
Out [26] ['c', 'c', 'c', 'l']
```

Next, let's explore how we can target multiple occurrences of characters in a row. Consider the string `"bookkeeper"`:

```
In  [27] word = "bookkeeper"
         word
```

```
Out [27] 'bookkeeper'
```

To search for exactly two `"e"` characters in a row, we can pair them in the search sequence:

```
In  [28] print(re.findall(r"ee", word))
```

```
Out [28] ['ee']
```

We can also search for multiple occurrences of a character with a pair of curly braces. Inside the braces, we declare the number of occurrences to match. In the next example, we search for two `"e"` characters in a row within `"bookkeeper"`:

```
In  [29] print(re.findall(r"e{2}", word))
```

```
Out [29] ['ee']
```

If we search for three `"e"` characters in a row with `"e{3}"`, the return value will be an empty list because there are no sequences of three consecutive `"e"` characters in `"bookkeeper"`:

```
In  [30] print(re.findall(r"e{3}", word))
```

```
Out [30] []
```

We can also enter two numbers inside the curly braces, separated by a comma. The first value sets the lower bound of occurrences, and the second value sets the upper bound of occurrences. The next example searches for between one and three occurrences of the `"e"` character in a row. The first match is the sequential `"ee"` characters in `"keeper"`, and the second match is the final `"e"` in `"keeper"`:

```
In  [31] print(re.findall(r"e{1,3}", word))
```

```
Out [31] ['ee', 'e']
```

Let's walk through this example in more detail. The pattern searches for one to three "e" characters in a row. When Python finds a match, it keeps traversing the string until the search pattern is violated. The regular expression first looks at the letters "bookk" individually. None of these letters fits the search pattern, so Python moves on. Then the pattern locates its first "e". Python cannot mark this match as final yet because the next character may also be an "e", so, it checks the next character. That character is indeed another "e", which fits the original search criteria. Python proceeds to the "p", which does not match the pattern, and declares the match to be "ee" rather than two individual "e" characters. The same logic repeats for the "e" closer to the end of the string.

We're making good progress, but all the previous examples have been mostly theoretical. How can we use RegEx when working with real-world data sets?

Imagine that we are running a customer-support hotline and storing transcriptions of phone calls. We may have a message like this one:

```
In  [32] transcription = "I can be reached at 555-123-4567. "\
                         "Look forward to talking to you soon."

         transcription
```

```
Out [32] 'I can be reached at 555-123-4567. Look forward to talking to you
          soon.'
```

Let's say we'd like to pull out a phone number from each person's message, but each transcription is unique. We can assume, however, that a phone number has a consistent pattern consisting of

1 Three digits
2 A dash
3 Three digits
4 A dash
5 Four digits

The beauty of RegEx is that it can identify this search pattern irrespective of the string's contents. The next example declares our most complex regular expression yet. We simply combine metacharacters and symbols to describe the logic above:

1 \d{3} searches for exactly three digits.
2 - searches for a dash.
3 \d{3} searches for exactly three digits.
4 - searches for a dash.
5 \d{4} searches for exactly four digits.

```
In  [33] print(re.findall(r"\d{3}-\d{3}-\d{4}", transcription))
```

```
Out [33] ['555-123-4567']
```

Voila!

There's also a convenient + metacharacter that indicates "one or more" of the preceding characters or metacharacters. \d+, for example, searches for one or more digits in a row. We can use the + symbol to simplify the preceding code. The next regular expression holds a different search pattern but returns the same result:

1 One or more sequential digits
2 A dash
3 One or more sequential digits
4 A dash
5 One or more sequential digits

```
In  [34] print(re.findall(r"\d+-\d+-\d+", transcription))

Out [34] ['555-123-4567']
```

With one line of code, we can extract a telephone number from a dynamic piece of text—pretty powerful stuff.

E.4 *Regular expressions and pandas*

In chapter 6, we introduced the StringMethods object for manipulating Series of strings. The object is available via the str attribute, and many of its methods support RegEx arguments, which significantly expand their power. Let's practice these RegEx concepts on a real data set.

The ice_cream.csv data set is a collection of ice cream flavors for four popular brands (Ben & Jerry's, Haagen-Dazs, Breyers, and Talenti). Each row includes a brand, a flavor, and a description:

```
In  [35] ice_cream = pd.read_csv("ice_cream.csv")
         ice_cream.head()

Out [35]
```

	Brand	Flavor	Description
0	Ben and Jerry's	Salted Caramel Core	Sweet Cream Ice Cream with Blon...
1	Ben and Jerry's	Netflix & Chilll'd™	Peanut Butter Ice Cream with Sw...
2	Ben and Jerry's	Chip Happens	A Cold Mess of Chocolate Ice Cr...
3	Ben and Jerry's	Cannoli	Mascarpone Ice Cream with Fudge...
4	Ben and Jerry's	Gimme S'more!™	Toasted Marshmallow Ice Cream w...

> **NOTE** ice_cream is a modified version of a data set available from Kaggle (https://www.kaggle.com/tysonpo/ice-cream-dataset). There are typos and inconsistencies within the data; we have preserved them so that you can see the data irregularities that appear in the real world. I encourage you to consider how you can optimize this data with the techniques you'll learn in this chapter.

I'm curious how many different chocolate treats we can find in the flavors. Our challenge is to find all words that immediately follow the string "Chocolate" within the Description column. We can use the str.extract method on a Series to accomplish this task. The method accepts a RegEx pattern and returns a DataFrame with its matches.

Let's construct our regular expression. We'll begin with a word boundary (\b). Then we'll target the literal text "Chocolate". Next, we'll mandate a single whitespace character (\s). Finally, we'll match one or more word characters in a row (\w+) to capture all alphanumeric letters until Python encounters a space or period. Thus, the final expression is "\bChocolate\s\w+)".

For technical reasons, we have to wrap the regular expression in parentheses when passing it to the str.extract method. The method supports an advanced syntax that searches for multiple regular expressions, and the parentheses limit it to one:

```
In  [36] ice_cream["Description"].str.extract(r"(\bChocolate\s\w+)").head()

Out [36]
```

	0
0	NaN
1	NaN
2	Chocolate Ice
3	NaN
4	Chocolate Cookie

So far, so good. Our Series includes matches such as "Chocolate Ice" at index position 2 and "Chocolate Cookie" at index position 4; it also stores NaN values wherever it could not find the search pattern in the row. Let's invoke the dropna method to remove rows with missing values:

```
In  [37] (
            ice_cream["Description"]
            .str.extract(r"(\bChocolate\s\w+)")
            .dropna()
            .head()
        )

Out [37]
```

	0
2	Chocolate Ice
4	Chocolate Cookie
8	Chocolate Ice
9	Chocolate Ice
13	Chocolate Cookie

We're getting closer.

Next, let's convert the DataFrame to a Series. The str.extract method returns a DataFrame by default to support the potential of multiple search patterns. We can use the squeeze method to coerce the single-column DataFrame into a Series. You may recall the related squeeze parameter from the read_csv import function; the squeeze method accomplishes the same result:

```
In  [38] (
            ice_cream["Description"]
            .str.extract(r"(\bChocolate\s\w+)")
```

```
        .dropna()
        .squeeze()
        .head()
    )
```

```
Out [38] 2         Chocolate Ice
         4      Chocolate Cookie
         8         Chocolate Ice
         9         Chocolate Ice
        13      Chocolate Cookie
        Name: Chocolate, dtype: object
```

Our method chaining is getting quite lengthy, so let's assign the current `Series` to a `chocolate_flavors` variable:

```
In  [39] chocolate_flavors = (
            ice_cream["Description"]
            .str.extract(r"(\bChocolate\s\w+)")
            .dropna()
            .squeeze()
        )
```

We ultimately want to identify what ingredients come after `"Chocolate"`. Let's invoke the `str.split` method to split each string by the occurrence of whitespace. Instead of passing a string with a single space, we'll provide an argument of a regular expression here as well. As a reminder, the `"\s"` metacharacter looks for a single whitespace:

```
In  [40] chocolate_flavors.str.split(r"\s").head()
```

```
Out [40] 2        [Chocolate, Ice]
         4     [Chocolate, Cookie]
         8        [Chocolate, Ice]
         9        [Chocolate, Ice]
        13     [Chocolate, Cookie]
        Name: 0, dtype: object
```

The `str.get` method retrieves a value at a consistent index position from each list in a `Series`. In the next example, we retrieve the second element (index position 1) from each list or, equivalently, the word that follows `"Chocolate"` in the original string:

```
In  [41] chocolate_flavors.str.split(r"\s").str.get(1).head()
```

```
Out [41] 2         Ice
         4      Cookie
         8         Ice
         9         Ice
        13      Cookie
        Name: Chocolate, dtype: object
```

For curiosity's sake, let's invoke the `value_counts` method to see the most frequent words that follow `"Chocolate"` across all ice cream flavors. Unsurprisingly, `"Ice"` is the winner. `"Cookie"` comes in at a distant second:

```
In  [42] chocolate_flavors.str.split(r"\s").str.get(1).value_counts()

Out [42] Ice            11
         Cookie          4
         Chip            3
         Cookies         2
         Sandwich        2
         Malt            1
         Mint            1
         Name: Chocolate, dtype: int64
```

Regular expressions offer a sophisticated way of searching for patterns in text. I hope that you've gained greater understanding of the benefits of RegEx and how to apply it to various methods in pandas.

index